Due to a publishing er
during the printing proc.... . ... ,.u
could insert this page and keep it with 'Orpheus is
Another World' as these are some of the most
important and heartfelt words I wrote:-

Many thanks
Bernadette Seymour

I would like to dedicate this book to:-
Captain Pete without whom I would never
have set foot on a yacht. To Roy who
selflessly aided us in our search for a yacht
and to Dudley my friend, confidant and
lover who has encouraged and supported
me in every way since the day we met.

I would also like a special note of thanks
in memory of those who touched my life
during this time and are sadly no longer
with us; they are Richard, Janet, Jonathon
and Harry.

Remembering you always.

Orpheus Is Another World

Bernadette Seymour

Raider Publishing International

New York　　　London　　　Johannesburg

© 2009 Bernadette Seymour

All rights reserved. No part of this book may be reproduced stored in a retrieval system or transmitted in any form by any means with out the prior written permission of the publisher, except by a reviewer who may quote brief passages in a review to be printed in a newspaper, magazine or journal.

First Printing

The views, content and descriptions in this book do not represent the views of Raider Publishing International. Some of the content may be offensive to some readers and they are to be advised. Objections to the content in this book should be directed towards the author and owner of the intellectual property rights as registered with their local government.

All characters portrayed in this book are fictitious and any resemblance to persons living or dead is purely coincidental.

Cover picture courtesy istockphoto.com

ISBN: 1-935383-98-1
Published By Raider Publishing International
www.RaiderPublishing.com
New York London Johannesburg

Printed in the United States of America and the United Kingdom

Orpheus Is Another World

Bernadette Seymour

Dearest Peter & Liz,

It was definitely all your fault !!

Berni xx.

CHAPTER 1
EXODUS

Have you ever had an occurrence in your life that changed it forever? Maybe you met a person who had such an effect on you that your life changed direction. Well, for Dudley and I that was Captain Pete.

The tides of time had kept my husband and me apart until our respective lives were ready to accept a relationship. Our paths had crossed many times over the years but it was only when we met in 1996 that love blossomed and Dudley and I were married on my thirty-third birthday. We had met by chance whilst enjoying an evening's entertainment being provided by amateur "wanna-bes". I was talking to my cousin when a slightly balding, dark haired gentleman walked up, was introduced and immediately did the Roy Orbison "Pretty Woman" grrrrrrowl. Steel blue eyes met mine and white teeth smiled mischievously from within a slightly tanned complexion. I tried to hide my blushes, whilst inside my heart was racing to the beat of 'Nut Rocker' by Bee Bumble and the Stingers. One meal, one walk and a half of lager at the local later, we were living together and our love was sealed forever. Neither of us had planned a relationship so it was quite a surprise to both of us to find ourselves living with someone who seemed to be the other half of a whole. It was as though Dudley and I had always been together; our lives just blended without any effort on either part. It was with much happiness that just over a year since we first met we were married.

All my life I had dreamed of visiting Hawaii and we spent three weeks on the island of Oahu for our honeymoon. It was not quite the "Blue Hawaii" of the Elvis movies that I had been raised on, but it was magical. During a trip to Huanama Bay Dudley convinced me to try snorkelling. I have an immense fear of the sea; if anything brushes past my leg it just has to be a shark, nothing smaller, no matter how shallow the water! He was very patient and gentle with me and I slowly came to love it. I found the colourful fish and turtles enchanting, and was spellbound by their beauty and magnificence. I was so interested in the wildlife that I forgot my fear of the water – then I realised I didn't mind the shallow water around the reef as long as I could see what was touching me. Thus began my love of snorkelling and my ability to swim in the sea, even if it did still terrify me. To this day I still cannot bring myself to just drop anchor and dive off into the deeper parts of the briny.

Soon after the honeymoon, we bumped into Peter Boddy at a local charity event. Peter was an acquaintance and retired work colleague of mine. On the way home, at the end of the evening, Dudley asked me to contact Peter to see if it would be possible for us to make arrangements to holiday with him that summer. He had a boat moored in Levkas and for the past few years had sailed around the Ionian Islands. The Ionians are the most westerly chain of Greek islands in the Mediterranean. Peter seemed pleased when I called and suggested Dudley and I might like to go out to visit during the coming September. It was a summer none of us would forget and lasting friendships would be forged.

The nine months that followed, leading up to the holiday, were filled with apprehension. I would voice my displeasure at having to go on a boat to anyone that would listen. I had never sailed before and, as I just explained, had a great fear of the sea in general. I could not visualise living at close quarters, sharing bathrooms, having no electricity therefore no hair dryer and no showers. I had no wish to sleep in the 'pointy bit' with nowhere to get dressed and put my makeup on!! Without exaggeration, I was dreading every second of the fast approaching holiday. Nevertheless, I would go for my husband's sake. My boss at this time, another Peter, took great delight in regaling me with stories of Greece on board a boat. He cheerfully described the nightmare of a deck shower and teased me mercilessly about the many naked maidens from countries afar, knowing full well that I find flaunted bodies very distasteful. The deeper my blushes, the deeper my hatred of boating – before I'd even tried it. Anyone who discussed the topic with me will vouch that my favourite saying during these months preceding the holiday was, "Poke the boat, I don't want to go!" We Norfolk girls like to let people know how we feel in the most open and honest of terms. It would be fair to say that there is hardly ever any ambiguity about what I am thinking and feeling. It can sometimes be frustrating when your facial expressions give you away so completely and it's even worse when the over willingness of the mouth to open, before the brain is in gear, digs a big hole for you to step into. I am an open book to the world around me but I guess it's better the devil you know!

The months passed quickly, and before we knew it September had arrived and we found ourselves at Preveza Airport on mainland Greece. We took a taxi to Nidri where our holiday boat would be waiting at anchor in a place called Tranquil Bay. We were to be collected by Peter in a local taverna and transported from there. On the way I asked the taxi driver how to say please and thank you in Greek, I've always felt that these two words are most important in any country I'd visited. This quaint man in his broken English explained "Parakalo" was please – this I managed – thank you was another matter. He tried to pronounce it three times so I could understand, but the speed in which he said it left me confused. I retired in defeat promising myself I'd try again later. This was my first experience of Greece and the Greek people and within the distance of the taxi ride I was smitten with both. It was just a shame about the boating business...

We kept our rendezvous with Captain Pete and over an Amstel lager I asked him how to say thank you in Greek. Without any hesitation he said, "All you have to remember is to say: a ferret's toe." After making fun about this rodent's anatomy I listened to the Greek waiter who delivered three Mythos lagers to our table, another of the local beers, and realised it sounded exactly how Captain Pete had said it. That was it then, "a ferret's toe", or to a Greek, "Efhareesto".

I had known that the boat, which I was informed should be called a yacht, would be at anchor; but at no time had I considered how we would be transported out to it. Dudley and I followed Peter to the end of a pontoon and were faced with a small four-man rubber dinghy. It sunk in the water as Peter and the bags boarded and I was almost certain by the time Dudley and I got in it would be sinking to the bottom. A small outboard sat on the back of the dinghy, which looked encouraging, but as I took my first tentative steps onto this miniscule craft, that just would not stay still, I felt a certain amount of foreboding. I grabbed Peter's shoulder in one hand and Dudley's hand in the other and stepped down into the dinghy to all sorts of helpful advice from Dudley like, "Step in quickly, keep your centre of gravity low and then quickly sit down."

"Well that's easy for you to say," I thought to myself as I held tight, stepped in and quickly sat down just as a slop of water peaked over the edge of the dinghy, giving me a nice wet patch to sit in!

To my utter amazement, the dinghy did not sink, and, on the second pull, the outboard burbled into life and put-putted us out to the 'yacht' whilst the water lapped at its edges. For most of the trip I was too worried about not getting any wetter than I already was to realise that I had to go through the process for a second time to get out of the dinghy and onto *Admetus*. As I took my first step aboard *Admetus* she was a true lady, treating me very kindly by staying steady beneath my novice feet. She may have realised I had some QT tea and a jar of Marmite in my bag, two crucial pieces of victuals the captain couldn't purchase on the islands.

Having arrived, and having had the use of the ship's toilet explained to me, (nothing goes down it that hasn't passed through the body first!) I was told that the next day I would be taking part in the Ionian regatta!! Having never sailed before, terror was starting to sink in. I dared to speak up and asked my new captain what I would be required to do. The answer came, "Stand in the companion way, keep your head down out of the way of the boom and do nothing." The nothing bit I understood; if only I knew what a boom was, and where was the companionway? Out of self-preservation, I soon found out.

On the morning of the Regatta we attended the 1100 hours briefing where all participants had the rules and regulations explained to them. The weather forecast for the duration of the regatta was given, along with the warning to fly a white flag on your boat if you didn't want to take part in the games! Now I was curious. I just love games. Captain Pete didn't seem so keen and it wasn't until later I found out why. Just after lunch a local flotilla leader joined the *Admetus* crew to assist with the sailing during the race. We made our way to the Meganisi Channel and along with many other boats, were sailing and vying for a good starting position.

Admetus was flying a white flag on the backstay. No,

that's not part of a lady's lingerie drawer. It is a tensioned supporting wire from the back of the mast to the back of the boat (sorry, yacht!). The flag was apparently to stop the boats involved in the games throwing flour and eggs at us. Now that isn't my idea of a game; on this point I was definitely with Captain Pete. The first can of beer was opened and we were fired up for the start of the race. I didn't have a clue what to expect; indeed I wasn't really about to take part but the fun, games and sheer number of boats all together gave me quite a buzz. There was a gentle wind, we had an excellent starting position, or so I was told, and then the horn blew and we were off... no we weren't. I had never experienced anything like it in my life. Almost as soon as the starting horn was blown the wind blew out – nothing – nearly two hundred boats becalmed!

After bobbing about for an hour and not getting anywhere at all, we had our third beer and decided that we would drop out of the race and motor to the finishing point. We arrived at Sivota crestfallen, but in my case relieved, because I hadn't been tested in my sailing ability or my stomach ability – yes there was the possibility that I may be seasick. Who could know, I'd never done this before!

That evening there was partying and drinking; bands played and some yacht crews donned various costumes. Dudley and Captain Pete seemed keen on the yacht full of maidens dressed in red leather nurses outfits and white stockings – I can't think why – my mind was on the yacht full of men dressed in togas! In the morning it was all a blur, a pleasant haze of sunshine, sea and plenty of slosh.

On this morning, as with most mornings we were awakened with the sound of goats' bells up in the mountains, heralding the beginning of another day. After a relaxed beginning to the day, waiting for the wind to get up, which was usually at around 1100 hours, we could look forward to sailing somewhere new. From Sivota, our race day final destination, we sailed in a southeasterly wind to the island of Meganisi and moored at Vathi just in time, as the heavens opened and a thunderstorm commenced.

After a day of spectacular lightning and storms we managed to sail away again in a lighter wind. We stopped for a swim and lunch in a bay on Meganisi called Abeleike and then continued our light airs sail to the island of Kastos. During this leg of our journey we had our first sighting of dolphins in the distance off the northern tip of Kalamos. After another pleasurable evening of drinking and eating we found ourselves in variable winds headed for a swim on the island of Astakos and finished the day's sail in a bay just outside Frikes on the island of Ithaca. The day had seemed rather strange with the winds turning from northeasterly to southerly and then southwesterly. Captain Pete, as always, was very happy to explain to me the nature of sailing and I was becoming more interested in how the mountains turned and channelled the winds. Each mountain range caused the natural winds to be diverted to create a false wind and then again, it was explained, there was also an apparent wind. I won't even go there. It was all rather technical and I simply put it down to nature and was very glad our captain knew what he was doing.

The following day started slowly as we motored southwards. Things picked up when we sighted dolphins again and they were close enough to photograph. Captain Pete tried to get them to come and play with the bows of the boat but they were not interested just then. No sooner had this excitement died down than we rounded the southern tip of Ithaca and picked up a northerly wind force 4/5. The sails were out and we had an absolutely brilliant sail all the way to Eufemia on the island of Kefalonia. Apparently, we had recorded 7 knots on a beam reach with a 30 degree heel. I asked Captain Pete if this was good and he assured me anybody who knew anything about sailing would be impressed; so I hope all readers are making suitable sounds and nodding approvingly!

Both Dudley and I were helming the next day as we sailed close-hauled (this is when the wind is as close to the bow as possible whilst still allowing the boat to continue to sail). The wind was north, northwesterly and we made our way up to Fiskado, an anchorage on the northeast of Kefalonia. Just as I was starting to gain confidence and beginning to really love this new way of life the following day brought me down to earth with a bump. We sailed from Kefalonia to Vassiliki on the island of Levkada and during the journey I was making sandwiches in the galley, but by the time they were made and ready for eating I was lying prone on the side deck, seasick.

The following days were very hot and there was no wind at all, so, motoring on the engine, we headed from Vassiliki to

Sivota also on the island of Levkada and from there the following day to Spartachori on the island of Meganisi. "George", the name Captain Pete gave to *Admetus'* auto-helm, did a fine job and I felt obliged to do the difficult job of lying on the 'pointy bit' pretending to be a tourist whilst the men-folk talked. From here we made for Tranquil Bay the days having just disappeared; the holiday was nearly done but we had one last sail close hauled in a northwesterly force 4 as we made our way up the Levkas Canal to the mole (A stone pier at right angles to the town quay).

The fun of the previous fortnight over, I truly took stock of *Admetus*, a Sadler 32. Walking up the plank perched on her pulpit (metal frame around the bow of the boat) you automatically take hold of her furling genoa (foresail) and walk across her pale blue decks. Down the side decks she has wooden grab rails that guide you to the cockpit which has teak seating and floor. A carved beaver's head tiller sits beckoning at the stern along with the stern anchor locker.

Once down the companionway (stairway down into the boat) *Admetus* opens up into a galley on the left (port side) and chart table to the right (starboard side). Behind the chart table is a den-like cabin known as the quarter berth. Walking forwards brings you to the main saloon and living area and here is where we spent many special moments of fun, laughter and sharing. *Admetus* with her rich wooden surrounds and many hidden lockers held Captain Pete's life admirably and when we got to share her she held us inside and made us very happy. Forward from the saloon you find the heads (toilet) and wet locker; then forward again the forepeak cabin (bedroom), which is where Dudley and I slept. It might not sound much to the average person, but to us, during the two weeks we were on board, she became wonderful; the mere mention of her name came to mean freedom and happiness. Even now, looking back, Dudley and I still agree we shared some of our best sailing days with Peter and Admetus.

The patience of *Admetus* and her Captain Peter were to be admired. Over the two weeks of our holiday with their gradual, gentle, coaxing encouragement, I was at the helm. How did that happen? I was winching in sails as Dudley put in a tack – what was a tack? I was learning knots and putting out fenders with a professional looking clove hitch with a half hitch and making ready for when Dud dropped the anchor and we moored for the evening. Who was this person I had become?

I came to love the feeling as the boat lifted out of the water heeling in the wind, and the sight of the sails as I sat and looked up between the mainsail and the genoa, never ceased to captivate me. The concentration of sailing close hauled, watching the tell-tails, feeling the wind, the pull on the tiller, watching the water lap the hull of *Admetus* in a poetic dance of shimmering light and cobalt blue, enthralled me. I was in love. I was hooked. She was a perfect, understanding teacher. Captain Pete wasn't all that bad either. My smile was now like that of a bride's on her wedding day. It was there all day and you just never knew why. I had known why on my wedding day and I knew why now - I was in love – with Dudley and with sailing.

I found deck showers using water heated by the day's sunshine exhilarating. Even more fun was walking through a supermarket to the rear garden and using one of the make-shift showers available there. Who needed make-up? Nature gave my skin a sun kissed glow that no amount of make-up could ever create. Hair was dried on deck in a setting sun with a 'sundowner' in hand, usually one of the excellent local red wines. After sunset, a trip ashore for an evening meal in a local taverna meant we would be meeting more friendly Greeks and trying local cuisine. What a perfect end to many perfect days!

Our holiday fortnight ended too soon and it was with tears that Dudley and I got on the bus to leave and fly back to England. Someone had stolen my life for such a short time and it would never be the same again. Both Dudley and I could never be the same people as something special had happened to us during the holiday and it had come in the form of Captain Pete and *Admetus*.

We spent the remainder of the year following our holiday, thinking of *Admetus*. Our lament followed on into the following year and we just couldn't seem to be able to get the thought of sailing out of our minds. I faced the humiliation of everyone saying, "I told you so," as I had to hear recounted my months of complaint prior to the holiday taking place. My boss, Peter, couldn't stop laughing at the complete turnaround and friends who knew of my fear of the sea couldn't believe I was the same person. Of course, I wasn't. Things that I first thought important, possessions and surroundings, meant nothing to me now. I had always been aware of the wonderful things God had created and now I had found the most perfect way of enjoying all of his wonders. I couldn't wait to go back and be part of it again.

Throughout the following year, life moved on and, for some reason, fate packed it with troubles. Without Dudley by my side I would have been desperate and doubt very much that I would have coped. I had problems at work and it seemed as though these bad times would never end. Of course, this meant that there was to be no visit to *Admetus* this summer. My faith was being tested through these long months that turned into a long year and through God's love I regained an understanding of humility and sacrifice. Another year arrived with the usual pomp and parties and although life was still troubled, we made plans to visit Peter during the latter part of this New Year. If only we could have seen ahead! This New Year was about to bring another change to our lives.

We were due to fly out to be with Captain Pete on Saturday 15 September. On the 11 September, whilst I was at work, I heard that the unthinkable had happened. Two passenger aircraft had been hijacked and flown straight through the twin towers of the World Trade Centre in New York, closely followed by a further aircraft flying into the Pentagon. Disbelief was only one emotion I felt. That evening Dudley and I reflected on how short life was. We thought about all the plans those families must have made; relatives of all the dead were now mourning, their lives changed forever. It was an eye opening and heart wrenching experience, not only for us but for the whole world at that time. When such evil visits the earth it is difficult to keep faith, but this incident made me more determined to lift myself from my own problems, which now seemed very minor. I grasped my faith and clung to it. Suddenly I felt stronger than I had in a long time; strong enough to move on in my life.

We set off for our second trip aboard *Admetus*, taking with us the biggest jar of marmite money could buy. As per the first time, Dudley and I loved every second sailing with Captain Pete, who proclaimed I was "a fine helmswoman". On a yacht such as *Admetus* it wasn't difficult to helm. She purred beneath my hands in a rhythmic pulse and responded to my every touch. She had taken us from the mole in Levkas down the canal and south to anchor off in Abeleike on the island of Meganisi. We walked over the hillside on a roughly made road - no houses, just lush greenness - and had our evening meal in Vathi. These sort of places were now familiar to us and it was good. I was becoming more aware of my surroundings and the places we had visited previously. I was finally seeing the Ionian for what it was - a very beautiful piece of the Mediterranean dotted with tiny islands that hid nature's treasures.

Whilst having another fun day on the helm in a south-westerly 5 Captain Pete went to pump out the holding tank. All of a sudden there came a cry of "Oh S***." This, we were about to find out, was a literal comment as the pump had broken. Necessary action meant that we were now heading for Nidri and Tranquil bay instead of Kalamos as originally planned. I hinted to Dudley that this was obviously a man's area of boating and being the only lady on board I did what ladies do – I sunbathed whilst poor Captain Pete was up to his elbows in it.

Admetus back together and all vital components working correctly, we sailed to St. Nicholas Bay on the mainland for a swim and lunch and from here we headed to Spartachori. It was a hot afternoon and Dudley had decided to go below for a siesta. This left me at the helm sailing in a north north-easterly wind under the watchful eye of the captain and in the caring arms of Admetus. Pete asked if I would like to 'Goose-wing'. This required skill to keep both sails evenly balanced, he explained. "Why not?" I said. After all, I was an old salt now with much experience ... all two weeks of it! What a sight, what joy, what a thrill! It gave me goose bumps, never mind the goose wings. Admetus unfolded her sails before me in a magnificent display, proud as a peacock in the mating season. I looked up her mast to see her wings completely unfolded in all their glory. I asked Captain Pete to take the helm so I could just sit and soak up the wonder of it. "Quick! Get the camera. Capture this moment." I thought to myself. But it's impossible. No amount of pictures could show what I felt inside. The majestic way she glided through the water, wings gently flapping, I decided geese had nothing to do with it – *Admetus* was definitely a swan, proud, graceful and oh so beautiful. I came to love everything about her and her captain. They would both hold a very special place in my heart for the rest of my life and to this day I still call it 'Swan-winging' when referring to *Admetus*.

At Spartachori that evening we relaxed and watched the sleepy Greek villagers amble through their day, unrushed, friendly and co-operative. Suddenly I realised the following day would be our second chance in the Ionian Regatta...

Bright and early in the morning, our Captain briefed us, 'the crew', on how to put in a speedy tack. The challenge was on this time. We were going to win. Our fight plan was discussed and we attended the full briefing as before. As soon as the wind was up we took Admetus out for a practice run so Dudley and I, the foredeck gorillas, could be sure we were ready for the task ahead. Just as before, the games and the boats were playing with each other and vying for a good starting position. Suddenly, a huge yacht with the smell of money about it was heading straight for us and I was at the helm steering. "Captain Pete!" I gasped.

"Hold your course," he said firmly. I wasn't going to argue. He was a man possessed, rage in his eyes. In a flash I heard him shout "STARBOARD!" At this, the other yacht immediately turned away. Well, that did the trick. "Let's try that again I thought and get them all out of the way..." It was only when the redness had disappeared from the whites of his eyes I dared to ask why he had held course and shouted in a manner not consistent with his normal character. He gruffly said, "The rules of the sea. Port tack gives way to a yacht on a starboard tack." By this time I knew my left and right in the boating world and thought that this was a nifty rule to have, especially on race day. I also realised that I should make more effort on my return to England to learn the rules of the road to make for safer sailing in the future.

The race took off this time to a flying start and at the sound of the horn we set off initially with short tacks due to the number of boats and the narrowness of the Meganisi channel. We settled into a long tack and noticed we had made good headway; only the larger yachts were ahead of us. The majority were behind, including the only other Sadler 32 in the race, so we were looking good to win first in class. Joe Charlton was the owner of the other Sadler being raced, a very helpful chap who took care of *Admetus* over the winter months when Peter returned to England. Just for today, race day, he was the enemy. As we made our way to Arkoudhi Island we were ahead of Joe, but as we rounded and cleared the island we suddenly realised we were behind. A strategic move to put in a long tack towards Sivota had bitten us on the backside as close to the land, unusually; we lost the wind and spent the last nautical mile of the race almost becalmed. We watched Joe cross the line just minutes before we managed to crawl across. The only gratifying part of our finish was to look behind and see the number of yachts that were still in our wake trying to make for the finish line. We had managed to place eighteenth out of one hundred thirty yachts – Well done, *Admetus* – That deserves a drink! Naturally, during later conversations, the number of yachts we beat increased somewhat.

We had no time for post race day blues and though there was no wind, but it was still a beautiful sunny day, we decided to motor to what was now becoming 'our' bay, just outside Frikes on the Island of Ithaca. I felt obliged to have another 'pointy bit' moment, which obviously entailed my lying on the bow, sunbathing. From here we spent happy days and nights in Port Vathi on Ithaca and then around the southern tip to Eufemia on Kefalonia. The wind still evaded us, being only variable force _, so we motored to a bay just outside Fiskado and then from here back to Sivota on Lefkada. This last stretch brought the delight of seeing dolphins for the first time this trip and this time they came to play with the bows for a short while. I hung over the side deck trying my hardest not to miss one moment. Alas, it was over all too soon and they were gone, but it was a shared special moment that Dudley and I could treasure.

Typically, the following day we remained in Sivota as the wind, that had been missing for many days had decided to make up for it by blowing through full force. After a lazy day of reading and hiding from the weather, we managed the following day to have a gentle sail in a southerly 3 and spent the evening in what we now referred to as Little Vathi on the island of Meganisi. On this trip we had learned that there was a Big Vathi on the island of Ithaca and so, to distinguish between the two ports named Vathi, they were referred to by size.

The next day sadness began to set in, as we had to make our way back up the Levkas Canal and back to the mole. I was starting to hate the sight of the canal, as it seemed to portray the end of something that was so good and which neither Dudley nor I wanted to end. We had rested and sailed our holiday away and all too soon it was over.

Each time we left it became more difficult to say goodbye. There would be tears and a wrenching in my heart. For us, Captain Pete and *Admetus* would be gone again for a little while but we promised ourselves we would be back. We would be seeing Captain Pete when he came home for the winter months but it would be different. The detached life in England could never replicate the closeness and happiness we had found in Greece aboard *Admetus*.

When we landed in England we were met by angry, pale faces, people rushing around and pushing to get nowhere. Rules and regulations jumped up to slap us in the face at every turn. What a difference in the cultures! I looked at Dudley, thinking of the lovely little shops and smiling faces and he looked at me, longing to be back where we had just come from. At that moment, a well-rounded lady pushed past me, nearly knocking my off my feet, in an extreme effort to get to the front of a crowd to collect her luggage – which didn't appear for another hour and a half. It was then that both Dudley and I realised that England held nothing for us anymore and that another place was calling to us. We knew that, thanks to Captain Pete and *Admetus*, our lives were about to change forever. We knew we wanted to begin our lives again around the places *Admetus* had taken us to. From there, who could know, I was happy to go anywhere Dudley wanted to take me as long as we were together.

CHAPTER 2
WISHING AND HOPING

After many evenings of soul searching and discussion that involved considering family commitments and ties to England, we made the decision to set sail. Dudley immediately set about looking for a boat that would suit our needs and fulfil our plans to become "live-aboards". He had various contacts in the boating world, thanks to good friends Mike and Janet Harvey, who had been close to Dudley before we had met. Mike had owned a Marina in Stalham, Norfolk, and during their friendship Dudley had gained a great deal of experience and knowledge from them in the areas of both, flying and boating. Sadly, at the time Dudley and I met, Mike had been taken from this world prematurely as a result of a flying accident. I prayed that under Mike's watchful eye Dudley would embark on a successful boat hunt.

Dudley gave me a book to read entitled *Sell Up and Sail* by Bill & Laurel Cooper. This inspired me and made me think, "What if?' What if we got ill and needed the hospital, dentists, doctors, vets?" We had a little Westie called Harry whom I would not dream of leaving behind. There will be very few questions you can think of that we did not ask ourselves during this searching time; Dudley was driven mad by my constant worrying. My experience of visiting foreign countries was so limited that the reality of what we were planning caused me to spend hours of debate considering whether we were doing the right thing. Soon, my "What if?" turned into "So what?" Do you stay in a life that makes you unsettled and unhappy just to be near a hospital? Do you stay in England just to visit the same hairdressers and shop at your favourite supermarket? Or do you take the risk and follow your heart? We both agreed that giving up what we had to live a basic life on a little money in Greece was better than the alternative of sweating buckets, working to break even in England.

Dudley would say, "If you are that worried about things, we do not have to go." This would make me think, there was no pressure and I was being given the option to be sure of the road ahead. Being younger than Dudley, it was not simply a matter of starting a new life abroad. The life we were about to choose would mean that I was retiring from work very early. This meant that on reaching my recognised retirement age of sixty-five my pension would be very small and certainly not enough for me to live on. Whatever decision I made now would effectively mean the end of any career I might have and would result in a very meagre income for the rest of my days on this earth. It was not a very easy decision for me to make as I had worked for the Norfolk Constabulary for twenty-one years. I had joined as a junior clerk and through promotion now held the position of Executive P.A. I had a very good income, a very nice home and a guaranteed pension. I would be walking out on a very secure future and everything that I had spent my life working towards.

Something had happened to me. I had seen and experienced something that had touched me deeply. I felt I had found a perfect forum for me to build myself a new life, a good life, a life guided by God, a chance to make myself a better person and be closer to nature. Once I realised I wanted to go more than I wanted to stay I let nothing stand in my way. I became positive and pro-active and with each worry I found a solution.

As the captain of any great ship must have said at least once in his life, "Hold your course steady, sailor – dead ahead." We had both chosen and were committed to our new course and this is exactly what we did. We remained steadfast in our pursuit of achieving our aim.

If, as a reader, you have ever considered taking a giant step in a different direction, then I hope reading this will give you the courage. Each individual holds their own fears, needs and wants and I suggest your own strength of being will help you overcome your hurdles and shape your future. As you will see by reading on, much can be achieved with very little. All it takes is a little faith and a lot of determination or vice versa if you prefer.

Even with Dudley's many contacts, it took some time for us to find a yacht with our specifications. For many months we had plagued our dear friend Roy, who owns a Piper Lance, to fly us to places such as Ipswich, Falmouth and Rye near Lydd. We searched the internet, made visits to yacht auctions and sales and contacted reclaim companies. We talked to customs officers in the hope of buying a cheaper boat in need of some care and attention or one that had been seized and would be sold following a subsequent court case. For such an important purchase we would have to wait a long time until the right vessel came along.

Dudley and I had decided on the layout of the boat we wished to purchase and were determined not to waver. This was to be our first time living aboard and we wanted the best possible chance of making it a success. We had considered space for us to live in; family visits, having children on board and of course Harry, our little sailor boy Westie, who absolutely hated water!! We had decided on a forty-foot boat, fibreglass hull, at least two double cabins and two heads. These would preferably be at opposite ends of the boat to allow for maximum privacy when people came to visit.

We looked at boats with heating and baths on board, which obviously were completely inappropriate for living aboard in the sunny Mediterranean. We saw boats that had been left to go damp and were not cared for, boats that had been seized from drug smugglers and boats that we were very keen on but just never were successful with the sealed tender we put forward. We had even considered ex sailing holiday boats that were chartered around the Greek Islands by the big companies; alas for us these were all too expensive. We discovered a Ferro Ketch (a yacht with a concrete hull) anchored off the island of Meganisi in the Ionian. We contacted Joe, our race day enemy, who inspected it for us but were told that all was not as it first appeared. During our long search we considered anything and everything. We stumbled across a steel hull; nothing else, just the hull. It would have been a wonderful project for someone with the knowledge to re-build it but for us, it was too much to contemplate and would take too much time.

Whilst we continued to search for a yacht and in an attempt to gain more sailing knowledge we decided to go dinghy sailing. On the recommendation of Captain Pete the month of November saw Dudley and me attending a "try out" sail at Filby Broad in Norfolk with a dinghy sailing club. It was a bright, crisp, sunny day as the sun glistened on the broad water. Trees were either bare or coloured with bright orange autumnal leaves and ducks were picking around the banks and reeds. What a wonderful world! ... Back in the bosom of his family for the winter months, Captain Pete had come to see us off and to make sure we were okay.

A Wayfarer is a far cry from a thirty-two-foot Sadler, but Paul, our captain and tutor for the day, assured me that this was a stable boat and excellent to learn in. One step on board, and I began to doubt his sincerity. This strange dinghy was made of very light fibreglass and seemed not much bigger than a bathtub but I had been assured there was no need for me to wear a wetsuit as nobody ever fell out of a Wayfarer! There were ropes lying loose all around the boat and I noticed there were no winches or winch handles. Closer inspection revealed that the tiller was some elbowed contraption that seemed to go the opposite way to the one you wanted it to. My ponytail of long blonde hair kept catching on the boom as it was so low and any amount of movement seemed to send the whole boat careering off in the wrong direction.

The Wayfarer and her captain were certainly not as forgiving as I was used to. Why was the song, 'Ride White Horses' coming to mind? "Put your bottom over the edge," Paul said. "Lean out," he said. "Lee ho," he shouted. "Jibe ho." – JIBE – HELP! I no longer saw the sun, the trees or the good things around the broad. In fact, the last thing I saw was Dudley's worried expression as I sank backwards off the side of the boat and into the icy cold water of the broad. The lifejacket kicked in and I bobbed to the surface like a cork out of a champagne bottle just in time to see the boat disappearing. "Will they come back? Can I get back on board? Lord, it's cold in here...."

I made a mental note: Always wear a life jacket AND a wetsuit when sailing in a smaller boat!

This was Dudley's first real man-over board practice. He did quite well really. Well, at least he came back for me. For a husband and wife sailing team, I suppose that's a show of love! Getting back on board was not at all easy; my clothes now weighed a ton and it took all my strength and that of both men to haul me in a most unladylike way back on board. My embarrassment was not spared when Paul said, "That is the first time I've ever seen anyone fall out of a Wayfarer. They're quite stable boats." How I missed *Admetus* and Captain Pete, who by this time had gone home for Sunday lunch and left me in the clutches of this madman. I persevered with the day's sailing and dried out in the winter sun and eventually began to enjoy it, but quite clearly I had a long way to go.

Peter looked amused as I told him of my clumsy exit from the Wayfarer. At least his lovely wife Liz looked concerned. Every Tarzan has a Jane and Captain Pete, hairy cave man with prominent forehead, gentle blue eyes and caring nature had slim, blonde, blue eyed and beautiful Liz. She was a devoted mother and grandmother as well as a patient, understanding woman because she stayed home whilst the captain went off sailing all summer. It had been three years since we had been introduced to each other and happily all four of us had bonded in a comfortable friendship. We loved to spend time together during the winter months reminiscing and swapping tales of summer sailing and family fun. I soon realised that Liz and Dudley were very much alike and had the finesse that Peter and I were lacking; you could say that we were 'the bit of rough'. Needless to say, the combination worked wonderfully and our friendship blossomed because of it.

In February, 2002, I took my first steps towards increasing my sailing knowledge. I enrolled into an evening class to obtain my day skipper theory navigation certificate. This meant I would be learning not only navigation but safety rules at sea, buoys, lights, terms for parts of the boat, plotting a course and many more confusing things. I must confess that I am a woman with no sense of direction whatsoever; I could get lost in my own back garden. Indeed, having lived all my life in the city of Norwich, I still would not be able to give clear directions to any particular place if a stranger stopped and asked! It is with many thanks and much credit to John, who did a fine job in teaching me navigational skills that I passed my day skipper written with flying colours.

Having gained this qualification I was determined not to be the kind of sailor that became snobbish about the terms. Living within close proximity to the Norfolk Broads and many sailing clubs the nuances of raised pinkies and select groups had not gone unnoticed. It may be my inexperience, my Norfolk upbringing or just my simple bloody mindedness but to me it would always be the "pointy bit".

Dudley had previously passed his yacht master written and had taken the opportunity to be a member of a five man crew crossing the Atlantic to St. Lucia. This had taken place on a Ferro Ketch (a two masted concrete hull yacht) and had required the crewmembers to helm twenty-four hours a day. The experience he gained during this trip was immense, including his two trips up the mast to fix the rigging; that's what you get for being the lightest man on board! Undaunted by my husband's experience, because Captain Pete had said I was "a fine helmswoman", I knew if I tried I, too, could be a great sailor one day.

I had a lot to live up to within my family as I had been born and bred into seafaring stock. My father and brother had been Royal Navy men and my father's grandfather, Solomon Brown, had been Coxswain of the California Life Boat in Norfolk. He had received the bronze medal of the Grand Duke of Mecklenburg and had been part of the Caister Life Boat crew. Sadly, he died during a rescue of the crew from a boat named the Soudan of Liverpool. I certainly hoped that if he were looking down he would not be disappointed in his latest descendant to take to the sea.

June found us again enjoying the delights of Admetus and Captain Pete. We missed the opportunity of seeing Liz as she had gone home on a flight just before we landed. However this meant that Captain Pete was already at the airport and, happily, was able to meet us off the plane. It was an excellent start to our holiday and, as always, the fun we were about to have would be etched into our very being forever. In addition to the fun we knew we would have this holiday we also had an ulterior motive: to take the opportunity to make as many contacts as we could in our search for that special yacht to sail away on.

We left Levkas via the Canal in a northwesterly force 3 and were sailing well until we came out of the Meganisi Channel and the wind increased to force 7 and also changed direction slightly so it was now directly on the bow as we headed for Sivota. The sails had to come down and we motored the rest of the way to our night time mooring. A yacht alongside us that evening indicated that a local taverna owner had a yacht for sale that we might be interested in. The taverna owner, being a good Greek father, was away at the time on a school trip, so any boat viewing had to wait.

The wind was blowing in a westerly direction the following day, which meant all chances of boat buying had gone and we were out sailing towards Vassiliki. The winds slowly increased to force 6 but not before we managed to reach the harbour and moored in a protected corner.

Passing a butcher's shop in Vassiliki Captain Pete asked if we would like a barbecue. This would entail anchoring in a quiet bay, watching the sunset, cooking the food whilst drinking wine and that done, playing the harmonica round the campfire. What more could a girl ask for, scenery, good food and entertainment! The decision made, we walked into the butcher's and were immediately faced with a big round wooden slab in the middle of the room. The block was dirty with blood and there were flies everywhere. Standing behind it was a rotund butcher with a cigarette hanging out of his mouth. *What would Health and Safety in England make of this?* I thought. We asked for "Kotopoulo" (chicken) and "Moskhari kima" (minced beef) without hesitating over the cleanliness issues that seem to burden the rest of Europe.

This encounter again highlighted the differences between the Greek culture and that of England. Sadly, we feel, Health and Safety issues in England have gone so far that they should be held responsible for the outcome of creating an extremely sterile environment. In spite of that, or perhaps because of it, we now have children with more allergies than ever before and hospitals with super bugs. These things are almost unheard of in Greece and after four years of living with their culture we have never been ill and have never heard anything but praise for the Greek people's relaxed attitudes. We have seen a slow increase of the more modern butchers with their clean looking stainless steel counters but we much prefer the original more relaxed experience of the local butcher's block.

Armed with our lean and healthy meat, we made a plan to sail to Sikidi Bay on the island of Kefalonia. Having learned about navigation and acquired a logbook to record my sailing hours, I asked the captain to fill it out with details of our past trips. The entry he made for the present trip included not only helm and deck work but also navigation. The next morning Captain Pete invited me to look at the charts and plan our course for the day's sail.

Rising to the challenge, I spent a good half hour

calculating speed and measuring distances. I estimated arrival time, course to steer and suitable time for departure. I had it all worked out and felt very smug with myself but it didn't take very long for me to realise that although useful, my efforts meant nothing once we were underway. We motored out of the harbour, assessed the wind direction, set the sails and as any experienced sailor will understand, days of perfect wind directions are very few and my calculated heading headed off in a different direction! It had been great practice reading from the charts and picking up landmarks, using the land heights to work out which headland was in front of me and using the hand-bearing compass to make a three point fix. What I learned more than anything else was that my lack of practical sailing experience made it impossible for me to apply the theory in a realistic way. I needed more 'hands on' time to enable me to combine the theory and the reality to make it a useable tool.

Once anchored safely in Sikidi Bay with shorelines secured, the barbeque plans went full steam ahead. The meat cooked up perfectly with a Greek Salad and Captain Pete's recipe for Metaxa soaked peaches rounded the meal off nicely. The sun had set behind the mountains in an unassuming display of muted colours and the entertainment began.

The following morning we all awoke in a wine induced haze and remembered the fun of the previous evening. As the fog lifted from our brains I recalled that I was married to a latent arsonist who had turned into a man possessed when given a camp fire to play with and that Captain Pete was a budding Larry Adler; me, I was just a trainee drunken sailor! Over breakfast, we decided in a democratic way, that we would sail, with a following wind, to Poros on the island of Kefalonia; there were so many places to see and so little time of our holiday left.

Liz, Peter's wife, had told us at the start of the sailing season that problems were being experienced with over-zealous port police. She made me promise that whilst we were there I would not let our captain get too upset if the port police asked to see the ship's papers. It was a simple matter of producing the boat's registration, Transit Log and Cruising Permit, then paying a small fee under the heading of 'Harbour Dues'. Now most sailors within European waters will know that European Law stipulates that we should have the right of free passage. Captain Pete knows this too and is not afraid to voice objection. I promised Liz I would do my best to do my duty in preventing a confrontation because, after all, the fee was for the upkeep and development of the harbour.

We arrived in Poros and no sooner had we secured the boat a man in uniform appeared from nowhere and shouted, "Office, ten minutes".

Captain Pete drew himself up to his full height, his chest expanded by at least four inches. "Who are you?" he asked.

"Port police," came the reply.

"What do you want?" asked Peter.

"Papers, ten minutes," said the Greek pointing his finger in the direction of the office. I looked at the captain's face, which was becoming rapidly more rigid and I saw the signs of a man about to cause trouble. Thinking of Liz, I reminded him of his promise to her that he would not quote his human rights and the right to freedom of travel. Dudley went along with Pete to the Port Police Office whilst I stayed on board. When they returned they were laughing. I always twitch when men are looking pleased with themselves. What they got up to I hate to think but at least what I didn't know I wouldn't have to confess to Liz!

As we walked from the harbour around the winding road to the village in search of a restaurant, Dudley saw a sign reading "Local Karaoke Evening Tonight". Before Dudley and I met he had compered karaoke evenings himself. He had found this a great way to meet people and make friends in England and planned to host the occasional sing-a-long when we were eventually living in Greece. Dudley was interested to see what response Karaoke received amongst the Greek people and as we both liked to sing, it was natural that we would end our evening at this establishment.

After our meal Dudley guided us back to the local taverna, saying, "Just one song, just to see." By 2 a.m. in the morning we all had sung several songs and drunk enough Metaxa to sink a ship. Captain Pete sang Delilah to rapturous applause and the karaoke man said instead of the normal two prizes, that evening there would be three. One for the best singer, one for the worst singer and one for the special talents of Captain Pete!

In the morning we set sail for Big Vathi on Ithaca and whilst Dudley was at the helm Captain Pete invited me to navigate. It was his valued opinion that I was 'getting the hang of it' so it was with a puffed up chest that I sat on the side deck as the wind got ever stronger. Just as we rounded the headland at the southern tip of Ithaca a gust caught us and we were millimetres from a knockdown, the genoa just dipping into the water. Luckily Dudley did not fight against the helm and relaxed his hold on the tiller allowing the bow to naturally come round into the wind and *Admetus* did what she was designed to do and righted herself. We put a reef in the mainsail, reefed the genoa and off we sailed, safely arriving at Vathi in one piece!

With our holiday fast slipping away from us we decided to provision for a further barbeque and made our way by motor to 'our' bay just outside Frikes. These places were starting to feel like home and made us wish more than ever that we could find that perfect boat. With this in mind Captain Pete suggested we go back to Sivota to see if the taverna owner with a yacht for sale was available to see us the following day. Luckily for us, when we arrived the following day he was available and was happy to show us around his yacht, a Dromor Apollo, Greek built boat, 39 foot, double cabin and heads in the bow and two double cabins in the stern with separate heads. At last! Could it be true?

Being respectful of the local culture I stayed back aboard Admetus whilst Dudley and Captain Pete (the men folk!) went to talk business with the taverna owner. I was left alone for over an hour to wonder what was being said, I was anxious, nervous and somewhat excited. My anticipation and excitement disappeared when the men returned, as they were not sure if the boat was for sale. The owner of the yacht had said it was for sale and he wanted the money immediately but we could not take possession of the boat as he had lets to the end of the summer. We later found out that he had also taken lets for the following year!!

We were so disappointed! The whole affair of boat hunting had become a bit of an emotional roller coaster and we began to think that we were never going to find a boat. It had been almost a whole year since we first started looking for a yacht that could become our new home. So far, whatever we had looked at had been suitable or had been out of our price range.

Faith can be a funny thing. When things are going well faith is strong. When life becomes difficult, faith can become weak. I know in the past when bad things have happened I question faith; I question, "Why me?", I question if I am really being looked over. This time I was determined to trust in my faith, I knew that what we were planning was right for our future and I was positive that if my faith remained strong something would come along. More than that, it would come along for us at the right time in our lives.

Whatever happened, Dudley and I were not going to let our disappointment spoil the rest of the holiday. All thoughts of the Dromor disappeared when on this bright, sunny, calm morning we received Navtex information indicating a storm warning. We motored to Tranquil Bay, there being no wind at that time, and passed through into an adjoining bay beyond known as Vliho. When the wind eventually came, it did so with some force, but we were safely anchored and well prepared to ride out the storm.

Captain Pete indicated that I might be about to have my first night on anchor watch. For those not in the know this is exactly what it says. You sit and watch in case the anchor drags loose in bad weather. As the weather worsened we decided that we should not leave the boat and we would eat on board. This was to be my first experience of cooking on board Admetus or any other yacht for that matter. I was pleasantly surprised that although the cooking area appeared small in comparison to the kitchen at home, wonders could be achieved. A chicken curry and rice kept the cool air out but did nothing for the increased wind inside the boat!! Luckily the full storm never reached us and we all managed to have a full night's sleep.

The following day brought light south-easterly winds, and Captain Pete in his wisdom, misguided or otherwise, turned Admetus over to us to sail alone without his input. I still could not seem to grasp which way to head the boat to catch the wind in the sails. When close hauled, I was fine because the 'tell tales' indicate which way to steer but in other sailing directions once I lost the wind from the sails, I got confused as to how to find it again. It's a weird sensation, a little like when I first took driving lessons. When I looked behind to reverse I could never seem to co-ordinate left and right to steer the car in the correct direction. Captain Pete, as ever, was patient and said it would come. Well, we'd just have to wait and see on that one! The day ended with us moored in Little Vathi and another pleasant meal ashore whilst Dudley explained wind directions to me. Being a pilot of light aircraft, he explained that the principles and wind effect on a sail were the same as that of an aircraft wing. He obviously grasped what was happening and could helm accordingly. I, on the other hand, didn't have a clue. What he was talking about?

The new day brought a south-easterly force 5 and we had a wonderful sail around the corner into Abeleike for a lunchtime swim. Dudley and I were snorkelling under the watchful eye of the captain when another yacht came squeezing into the space between *Admetus* and the shore and nearly dropped their anchor on top of me. I was glaring at the crew as I swam back towards *Admetus* trying to avoid further hazard when I noticed the yacht was flying a German flag and it was full of naked men, one of whom sat with his legs at 'ten to two' as I swam past. Well excuse me, that was a sight I could have well lived without. This kind of behaviour I find totally unnecessary and not the sort that makes friends of other sailors, especially not this novice one.

The wind still good, we set off for our anchorage of the night on Kalamos. As we came through the channel between Kalamos and the mainland the wind was gusting as it was being channelled in such a way that the wind force was increased. One gust came with such force we almost instantly heard a loud bang. We saw a jolt of the boom and we all jumped up and looked to see what had happened. The kicking strap under the boom had snapped with the fierceness of the wind. We took the sails down to prevent further damage and motored into the harbour to see about temporary repairs. Captain Pete had noticed a tear in the UV strip on the genoa and decided that it too needed to be taken down in the morning for repair.

We were starting to prepare for our evening deck shower when another boat limped in alongside us, having lost the use of its engine. Both men on board *Admetus* jumped into action and, with little pomp or nonsense helped the boat in distress to moor safely next to us - just another good deed for the day! Back to my deck shower, I sat on the cockpit floor washing my hair and Dudley, as usual, had control of directing the hose for accuracy. "Dudley," I had to moan more than once, "What are you doing? You are not aiming the water very well." I couldn't understand why he was being so careless with the water; normally he had a direct aim and would constantly tell me to hurry up and not to use so much water. I came to the conclusion that because the other boat was so close, he dare not say anything and was being polite. Wrong. When I stood up following my shower I noticed the lady, or should I say woman? No, let us be brutally honest. The tart next door stood there in front of the whole harbour, with not a stitch on, washing her frontal lobes with great delight and taking far too much enjoyment in over zealous massaging.

I was furious. Dudley's silence was obviously because he was too busy looking at her rather than paying attention to me. That was it- divorce. How unfaithful could my husband get? It was so completely unnecessary. Why do women with low morals force themselves onto others with more decorum? As you may be able to tell, I disagree with the need to be naked in front of anyone other than my husband. Captain Pete tried to calm me, explaining if I wanted to live a life on board a yacht abroad, this was something I would have to come to terms with. "People should be allowed to express themselves as they wished," he said. I knew he was right but it went against everything decent inside me. I prayed for guidance and understanding for the sake of my marriage and our planned future life together.

Speaking grudgingly to my husband the following morning, the genoa was taken down and an unsuccessful attempt to repair it was made. Not having a sail to sail with and there being only two days left of our holiday, we therefore decided to leave Kalamos and head straight back to Levkas. It was a bright sunny day as we left, heading back under engine. Within ten minutes of our departure the clouds filled in and all of a sudden we were surrounded by what appeared to be three separate storms. Within a very short space of time the winds increased and the seas became very choppy as the storms moved around us. Conditions worsened as the rains came and Dudley and I got the opportunity to christen our waterproof jackets. The storms swirled around us as we sat in the cockpit getting absolutely drenched. The sea spray crashed over the side decks as poor Admetus heaved up and down on the waves. The propeller was whirring and whining as it tried to turn in nothing more than air as the stern of the boat was pushed up by waves that were disappearing underneath the yacht. So we continued on, going up and down, round and round, until the *Admetus'* crew of three, salt crusted and looking very much the worse for wear, arrived in Levkas. We still had full wet proofs on as we came into moor on the mole, as it hadn't been until we reached the end of the canal that we left the rain behind and motored into blue skies. Now we found ourselves being stared at by people lounging about in bikinis, seemingly thinking, "How strange". Trying to break the ice and finding an opportunity to explain our appearance, we discovered that Levkas town itself had had a nice, calm, sunny day. They must have thought we were mad but not as mad as the strange weather patterns that prevail around this particular area of the Ionian.

Our last two days on the mole disappeared too quickly and all too soon we were on the bus headed back to England. This was more heart wrenching than ever before. We so longed to be able to stay, yet our search for a yacht had been fruitless. We didn't know when we would be able to come back again and this not knowing increased the sadness we felt. We knew that to be able to afford to buy our own boat there would be no more holidays for us and we would need to save as much money as we could in all areas of our life to make this dream come true. With the deepest sadness, Dudley and I tore ourselves away from Levkas, Captain Pete and *Admetus*; we held in our heart the words, "until we meet again."

Once home, and spurred on by our holiday, Dudley began to call all yacht brokers and charterers around England. One particular Broker in Lewes, Sussex, thought he might be able to help. It transpired he was an agent for a Sailing Holiday company on the Island of Corfu who, as it was the end of the holiday season, were selling off one of their boats. We couldn't believe our luck, the details were faxed through to Dudley's office and the yacht in question turned our to be another Dromor Apollo, only this one was a forty-foot and had exactly the right specification we had in mind. Indeed it was almost exactly the same as the yacht we had been trying to purchase on our holiday, the difference being it was slightly longer and wider.

With the helpful assistance of the broker Dudley hopped on a plane to Athens. Outside of holiday season, the only flights available were scheduled flights to Athens. From here, Dud picked up a connecting flight to Corfu to view the boat. The journey having been arranged for Dudley, things went smoothly and the only contact I had with him was when he said he had arrived safely and he would view the boat the following day. The following five days were torture. I dared not hope for too much but at the same time was praying that this was the one. Dudley came home smiling and feeling very proud of himself as he told me we were now the proud owners of a yacht named *Orpheus*.

He had taken photographs of the inside and outside to show me but it would be some time before I would get to see the real thing. When the initial excitement wore off and reality set in we realised that this was just the beginning. We now had our whole lives to sort out to enable us to leave England and start our new life on board.

For those who have never heard of "Orpheus in the Underworld" I shall briefly give you an insight into this part of Greek Mythology. Orpheus was son to Apollo and the muse Calliope. Apollo presented his son with a lyre and taught him to play it. It was said that the skill of his playing could charm wild animals and uproot trees. Orpheus fell blissfully in love with a nymph named Eurydice and they were wed and lived happily until one day a minor deity Aristaeus pursued her. In her eagerness to escape, she stepped on a poisonous snake, was stung and died. Such was Orpheus' grief he resolved to find his dead wife and beg for her release from the underworld.

Finding a cave, which led to Hades, he used his musical charms to persuade the devil to let Eurydice return to the land of the living. Such was the beauty of his playing the ghosts and demons wept as he played. It was agreed that Eurydice would be released on the condition that as they returned to the world of the living he should not turn around to look at her until they reached the upper air. In a moment of forgetfulness, to assure himself that she was still following, Orpheus glanced behind him and she was instantly pulled away and returned to the underworld.

In his grief Orpheus vowed he would never love another and hid himself from all women. One day, the Thracian women stumbled upon him and tried to entice him but he showed no interest. In frustration, the women attacked him, throwing stones and javelins at him and tearing him limb from limb in anger. The muses then gathered up the fragments of his body and buried them at Libethra, where the nightingale is said to sing over his grave more sweetly than in other parts of Greece. Zeus, to mark his grief, placed Orpheus' lyre amongst the stars.

Once in the underworld, Orpheus sought out Eurydice and embraced her with eager arms. Now they are said to roam the skies together taking it in turns to lead as they dance across the sky, together forever.

This Greek legend amused us both because Dudley, as previously mentioned, was otherwise known as 'Cuddly Dudley' running a Karaoke Road show. The musical and enduring love connections delighted us. It felt so right. This was the one meant for us and we had a good feeling about life. We focused on nothing but ensuring we put our lives in order to allow us to fly out to *Orpheus* at the earliest opportunity. Nothing could take the shine off the happiness we both felt and to some extent we felt relief. At long last our dream was looking like it could become a reality.

CHAPTER 3
PLANNING AND PRAYING

Now we were the proud owners of *Yacht Orpheus*, it was time to think about the practical side of things. It was now a reality. It was going to happen. *Orpheus* was in dry dock in Corfu being cared for over the winter by Dimitris, the owner of the Sailing Holiday organisation we had purchased the boat from. He had agreed to make a few alterations for us as part of the sale, such as cockpit speakers for the music system and a spray hood for winter sailing – cosmetic things that Dudley and I had wanted to make our dream boat complete.

There were hard and definite decisions to be made to make our dream a reality. We now had the boat but we needed to take stock of what we already had on board and what equipment we would need to purchase. The only sailing experience I had was gained on board *Admetus*; I felt I needed more than that if this was to be my future life. Most importantly, there was Harry. How were we going to get Harry out of England and into Greece? I also had to consider girlie things such as blonde highlights, which at the time I had and quickly realised that nipping to the salon to have them enhanced was not always going to be an option open to me. I decided to grow them out and return to my natural mouse blonde.

January arrived and we took ourselves along to the boat show at Earls Court, London. We had our shopping list for Orpheus and were determined to get only what we wanted and needed and not to be led astray by all the wonderful things that were there. Item number one on the list was a life jacket for our Westie, Harry, closely followed by a Furuno GPS that had been voted best buy in a monthly yachting magazine. We also considered the practical side of living aboard a boat in a hot climate and decided we wanted an independent 12V/240 fridge that could operate from the domestic battery on board and not draw energy from the main battery used to start the engine.

This all turned out to be just the pinnacle of our independent lives - using 12 volt. We looked for battery operated lights, solar powered torches, a 12v shaver (for Dudley of course) and a 12v television. We even invested in two second-hand folding bicycles so we could explore the islands under pedal power. We enjoyed every minute of our search for equipment and things to make our new life comfortable. It would be fair to say it was great until we reached the part where we had to look at computers and mobile phones.

At the end of January I was convalescing following an operation. With time on my hands I tried to decide the best way for us to stay in touch with family and friends whilst living on board a yacht. I finally decided the easiest and best way would be to take along a laptop, invest in a new mobile phone and email home regularly. We thought a digital camera would also be a good idea to enable us to attach some photographs to emails. Conversely this arrangement would also allow Dudley's four children and six grandchildren to keep in touch and send us photographs of themselves. It all sounded ideal, until the reality of our technical knowledge kicked in.

My experience of computing had been to turn up at work as a PA and type away on a centrally driven system utilising Windows. If anything went wrong, I called the help desk. Dudley's experience was specific to insurance quotes, which didn't feature in our future life. We soon began to realise that people in the computing world would take advantage of the fact that we didn't know what we were talking about. I am quite a sensitive person and can normally tell when I am being taken for a ride. Luckily for me, on this occasion, coming from Norfolk was a gift as we speak our minds and are not afraid to say no, forcefully if need be. We wanted to buy second hand as we had read that damp and salty conditions meant the life span of a laptop was approximately two years. We also wanted the ability to email, to store digital photographs and also to allow me to write a book! A good friend of Dudley's, Joe Aldridge, owned his own computer business and, on hearing of our difficulties, kindly and patiently helped us to find the right laptop for our purposes.

We purchased a digital camera with little hassle, from Pat at Capricorn Cameras and apart from reading the book and learning how to use it, all was going well. This was not to be the case with the mobile phone. We purchased a mobile with GPRS capability. At this time, this was still a relatively new thing and we had to rely on the staff selling us the mobile to explain what this meant and what its use was. GPRS stands for Global Positioning Receiving Satellite, a system used to transfer electronic data i.e. an email. The benefits of this were we would be charged per megabyte of information sent and received, as opposed to the amount of time we were logged on to the Internet. The only hiccup with this was that the phone company who sold us the phone didn't supply the data cable to link it to the laptop. This we had to purchase separately from the telephone company. However, neither company supplied us with the software to load onto the laptop to enable the use of the GPRS. The telephone company said the shop where the phone was purchased should have provided it. The shop said we could have GPRS on 'pay as you go' but would only provide the software if we were on contract. Without the software we could not use the GPRS – (are you keeping up with this?)!

To conclude what could turn into a very long saga and sequel to this book, we asked for our money back from both the shop and the phone company and started again. Along the way we had learned that buying a local sim card meant cheaper calls because we would be paying local rates instead of international rates. If we bought a phone in England it would cost £20 to unlock the phone to enable a local sim card to be inserted when we got to Greece. We decided we would wait until we went away and purchase the phone and sim card then. This was a decision we should have stuck to but you will see, as you read on, in our eagerness to ensure contact with family and friends we added further torment to what was already a nightmare.

Dudley and I discussed how we would travel out to join Orpheus. We decided we could have a big adventure travelling across Europe seeing France, Luxembourg, Switzerland and Italy along the way. We thought we could purchase a vehicle and caravan, pack up our belongings and travel over two months having some fun with Harry. All thoughts of fun and adventure faded when I contacted DEFRA (The Department for Environment, Food and Rural Affairs) to see what veterinary services I would need to take Harry across Europe.

I was informed that my local vet could provide me with a letter and certificates of health for Luxembourg and

Switzerland under the PETS scheme, however, DEFRA would issue the export licence to travel through France, Italy and Greece, our ultimate destination. The trouble with what appeared to be a very user friendly system was that each licence had a time expiry date. From England we were allowed 30 days to get to Italy but only ten days to get to Greece, which was considerably further away! If we did not make it to Greece in time we would have to take the chance that the Italian authorities would renew the licence allowing Harry to travel on to Greece. This was a risk we were not prepared to take. Harry meant too much to us to have him taken away for even a second.

When we had first made the decision to buy a yacht I had taken Harry to be chipped. I would highly recommend doing this as soon as possible as once they are inserted under the skin they can move. Harry's moved from the back of his neck down to the shoulder on the left leg. This is apparently normal and nothing to worry about. We were advised that before issuing the certificates Harry would require rabies vaccination and that we should arrange for this in good time before leaving the country. It is at this stage that the vet marked on Harry's record card where his chip was located, hence my suggestion to get your pet chipped as soon as possible. It gives the chip time to settle in the body and allows for an accurate identification of the animal on the record card.

After the first injection we were asked to return four weeks later to allow the vet to take a blood test from Harry. This was required for testing to see if the rabies vaccination was offering sufficient protection. The actual ruling was in fact THIRTY DAYS after the vaccination had been administered NOT four weeks. Therefore I had returned to the vet three days early and they would not test him – quite right, but frustrating for everyone concerned. If the blood test came back with an unfavourable result a second vaccination would be necessary and there would be a further wait of thirty days prior to a second blood test being undertaken.

Luckily for us, Harry's blood test passed first time at a cost of £78 but this in itself was not without problems. It took six weeks for Harry's blood test results to come through. Initially the testing company had sent the results to the wrong vet, who had done nothing with them, causing an unnecessary delay. This was only discovered after six weeks because I felt the length of time I had waited was unreasonable and I insisted my vet chase the company for the results, which was when the error was discovered.

Once the blood test was confirmed the vet could issue the PETS certificate and as long as a booster rabies injection was given prior to the date of expiry the PETS certificate could be renewed without having to start the process all over again. It was our experience that being well prepared and obtaining the necessary injections and PETS certificate well in advance of travel made the whole system more relaxed and bearable. A word of caution for those who leave it late and wish to return to the U.K. within a short space of time: your pet will not be allowed back into the U.K. until six months has passed from the date of the first successful rabies vaccination and subsequent blood test.

All the necessary medical requirements for Harry were in place. The only thing left for us to do prior to travel was for us to make sure Harry, received treatment for ticks and tapeworm within twenty-four to forty-eight hours prior to travelling. This timing is VERY important because if the treatment is given over forty-eight hours prior to travel, authorities will not permit the pet to travel. A further treatment would need to be administered to allow travel the following day. This type of delay can make for a bad start for you and a stressful start for the animal so think ahead and be prepared.

With Harry sorted, we went back to making our decision as to how best for us to travel to Greece. Obviously with only 10 days to get to Greece we needed to get there as cheaply and quickly as possible. We had already planned a provisional route over land so we carried out a costing analysis including purchase of vehicle and caravan, petrol, toll fees and living expenses. We estimated the total to be approximately £2,400 to £3,000 depending on how much we had to pay for a cheap caravan. As an alternative we considered taking just a car and staying in bed and breakfast accommodation. This meant we would have to ship our belongings out to Greece; the cost of this was to be £420 for two pallets. It also meant we had the problem of finding accommodation that would allow a dog into the bedrooms.

Looking at all alternative routes of travel I contacted various airlines to obtain quotes for flight prices for both Harry and us. I was informed that a set air fare price was paid for any animal with an additional fee per kilogram of weight. I was glad I had kept a healthy life style for Harry and that he had not gained a middle age spread over his nine years on this earth. I was very concerned that we would be able to fly with an animal only from England to Athens; this would cause us problems getting from there to the boat in Corfu. We were advised we would have to wait until the commercial holiday flights started at the end of May to be certain we could get a flight out to the Ionian.

Having carried out this, what we thought to be, very helpful exercise; we agreed it would be best for all concerned for us to ship out our equipment and for Dudley, Harry and I to fly out direct to Greece. Hopefully this would result in a saving of one thousand pounds, or more. It also meant all I would require from the vet was a PETS certificate and an Export Licence from DEFRA for Greece. We were disappointed that we would not be able to enjoy the journey as we had first planned but Harry was our priority and I wanted to make his life as easy as possible. As with most things in life, the best laid plans are sure to fail and ours were no different. We faced further dilemmas and had to remain flexible as to how we would finally make our way to Greece.

We had planned to travel to Greece in the latter part of August so things were well underway. By the end part of April I was in possession of the PETS Certificate (at a fee of £28) and was contemplating the completion of the EXA1 Application to DEFRA for the Export Licence to Greece. Knowing that the licence was valid for only ten days, DEFRA asked for 10 days notice prior to travel. During my dealings with the staff at DEFRA I found them to be very informative and very helpful; such was my confidence, I put any further Harry planning on hold until the end of July when I would have to again approach the matter of available flights.

Spring was upon us and we were happy to wave off our friends John and Diane Essam. Like us, John and Diane were taking off for a life aboard their yacht named Jess. They planned to sail from their mooring at Brundall, Norfolk, along the coast to the Solent and across to France. The French West Coast was calling them and their sailing date was getting ever closer.

John had known Dudley for several years and they had become good friends. John's talents were such that he had started building Jess in 1985 and completed her in 1990. Five years of dedication had resulted in a wonderful yacht. As a couple they had enjoyed sailing her over the years and were now planning to leave England for French shores. How we longed for our day to arrive to start our lives aboard *Orpheus*!

With things on course, Dudley and I were navigating our way to a successful getaway. I decided the time had come to book myself onto the Day Skipper Practical to boost my sailing skills. Dudley was to undertake a one-day assessment to obtain an I.C.C. (International Certificate of Competence), which we were advised was a requirement to sail European waters. When we finally made our way out to Greece and took delivery of Orpheus we suddenly realised that to be able to sail *Orpheus* from Corfu to Levkas and waters beyond Dudley would need to ensure that he had qualified for the I.C.C. So he booked himself onto the first available course.

He arrived early in the morning to be told that the weather forecast did not look promising and the practical sailing may be cancelled for that day. However, the written classroom part of the assessment could be completed. It had been twelve years since Dudley had passed his Yacht Master theory work and we had been revising together to refresh his memory. To him the practical sailing was the easy part of this qualification so he was relieved after spending a morning in the classroom that they told him he had passed the theory assessment. The weather did not improve during the morning so the practical sailing was cancelled and re-arranged for three days later when the projected forecast showed an improvement.

Dudley left early in the morning for Shotley to complete the practical assessment for the I.C.C. When he arrived he was informed he would be sailing that day under the supervision of three new instructors. The tutor for the day would be assessing the new instructors whilst they were assessing Dudley!

During the day Dudley was assessed on his ability to motor to a mooring, sail to a mooring, moor alongside a pontoon, recover a man overboard and prove an ability to sail with the wind in all directions to the boat utilising tacks and jibes. After a full day of sailing, and a few more tidal miles in his logbook, Dudley was informed that he had passed. He came home proudly announcing his success, which was excellent news as we could now legally sail *Orpheus* during our forthcoming trip.

Life moved at a hectic pace that spring: friends leaving, trips to the vet, the house to clear and Dudley in the middle of a building project. I had fully recovered from my operation and had returned to work to be informed within a few weeks that my then boss was leaving for pastures new and was not to be replaced. I was given the option of remaining in work at my current rate of pay or taking a voluntary redundancy with a cash incentive. I couldn't believe my luck. Knowing that I was going to be leaving my employment later in the year, to have the opportunity to leave with a redundancy package after 21 years was an absolute gift from heaven. This not only meant extra cash to help with the purchases for the boat but it meant that I would be free to help Dudley with the building work and sort the house out with less stress attached. I was realising that trying to clear a house was a mighty task and one that I was struggling to keep up with on top of everything else. This was the icing on the cake to help us start our new life.

My working life had not been an easy one in many senses. I had left school at the age of sixteen, not really being encouraged to pursue further education. I had taken many evening classes to qualify in secretarial studies and had worked my way up through the ranks the hard way. I had had many happy years with my employers and although I would miss those I worked with, I would not miss the reality of my life so far.

From the age of sixteen I had seen the worst side of people: the bad in the community and the negativity of people who live their lives to commit crime. I had worked in several units through the years dealing with drugs, surveillance, criminal records, the court system and even murders. When I finally walked out of the station doors on my last day of work I felt relieved. It was as though I had taken off a rather large, dirty, heavy coat and left it on the doorstep to replace it with a nice, new, clean one. It felt good.

I was now free to go along each day with Dudley, who was self employed, and help in the office. I played at being brickie's mate, decorated, dug the garden and generally did anything other than typing. I loved every second, feeling very much appreciated for what I was doing; a feeling I hadn't felt for many years. The sun shone as Dudley, Harry and I spent our days and nights together, enjoying being with each other and feeling closer than ever before.

We made plans to let the house at the start of the new academic year and to lease Dudley's work premises as soon as possible. We had estimated income and outgoings; the house had been re-mortgaged to afford the purchase of the boat, and we hoped that if all went well we could just about manage to live in Greece on what little income we had. Dudley was keen to take his karaoke equipment with him, convinced he was going to become the 'Cuddly Dudley' of the Greek Islands. "Angaliazo Dudley" in Greek just didn't have the same ring to it but there was an irony that 'Anglos' meant Englishman so maybe it would work after all!

Orpheus, we had been told, had been launched back into the water and was ready for us to collect. Because of delays in the building works we were not ready to leave England and so had to make a plan to take delivery of the boat and then come back to the U.K. to finish our build. Roy West our dearest friend offered to fly Dudley, Captain Pete and myself in his private aircraft, a Piper Lance, to Corfu. From here we would all sail down to Levkas where Captain Pete would stay on *Admetus* for the summer. *Orpheus* would be left on guardianage with Joe Charlton and Roy and Dudley and I would fly back in the Piper Lance to Norwich. We gratefully accepted this kind offer as this gave us the opportunity to transport far more out to Orpheus than we could have done any other way. May was approaching and it was time to fly out with some of our belongings, make our final payment of purchase and move *Orpheus* to Levkas.

The realisation that very soon I would be taking my first steps on board *Orpheus* were quite nerve racking. I hoped the real thing would live up to the promise of the photographs, and, more than ever, I wanted Roy and Captain Pete's approval for our choice. Both Dudley and I were looking forward to spending a week with our close friends; it served as a stark reminder that very soon we would be leaving them behind for a very long time.

CHAPTER 4
MAY DAY DELIBERATIONS

    For several months Dudley and I had laboured over what possessions we could take on board and what should be packed away. Boxes and newspaper everywhere, we had bit by bit packed up our home ready for storage with my mother. We knew we did not want to vegetate aboard *Orpheus* so we planned to brush up on French, learn Greek, Spanish and any other language that was necessary. The appropriate books were packed to be taken along with various musical books and instruments.

    Dudley has a musical gift in that if left to "fiddle" for a few moments on any instrument, and once he can play a full scale, he can play almost anything. Not being able to read music he plays by ear. As long as it's a tune or song that he's heard he can play it. He had told me once the only instrument he had not been able to master was a concertina. I decided that with time on his hands he should not be defeated and this was my boating gift to him: a shiny red concertina to keep his musical mind occupied.

    We packed holdalls full of kitchen equipment, cockpit cushions, clothes, and even Christmas decorations - literally everything we needed to live a normal life on board a boat. Poor Roy, I don't think he really knew what he had let himself in for when he made the kind offer to take us out to Corfu. Roy is a quiet, unassuming man, short, cuddly and generous to a fault. He seemed unfazed by the number of holdalls we planned to take, only too happy to help us deliver our chattels and spend a week aboard *Orpheus*. Dudley and I were amazed he was going to stay on board as Roy likes the comforts in life; a five star hotel would be his usual accommodation requirement. What a true friend he really was! He was prepared to sacrifice all to be with us!

    Our rendezvous point with Roy and Captain Pete was arranged at Norwich Airport. We arrived at 0600 hours bleary eyed but eager to start our journey. The Piper Lance GN-ROY was bursting at the seams with all our bags but with all the necessary weight and balance calculations done, Pilot Roy and Co-pilot Dudley were ready to take off. Using more runway than she normally would, due to the heavy load, she took to the sky and we were off. A lovely, clear blue sky lay before us with the promise of a sunny day ahead.

Captain Pete and I sat happily in the back of the aircraft looking at the sights as we waved goodbye to England and hello to France, passing a very tall Mont Blanc. Flying alongside the French Alps, not too close, we worked our way down to the South of France. It was easy to tell when we were getting closer to the South of France as the houses seemed to get bigger, every garden contained a shimmering blue pool and the marinas were full of expensive looking yachts.

Four and a half hours later we were landing at Cannes to refuel not only the plane but ourselves, too. It was midday, local time, Cannes being one hour ahead of England. We had a quick stretch of the legs, diet coke and a sticky bun and back to the Piper to take off once again for the second leg of the journey. Even though I say so myself, the trolley dolly on board did very well. I had packed sandwiches, cakes and sweets, as well as drinks; but with no toilet on board everything was consumed in moderation!

We left France heading for the Northern tip of Corsica and on from there to the coastline of Italy. Original planning had to be re-assessed when the Rome air traffic controller, as busy as he was, insisted we lower our altitude to one thousand feet – three times! To avoid flying this low Roy decided to stay outside Rome air space and flew down the coastline and cut across at "the ankle of the boot". I am assuming that readers will be au fait with the shape of Italy.

From Italy we made the long stretch over the water to Corfu. It was a very welcome sight, as the last two hours had seemed an eternity. A further four and half hours had passed and we landed local time 1900 hours, Greece being two hours ahead of England. Relieved to be there we fell out of the aircraft and started to unpack our many holdalls. I was beginning to wonder if we would be stopped because of the amount of luggage we had and feared the worst. What would they think if they found all my kitchen knives?

The sun began to set and we were still standing with our

luggage, awaiting the arrival of a bus to take us to the terminal. Darkness crept on and the gnats came out and still we waited for the bus. Captain Pete and Roy took off to see if they could speed things up and almost an hour later a bus appeared with Peter and Roy on it and the bags were loaded on. The bags were loaded off again as we stood on the edge of the airfield just outside the terminal building. The bags had to be loaded onto a conveyor belt and we all then rushed upstairs to take them off again before anyone else did! By the time we had loaded them all into two taxis we were exhausted and very hungry.

Because of the delay at the airport we arrived in darkness, and tried to find *Orpheus*. We found one yacht with the same name but quickly realised this was not the one and found our *Orpheus* a little bit further along the quay. We had emailed Dimitris telling him of our evening arrival and had requested he leave the boat unlocked for us. We had also indicated our wish to leave immediately the following day to head southwards. We loaded the bags inside *Orpheus* with barely a thought for the boat and rushed out to eat before it was too late.

Feeling a little more relaxed after our meal, we returned to the boat ready to sleep, only to find no bedding. When we looked around the boat it was bare, no cooking equipment or kettle, no duvets, no pillows, not even a toilet roll. We had to make do with the throws and cushions we had flown out for the saloon and were very grateful that my parents had bought us a yachting kettle to bring out. I was not impressed. Where was the full inventory of equipment that should be on the boat?

When morning arrived I was a woman possessed. We had taken with us the full inventory of equipment that formed part of the purchase of the boat and none of this was present. The cockpit speakers had not been fitted, there was no spray hood, and the anchor hadn't even been tied on. I looked along the line of boats and it suddenly struck me: *Orpheus* was the only one with an old tatty Greek flag; all the others had new ones. As the morning passed I was getting more and more angry. Dudley says it's because I'm young and impetuous and that I will become more patient with age. I can't see that happening myself.

Dudley had left several messages for Dimitris to come to the boat and it appeared he was ignoring us. I was now furious, I bargained with Dudley that he could have five minutes with Dimitris and then I would let rip if I didn't get what I was paying for. Being the calm person he is, wise as an owl, he sat and waited. He politely greeted Dimitris when he finally arrived at midday, and quietly told him of his displeasure at the emptiness of the boat.

Dimitris appeared to be surprised at Dudley's complaint and understood his wanting satisfaction. He said he would have his men come and fit the speakers and bring the full inventory of equipment. He asked us to write a list of things missing and he would ensure all was put right. I couldn't believe it. This man I had spent all morning hating was kind, understanding and caring. I ate humble pie. Dudley had been right; negotiate and give others a chance before rushing in.

By 1600 hours that afternoon the boat's inventory was complete and I had managed to pack away all the equipment we had flown out. It had been a long and busy day and I was frazzled. The weather seemed so hot and there had been much to do, I was really looking forward to my first sundowner on board. I had been so tied up in the day's events I had not really considered whether I liked the boat. That initial feeling of delight and pleasure had passed me by and the May Day celebrations I had anticipated for so long had turned into deliberations.

Tuesday morning we prepared ourselves to sail towards the island of Paxos. We filled up with water and diesel and were on our way. I still didn't really consider the boat as my future home and felt somewhat indifferent. I just wanted to get to Levkas. The first time I took the helm it felt awful. I had only ever sailed with a tiller on *Admetus* but *Orpheus* had a wheel, which I found difficult to steer, as I could not feel the boat responding to my control. It was cold and unfeeling and I was starting to miss Admetus very much.

There was very little wind and the heat of the day was more like that of July instead of May. We motored along with the bimini up for shade and just a gentle breeze over the deck of the boat keeping us cool. In the afternoon Dudley and Captain Pete took time out for a siesta and I navigated whilst Roy took the helm. I was amazed at how well he had adapted to the boating life style but I wondered whether sailing was quick enough for him. He was used to fast aeroplanes and cars; six hours sailing to travel such a short distance was alien to him.

We made our leisurely way to Gaios on Paxos by which time all crew members were awake. On board *Admetus* we were used to mooring bows to the quay and so decided to do the same on *Orpheus*. We were coming into anchor for the first time and it was agreed Captain Pete would take the helm whilst Dudley dropped the anchor; he would then come forward to sort out the shorelines. Unfortunately the anchor rope had a knot in it and became snagged which took some time to clear. By the time we got close to the quayside there was a man waiting for the shoreline so I threw it to him and he passed it back on board. I asked for him to pull us in a bit closer so I could jump ashore and sort out the other line.

I stood on the step plate in front of the forestay waiting to be close enough to jump. I launched myself ashore to take the second rope and all I remember is landing. My shoes slipped off my feet – blood – hole in my bottom lip – people dragging me asking me to walk – sitting with blood all over me and a leg that had been badly grazed, looking at a sea of worried faces.

An Australian lady was dabbing iodine all over me whilst a flotilla leader was finding numbers for the doctor and a taxi. People rallied round to help, showing an interest but I was too stunned to realise what had happened. My head felt light and I wasn't sure if I was in pain or not. I knew from the amount of blood I should be feeling something but I wasn't. I kept fading in and out, catching snippets of time, glances of faces and the occasional grip of my hand as Dudley kept saying, "Grip my hand if you can hear me."

Roy managed to flag down a car and I was taken to the local hospital. I was ushered into a small, pure white room with a lady dressed all in white. The only colour I could see was her black hair and the Red Cross on the front of her white overalls. Red; pure red; blood red. She said I needed the doctor and luckily the local man had waited, as I had to go back from whence I had come. The worried expression on the man's face emphasised his aging wrinkles and I remembered thinking, *What a nice man*.

The next thing I knew I was walking upstairs and guided into another small room with a bed in it. A bed at last! Let me lay down, let me sleep; please, just let me sleep. I lay down and Doctor Kostas went about repairing the damage. I had tiny stones imbedded in my face, which were gently removed. Once clean, with Dudley's assistance, the doctor numbed my face and put seven stitches under the chin and five in the bottom lip.

Kostas said he would not have given so many stitches for a man, but so I would still look beautiful he put in a few more. What lovely eyes he had. Inside the bottom lip was another matter. He could not give me any more painkillers and he had to put three stitches inside. Stinging agony; my mouth watering; feeling sick with the pain. I faded in and out and could still hear Dudley asking me to grip his hand. For a moment I thought I heard him crying but then this could be my imagination. What on earth had I done?

I became aware from time to time of people looking through the door- local people who had come to be treated by the doctor. On seeing that he was busy they would patiently wait outside the door. I could hear Roy chatting to a lady in the reception area and it seemed so surreal. This wasn't me; it must be someone else. Why couldn't I feel my face, my jaw, my teeth. I had already twisted my front tooth back into shape, it having been pushed in when I fell. Now it was numb.

On finishing his handiwork I was given a tetanus jab, given antibiotics, painkillers and anti-inflammatories by the doctor. He wanted me to return in the morning to clean the wound and to settle his bill. "I hope you did our holiday insurance," I said to Dudley on leaving the doctors.

"No," came the reply. However much was this all going to cost? On top of everything else we were going to have to pay for the treatment.

I took to my bunk on returning to the boat and Dudley came and lay with me, comforting me and ensuring I took my medication on time. All night I could hear people outside the boat talking about the incident and what had occurred. I felt so ashamed; I was the topic of the harbour. How embarrassing! It reminded me of the time we sat on *Admetus* and a husband and wife team came into anchor so quickly they burst their bow buoy. Everybody was talking about it all evening and took great delight in relaying how loud the bang was and how the male, who had been at the helm, tried to cover his embarrassment by blaming the female, who at the time was visibly shaking as she stood on the bow when the buoy burst! My sailing reputation was never going to be the same again.

Sleep evaded me. I lay awake wondering what awful thing I had done to deserve such a punishment. I questioned my actions and prayed for an explanation as to why this could have happened. All I could remember was landing, so what had happened. In the morning I asked Dudley to look at the quayside because I thought it had given way under my feet. When we both looked the square quayside was not square, it was bevelled like a 50-pence coin. I had obviously jumped and landed on a slope and my feet had slid backwards down the slope, scraping my leg and landing with my whole body weight on my chin.

With my eyes bleary from lack of sleep, Dudley took me back to Doctor Kostas to have the dressing changed and the wound cleaned. It wasn't until we tried to find the building housing the doctor that both Dudley and I realised how little we had remembered; a sign of how distressed we both must have been. We eventually found Kostas who, on inspection of the wound, was pleased with his craftsmanship. This morning I could concentrate on more than his eyes and I maintained my original opinion: he was a fine looking man. Dudley didn't agree but then I would hardly expect him to. The doctor told us that a Dutchman had done exactly the same thing the previous year, only he had fallen completely in the water and sustained a compound fracture of both shins. This started both of us thinking, what if... What if I had broken something? What if I had bitten my tongue? What if my glasses had smashed and splintered into my eyes? What if...

Suddenly it began to dawn on me. I had not been punished I had been saved. I left the doctor's office with the feeling that I had been protected in my hour of need. I no longer searched for answers or complained about the pain. I felt very grateful. On considering what could have happened to me, I was happy to have only suffered a few stitches and a scraped leg. I had been very lucky indeed.

Dudley asked Doctor Kostas how much we owed him for his services and I stood holding my breath, fearing the worst. In the translation from Euros to Sterling, the cost of having stitches, tetanus, painkillers, antibiotics, anti- inflammatories and a re-dressing came to £70. I couldn't believe it. His treatment had been worth every penny! And did I mention how handsome he was?

I had received first class treatment and had been surrounded by lovely, friendly people who had been prepared to help when it was needed. I felt so lucky and knew that when we came to live in Greece permanently, I would never again be afraid about getting medical assistance if it was needed. I was very impressed with the quality of service, in such a small village, on a very small island.

As we left the doctor's surgery I recognised the face of a man crossing the square in front of us. Greying hair and worried wrinkle lines that faced North instead of South as he smiled across at us. I waved my best Greek wave and squeezed out, "Kaleemera," through swollen lips. My good morning greeting worked and he said, in broken English, that I looked well and would we all like to have a coffee with him. We gladly accepted, wishing to thank him for his help the previous evening.

Dudley, Roy, Peter and I followed along the road to his taverna and sat drinking coffee with him. His English was limited but he appeared to enjoy sitting and listening and sharing in the conversation when he could. I explained as best I could, my face now very tight with swelling, that Dudley was my husband, "Andras Mou," and that the other two gentlemen were "Filos Moo, ton Iene Roy keh Peter." - my friends, their names being Roy and Peter.

This was what Dudley and I longed for: meeting people, breaking down boundaries of languages and enjoying the relaxed culture of the Greek people. As sore as my face was, the incident had not stopped me loving the place, loving the people. I felt so very lucky and so grateful for having the fortune to be around such caring friends and strangers. When we got back to the boat I had the opportunity to thank the Australian lady who had dabbed her best iodine all over me. Again and again I thanked God for my life and for surrounding me with such love and beauty. I felt so cared for, that by the time we pulled up anchor to leave I had almost forgotten my stitches. I guess a part of me would always love and remain in the pretty village of Gaios, literally.

We headed off for our second leg, 180 degrees due south to Levkas. We bobbed along under engine power, there being no wind again today. The men took it in turns to helm whilst I hibernated under the bimini. The sun on my open wound stung, so I decided to stay in the shade and be treated like a lady. I was being fussed over and treated like a rare orchid by three caring and loving men. A few attempts were made to get me to take the helm but I just didn't want to. All I wanted to do was get to Levkas and visit Admetus; she would understand and make me feel better.

We arrived at Levkas harbour late afternoon. We introduced ourselves to Joe and his staff and made arrangements for him to look after *Orpheus* when we returned to England. We had two days to sort out the boat so Roy hired a car to explore the island leaving Dudley and me to plan our future. Of course, Peter went along to *Admetus* to settle himself for the next six weeks on board. We planned where our equipment would be stored, cupboard space, clothing, curtains; it was just like setting up home. It had been lovely having all three men on board but now we were alone, it was our first taste of what our life would be like together. We were happy. The boat was very clean and very cosy. I was happy with Dudley's choice and my new home. I had been on board three days and it was only now that reality was sinking in and instead of fighting the boat I was actually paying attention to it. I was very pleased with the way I felt and was very much looking forward to August when we could finally come back to stay. The only sadness I felt was due to the helm wheel. I simply had not enjoyed the sailing aspect of *Orpheus*, I knew it was going to take some time and practice before my views would change.

With wings on my feet, Dudley and I went off to meet Captain Pete aboard *Admetus*. There she sat, blue as the sky, nodding a gentle hello. It was good to be aboard. I took myself to the 'pointy bit' and had a quiet moment with her whilst Peter showed Roy around her lower quarters. She had a few more scratches on her deck but still looked and felt good beneath my feet. It seemed strange knowing that I was not going to be sailing her this trip. I felt quite sad. Would I ever be sailing her again? Would I have that chance or would I be so wrapped up in *Orpheus* that the occasion wouldn't arise?

Saturday morning arrived and it was time to say goodbye to Captain Pete and *Admetus*. He would be staying until the end of June enjoying life, sailing and being free. There were no tears this time because it would only be four months and we would be coming back for good, but there was heaviness in my heart and I felt a great loss. I missed *Admetus* already. Would I ever be sailing her again, feeling the thrill, admiring her beauty? I so very much hoped I would.

Dudley, Roy and I drove from Levkas to Igoumenitsa to catch the ferry back to Corfu. It was during the journey that Roy thought it might be a good idea to board the Piper and make our way to Cannes that afternoon to break up the long journey home. We thought it an excellent idea and took off from Corfu around 1300 hours.

We arrived in Cannes in good time to book into a hotel and visit the restaurant. The menu before me was very unforgiving for a person with a mouth that would hardly open, a jaw that couldn't chew and teeth that couldn't bite. I had spent two days unable to eat anything but soup through a straw and had now reached the stage of being able to squeeze little bits of soft food through a half inch gap in my lips. Nothing on the menu seemed appropriate so I would have to struggle. I was reminded of our night out at the Lighthouse Restaurant in Levkas. Steve was a cheerful man with a big smile and bigger waistline who worked very hard whilst his wife, the chef, worked even harder. On seeing my face when we arrived he had asked his wife to make me a special soup that I could suck through a straw. It was delicious and very welcome to a stomach that hadn't eaten for so long. His wife had cut little pieces of spaghetti into it so if my aim was good I could suck that up too. Nothing so caring in Cannes, and two hours later I was still trying to cut up and chew the chicken I had chosen.

The next morning we set off again for England. All the same sights passed me by and my tiredness caught up with me, as I closed my eyes and drifted off into the land of nod. Roy and Dudley flew us safely home. We landed just in time for Sunday lunch at Autopilots Bar. If only I could eat it! I tried my best but everything was an effort. We picked up Harry, our Westie, from Doreen, a friend and neighbour who had taken care of him whilst we were away. We sat in our home, unpacked and started wishing that August were closer than it was. However, there was still so much for us to sort out before we could leave the country, the most important of which was for me to get Harry used to being in a carrying case ready for his flight out. The accident had given my confidence a savage blow, I was hesitant about moving around the deck and mooring and thanks to the helm wheel my sailing ability seemed to have hit rock bottom. I was going to have to get over this rather quickly because the Day Skipper Practical course I had booked myself onto was just around the corner. I hoped my face would heal in time, as we would be eating on board!

CHAPTER 5
DAY SKIPPER

I contacted the company co-ordinating my Day Skipper course to make them aware of my continuing difficulties due to my recent accident. My facial swelling was now gone, my jaw opened a little wider but I still had difficulty eating some foods that required lots of chewing. As food was being provided for the five days of the course I felt it only appropriate to warn them in advance of my facial disability. They didn't seem to think there would be a problem so off I went to complete my practical sailing course.

The Sunday morning arrived for the course to commence. Dudley helped me to pack the essentials such as sleeping bag, waterproofs, sailing gloves and warm clothing. As the day passed I was getting more and more nervous. When booking onto the course the co-ordinating couple had cast doubt on my ability to cope because I hadn't completed the competent crew practical beforehand and had never sailed tidal waters. Now the day had arrived, their doubts had become mine and I was starting to feel quite sick with nerves.

All the way to Ipswich I begged Dudley not to make me go. I didn't want to go any more, I couldn't do it. I sent a text message to Captain Pete for support but the answer came back, "Make sure you wear sensible shoes". Both he and Dudley were still convinced my feet slipped on the quayside in Gaios because I was wearing sandals and not proper sailing shoes. I appeased him by letting him know that I would be wearing proper deck shoes and boots.

We arrived at Suffolk Yacht Marina and found the yacht that would be home for the next five days. Dudley came aboard and I clung to him trying to drain every ounce of confidence he had, to use it for myself. I sat quietly whilst he talked to the couple taking the course, sharing boating stories, hoping that nobody would ask me anything. I was just the dumb blonde who jumped off boats, smashed her face up and has never sailed tidal waters... Oh, why did I come?

A quietly spoken gentleman arrived and was introduced as Steve. He appeared to know the couple already and I thought to myself, *I really am going to be the odd one out.* As we sat drinking tea I was asked what had happened to my face that caused me to have such eating difficulties. It was a fair question, so I regaled them with my story of flight from the bow to the quay; no comment was made other than to remark how quickly the wound had healed. It had. It was only two weeks since it happened and the stitches were out and externally all looked well.

Steve was very polite and almost as nervous as myself. He explained he owned a yacht called Scylla, which is the Latin name for bluebell, and had sailed the Ipswich waters often. "Oh no," I thought, "he can sail and has experience in tidal water." The doubts I already had just increased ten fold. I really did feel the biggest bimbo out and I didn't want to stay. Please don't make me stay, Dudley!

Dudley drove away leaving me on board, after hugging me and telling me to just do my best. Everything would be all right. It was only five days and if I didn't pass it didn't matter. At least I would have tried. The husband and wife tutors, Steve and myself went for a drink in the marina bar to acquaint ourselves with each other prior to setting off.

During the evening I warmed to Steve. He may have been experienced but he was unassuming, friendly, funny and quite charming. If nothing else, I hoped I had made another friend during the week of torture that lay ahead. The couple explained to us briefly what the week would consist of and then we meandered back to the boat for a good night's sleep – or so I thought.

Because we were two males and two females it was natural for the sleeping arrangements to take account of this. The females took the forepeak cabin and the males the saloon bunks. I snuggled down into the sleeping bag and missed Dudley very much. I was asked if I minded if my cabin mate read for a while. Of course, I didn't. I regretted this decision later when I discovered she was a paper rustler as she read, never mind that it wasn't for long. When at last the paper slapping and rustling ended, it only took seconds and the snoring started; it went on and on, and on. Tiredness overtook me in the wee hours of the morning but it was only when my cabin mate rustled and banged her way out of the boat at 6 a.m., heading for the showers that I finally slept soundly until breakfast.

Over breakfast the natural question arose, "Did you sleep well?" What should I say? Should I be honest? Should I tell a little white lie? "Why change the practice of a lifetime?" I thought. "Just tell it how it is."

"Not really," I said. "You snore like nothing on earth." A hush went round the boat.

"That's it you've just blown your certificate," I thought to myself. Luckily, after a short period of denial the excuse of having a slight cold was given and all was forgotten.

Steve and I were shown around the boat and as we went the various ropes, or sheets as they are called, were explained to us and we were shown how to hank or hook on and hoist the genoa (foresail). This was all very interesting to me as my sailing had only been on *Admetus* and she had a self-furling genoa. Having prepared the sails and tidied them ready to hoist when required, we were given tuition on how to start the engine. The course and plan for the day's sail had been made for us and we set off together.

I was at the helm as we motored along, feeling very content as this particular yacht had a tiller and not a wheel. I was told we were going to pick up a mooring buoy under engine power. We had only been out ten minutes and I was a little surprised by the speed of the action. I had expected to be broken in more gently than this. What the heck – in for a penny, in for a pound. We were asked what effect the tide would have on the boat as we approached the mooring; obviously I didn't have a clue. Steve knew and volunteered an answer that only promoted another question and another answer. This was the first of many such bouts, testing our knowledge. It almost felt like they were trying to trip us up, catch us out in an attempt to make us feel ignorant. The ploy was working and my self-esteem was crashing at the rate of knots.

It transpired, after what seemed like seven rounds in the ring, that looking at the boats that were already moored was the best thing to do. Knowing this made the whole affair more sensible. I could see where the wind was from the ribbons on the cross trees as they fluttered an indication of the breeze. I was aware that a boat would naturally turn bows into the wind. The boats around us were not bows to the wind; they were laying with their beam to the wind. Therefore the tidal effect was stronger than the wind and had turned the boats on their moorings.

Armed with the knowledge that a mooring buoy should be collected down-wind, to allow for an escape route if necessary, I was ready to have my first go at helming to a mooring whilst under motor. Steve stood on the bow with a boat hook reading to collect the buoy as I passed but he wouldn't bring it on board; it was simply to prove it could be done. I was pleasantly surprised that my first attempt was not too far off the mark; the wind had just blown me too far away from the buoy. Around I went again. My second attempt was spot on and so was the third so it was time to swap round, Steve at the helm and me on the bows. Steve was straight into it and after his third successful pick up we were feeling pretty good. I couldn't believe we'd only just begun the course and we were doing it – I was doing it! My confidence began to increase with the success of my first task and I was ready to face the next, until I found out what it was!

My renewed vigour and confidence were soon shattered when we were told the next task was to pick up the mooring buoy whilst under sail. How could this be done? Surely, this was impossible! With the wind in the sails, how could anyone sail to a set point so accurately and at the correct speed? Steve was making ready to hoist the genoa and get under way again, I joined him and together we turned the boat into the wind hoisted the main sail, went to the bows and hoisted it. The engine was turned off and we were sailing. I took a few minutes to enjoy those first hushed moments as the peace and quiet enveloped us.

With no time to relax, I gladly took the helm; it felt good to be sailing again. I enjoyed the feel of the wind on my face, a tiller in my hand and a very nice sailing yacht under my command. This was the second yacht I had sailed. It felt even and steady under my hands, responsive and fast; I was very pleased it didn't have a wheel.

My peace of mind was short lived as I was asked to come into the mooring under sail. All I could think was, "How?" I was given no time to think, so I did exactly the same as before, when we were motoring. Wrong, completely wrong. The steering and aim of the boat was completely different. I was shown how "releasing the main sheet" and letting the mainsail lay out to the side, lessened the power of the sail and reduced the speed of the boat. By 'sheeting in' the mainsail bringing it to mid-ships or up to windward on the traveller, we not only gained speed but were also able to steer up to windward. In simple terms these two actions allowed us to manoeuvre left and right as well as gauge the speed of the boat. This allowed us to crab slowly forwards towards the mooring buoy affording plenty of time to hook it. Steve was on the buoy first time around and, quite rightly, looked very pleased with his efforts. As Captain Pete would say, he was a fine helmsman.

  I began to really enjoy the sailing; my fellow student was knowledgeable but never once made me feel like the bimbo I thought I was. I felt we were becoming good friends and I had already learnt so much from him and the gentleman taking the course. All of this on the first day and it wasn't even lunchtime!

  Talking of lunch, I started to feel peckish. All this physical exertion was taking a toll and hunger pangs were starting. Steve took the helm and I grabbed the boat hook. This time it was for real. We were stopping for lunch and I had to hook the buoy, pull it on board and secure it. The A Team was not going to fail. Neither of us wanted to look bad in front of the tutors and both of us were hungry enough to be determined to succeed. Steve brought the boat around and did a fine job of bringing us to the buoy. As I was the bimbo on the bow I bent my knees, successfully hooked the buoy and pulled on board a horrible green slimy rope that was secured to a cleat on the bow. The feeling of success was good, and both Steve and I had smug, fixed smiles on our faces as it started to rain.

  As we had sailed during the morning, the lady of the boat had prepared us a small organic offering. The meal was big enough to keep hunger at bay, but no bigger, and everything was organic. I paused for a moment to see if I could remember having been warned about this prior to booking the course. I had contacted them regarding my difficulty with food but at no time had they thought to share their eating habits with me. I had been expecting normal food with normal sized portions and to at least have a choice. I sat down to eat the food and did the best my face and teeth would allow.

  The rain eased and we were off again for the afternoon

when we were taught how to reef the mainsail should we encounter bad weather. Everything about the yacht had been made simple so students could quickly identify with things around the deck. Ropes had been colour coded and appropriately placed stickers gave a complete novice a feeling of comfort and support in times of need. The first reef on the mainsail was coloured blue, the second reef red.

First of all, Steve and I put in the first reef and then the second. We next had to take the reefs out again and took it in turns, Steve first, to each put in and take out the two reefs. Whilst I took my turn I forgot to let the blue first reef go and so couldn't tighten the red second reef. Whilst I stood saying, "What should I do with the blue thing?" I got my first unspoken glare from the male tutor that said, "Bimbo."

There had been no answer to my question forthcoming but a responding question, "Do you mean the reefing pennant?"

"Yes, the blue thing," I repeated and was rewarded with the glare. I made a mental note not to wind the teacher up and to play his game of calling everything by the proper name. I could understand he needed to be assured that I knew the correct names- after all this was all part of obtaining the certificate; it was simply the pig headed Norfolk girl in me coming out. There was only one blue rope on the boat, so, short of someone being colour blind, everyone knew what I was referring to.

The next time I was at the mainsail and it was again my turn to reef, my friend Steve whispered in my ear, "Don't forget the blue thing." Good old Steve, I could not have wished for a more suitable sailing partner. I only hoped Dudley was going to be this understanding when we were making our way around the Greek islands.

We sailed up and down the River Orwell, Ipswich, reefing in and out – I'm sure the exercise did me good. We eventually came to rest at Woolverstone Marina where the mooring up process passed me by completely. It all happened so fast. First we were coming into the marina and I was looking where we were going. I saw Steve stepping ashore with a line and "hey presto", we were securely moored to the quayside.

Over a cup of organic, English tea the male tutor debriefed our day's sailing saying we had done well but he would be looking for improvement. I was warming to him as he had taught me many things through the course of the day and I was very impressed with his ability to sail and his patience when teaching me. I had not seen the female tutor on deck all day and I wondered what role she was to have. I shared my thoughts with Steve who told me that she would be teaching the navigation.

Our cup of tea finished, we faced our first navigational lesson. Before commencing this we were informed that she would cook this evening's meal but in future she would be looking for a chef for lunch and dinnertime meals! "What did cooking have to do with sailing?" I thought? I've paid £300 plus to learn how to sail, not cook. Oh well, anything for a peaceful life – I guessed that Steve was thinking the same, but it may have been the case that he had been forewarned.

The lesson consisted of Steve having to measure distances on a chart, between set points, using a piece of string. At this point it became clear to me that Steve had done his theory work with this couple and that was why he had known them when we first arrived. I thought back to my theory work with John. Never once had I used string. I had been taught to use dividers to measure distance, obviously this was an alternative method. "Somewhat strange," I thought. But who was I to judge? As I watched Steve measuring between the points I began to realise that this was the course we had sailed during the day. His task for this evening was to measure the total mileage we had covered.

My task for the evening was to plot a course for the following day into Walton-on-the-Naze. This was difficult because unless the tidal times were calculated correctly we wouldn't get in, the draught of the boat was two metres and I was to allow a one-metre clearance. I took the bearings as instructed and wrote them down with the number of nautical miles to travel on each heading. Feeling pleased, I announced I had finished. This was not what she had wanted. She had wanted me to draw them on the chart. I started again and drew our trip on the chart but when I had finished she was still not happy. "I thought you would have traced the chart onto a plain piece of paper and plotted the course on that, not draw over the original chart," she barked at me. Oh, how I missed John! One of the crucial attributes of a good teacher is the ability to give clear and concise instruction on the task one is being expected to complete. Obviously this lady had missed this lesson on her teacher-training day!

Whilst barking orders at Steve and myself she stood at the cooker, preparing dinner, reminding us we would be cooking the following day. I looked at Steve and his eyes were indicating the same emotion as I was feeling – head down, bite your tongue, it's only for another four days. After eating organic pizza we had questions fired at us about navigation and boating and we finally fell into bed at 2230 hours. Sleep- I needed sleep. I wasn't going to get it though. The lady who had insisted she didn't usually snore, snored all night.

After snatching the odd bit of shuteye, in-between rustling bags and snoring, I arose Tuesday morning, determined she wasn't going to get me down. I shared my thoughts with Steve, who seemed sympathetic to my plight and his words of comfort were kind. The biggest lift from my tiredness was Steve's sense of humour. As we got to know each other his humour came forward, his innuendo and comment never passed me by without raising a chuckle, a giggle and finally a side aching roar. If nothing else, meeting Steve had been worth the trip.

As per the previous morning, we listened to the weather update from the Thames Coastguard and took it in turns to take the report down and interpret what this meant to the day's sailing. Today was going to be rough. The plan was to motor off the mooring, put up the sails and if the wind got too much, we would put in a reef or two.

We got into the main channel with the intention of heading towards Walton-on-the-Naze. The swell was increasing with every buoy we passed. By the time we were passing Shotley we had two reefs in the mainsail and conditions were worsening all the time. I took the helm and we sailed our way to Walton in a strong wind. I was having a fantastic time. Unfortunately, due to bad weather conditions, we had to abort any attempt at getting in when we arrived at Walton and turned back towards the channel. On the return trip we were sailing close-hauled and the helming was excellent; Captain Pete would be pleased that I was hooliganising someone else's boat. This particular point of sail was my favourite. I loved to feel the pull of the wind and the heel of the boat. The tiller rested lightly in my hand, just asking to be adjusted every once in a while.

The swell got bigger and the wind stronger. Soon we were sailing in forty-five-knot winds that classified as gale force.

We were soaked in salt water, the wind was stinging our cheeks and I was actually having fun. I laughed and laughed until I noticed poor Steve, who had been wearing a seasickness patch but was now feeling queasy with the swell. There was nothing we could do for him but repeat the same old stories that we had all been told: look at the horizon, take deep breaths, take the helm to concentrate on something else, have a dry biscuit or a sip of soup. Poor Steve, I recognised the look on his face, I knew exactly what he was thinking, "Leave me alone. Just let me die in peace."

Just as we were about to put in a tack we stopped dead in the water. There were shouts from the male tutor as he jumped to his feet, "Drop the mainsail now. Get the genoa down as fast as you can." Steve jumped to his feet, all thoughts of sickness gone. I went to help and we pulled the sails down and waited. We had run aground on a sandbank. We had left our 'lee ho' just a little bit too late. We waited to see if the wind was going to blow us off the bank but with each passing minute it became obvious this was not going to happen. It was decided to start the engine to see if we could motor back off the bank. This would only be an option if the propeller was free of the sand. Luckily it was. Apparently we had only just nosed on to the sand, so with use of the engine and a little tiller waggling the tutor managed to free us, which meant we wouldn't have to sit and wait for another five hours for the tide to turn.

After all the excitement, and having missed lunch because it had been too rough, we decided to quit for the day and go back from whence we had come. The up side of the incident meant that Steve took the helm and, in a short space of time, returned to his normal colour.

At Woolverstone Marina we congratulated ourselves on lasting the day and looked forward to our next organic portion. Under close supervision and much comment, Steve and I peeled and sliced the vegetables. "No, not like that... not round slices, slightly on the slant so they are oval ... You're peeling too much off ... That's too many ... You don't want to do that much." I was fast coming to the conclusion that she only wanted us to do the cooking so she could spend the best part of the evening berating us for not slicing things in the exact way she wanted us to.

Dudley always says that I nag too much. No way! This

woman left me standing. What I really could not understand was what she was telling us off for. She didn't want to cook and had asked us to do it, so why wouldn't she let us do it our way. I like round slices of carrot. If she wanted everything done her way, why didn't she do it? Steve sensing my rising frustration made light of the situation and gave me the giggles again. He promised if I was a good girl I might be allowed to join them all for a lager later.

After the meal we all took off for my promised half. I do enjoy a drop of beer but the taste soured a little when I noticed little plastic boats being placed on the table. We spent the rest of the evening answering questions and scenarios to do with collision at sea rules. I appreciated the importance of this but I was starting to wonder whether there would be any time this week that I wasn't going to be tested, questioned and observed. I thanked God for my patience and for Steve.

As I awoke Wednesday, very tired after another night of snoring, I was weak – so little food, no sleep and all this physical exercise. I missed Dudley. I needed Dudley. Why had I come? I longed for a hug and a kiss and to hear him say everything would be ok. I needed to speak to him. I had taken my mobile phone with me so I called him hoping that hearing his voice would comfort and reassure me. I love him so much and sharing my feelings with him made things seem quite trivial. I was above this and I could do this. I shared with Steve how much I missed Dudley and he said he felt the same about his wife, Jennie. They had never been apart for such a long time and the distance was difficult for him too.

My morning mope over, it was time for a tricky manoeuvre to get off our mooring. Steve took the helm and our first lesson today was to come into moor alongside a pontoon under power. Thank goodness Steve was first at the helm; this was going to be tricky. After two or three attempts Steve managed it, even though the wind was blowing the boat off the pontoon making it more difficult for him to actually get near it. Each time he failed I tried to learn from his errors. He was skilled at knowing what to do with the engine, how and when to slow it down and reverse it to stop. I had never done these things and it did not come naturally. I tried to tell myself it was no different from parking a car. I don't know who I was trying to kid.

Soon it was my turn and everything I thought I had learnt from Steve's attempts amounted to nothing. It was awful. All I could see was the pontoon. I simply couldn't tell where the boat was in relation to the pontoon at all. As I bent down to slow the engine I couldn't see anything at all so I would take us off course. By the time I got the engine slowed and looked up, we appeared to be so close to the pontoon that I thought I would hit the bow and beam with a crash! I was assured this was all okay; I needed to be this close and it was at this point that I should bend down again, put the engine into neutral and then into reverse to make the boat's forward motion stop. This close to the pontoon the last thing I wanted to do was bend down so I couldn't see anything. "How much did he like his boat this shape?" I thought!

After three or four attempts I managed a half-decent mooring but I still had difficulties in using the engine controls and maintaining eye contact with the pontoon. I was sure I would be tested on this again during the week and didn't really look forward to it. I was told all I needed was practice and that when I had a boat of my own I would become used to the controls and be able to do this without thinking. I felt he was being very kind but as I watched him bring the boat into moor I realised he had perfected a system whereby he could use his foot to change the boat controls thus alleviating the need to bend down and lose sight of the pontoon. I was impressed and finally understood what he meant about practice and becoming acquainted with different yachts.

We had a strong wind again so the sailing was interesting. I had hogged the helm the previous day and was happy for Steve to do his share today. We made our way to Walton-on-the-Naze and managed to negotiate our way in and stop for an organic soup lunch. After lunch we sailed out and in an open stretch of water. Fred, a scruffy old life jacket was brought out because this afternoon was to be man overboard practice. I was only too pleased to see Fred because after all the cheek from Steve and the giggling from me I wouldn't have been surprised if it was one of us that got thrown over instead.

The man overboard procedure was explained to us. When calling, "Man overboard," one delegated crewmember should point at and keep sight of the "man". The helmsman should immediately tack and "crash tack" the sails. This meant that as the boat tacked, the genoa would be unable to come completely across to the other side and would thus stall the mainsail by taking its wind. This would result in the boat stopping dead in the water. If the boat stopped close enough to the "man" a line would be thrown. If not, the genoa would be taken down, the engine started and the helmsman would have to motor in a sweep around the person approaching bows to and downwind. It all sounded very simple…

At my first attempt I came in too quickly and was told I may have seriously injured Fred had he been a human being. At the second attempt I didn't turn the correct way and recovered Fred bows to him but up wind. Although I did recover him I was told I would have been lucky to do so without injuring him, as the wind would push the boat onto him instead of the other way around. I was to try again. My third and fourth attempts were successful and I was grateful for the practice as this was one thing Captain Pete had never had an opportunity to show us. I knew how important it was for me grasp this particular procedure as Dudley's life might hinge on it some day.

During my attempts, Steve had stood point on the bows indicating where I should steer to for the recovery of Fred. I promised to try to do the same for him. However, I soon learned there was an art in the judgement of pointing to give the correct directions. His first attempt failed because I took him too close and we ran directly over Fred – poor Fred. Poor Steve, he had to cope not only with the task in hand but with a woman who had no sense of distance. His second and third attempts were successful and I realised I could do with a little more practice in directing the helmsman.

The stresses of a man overboard situation over and glad we had had the opportunity to practise, we sailed off talking about life. We both appreciated that when we were sailing alone with our partners it would be good to know what to do. We discussed how to bring the recovered person back on board; should it be at the stern or amidships, would it be with a rope or ladder? We decided the best sounding option was to throw the man overboard a line, winch them in to the beam and use a mast halyard and winch to bring them onboard. At last I felt I was of one accord with the male tutor and I was so grateful for his knowledge and the things he shared.

I wish I could say I felt the same way about the female navigation tutor. I felt she had interfered with the sailing all day and had done so in a manner that was winding this Norfolk girl right up. She was becoming one of the most contrary, rude and annoying people I had met in a long time. "Not long now," I told myself. The course was almost done.

We picked up a mooring buoy at dusk and were told that this evening we would be doing a night sail! We were relieved of our cooking duties to allow us to plot our course for that evening. It was planned that we would command half the journey each. I was to helm whilst Steve navigated from outside Shotley lock around the channel to Shotley spit cardinal buoy and back level with Shotley. Steve would then take the helm whilst I navigated from Shotley up the channel until we passed Suffolk Marina, turning at the red port can named Butt. We would then come back to Shotley and into Shotley lock. I now knew where the saying 'kiss my butt' came from!

Whilst we plotted our respective courses under the close annoying supervision of our female tutor, our male tutor cooked canned organic curry with organic rice. Again, pieces of string were brought out to measure the distances. We were shown a length of string used the previous week that she complained had been ruined. The previous students had taken a match to it and welded the two ends together making it a solid circle so she could no longer use it. I knew just how they felt and when Steve announced, "You wait and see what I'm going to do to you," my laughter was full blown and could have been heard the length of the Orwell.

We ate and waited for darkness whilst being tested on our knots. We had to prove that we could tie a bowline, a reef knot, a clove hitch, a rolling hitch and a sheet bend. Finally the time arrived for us to leave and the nerves kicked in. I am not afraid of the dark but I don't like to be doing things when I cannot see clearly, especially not things involving the sea, wind and waves. I tried to put these thoughts behind me. I was determined to do my best as I wanted this certificate. I felt like I had already earned my accreditation and I was not going to let one little night sail put me off. We started out about 2100 hours and to my dismay the female tutor took up a position sitting on the companionway top step and didn't move all night.

For the next four hours she sat there, barking orders in what should have been a still, quiet night. She gave us not the least bit of credit for common sense as she sat there saying, "Not too close ... Come right a bit ... Come left a bit ... Look over there ... Can you see it?" My tongue must have looked like a sieve having been bitten so much. In the end both of us took to, "Yes, we can ... "Yes, we're steering that already ... YES WE KNOW!" Just as we were rounding red port can 'Butt' I saw silhouetted sails against a night sky, no lights, nothing, just flapping sails. I raised the alarm and was concerned that they may be in distress. Nobody else seemed overly concerned but agreed it was a yacht sailing at night with no lights. How dangerous and irresponsible can one person be! We could have had a collision. We shone a light at the yacht to indicate displeasure at their behaviour and their response was to shine a light back. I guess it was an acknowledgement to say they were okay but they still didn't put their deck lights on.

After a long five hours of drizzling rain we had successfully completed our night sail and were headed for the Shotley Lock. This sail had been our last major test and although there was still one day left we were wondering if we had passed. There had not been one word of encouragement or congratulation. I didn't know if I had pleased or not. It was too early in the morning to worry about it; all I wanted was a good sleep.

Thursday morning, the penultimate day, neither Steve nor I were certain we had passed. We had covered most of the syllabus now and still nothing had been given away as to our sailing ability. I personally thrive on honest comment and encouragement and without this it was a struggle to even be bothered to try but *Orpheus* awaited and I wanted this certificate.

We had settled into the routine of taking down the weather reports each morning. I then enjoyed working out our day's navigation and tides whilst Steve readied the boat to sail. We were turning into a great sailing team, each knowing what the other liked to do and was good at. We were gelling not only in our sailing but our friendship; I thought I would miss him after tonight, our last night on board. Then I thought of Dudley, no more snoring and no more organic food. I began to feel happier already.

Today we were headed for the River Deben, another difficult river to navigate if the timing was wrong with the tides. Over breakfast Steve and I got a telling-off for not keeping a detailed log of our trips out and the female tutor insisted we kept one that day. I wouldn't have minded but there had never been any indication that this was something she had wanted us to do. I found telling us off for something we had been blissfully unaware of, somewhat strange. As always, Steve defused the situation with a joke, making me laugh and reminding me just to roll with it. Only just recovering from this rebuke Steve and I saw the she was making to put on her sailing jacket. As quick as a flash, he said, "Quick, shut the hatch and nail it down. She's coming out to sail with us today." We all thought this hilarious, including her husband, who by this time I had decided must be a saint. Our sailing days had been wonderful, only being spoiled by the appearance of this woman who insisted on interfering with everyone and everything.

    I was shown how to lasso a bollard when coming into a mooring or more specifically a lock. We had come through the lock the night before but in the dark and it had all happened so quickly that I had not really taken it all in. The lock layout and procedure was explained. Steve was to helm navigating us into the lock and I was to lasso a mooring and secure the bows. This all went smoothly, but as I stood watching the water flooding in I didn't like it at all. It all seemed a bit too manic and out of my control to be enjoyable. I really didn't enjoy it as tonnes of water foamed and flooded its way through the lock gates.

    After exiting the lock we had a lovely day's sailing, taking it in turns to helm and navigate. We even remembered to keep our detailed log! We arrived at the end of the Deben in time for coffee and organic biscuits. On setting off for the return journey the swell was getting bigger and the wind colder. All week we had either been rained on or covered in salt water. Why should today be any different? Steve did most of the helming and I was very pleased to see that the swell had little effect on him this time. We three sailors chatted in a friendly but cold atmosphere, enjoying each other's company in a relaxed way as the female tutor had stayed below. The boat was very well balanced and I had learned over the week that no matter how strong the wind was, if the sails were set correctly, it was very easy to helm. She was a fine boat and the tutor had great knowledge to impart. My confidence, whether I passed or not, had shot through the ceiling. This was exactly what I had needed, especially after the accident.

    That evening we had planned to eat out, it being our last

night together and we all hoped we would get a shower before sitting down in a proper restaurant. As we came back through the lock to moor in Shotley Marina, the female on board disappeared. Once we had finished mooring and sat down contemplating a shower, she appeared from the heads saying, "Come on, then, we'll be late."

"What about a shower?" I said.

"We don't have time now. You'll have to have one in the morning." As usual, this irascible woman who snored, expected everyone to jump when she said jump. We all jumped as expected and ate out with only one of us smelling of roses. Whilst we had been mooring the boat, she had been taking a shower. Her husband really was a saint.

Come Friday morning, the last day, I resembled an empty husk. I felt as though I had no physical substance or energy left at all. The lack of sleep was taking its toll. "I just have to get through today," I told myself. Over breakfast, Steve and I were chatting when the magic words were spoken. The week's sailing was debriefed. We were told that we had both done really well. The male tutor was pleased with our progress and improvement over the week and he was happy to sign our certificates. YES!...

It had all been worth it. I looked at Steve and he looked at me in disbelieving pleasure. We had done it. All we had to do was survive another day. Steve and I jumped to ready the sails and prepared to motor off the mooring. Today we were to sail up the Orwell and return to Suffolk Marina our drop-off point. Steve had offered to take me home to meet Jennie and Dudley would come to collect me from there. Before making our way to Suffolk Marina the syllabus was concluded with engine mechanics. As Steve was a qualified engineer it was clear that this briefing was for my benefit. Being more qualified than the instructor, Steve actually gave the brief! I was interested and keen to see where the main engine "bits" were but lacked the obvious enthusiasm of a man. Dudley had planned to take a diesel engine course and I was happy to allocate this responsibility to him when on board *Orpheus*.

The engineering lesson over, we were told that this final day we were on our own; there would be no input from either tutor at all. We would be required to set the sails and navigate our way back to the marina. Steve knew the stretch of river very well so navigation was no problem. We made a fine sailing team and I hoped, for both our sakes, we could reach the same comfortable position with our respective partners and boats when the course was over and we went our separate ways.

During the sail up the river Steve had suggested we tie Fred, the man overboard, securely to the boat just in case he was clumsy enough to fall off again. We laughed and shared our fun and delight at having passed with the male tutor whilst the female tutor scowled, wondering why I was always giggling.

I left Steve at the helm to prepare our lunch of organic pita bread with organic tomato puree and organic cheese on top. Now, even for my non-existent culinary skills I could have worked out how to cook this pita bread pizza concoction – but no, I needed close supervision. "Not too much tomato ... I want more oregano ... – organic of course – Not three slices of cheese, only two." Why did she bother asking us to help? It was obvious she didn't want it and whatever we did was going to be wrong.

After lunch we were on our last lap, our logbooks had been signed over lunch and the syllabus completed, or so we thought. The female tutor demanded our attention and handed us sheets of paper and commenced demanding answers to questions about light combinations and recognition of horn/sound signals. Some of them seemed rather complex so I tried to catch a glance of the title on the sheets, I noticed at the top of the page that she had been asking us questions from a Yacht master theory paper not Day Skipper questions! I think that was one point to us because we had managed to answer them.

We set off for Suffolk Marina with gusto; just another two hours and we would be on our way home. Unfortunately for us the forecasted wind increase came, making our entry into Suffolk Marina very difficult. To add to the problem, a regatta was due to take place and there were no moorings for us to come into. Realising we had to be dropped off and desperate to get ashore, we noticed there was a space at the end of a pontoon. We took advantage of it quickly before anyone else did.

Once there, Steve and I handed the bags out and took them to the car. Just as I thought we were off, Steve said, "No, we have been asked to wash all the decks down!" "Okay," I thought, "that's only fair". Of we went, scrubbed and washed down the decks and did a fine job considering we wanted to be getting on our way to our loved ones. Steve disappeared below and I thought to say goodbye to the female tutor. He came up the companionway with his arms full of mats and rugs saying, "We have to clean and sweep the rugs before we can go." At this I could have burst a blood vessel, no I was not going to sweep her b****y mats. The time was 1700 hours and I had to get back to Norwich from Ipswich in time enough for Dudley to keep a karaoke commitment at 1900 hours. She could sweep her own mats.

I couldn't believe that I had paid £300 plus to become her slave for a week; a hostage to be nagged, moaned at and bossed about in an obnoxious manner. THIS WAS THE LAST STRAW. Steve explained in his pleasant manner that we had to go and we were nearly off when the male tutor returned voicing concern about getting off the mooring in such a high wind. We agreed to stay long enough to help him on his way to ensure they were safe. I would miss him as he had taught me a great deal in a very pleasant way. I found him a very pleasant man and a saint to put up with his lot in life. At least it made me appreciate Dudley even more. We waved goodbye as they sailed out of Suffolk Marina and I made a mental note of the promises I had made to the tutor. I had promised that I would always clip on in rough weather and that I would always keep my fingers well away from the winch.

At last we were off, successful day skippers travelling home after five days of hard work and learning. Jennie was everything I had expected: friendly, smiling and loving. Steve was master to a lovely little dog who greeted him with lots of love and licks. It made me realise that I had been too busy to miss Harry but I was certainly looking forward to some of the same treatment when I arrived home. Dudley came to collect me and after a quick coffee we made our exit.

After a long night of sleep I awoke absolutely shattered. The stresses of the week had left me weak. I mulled over what had taken place and was glad I had done it. For any sailor who wants to be safe I could not recommend it highly enough. I learnt so much and gained so much confidence. It gave me the edge to ensure should any emergency occur, when on board *Orpheus*, I would not panic in ignorance but be able to react knowledgeably. The sailing tutor had been worth every penny but I had been left feeling cold by the navigation tutor. John had been much more useful to me. I had no regrets. I had done it and I had my certificate, which with the theory certificate I had already gained now entitled me to the I.C.C. (International Certificate of Competence). I was now qualified to sail around European waters.

My final word of wisdom concerning the RYA Day skipper course is – it is a must. The benefits I gained were many. Be safe and sail with knowledge; don't be a burden to those who sail with you and around you. Just remember you may stumble across my Captain Pete one day. He'll be the one scowling, hands on hips shouting, "Starboard!"

CHAPTER 6
COUNT DOWN

Life settled into a semi-normal routine whilst we prepared for the day that we would finally set off for Greece. I found myself searching pet stores for the appropriate carrying case to allow us to fly Harry out of the U.K. I found they varied greatly in price and size; some came with accessories others did not. Having contacted D.E.F.R.A. I was aware of the strict guidelines for the size of the cage; there would have to be room for Harry to stand up, sit down and turn himself around – oh, okey, kokey, kokey...

We visited local pet stores and were shocked to find an airline approved case sized for a Westie would cost £79 and £17 extra if we wanted wheels and a carrying handle. Our search continued and we eventually found one for £49 that came with wheels and a proper solid handle. It definitely does pay to shop around!

Not wanting to get the wrong case, as different airlines have different rulings, I started to ring around for tickets to fly out to Greece the last week in August. One airline assured me we could fly out from Gatwick to Corfu one way, with Harry, at a cost of £137 for the humans – the "animal" would have to be booked in as cargo. Unfortunately, despite numerous attempts to call the cargo booking-in office, there was never any reply.

I tried another airline that indicated we could fly the same route but should the flight be full they would remove the dog to make room for luggage. When asked if I would be informed if this was to happen the reply came back: "No." So in reality I could end up in Corfu and Harry might still be trapped in a case at Gatwick. Not having any luck, I rang a travel agent and entrusted them with my problem. Very helpful and efficient, I was told within a very short space of time that when travelling with a dog we would have to route via Athens. We could fly from Gatwick to Athens at a cost of £500 and from Athens to Preveza on a different airline for £71. These prices were for each person and the same again for the dog! This meant the total sum for us to fly out would be £1,724; not forgetting that this did not include the cost of sending our belongings separately as freight via cargo ship.

On discovering these costs Dudley and I went back to the drawing board and re-assessed our situation. We had already sold our respective vehicles in preparation for our departure and had purchased a £200 run around to keep us mobile until we finally left the UK. Previously we had considered the option of a caravan but found this only added to fuel consumption and ferry fees. With our options becoming limited we were forced to consider the viability of using our Mazda run around to transport our belongings, Harry and us to Greece and purchase a four-man tent to use for our overnight accommodation as we travelled across Europe. We had seen a tent locally for only £40 that seemed to suit our requirements. We estimated by travelling approximately two hundred miles a day, with overnight stays in campsites, we could arrive at Brindisi in Italy within five and a half days. The total cost of this, including ferry crossings, would be in the region of £500.

We had finally found a solution to all the problems we had encountered in getting us from the U.K. to Greece. Driving across Europe would mean we could look after Harry in the appropriate manner, save ourselves money and know that our belongings were being safely transported out to our new life.

Whilst considering the viability of travelling by land I had worked out a provisional route that took us from Dover to Calais, through France, Belgium, Luxembourg, Switzerland and Italy. We would then take the ferry from Brindisi to Igoumenitsa on mainland Greece. We had previously visited Igoumenitsa and knew it was only one and a half-hour's journey by car from there to where *Orpheus* waited for us.

Now the final decision had been made in relation to our route, it allowed me the chance to break the trip down into daily portions and assess where we would need campsites for each night. A search of several web sites resulted in several options for overnight accommodation each day at reasonable rates and dogs were welcome; our plans were well under way.

This final agreement on which route to take also meant

we were now clear as to which countries we would be passing through and I knew which certification to ask for from the vet to ensure Harry travelled safely across Europe. As we were intending to stay abroad for the foreseeable future, Harry's export request form had already been filed and the only thing left remaining to do would be the last minute trip to the vet for inoculation and signing of the certificates confirming him fit to travel through France, Belgium, Luxembourg, Switzerland, Italy and Greece.

Six weeks had passed since our return from Greece after taking possession of *Orpheus* and I received an appointment to attend the local hospital to review the damage to my front teeth following my fall. My jaw was still troublesome and my front teeth tender. A very thorough doctor diagnosed that I had severely traumatised my jaw. He explained in simple terms that the instructions from the brain that controlled the movement of my jaw were somewhat bemused and I should undertake daily exercises to re-train the signals to enable the jaw to do what it should be doing i.e. chew and bite food. I knew when I got home to tell Dudley that I was to do jaw exercises he would scoff and indicate he felt my jaw got enough exercise as it was, but I still left the hospital feeling better for knowing what was wrong. However, I wondered about the cost of repairs to my two front teeth that required root filling and possibly capping.

We had experienced a delay and extra expense with our building work project and had lived on a very tight budget in order to complete it. Having taken a voluntary redundancy from my employment I was no longer earning and had not signed on for benefit, as I knew within a matter of months we would be leaving the country. The cost of dental treatment under the current system of privatisation and the lack of National Health Dentists meant we would be struggling to afford the treatment I might need.

Voicing my fears to a friend I was reminded that unemployed people were entitled to free dental treatment so I decided to contact the local Social Services. I attended the local offices having made an appointment and explained that I had had a fall and as a result I required dental treatment that I could not afford. After working for twenty-two years and never taking a penny out of the country I was somewhat aghast when I was told I was not entitled to this help. I asked why not and was told it was because I was not claiming benefit!

I explained my situation, pointing out I was planning to leave the country in less than three months and this was the reason I had taken the decision not to claim benefit. However, in light of this unforeseen accident and hidden costs I needed financial support. If I couldn't claim my dental treatment I would need to claim unemployment benefit. In response to this I was told I could not sign on for benefit. I questioned why it was, as an unemployed person I was not entitled to this and was told because I had only just called their office.

By now I was getting very annoyed, I had never asked for anything from the country; whatever I had taken out I had paid for in my taxes. I had read articles about free housing, cars and various benefits being given to criminals, vagrants and asylum seekers but a hardworking, and I like to think, upright member of the community, was being denied any assistance at all.

A red mist descended as I insisted that if they were not prepared to fund my dental treatment I could no longer afford to pay my household bills, which I had previously been prepared to do. Therefore, I reasoned, I surely must be eligible for some sort of income support. Having excused herself to seek her supervisor's advice, she returned to say I was not only entitled to dental treatment but income support, incapacity benefit and council tax benefit. All I had wanted was for my dental treatment to be paid for, which they denied me but instead they wanted to pay me five times more than I was asking for! I was now starting to understand for the first time in my life why our Great Britain was becoming not so great and was on a slippery slope to destruction.

To better this further they offered to pay me "Job Seekers Allowance". I explained that I would not be seeking employment as I was leaving the country as previously explained. This apparently was the only benefit they could offer me so I would have to attend once a month to assure someone that I was trying to seek employment then I could receive the benefit. Desperate for financial assistance, I decided to play the game but this left no doubt in my mind why the country never seemed to have any money for crucial services. I was utterly astounded. As for the incapacity benefit I was being offered, I just looked disdainfully at the young lady and explained that it was my teeth that were the problem and as far as I was aware root fillings and caps didn't stop the rest of my body from functioning perfectly well!

The "game" commenced and I attended their offices once a month for three months. Each time I sat in front of the same person who asked me the same questions. Had I been actively seeking employment? "No," I would reply.

"You have to, for us to pay you the benefit," they would say and my reply would be, "I am unemployable as I am leaving the country in two months time."

"Never mind keep trying!"

To just jump ahead to the present I never did receive any free dental treatment. I paid for the treatment and filled in the claims form but since leaving England I have never received an acknowledgement yet alone refund for the treatment. As I had been receiving the "job seekers allowance" I never took the trouble to complain but wonder how many more people there are like me out there!

With my teething troubles sorted, our route out of England planned and Harry's certificates being arranged, Dudley and I concentrated on the project he had begun some six months earlier. In order to provide an income for our new life abroad Dudley had decided to build two new flats behind his existing office premises. Our already tight budget had been extensively stretched at an early stage due to the foundations needing to be piled. This had not only caused an over-spend but was the chief reason for our delayed exit from the U.K.

We knuckled down and spent long days, nights, and weekends at the site. It seemed our every waking moment was spent working on the buildings. We carried bricks, dug ditches, cleared rubble and generally did anything we could to assist our builder. Once the walls were up and the roof on we were faced with another slight delay as plasterers were in high demand and Dudley had trouble finding one available. I used this break in the building proceedings to settle some more of our domestic chaos.

Having previously made an appointment, I took myself to Dudley's barber armed with a pair of rechargeable hair trimmers. It was our plan that I would be the person to trim Dudley's hair when we left England and his barber had kindly agreed to spend half an hour showing me how to use the trimmers. He instructed, watched and guided whilst a very nervous Dudley sat in the chair having his hair cut by me for the very first time. It was a rather pale face that looked back at me in the mirror, but all in all he was a good sport about it. I was given the nod of approval by the barber who decided I was ready to be let loose on him at any time in the future.

As soon as one problem was solved another one would surface. One of the biggest problems we identified was that when we left England we would no longer have a postal address. Living on board a yacht travelling the Mediterranean meant receiving our mail was going to be very difficult. We tried to open a P.O. box with the post office but they indicated they would not forward on any mail abroad, as it was a collection only service. We tried to find an independent mail handling service but could not find a suitable one. With no other options open to us we asked my parents if we could use their address as a mail collection point.

With their approval to use their address I spent a day writing to all our contacts indicating the new address. I registered for Internet banking, negating the need for monthly bank statements but was informed credit card statements would still have to be sent, as the law required them. I found this law unusual as it contradicted my rights to privacy and probably broke a few banking laws that I am not au fait with. In simple terms, this meant the bank was prepared to knowingly give my personal account details to someone (albeit my mother) without my authority! For me this was not a problem as she was my mother but for Dudley it would mean an intrusion into his personal affairs. They would be giving my mother access to his most personal information concerning finances. When we pointed this out to the bank their answer was we could cancel the account at any time we wished! It appeared we had been given no choice despite our rights!

In one of our lighter moments, which at this time were becoming few and far between, Dudley agreed to run a charity karaoke night for our dear friend Roy in aid of Cancer Relief. Captain Pete came with Liz, which meant that Dudley and I could enjoy their company for the first time in what seemed a very long while. The evening was well attended by all the regular karaoke singers and whilst chatting, drinking and having lots of fun we made a lot of money for a very worthwhile cause.

Dudley, being the caring, yet mischievous person he is,

had set the rules for the evening: £1 per person to sing a song and if somebody wanted Dudley to turn the singer off they would have to pay £2. It did not take long for people to realise that there was more fun in seeing the faces of people being turned off than actually listening to them sing. Both Dudley and I were victim to the rules and of the three songs I tried to sing that evening I managed to sing two words before being turned off! We hadn't laughed and relaxed this way in a long, long time. Our lives had become so stressful with everything we were trying to co-ordinate that we had grown slightly apart. It had been a long time since we had done something meaningful together. This evening served as a catalyst to bring us back together and remind us what it felt like to be in love.

The only thing that marred the evening was when a fellow karaoke compere wished to sing. His turn came to sing and, as per the rules of the evening, was duly turned off. He pounced on Dudley shouting, "Nobody turns me off," at which Dudley pointed out, "Too late. I just did!" The situation was made even worse when he had the audacity to ask for his money back because he didn't get to sing. We later found out that the money in question wasn't even his but his friend's! Needless to say he gained fame as the "Rotter" of the evening and served to spur everyone on to pay £2 to turn even more people off.

A rather beautiful lady, with an excellent voice was turned off. Her husband paid £5 for her to be able to sing her song again. All the way through her song my brother, another mischievous imp, wanted to know how much he would have to pay to turn her off again. The sum of £25 was agreed and the lady's husband was agog and wondered what it was about her voice my brother didn't like. "Nothing. She sings wonderfully. It's just for charity," came his reply. The hero of the evening was one of the regulars who paid £50 to sing an Elvis Presley number. Nobody was daring enough to pay the required £100 to turn him off!

Wonderful people with big hearts raised a total of £350 that evening. A night that Dudley and I will never forget.

July arrived and so did the plasterers. We were back, busy at the flats and life took on its very, very stressful pattern of decorating, tiling, picking kitchen units, fridges, etc. Dudley was spending more and more time in the office sorting out the closure of his business, trying to wind down thirty years of trading in insurance and estate agency. He was also trying to deal with the electricity, gas and water companies to get services connected at the flats. I was left to do much of the manual labour and this was taking its toll on me both, physically and mentally. The first lot of kitchen units were delivered late afternoon one day and were promptly stolen overnight as the front door to the flats had yet to have locks fitted. How had they known they were there? It must have been an inside job and whoever delivered them must have either come back and taken them themselves or had tipped someone else off. What did the police do? Nothing. Oh well, another big chunk of the budget gone. We were now quite deep in debt and we had the first of what was to be many big arguments about our financial status.

In amongst all this aggravation, instead of Harry being his normal comforting self, he was testing my patience more than a little. He obviously sensed something was going on with all the changes and different routines in his little life. Whilst out walking one morning Dudley and I were talking about our problems and not really paying attention to him. A milk float passed by and still we paid no attention until we heard an immediate screech of brakes. We looked around to see Harry standing in the middle of the road. I yanked on his wander lead too late and had to quickly let it go slack as he disappeared under the milk float. He rolled over and over underneath the float until it finally came to a stop. Hardly daring to look and fearing the worst I just stood and stared. My stomach was churning and I felt quite sick as Harry picked himself up and came running out from under the milk float! I couldn't believe that he was completely unscathed. The poor milkman jumped down from his float and gave us a few gruff and rude words and took off. We couldn't blame him. It must have shaken him as much as it had us.

For the first time in many, many weeks I thought about God and thanked him for the life he had spared. My life over these few weeks had become empty and faithless. I couldn't even remember the last time I had thought a pure thought. I suddenly realised that being so busy, so stressed and not knowing which way to turn, I had completely detached myself from everything. I was wallowing in my own small world of self-pity and it took Harry's near death to shake me out of it.

This drama over we took ourselves back to building and

decorating but when Harry decided he'd try to eat the plumber's blow torch it was the last straw. I decided the building site was no longer suitable for Harry and from then on my mother had to baby-sit during the working week days. This went a long way to reduce my stress as worrying about him amongst everything else was too much.

I am ashamed to say that it took only a matter of days for the stress to build to such a level that I again forgot who I was, what I was and what I believed in. It is true to say that both Dudley and I were now living separate lives. We got up together, we spent our days working at the site- Dudley inside and me outside and then we went home together. Outside of this, we were almost strangers; neither of us happy and both of us very, very tired and stressed.

Sadly, to add to our troubles, our dear friend Richard Maxwell passed away. I had met Richard on a regular basis with Dudley, when we attended a local flying club with our friend, Roy West. Over lunch, Richard would chat in a relaxed way about his exploits in the armed services, which were many as he had reached the rank of Major. He regaled us with wonderful stories such as the time he met and fought alongside Monty. He was a gentleman who, although he'd reached 86 years of age, still had a twinkle in his eye and impeccable manners. He was a far travelled man who had a zest for life and loved to explore, pushing past the limitations of age. Indeed, such was his determination it was at the age of fifty-eight that he first became determined to qualify for a private pilot's licence. Only once before had I ever met a man with such an interesting and varied life and that was Wing Commander Ken Wallace of Autogiro fame.

There is so much I could say about Richard. However, as we entered the small chapel and took our seats, Dudley to my left and Roy to my right, all I could do was remember. The sun shone through the stained glass windows creating a heavenly glow and a warming peace around the chapel. People filled the seats to capacity and were then forced to stand around the edges, eventually overflowing into the gardens. Richard lay before us and as the service drew to an end you could feel the love for this man filling the air. The final piece of music began to play as Richard left us in this life. He had chosen the music himself, a Russian anthem. To you and me it is more commonly known as a song called, "The Carnival is over". Music filled the chapel and as it dawned on us what the title of the song was, I cried. Dudley and Roy with bent heads, cried, and I cried some more. Then I cried because I was wondering when my carnival would be over, when I would get my life back. My life seemed dead, on hold and numb. I left the chapel praying that I would again have the pleasure of meeting Richard in the afterlife.

With a heavy heart I went back to decorating and it was becoming clearer by the day that we were not going to make the end of August getaway we had hoped for. Another argument, another look at the finances and we concluded that the earliest we would be able to leave would be the end of September. Every month it took us to leave England was another month's guardianage we would have to pay to keep *Orpheus* safe in Greece. This was another expenditure that we had not taken into consideration when we went to take delivery of her in May.

Wanting to rent our house for a secured income when we left England, we placed an advertisement in the local newspaper for a student let. In a short space of time we found four city college entrants willing to take the house. We were obviously relieved to have the income but this rental caused another problem. The students wished to take up residence the end of August; we had delayed our departure to September so this meant we would be homeless for our last three weeks in the UK. We knew we didn't have the spare funds to move into accommodation and resigned ourselves to the fact that we would have to camp out in the flats whilst trying to complete them. The flats would be secure but at this time had no water, gas or electricity. Dudley had been trying to get these services connected for over a month and was still experiencing problems.

We had already managed to find tenants for the flats we were building and had also let Dudley's office premises. We had three mortgages to pay but the way things had come together it looked as though we would have enough income to cover these and just enough to live on once we got to Greece. At last our affairs seemed to be getting sorted. The last of our personal items had been packed and deposited in my mother's loft. Our final hurdle was simply to complete the flats.

One Sunday, whilst I was painting and varnishing a cupboard, I became aware of a sudden sensation of quietness. I am sure every mother and father reading will relate to this sensation. You have noisy children or animals playing around fussing and demanding but as you are busy you concentrate on the task at hand cutting out all other noises – or so you think – until the noise isn't there any more and then suddenly you think what's wrong? Why is it so quiet? Where are the children? In my case it was, "Where is the dog? Where's Harry?" I ran out into the yard that had been sealed off to stop him getting out. The gate was still across but no Harry. Hearing me call, Dudley came running to see what the matter was. We both ended up running around the building site and yard but to no avail. We couldn't find Harry.

    Dudley immediately got in the car and started to drive around the streets. I was beside myself, shouting his name, crying, walking the streets and grabbing people to ask if they had seen a little white dog. We were just four weeks away from leaving the country and all sorts of thoughts started going through my mind. "What if he didn't come back, would I leave without him? What if he was found after we left England, how would we get him to Greece or would we have to leave him behind?" I sat on a pile of shingle at the end of the yard and howled. My whole body shook as my heart broke in two.

    Dudley came back having found nothing and called the local police section box to report him missing. He told them we would leave our mobile phone on should anyone bring him in. They could call any time of night or day. Dudley then took off again on foot, looking for Harry whilst I sat in the yard, a broken woman, I held onto the phone not knowing what to do just begging and praying for it to ring. I was startled back into reality as the phone did indeed start to ring. I expected it to be the police. However, it was a local pet shop with an in-store veterinary service. Somebody had found and taken Harry there.

    It was just pure luck and fortune that two days earlier I had contacted the company with whom Harry's chip information was held. I had updated our contact details in readiness for our departure and I was now so grateful for a system that obviously worked very well in an emergency. Dudley came back to find me sobbing and laughing and babbling away. He must have thought I'd had a complete breakdown. He held me close as I told him Harry had been found and suddenly the realisation hit us that it had been a long time since we had been this close, both physically and emotionally. I loved Dudley and needed him so much, but the stress of building the flats was almost bringing our marriage to an end.

We went to collect Harry from the store. I was almost running through the store to get to the veterinary section at the rear. One look at my face told the receptionist why I was there as through sobs and smiles I said, "I've come to collect the Westie." He was handed over the counter and I hugged him so tight and kissed his cute little face, while he in turn sat looking at me as if to say, "What's all the fuss about?" It appeared that he had managed to climb up a tall grass bank at the side of the building, into some woods and out the other side where he had been found wandering around a housing estate! So we were forced into the decision that my mother would have to become caretaker to Harry even at the weekends.

In the last week in August we moved out of our house to make room for the tenants. It had been our home for the past seven years and a place I had lived in alone for three years prior to that. We took our remaining possessions and camped out in the flats where the water, gas and electrics were still waiting to be connected. We had run a cable from the office next door to provide us with electricity and heat and were forced to use the sink and toilet at the rear of the office premises for the necessary ablutions. Mother and Father came to our rescue again providing us with clothes washing and showering services.

Suddenly life became a blind panic. We had one week left before our departure date. Our personal property had been stored and packed and the flats were almost complete. We had the fixtures and fittings to complete inside both flats and although it looked like we wouldn't get these done in time we were both determined we would. During one of these determined last seven days in England we received a telephone call from Mother to say there had been an earthquake in the Ionian Sea. We watched the news and listened to the radio. Both confirmed there had indeed been a very serious earthquake in the Ionian but there had been only a few casualties most of the damage being structural. Levkas, where *Orpheus* was moored, had been badly affected. Not wishing to be selfish and tactless we spent a whole twenty-four hours worrying about the friends we knew who lived in the area and also wondering if our yacht had sustained any damage. We had been through so much; to lose it all now would be unthinkable and the consequences shattering for us.

The following day we couldn't wait any longer and we telephoned Jeanette, our contact point at the Contract Yacht Services office. She described to us how frightening it had been but all our friends were okay and *Orpheus* had been completely unaffected. She went on to describe that many yachts had not been so lucky. A shipyard in the village of Vliho had suffered badly. Almost all of their boats "on the hard" (which means out of the water and propped up on stilts), had fallen in a domino effect and were quite severely damaged. Our emotions were confused. Whilst we wanted to celebrate our near escape we felt very sorry for the owners of the yachts who had not been so lucky.

To help us recover from this shock and to wish us well on our adventure, Roy arranged a leaving party for us. We arrived at his club to find that he had decorated the familiar room with balloons, streamers and well wishing banners. Roy had been a true friend to Dudley and I and we were starting to miss him already. He had been such a big part of our lives on a daily basis and leaving him behind was a wrench. We had shared many meals together and enjoyed many Friday night karaoke evenings at his club. Sadly, our last Friday night had arrived, albeit in party form. It was wonderful to have all our friends together to see us off but as we were both very tired emotionally and physically it was almost too much. We were near to tears for the majority of the evening even though we felt happy. We were looking forward to our new adventure but at that moment in time it felt as though it was never going to happen. My family was naturally there to wish us well. Mother and Father began to realise the inevitability of it all and began getting very upset. It had been a wonderful evening that ended in a special gift from a special man. It was terribly hard for us to say goodbye to Roy. He was our closest friend and there are no words to describe the sadness I felt as we walked away that evening.

Mother and Father had cooked my favourite meals for the last week of our time in England and we had enjoyed a wonderful evening meal the night before we left. They had agreed it would be best to say goodbye that evening rather than stand and wave us off when the time came. It was hard to tell how upset Father was, but Mother was really getting upset. It was a very difficult time. I knew the decisions we were making for our future were what we wanted but it was having a very upsetting affect on those close to us and it was becoming very hard for us to just walk away.

We finally got the flats finished apart from a few minor things such as affixing bathroom towel rails and accessories. We wondered whether we should delay our departure to get these last few things completed but I argued that these could be left for our builder to complete. I pointed out truthfully to Dudley that our lives had become so stressed and our relationship stretched to such a limit that I felt if we stayed any longer instead of leaving for a new life together, we would probably be seeking divorce. We had been arguing constantly and disagreeing about money. Both Dudley and I had lost a lot of weight and I was sure neither of us could stand a further delay. Dudley agreed to leave the last few jobs to the builder and paid him a week's wages in advance.

The morning of our departure arrived and we packed all our belongings, ready to load them into the car. I managed to finish the last of the grouting in the bathrooms an hour before we were due to leave. Dudley had loaded the car with all our belongings leaving a hollowed out hole in the middle for Harry to sit in and the roof rack was piled as high as we legally dare.

We were just starting to see the light at the end of the tunnel and were preparing to leave the site. We had hoped to leave by midday but it had not been possible and we were already delayed by two hours. We were making to get into the car when one of the tenants for the flats came to tell us that she would no longer be taking up residence. It had obviously been a cowardly attempt to inform us after we had already left but due to the delay she had been forced to tell us to our faces then. What now? We had mortgages going out and now, until we found another tenant, we would not have enough money coming in to give us anything to live on. What should we do? Should we stay and find living money in England, and guardianage for the boat in Greece? Or should we just leave and take our chances?

Under the cloud of yet another argument, my marriage looking to be ruined and stressed beyond anything I've ever known, we got in the car and left England.

Sadler 32 *Admetus*

Capt. Peter Boddy

Dudley helming *Admetus*

Roy West flying us to Corfu

Orpheus on Levkas mole

The Three Amigos

Harry's first trailer trip

Oxi Day Parade – Levkas Band

Kathisma Beach

Levkas Town

Nidri and Scorpios Island

Porto Spilla ("The Brothers") Pontoon

Vassiliki habour Lefkada

Ionnina, mainland Greece

Christmas decorations onboard *Orpheus*

Orpheus' winter cover

Christmas tree Levkas Town Square

Epiphany celebrations

CHAPTER 7
SEVEN DAYS ACROSS EUROPE

The plan was for us to travel to Worthing, spend the night with some of Dudley's children and say our goodbyes. After our hectic and upsetting departure the relaxed atmosphere of the evening was very welcome but as I looked around the table I began to get pangs of guilt. I realised Dudley and I had agreed and made our future plans together but now, looking at their faces, I felt terrible. I was taking Dudley away from his children and grandchildren not knowing when we would be able to see them again. We had obviously discussed our plans with family before making our final decisions and Dudley had taken into consideration that he would be missing out on the grandchildren growing up. Now the time to leave had arrived and I felt selfish, self centred and heartless.

We awoke at 4.30 a.m. the following morning to travel from Worthing to Dover to catch the Dover Calais ferry. Due to the lengthy stretch of road we just missed the 7.45 a.m. sailing so booked ourselves in on the 8.45 a.m. at a cost of £139 one way! We had all the necessary PETS documentation for Harry; the flea, tick and worm treatment had been administered and I had a certificate from the vet to say that he was fit to travel. This, however, did not stop me starting to worry whether everything would go smoothly.

Knowing that Harry would have to remain in the car for the length of the journey across the channel, I had asked the vet for a sedative. He hated to be left in the car and we knew the minute we had to go to the upper deck he would sit and bark and get extremely upset. This had been the main reason we had decided to start our journey from Dover. There had been easier, closer places to start but Dover gave Harry the shortest amount of time left alone in the car. The time arrived to administer the sedative and hope he would settle when we left him. Thirty minutes later he had a droopy head and couldn't walk in a straight line. He reminded me of myself after two pints of Guinness! As we passed through the gate to board the ferry the moment of reckoning arrived. "Would they allow him to travel with the documentation we had?" I wondered. As we approached the gate they looked at our tickets. They did not ask for any documentation in relation to Harry, never questioned anything and just waved us through!

The ferry left on time. The announcement was made that the car deck should be cleared and we left the car with a sad, little face watching us as we walked away. It was then the barking started. We asked if we were allowed to stay with him in the car but were told we could not stay in the loading area. We had no choice but to hope the sedative would kick in and calm him a little bit more. In no time at all, it seemed, we arrived in Calais local time 11 a.m. When we returned to the car we found a sleepy sedated dog who, prior to sleeping, had managed to shred to pieces a plastic bag full of sweets and goodies I had packed for the trip. He hadn't touched any of them but had in a very overt way made it quite clear to us his displeasure at having been left alone!

We headed off towards Dunkerque taking the A25 to Lille. The scenery was nothing spectacular, but due to the excellent French roadways we made good time. Lunchtime arrived and due to our early start Dud was feeling tired. I started to regret that I had never learned to drive on the 'wrong side of the road'. As all the driving was going to be done by Dudley we made the decision to take a much-needed rest. We parked amongst the lorries in a roadside garage and after some lunch I took Harry for a long walk whilst Dud, reclining in the car, closed his eyes and slept.

As I walked with Harry, my mind started to wander around the turmoil we left behind - our increasing debts and no income. It made it very difficult for me to relax and enjoy the countryside. I prayed for support and guidance realising that if I carried on the way I had begun I would make myself ill in a very short space of time. It was good to have some quiet solitude and to be in touch with my inner self as I walked the field next to the garage. The 'rat race' never allowed pockets of peace, moments of contemplation or simply the chance to enjoy the simple things in life. We were looking forward to enjoying these moments more in our new life.

We were soon off again on A16, A15 headed to Arlon, our final destination, for our first day's travel. Before we could reach Arlon, Dudley felt too tired to continue and I suggested we stop at the earliest opportunity. At Namur I spotted a sign, "Camping Rustique" and we decided to call it a day and stop for the night here. The campsite was completely empty but nevertheless we were greeted with a big smile and told to take our pick of the sites. The showers were pointed out to us and directions were given to a local restaurant where we could eat that evening. As it was out of season many places were closed so an offer was made to bring us bread in the morning and we happily accepted.

As we were left alone to contemplate our first attempt at erecting our tent, I took the opportunity to look at our surroundings. Beautiful! We were high on a hillside overlooking a very lush, green scenic valley. Cattle were grazing in the opposite field and there was peace all around. Not a sound to be heard. After several lungs full of FRESH air and a moment to reflect, Dud and I set about fixing the tent.

One sunny afternoon before leaving England, we had had a practice run on the lawn at my parents' bungalow. Whilst mother cooked Sunday lunch, Father had been entertained and amused at our attempts but right at this moment we felt quietly confident that we could erect the tent with little trouble. With a few minor altercations and marital huffs we managed to get the tent up. Next, we laid out an airbed inside and inflated it. So far so good. I made the bed and arranged our things and felt pleased with the end result, which was a homely looking interior to our £40 easy to erect four-man tent. Then it started to rain...

It rained harder and harder and harder. Ensconced inside the tent, which was remaining dry, we decided to text our friends John and Diane who were still sailing around France. We let them know that we had finally made our escape from England and were spending our first night in our tent in Belgium in the pouring rain. I shall never forget the text message we received in reply – "What the **** are you doing in Belgium? Everyone knows that it always rains in Belgium." I think this was John's way of letting us know that perhaps we hadn't made a wise choice!

The rain eased enough for us to take Harry out for a walk and ourselves down to the village for a meal. It was fantastic to think that, for the first time, Harry would be allowed into the restaurant with us. Before this exact moment I had never considered if he would behave. Obviously he had never been trained in restaurant etiquette as, in England, animals are not permitted inside. We were shown to our table and once we were seated I gave Harry the command, 'Under' which we used when entertaining at home. Harry took himself underneath the table, laid down and never moved. I was so pleased with him and was so happy because this meant he would be able to come with us again in the future. During our meal the heavens opened again and we realised we were going to get very wet getting back to the tent.

We arrived back at the tent soaked through but were relieved to see that the inside of our cheap little tent was completely dry. Zipping ourselves in for the night we looked at each other with love in our eyes. It was the first occasion in a long time. Neither of us had been this relaxed for such a long time. I could have cried. We snuggled down the duvet in a cuddle and had a wonderful night's sleep. Harry, who had been given a summer time hair cut, started to shiver in the wee hours and soon found himself a warm spot between Dudley and I. The bed being only ten inches off the floor made it an easy reach for his little legs and he was certainly wise enough to take advantage of the situation.

We were awoken at 8 a.m. to the sound of the bread delivery. Once we were dressed and surfaced the site manager brought us a steaming hot flask of strong coffee. It was very welcome indeed and as we say in Norfolk, "It could put hairs on your chest". As the morning awoke around us, brilliant sunshine appeared. We took the opportunity to dismantle the tent and laid it out to dry prior to packing it away.

Dudley took Harry off for a morning walk whilst I showered. He couldn't wait to tell me, on his return, of Harry's encounter with some Belgium cows. Packed up and ready to go we paid the bargain price of €10 for our one night stay. Picking up the A4 we continued to Arlon leaving Belgium and entering Luxembourg. Belgium had impressed me with its countryside of green rolling hills and lush valleys; a very pretty place indeed if only a little wet!

Harry, from the time he was a puppy, had always liked to jump up and down in a car and I had never been able to train him out of it. He liked staring out of the windows at the scenery and barking at motorbikes. No matter how hard I had tried to train him, which had included the water spray treatment, he still jumped up. Now it seemed, in a very short space of time, he had settled quietly to ride out the journey. As we had packed the car so full we had left him a space level with the tops of our seats, packed our duvet over the boxes to cushion him from them and laid his bed inside. After the first few hours he simply lay there, his head level with ours, either staring out the front window or sleeping peacefully. Never before had I seen him so relaxed and content in a car. Maybe you can teach an old dog new tricks after all!

Taking the A6 and A3 we travelled through Luxembourg in no time at all. I seemed to have no chance to gain a perspective of the place apart from how expensive the food was when we had stopped for lunch. We had been amused, whilst driving through Luxembourg, at the extremely polite lorry drivers. If you allowed them to pull out of a slip road or gave them room, they always thanked you by flashing their indicator lights left, right and left again; a very nice touch and maybe a good lesson in etiquette to lorry drivers everywhere.

We found ourselves entering France again on the A31 passing Metz and A33 to St. Die and Colmar. The day's journey had again taken a toll on both of us; Dudley from the driving and myself from trying to navigate and keep up with the road signs. As we carried quite a heavy load we had kept our speed to 65 mph not wishing to push our "G" registered Mazda too hard. The Auto-route directions had been excellent but whilst going through villages they indicated we should take "local roads". In these cases it was eyes down, look in, and twice we had found ourselves quite lost and asking locals how to get back onto the correct road.

It was getting near dusk, later in the day than we wanted and we still had to find somewhere to stay for the night. We were on the A35 heading towards Mulhouse. The light was fading fast and in my tired state it would be very fair to describe me as a volcano just starting to smoke and bubble. As we descended a very long, mountainous hill I could smell burning from the brakes, Dudley didn't seem to worry. This only added fuel to the lava and as thoughts of crashing at the bottom of the mountain came to mind a full eruption took place. I threw the biggest 'paddy' you ever saw. When we reached the Swiss border fraught and angry we asked the guard for directions to Basel. We needed to be there as soon as possible as we probably had only half an hour's daylight left.

We followed his directions and found the campsite I had researched on the Internet prior to leaving, which professed to be "a clean and quiet pitch". On the track leading to the site I saw many signs depicting a witch's hat. I found this somewhat strange but at this late stage of the day we had no choice. In the twilight we erected the tent on a pitch that was very muddy, cold and wet. Over a cup of hot soup cooked on a camp stove donated to us by David, one of our friends, we reflected on the day's travel. We felt that €3.97 for a tube of crisps in Switzerland was extortionate and the €21 we had to pay in advance for this campsite was daylight robbery, or, in this case, night time robbery. I decided however that "ausfahrt" was an excellent name for a motorway exit. I guessed an exit was an exit by no other name! Having not made very good time during the day we decided we should try for an earlier start in the morning.

I decided to check out the site and found that it had wonderful shower facilities that were being spoilt by campers trampling in the mud from outside. Nonetheless, I would be grateful in the morning for the warming flow of water. As for the quiet boasted of in the Internet literature it was clear our night's sleep was going to be disturbed by the noise of heavy traffic from the motorway that was strategically hidden behind some trees and from a train that whistled past every hour. To cap it all and to add to the noisy crescendo, a dog barked all night.

Needless to say, I awoke in not the best frame of mind and began to hate camping with a vengeance. I walked out onto the muddy sod and watched Harry running around with great gusto, piddling on anything that wasn't moving and looking like he was having the time of his life. To add fuel to my ever-worsening mood, Dudley was refusing to take the shower bag off the roof of the car because it would mean him re-packing it. After a not too civilised exchange of words, I took myself off for the shower. I needed to warm my now freezing cold and aching body.

We managed to make an earlier start and as we left the site I heaved a sigh of relief. I then noticed a wooded area and large signs saying private land, members only. I had not noticed this the night before and looked between the trees with interest expecting to see a building, clubhouse or something similar. No, all that could be seen was a circular clearing in the centre of the woods with an alter type table in the middle. My very tired and rather dramatic mind came to a very quick conclusion: "a witch's coven;" I didn't like this place. It felt and looked evil and I decided I was never coming back to this campsite.

We picked up the A2 to Lucerne and Lugano on the Italian border. Not being deterred by our bad first night in Basel we gave Switzerland another chance to prove itself and it turned out to be everything I had ever dreamed of. It truly was a picture postcard of green mountainous terrain, snow-capped and glistening in the end of summer sunshine. With autumn just around the corner there were wonderful colours in the trees and plant life. Even the houses we saw looked like something from a fairy tale. We both agreed that this was a place we would definitely be coming back to. We were enthralled with the stretch of road from Altdorf to Andermatt where the road sparkled in the sunlight. It was so mystical I expected to see a tin man, a scarecrow and Dorothy dancing up a yellow brick road. The tunnels were the longest I had ever been through, one being approximately eleven miles long. Different places touch people in various ways but Dudley and I agreed that Switzerland was a magical and heavenly place. We only wished we had more time to explore it. Luckily for us, on this trip, we were blissfully unaware of the Swiss Road Tax that you are forced to purchase upon entering the border. For some reason we had not been asked to pay for this.

No time to delay, we found ourselves all too soon by the Lake at Lugano. As we travelled further South the weather was warming up which went a long way to lifting tired spirits but did nothing for our patience as we drove around the bendy roads. The local bus drivers must not only have a lot of skill and ability but also be very even tempered. Whilst it was fun, amusing and picturesque for a while, the day was drawing to a close and we realised that it had prevented us from making the distance we wanted to that day. As a result, rather than risk a repeat of the previous day and to try to make it to Bergamo, we decided to settle for a campsite by Lake Como.

We were shown to our pitch for the night that turned out to be rocky, hard and unforgiving. The wind started to blow and

I began to get a bad feeling about the night ahead in our tent. We managed to erect the tent in the wind by hammering the stakes into the ground. To calm my rattled nerves I took Harry and went for a walk around part of the lake. The sun was setting and it felt good as it warmed my face. Slowly I was calmed by the sound of the rippling water. I took a moment to think good thoughts and tried to be reasonable about the whole affair. This was a means to an end. A few nights in a tent would find us in Greece with Orpheus and a new life.

I returned to the tent and set about lighting the camping stove ready to cook our evening meal. Although the little stove served us well it did limit our options so this evening would be a quick pasta dish. As I sat cross-legged on the bottom of the airbed, stirring pasta and opening a jar of sauce, I became aware that I was sinking to the ground. In that second reality dawned that the airbed had a puncture and was slowly deflating. "Bong!' A church bell rang out the hour. I didn't know if it was God's way of having a laugh at me or just warning me of the sleepless night to come.

Dud pumped up the airbed again but by 1am it was flat and as the wind howled I lay on a cold, hard floor, listening to a dog bark, a train passing every hour and the church bells chiming in at every chance. In the morning I begrudged every single penny of the €28 it cost for the sleepless night and in all honesty, although it was a pretty place, Como had not instilled in me the enthusiasm I had seen in many others who had stayed here. Friends who had taken holidays around the lake had said how wonderful it was but all I could say was it was nice but noisy. I knew I was certain about one thing and that was I hated camping.

We remained on the A2 to Menaggio where we caught the ferry across Como to Varenna; the cost of this trip for one car and contents was so insignificant it is not worth mention. It was fantastic value and saved us a lot of time, as we didn't have to drive around the whole lake. We were soon taking the SS36 to Lecco, SS639, SS342 and SS671 to Bergamo. This may sound complicated but it was easy to follow. However, it was again taking us too long on the winding roads to make the distance we needed to. Our plan from the outset had been to take the secondary roads to avoid paying toll fees and to allow us to enjoy the scenery. We now realised it was more important for us to make the distance each day to ensure our timely arrival in Greece for Harry's sake. We relented and picked up the Autostrada.

We tried to stop twice at a roadside restaurant on the Autostrada for lunch. It was impossible as they were like crawling ant heaps and were so busy. It finally dawned on us that it was Saturday and the local Italians were probably taking off somewhere for their weekend relaxation. Luckily I had packed some food in the car, so, as the sun was shining, we parked in the shade of a lorry to eat lunch. We had travelled so far south that the days were now warm enough for shirtsleeves; it was quite a contrast to the temperatures we had left behind. As we ate, a Dutchman approached the window with a half eaten sausage in his hand and thrust it through Dudley's window, saying, "For you."

Dudley with a somewhat shocked expression was shaking his head saying, "No, no."

I was saying, "Yes, please, thank you." The look Dudley gave me was one of absolute horror. He quite clearly thought I was going to eat this half eaten sausage the man was offering. "He's offering it for Harry," I pointed out as patiently as I could! I took the sausage and Harry devoured it in one big mouthful. The man looked on and laughed as Harry enjoyed his moment of glory and Dudley's face took on a look of relief.

Off again on the A4 to Brescia and Verona, A22 to Reggio Nell'Emilia, A1 Bologna and A14 to Pesaro. It was a long drive but all on the Autostrada, which is a very well maintained three-lane motorway. Just prior to Pesaro we exited the Autostrada and we began to wonder how much the day's travel was going to cost. When we reached the toll and offered up our ticket we were asked for €10. We were amazed at how cheap this was for such a well-maintained stretch of road especially considering the distance we had travelled.

Once off the main road we found a campsite with little trouble; fruit trees, ducks, chickens and other domestic animals surrounded it. Things were starting to look up; especially when we found out that they had a restaurant on the site that we could use. Real food, at last! The tent was erected with expertise and I looked forward to the wonderful evening ahead but the prospect of sleeping on the floor again this evening loomed heavy. Dudley did his best to pad the ground underneath us, trying to make it warmer and more comfortable but, in the morning, I awoke aching all over. I was feeling so very tired having only managed to snatch pockets of sleep in between the sound of trains, church bells, barking dogs and a cockerel crowing at sunrise! By now I had decided I hated camping more than anything else in the whole world.

I was heartened as we left the camp, which in itself had been wonderful, when the gentleman said as it was out of season he would only charge us €10 for the site. It was good to know that there were still some honest businessmen in the world. Sadly this was not to be the case the coming evening.

We made our way back onto the Autostrada down the east coast of Italy, A14 to Ancona, Foggia, Barletta and Bari where we found a campsite. Bari appeared to be an industrial town and as we drove through we kept a look out for campsites. It was again getting dark so when we found the first sign indicating a site we felt we had little choice but to take it. A grumpy gentleman showed us to another very hard, cold and unforgiving pitch and indicated where the showers were. Once the tent was erected, I went to the showers to ease my aching bones. I stood undressed, ready to relax – nothing – the showers were not working as it was out of season and maintenance work had begun to ready for the following season. The grumpy manager obviously forgot to mention this detail when he had showed us where they were, whilst giving us a two-faced smile.

In an effort to cheer me up, Dud took Harry and me for a walk and a beer by the seaside and we watched the sun set. He's always known how best to calm me when I'm angry or annoyed. We sat enjoying the last heat from the setting sun and listened to the restaurateur and his wife singing songs as they cooked. We watched as the local villagers strolled around the harbour in their daily ritual and everything seemed right again in our world.

Since our first night in the tent I had be unable to sleep but this evening I found sweet oblivion. The floor had been hard and cold but there had been no noises, just the gentle sound of rolling waves on the rocks just behind the trees. I was lulled and caressed to sleep by nature and awoke in the arms of a man who was definitely starting to look tired. The long days of driving were starting to show, but we were nearly there.

As we left the site the same grumpy old man who had booked us in, booked us out. He looked old enough to remember

Mussolini and with a very sickly smile on his face he said, "Twenty euros and I will not charge you for the dog." This flummoxed me somewhat because as he said this I looked at his list of charges that clearly stated 6e per tent, 3e per person, 3e per dog. My mathematic ability could never set the world on fire but even I could see that the listed figures did not correlate with what he had just said. He was making it sound as though he was doing us a favour whilst smiling and over charging us 5 euros!! Being Norfolk, I'm known for speaking my mind, but sadly, I am also terribly English. Dudley would never dream of arguing over something like this so neither of us said anything. We paid the money and left with a bad taste in our mouths.

We made the last short leg through Italy on the SS16 to Brindisi where we found it easy to find a ferry booking office. We had originally planned to travel overnight for only one reason. Knowing Harry would have to be left in a kennel we wanted to slip him another sedative in the hope he would sleep through the night so when he awoke we would be at Igoumenitsa on mainland Greece. It turned out there was a second good reason for overnight travel. Dudley was now desperate for a good long rest and a decent night's sleep. He had concentrated for many days on the long hours of driving and along with me he had suffered sleepless nights. Now all he wanted was rest.

We purchased our tickets and booked a double cabin with shower. Including the car and Harry, the total cost came to the sum of €128. We compared the length of journey and the facilities we were going to take advantage of whilst on board and again compared them to the cost of the one-way journey across the English Channel and realised what a huge "rip off" that trip had been.

With time to spare before boarding, we took Harry to the nearest beach so he could have a good run around. We were hoping to wear him out enough that sleep would overtake him on the ferry. I was amazed and thrilled to find that the beach we walked on was not made of sand or stones but millions of tiny little shells. I was in my seventh heaven. I love to collect shells and I never take a walk on a beach without leaving with something oceanic.

During the day we stopped at two restaurants to have a half beer each and were not too surprised to find it costing 9 euros in one and €7 in the other. These prices, although extortionate, were to be expected. There was nowhere else to go and the businessmen of Brindisi were making the most of their prime positions in this busy harbour.

At around 7.30 p.m. we were allowed to board the boat. I decided it was time to slip Harry his sedative. We had been informed that he would not be allowed in the cabin and would have to remain in a kennel on the upper deck. This was bothering me greatly as he had never been shut in a kennel or even a single room; I had always left him with the run of the house and had given him as much freedom as possible. We set sail and the time came for me to leave Harry in the kennel. I settled him on his blanket and he looked as though he would sleep, but the minute I moved to leave he started barking. I left him to bark in the hope that if he thought I would not return he would be quiet. Not a chance! I knew for me to return to the kennel would only make matters worse so I walked away crying, my heart aching and breaking at the sound of his cries. I begged Dudley to let me sneak him into the cabin but he dare not take the risk of us being caught. He needed this night's sleep too badly to risk us losing the cabin.

Making sure he was unaware we were there, both Dudley and I, throughout the evening, went to the top deck to check on Harry to see if he had calmed down but he had not. We tried to enjoy a Metaxa Brandy but at a cost of €9.85 it left a bitter taste in our mouths. We were well aware that a bottle of Metaxa at this time cost a little less than €7. Some four years later it still only costs €8.50. This mark up could never be justified. At bedtime, one last check revealed that Harry was still barking and, although I was longing for a good night's sleep in a proper bed, it was not to be. I must have drifted off sometime during the night as it was with a shock that the knock on our door announced it was time to disembark. By 5 a.m. I ran to the upper deck, flung open the kennel door and found my frantic furry friend giving me a look of pure hatred. He ran around the deck not doing a thing I commanded. He glared and ignored me until, finally, many cuddles later, he calmed down.

It was whilst we were waiting to dock that I took the first opportunity to consider what impression Italy had made on me. We had travelled the length of the east coast and had not really had an opportunity to see much of the countryside. What little we had seen had been pretty but the things that stuck out in my mind the most were the number of magpies flying around, the amount of near miss and full accidents we had seen on the Autostrada, and the extreme number of men who seemed to want to pee on the roadside in full view of everyone!

Sitting in the car park of the ferry terminal, we ate breakfast and waited for the sun to rise, which in glorious fashion appeared to warm the day. We took off for the last leg of our journey on the familiar road from Igoumenitsa to Levkas where *Orpheus* awaited us. Relief washed over us when we realised that we were here, that it was over, that this evening we would be in our new home, sleeping on our own bed. It felt so good to be back in Greece! We both loved the country and the people and were already looking forward to our new way of life.

During our journey across Europe we had kept a record of expenditure and had a quick count up of the total costs so far taking us from England to Greece. We estimated, taking account of food, petrol, toll fees, campsites and ferries, that in total we had spent just over £500. This equated roughly to the quoted cost of flying Harry from the U.K. to Athens. It had been worth every penny to ensure that all three of us stayed together and arrived safely at our destination. It had definitely been the easiest and cheapest way for us to travel. If only I had enjoyed the camping more!

To update on this journey, we took a similar route again some four and a half years later using main motorways across France but not toll roads, were obliged to pay the €30 Road Tax in Switzerland and used the autostrada through Italy. The total cost of the trip was £696 and, interestingly, the U.K. ferry cost had reduced to £92 and the Ancona to Igoumenitsa inflated to €258!

We arrived at Levkas at 10 a.m. in the morning and felt like we had finally come home. We went on board *Orpheus* and slept. We ate and we slept some more. All three of us were shattered from the journey and our bodies just needed to rest. George and Helen, a couple we had met on holidays with Captain Pete, came to welcome us and invited us out to dinner. It was good to see a friendly face welcoming us and giving us a few tips on how to survive living on board. Holidays were one thing, but living on board full-time was going to be completely different. Sailing together, just the two of us, was going to be a new experience and to help us through these initial days the words of wisdom imparted by George were, "Remember to panic slowly!"

That evening I gave thanks for our safe arrival and for the opportunity to live this new life amongst old friends and the new ones we hoped we would meet – and we all slept.

CHAPTER 8
SETTLING IN

We suddenly found ourselves sleeping like never before. We took to bed early, got up late and even enjoyed the wonderful Mediterranean tradition of siesta. In between times we were cleaning the boat from top to bottom and unpacking all our belongings. It took three attempts at arranging all our chattels in the various lockers before I finally found a system that seemed to work. Dudley had taken on the task of sorting out the cockpit lockers and looking at the warps, sheets and halyards we had on board. (For the non-sailors, these are the spare bundles of mooring line and the ropes used for pulling out, handling and adjusting the sails.)

Gradually we assessed what we had, what we thought we would need and slowly turned *Orpheus* into our home. Across the harbour, already out of the water on the hard for winter, was *Admetus*. She was a pale blue vision in the distance, overseeing our endeavours to make *Orpheus* safe and ready to sail.

It was whilst lying in the forepeak bunk on our third night on board that I smelt a foul smell accompanied by a dripping noise. I awoke Dud, drawing his attention to the increasing odour. When he put the lights on, our worst fears came to fruition. We had forgotten to empty the holding tanks before flying home in May. Thus, with the summer heat, fermentation had taken place, gaseous liquid was leaking everywhere. A lot of mopping up and manual pumping had to take place before I could finally disinfect and sterilise everything in sight. It was a bitter lesson and one I shall never forget. Don't ever forget to empty your holding tank before coming into harbour, especially when it's going to be for a long period of time.

During the ensuing days Dudley discovered our batteries were flat and, on seeking advice, found they were of no more use and it was recommended that we purchase new ones. A suggestion was also made that we would benefit from the installation of a battery master and booster, so we decided to follow the advice given. This work, along with the guardianage fees, cost us approximately €1,794 and this left us on even more of a sticky wicket financially. To add to our troubles, during one mealtime, whilst contemplating what on earth I could cook with only two gas rings, no grill and an oven that wouldn't work, I smelled gas around the galley area.

A tanned gentleman named Pip, who worked for Joe, came to the rescue and discovered a gas leak at the back of the oven. Whilst fixing the leak he gave Dud a few tips on how best to clean the oven in order to get an even flame and one that would not keep extinguishing when the oven door was closed! We later met Pip's wife Clare and as they were living on board a yacht on the Levkas mole we became friends. I mention this couple because, without them, our first winter on board could have gone so differently. Right from this first meeting they were very willing to impart information on where best to shop, where to get the best meat and wine and so on. These small snippets of information were extremely useful when trying to live on a budget in a place that seemed almost strange, despite our numerous holiday visits.

After spending a long week of settling into the boat and finding our way around daily life in Levkas, we found ourselves relaxing on Sunday 21st September. We had finally found time to have a day of rest. Harry had taken to the boat very quickly and already knew where all the vital accessories to his daily life were. His bed was under our forepeak bunk and his bowls were by the galley area. He had worked out which locker contained his food and was already showing us exactly what he wanted and when! He moved about the boat well but we were very perturbed to find him launching himself down the companionway steps, top to bottom in one movement. On board *Orpheus* these steps are about five feet tall with a gradient incline of 75 degrees. Although he looked somewhat shaken up after the first fall it didn't stop him doing it for a second time so we discouraged him as best we could. He walked around the decks confidently and thoroughly enjoyed sitting on the helm seat at the stern, watching the world go by.

A very enjoyable part of our holidays with Captain Pete

had been "Car Park", the name given to a local stray dog. Car Park lived on the 'mole' (a jetty off the main quayside) and was fed by the local fishermen. Pip and Clare minded him and so he spent much of his time at the back of their boat, which happened to be not so far from ours at this time. So Harry and Car Park, a golden Labrador with a very nice nature, met for the first time and, without a doubt, Harry liked Car Park very much!

As the weather was so nice we decided to take off for a few days sailing. It was to be our first trip completely on our own. We wanted to see how we would get on sailing together and both felt a little apprehensive. We knew that we needed to flush out our holding tanks and we also needed to scrape the bottom of the boat. *Orpheus* had been still since May and there was no doubt in our minds that the hull would be covered in weed and barnacles that would dramatically reduce our speed. They would need to be cleaned off as soon as possible.

Right from the outset of our journey everything seemed strange and different. Dudley helmed and I, using the electric windlass (anchor hoist), pulled up the anchor and we were off. I set about taking the fenders off the guardrails and then realised we had nowhere to put them. *Admetus* had stowage under the cockpit seats but *Orpheus* did not, so after a quick discussion we decided to tie them at the back of the boat against the push pit. This seemed to work well and later Dud realised there was an added benefit to this. When he was helming it gave him something to lean back on for a little bit of comfort.

We decided to pull alongside the fuel pontoon to ensure the tanks were full and managed to moor safely on the second attempt with the assistance of the fuel man taking our lines. The re-fuelling complete, Dud tried to start the engine but it was completely dead- nothing, not even a cough. Conscious that Joe closed his business on Saturdays at 2 p.m. Dud ran round the corner from the fuel quay to his offices just in time to get Spiro called back to attend to our problem. We thought we were going to be stuck on the quay for some time as Spiro started the long drawn out task of elimination, trying to establish what the fault was. Luckily for us, Joe decided to come and take a look. "Check the fuses," he said. There's one thing I can say hand on heart: my fellow Norfolk-man has never led us astray in all the years we've known him and his judgement was spot on. A new fuse box was fitted and we were on our way.

As we were taking off down the Levkas Canal I asked Dudley what his depth was. I looked at the instruments and they were still covered up. They had not even been switched on. I could tell that we were off to a shaky start. The Levkas Canal is dredged when necessary but this left the sides very shallow. It was essential to monitor the depth of water under the keel to avoid getting stuck in the mud. Sailors with a great deal more experience than us had gone aground here and it appeared Dudley wanted to join them.

We dropped anchor at the first bay we came to as we exited the canal so we could scrape the bottom. An hour later, having removed the weed and cleaned a heavily barnacle covered propeller we got back on board, feeling quite cold. All the time we had been in the water Harry had been creating a ruckus on board. He had obviously decided he didn't like or want to go in the water so he didn't want us in there either. We pulled up the anchor and realised that the forecasted wind of northwesterly 3/4 was blowing nicely. This being Harry's first time on a sailing yacht we decided to sail on the genoa (foresail) only. The wind filled the sail easily and we had little difficulty in getting the sails out. It was such a relief to find that we hadn't forgotten everything during our break away from sailing. *Orpheus* heeled nicely and had a steady pace; we were very pleased with our choice of yacht. Harry instinctively sat on the high side of the yacht with the heel and every time we put in a tack he changed sides. It made us relax further, knowing that his basic instincts were teaching him the right things to do at the right time.

I tried to take the helm but, being used to a tiller, I just could not take to it. It was going to take me some time to even begin to get used to the feel of it. I so missed *Admetus* and her wooden tiller. The cold, steel wheel was hard, unfeeling and unforgiving and I really did not want to try to take the helm; it simply felt too alien. Luckily, Dud understood my feelings and for this trip I handled the ropes whilst Dudley steered. We had a wonderful sail in warming sunshine and realised this was what we had fallen in love with and the reason we had come to live on board a yacht in Greece.

With the sail put away, we motored back to the Levkas quayside. I watched as Dud reversed us into a mooring. I went forward to drop the anchor when it was appropriate but had difficulties getting the anchor to drop. The links in the anchor chain appeared to jam and not run out smoothly. When I finally sorted it out, I looked round to see Dud flush faced, wide eyed, throwing mooring lines with one hand and steering with the other whilst wishing he had a third hand to fend off the neighbouring boats. If I had been an observer of the situation, I believe I would have stood and laughed, but as I wasn't, I rushed to help him fend off and secure the mooring lines. I made a mental note that we would have to sort the anchor chain and anchoring process to enable me to help Dud with the mooring. We had a quick de-brief of what had happened and realised we still had a long way to go to settle into any sort of mooring routine and the words, 'Panic slowly' echoed loudly in our ears.

Our day of fun over, we went shopping for a local sim card and mobile phone. Since leaving England our Vodaphone Datacard had failed to get a signal or operate. On arriving in Greece we were surprised at being charged 79p per text message and even more surprised to get our first statement for the datacard indicating we owed them just under £10 for the privilege of owning it! This was not as it had been explained to us and I was astounded, especially as the card had not worked since the day the man in the shop had sent a test text message – for which I had been charged £1.50!! Needless to say we were not too enamoured with Vodaphone and searched locally for a new sim card.

A local shop supplied us with a new phone, charger and sim card with €9 free calls all for the sum of €89, approximately £63 at the time of purchase. Each text message was going to cost us 11¢ for text under one hundred characters and 24¢ for over, a huge saving. We never looked back and were very pleased with the purchase. On asking around, most people had discovered the same as us and had ultimately decided to purchase local sim cards. Of course, since then, times have moved on quickly and prices have been driven down further, but we think buying locally still remains the best and simplest way to keep in touch.

Not having the time, money or ability to buy a tender in the UK and bring it out with us, we took many drives around local sailing holiday places and second hand shops trying to find a cheap dinghy to use as a tender. It was going to be awkward until we had one, as anchoring off would not be an option with Harry on board. As much as we had tried, Harry was definitely refusing to do his business on board and so he needed to go ashore at least twice a day. We could not find a dinghy within our price range anywhere at this time and so decided this was going to have to wait. This then prompted us to sit and write a list of requirements for the boat. Various things on board needed updating and some of the lines needed replacing. As we were cash poor we decided to make a list of priorities. Just to forewarn you, some years on, it seems our 'wish list' is longer than ever. For every item that gets purchased another seems to get added to the end!

It was during our dinghy search that we took a drive to Vounaki on mainland Greece. We knew where we were headed for, but without a map it was a little hit and miss. Our drive took us over the swing bridge from the island of Levkada onto the mainland. This bridge, which in reality is a barge, is all that separates the mainland from the island and is the reason they manage to keep their island status. Over the bridge and along the coast road, we travelled up mountains on tiny roads that were almost covered in tarmac. Olive trees and wonderful wild flowers that were sprinkled between the rocks and growth surrounded us. The views at certain points were breathtaking; an artist could spend hours at an easel soaking up the scenic splendour. We passed through tiny villages that consisted of a handful of houses and at other times we found just one isolated house with nothing else for miles around. These little houses all looked ramshackle but on the other hand were functional and self sufficient in animal stock and vegetables. At times the silence was almost deafening and a little unnerving.

Rounding a tight bend in the road we suddenly came face to face with goats; not just a few goats but hundreds of them, all lying in the middle of the road. Dud stopped the car and waited for them to move, but there was no such luck! Harry was on his feet sniffing the air and deciding whether to bark or not. Dud inched the car forward and it wasn't until the bumper was nudging the front goat that it decided to get up. As he did so the rest of the herd decided to lumber reluctantly to their feet, glaring at us for disturbing their afternoon siesta. Some ten minutes later, we had managed to nudge our way through the remaining goats and were off again. We passed unfettered horses and cattle, roaming around and grazing on the grass. Such a different way of life! God's creatures roaming wild, free and safe from harm! It was wonderful to realise that the farmer had no fear of his cattle being stolen or of being sued for his loose cattle causing an accident. That certainly would not be the case in England!

Carrying on, we came to a village that looked the worse for wear. The buildings were in a bad state of disrepair and some had half their walls missing. We then realised that all the houses were vacant, apart from the odd goat roaming around inside, eating and sheltering from the sun. When we returned we asked our friends about the deserted village and it was explained that during the 1953 earthquake the villagers had suffered badly. Instead of repairing their houses they had all decided to up and leave and had re-built the village a half mile down the road. This was not an unusual tale of courage as, after the World Wars, many have found themselves homeless and have had to rebuild their lives. Nonetheless one could only admire their determination.

We now found ourselves filled with our own kind of determination as, whilst enjoying our new life we had delayed the inevitable visit to the local port police to purchase our cruising permit, transit log and pay our harbour dues. We were hesitant for prior to leaving England we had registered *Orpheus* on the British Registry and were unsure whether it was still registered in Greece. If this was the case we would have been committing a crime, it being illegal to have a yacht registered in two places at any given time. It had been impossible for us to de-register the yacht in May when we took possession, because this would have meant us appearing in person at the place of registry, which in our case was Piraeus, Athens. By taking the opportunity to register *Orpheus* in England prior to leaving the U.K., we had created a dilemma.

Having explained our situation and plight, it is timely for me to introduce to you Jeanette and Vaia (pronounced Via) who worked in the office for Joe at Contract Yacht Services. Jeanette, a tall, blonde beauty, with the bluest eyes and the biggest white smile was not just a pretty face- she could speak five languages. Her assets went a long way to complementing her workmate, Vaia, whose olive skin, dark hair and delicate frame made her look typical of a young Greek. She oozed sex appeal and lured you with sultry, brown eyes whilst putting you at ease and solving all your accountancy problems. Captain Pete had entertained himself on many a rainy day by tormenting both the ladies within the office. But for us, thanks to them, our life had been made bearable.

We were finding ourselves outside of our normal living environment; we needed to understand the culture of those around us and desperately needed someone who could help us with our dilemma. Not being able to speak the local language we needed help with translation and both ladies were willing to help. Over the years of sailing Dudley and I have heard many complaints about the cost of yacht services but speaking on a personal level, the assistance Dudley and I received from Jeanette and Vaia was worth every penny and far exceeded that of general yachting services. As delicate and beautiful as Vaia looked she was a latent Rottwieler. Contacting the port police on our behalf she managed to ascertain that Dimitris, from whom we had bought the yacht, had de-registered it on selling it to us. What a relief! We could now approach the port police without fear of dual registry and obtain our necessary documents.

We presented all our documentation to the port police and answered their questions. I had to sign a declaration indicating I would be remaining in Greek waters for more that twelve months to enable us to purchase a three-year cruising permit, which was a cheaper option than a yearly one. To bring this matter up to date, twelve months later they dispensed with the need for the cruising permit in Greek waters, so we could have saved money by getting a one year permit but we were not to know. It has been our experience that documentation requirements come and go like the wind in Greece; changes are so frequent you must just be prepared to go with the flow.

We also acquired a Transit Log, which would have to be presented at any harbour we visited from now on and that had a port police office present. There would be no Port Police fee to pay, as this had also now been dispensed with but the log would be stamped and a harbour due charged! It was explained to us that harbour dues were collected to assist with repairs and improvements to the quayside, such as the introduction of water and electricity. In some respects these dues should not be frowned upon, as they would benefit all visiting "yachties" for years to come. After discussing harbour dues we were charged for three days mooring and left the building €95 down but knowing we would be cruising with all the necessary documentation and peace of mind.

We felt like we had the essentials on the boat sorted so we decided to stock the boat with victuals, make sure *Orpheus* was seaworthy and take off for a few days sailing to see if we could settle into a sailing routine. This was to be our first big adventure together, making our own decisions and taking responsibility for the decisions made. Naturally it was also going to test my navigation skills, both of our sailing skills and assess our ability to sail together. We wondered what was going to happen.

CHAPTER 9
SAILING AWAY

We left the Levkas Canal heading for the Meganisi Channel and making our way to Sivota. The winds were Northwesterly 3 gusting 4. We were happily sailing along and I was again amazed at how well Harry had taken to the boating life, when the wind suddenly changed direction 180 degrees and the gusts became stronger. I became spooked by the change and we both agreed that we didn't need to risk anything our first time out. We pulled in the sails and motored the remainder of the way to Sivota. As we arrived we couldn't believe how busy it was and soon realised that in the short time we had been away from the Ionian another flotilla company had made this protected harbour their base. It was changeover day so all their yachts were moored along the quayside indicating the end of a holiday for some and the beginning for others. We found a mooring space and began laying our anchor as best we could in our inexperienced state.

I was suddenly aware of movement near our bow and was aghast to see another yacht chasing us into the mooring. They let their anchor go and were coming full steam astern with little or no respect for anyone or anything. As I was becoming aware of this threatening yacht Dud had thrown our mooring lines ashore and I went to help him finish securing them, while the other yacht barged through and used us to hold onto whilst sorting their lines! We looked at each other aghast and couldn't really believe what had just happened. Their actions portrayed the worst of manners and were totally against the yachting etiquette of standing off until the first yacht has been secured and then coming into anchor alongside. Considering it rude and ignorant to the extreme, we were even more surprised when we looked at the flag of the yacht to find it was Swiss. These countrymen are usually very polite. It just goes to show you get rotten apples in every country world wide, not just in the countries that are constantly being targeted!

To recover from our rather hectic arrival at Sivota we went to a local taverna to have a Mythos lager. We were definitely going to have to budget our lifestyle closely. Over the two-year period that we had not been able to come to Greece, being busy planning our departure from England, the prices had risen dramatically. The cost of living that we had initially budgeted for had definitely increased and we decided in an attempt to monitor our expenditure that we would record everything we spent. We divided expenditure into categories of food, diesel/petrol, gas/water, communications and yacht improvements. The beer we had drunk in the past had cost us €2.50. It was now costing us €4 so we decided we would not be eating and drinking out for a while.

The following morning brought a burst of sunshine over green mountainous terrain. We saw a small harbour fully surrounded by lush beauty with a few houses and villas dotted around. Sadly, it appeared many grey carcasses were in evidence everywhere, indicating the arrival of new buildings that would soon spring up. I couldn't help but think that once the meat had been put on these bones things would surely change around this little bay.

We had not yet fitted our speed log as the boat had sat still for so long and it had been left out. Dudley decided that this morning was a good opportunity to fit it. The waters at Sivota in the mornings, before all the yacht anchors stirred up the bottom, were crystal clear with a healthy fish population. With the increased arrival of the flotilla boats we did wonder how long this would last, as, alas, on changeover day, the water pollutants would increase dramatically.

Dudley explained to me how he would remove the plug from the floor underneath our sink, which would let a little water in, and then re-plug the hole with the speed log. He needed me to shine a torch over his shoulder to enable him to see in the darkness inside the cupboard. "And, remember," he said, "there will be a little water when the plug comes out".

Torch poised, at the ready, Dudley pulled the plug out – "OH NO!" I screamed as the brightest, bluest water I've ever seen spurted up in a huge fountain – under my sink! "OH NO!" I said as I envisaged the boat filling with water and sinking to the bottom and then I said a few other things not repeatable. My legs turned to jelly. I felt sick. I began to shake and by the time Dudley had replaced the bung with the speed log (which must have been only seconds) I was holding onto the kitchen worktop to stop myself falling over. Near to tears, it was time for a cuddle as I shook. Dudley seemed to think this was all too hilarious for words but I can assure you I was not laughing. I promised him there and then if he was ever going to do that again he was on his own. I was going to be ashore, somewhere safe, and as far away from the boat as possible.

As if we hadn't had enough of water for one day, Dudley went off in search of fresh drinking water so we could fill our tanks. The Swiss yacht alongside had managed to find some and were filling their yacht so Dudley went to find the source a few yards down the quayside. Whilst he was gone an almighty ruckus kicked up and I heard screaming and shouting and wondered what on earth it was all about. I looked to see Dudley in the middle of it – what on earth was happening? Arms were flailing about as a heated discussion was taking place between the Swiss man and two local Greek men. Dudley was there and I couldn't make out if they were shouting at him too. I began to worry. Dudley returned to tell me that the Swiss man had stuck a screwdriver into the water machine as he had put 6 euros into it to pay for the water and none had been forthcoming and he couldn't get his money back. "Fair is fair," we thought but the local Greek men saw this as theft and called the local police. Having created the whole unpleasant scene the Swiss man pulled up anchor and left the harbour in the same arrogant manner that he had arrived; and no, we didn't get any water!

We took off from Sivota in very light winds and tried to sail, but, as is the way of the wind in the Ionians, we ended up motoring to a little bay outside of Frikes on the island of Ithaca and anchored off. Dudley wanted to clean the bottom of the boat and I wanted to get my hands on the teak decking which was looking very dirty. We had a lovely swim together and Dudley dived down to retrieve a few shells for me, "booty", as I liked to call it. I scrubbed the deck, which, on *Orpheus*, is non-slip fibreglass laminate, and then tackled the teak seating and flooring in the cockpit area. By the time I had finished the water around the boat looked like a massive pool of octopus ink. Being good healthy dirt, the fish seemed to be having a field day sucking in the goodness. Thinking to aid their digestion we threw some bread overboard and watched while the fish fed. It's such a wonderful sight watching fish feed as they have the ability to relax a person simply by just being there. I love nature so much; its beauty and complexities never fail to take my breath away.

From our little bay we went into the harbour at Frikes and managed to come alongside at the first attempt. I managed to lasso a bollard as Dud helmed us in and, before we knew it, we were tied up and secure for the night, just like that, without any hiccups or mishaps. We couldn't believe it! We were getting the hang of things so quickly – or so we thought.

The evening brought a very bad swell into the harbour and we rode the quay wall all night, up, down, round and round. Sailing was definitely feeling rather strange and very different without my Captain Pete around. He always loved Frikes and would never fail to visit one of the local tavernas for a glimpse of Katerina, one of the many beautiful Greek girls around the islands. For those readers who are thinking badly of my Captain Pete, please don't. Part of his charm is that he is a huge flirt; I would affectionately call him a 'tart'. I missed him very much.

We decided the following day to sail to Little Vathi on the island of Meganisi but I was feeling very queasy. We set sail and it wasn't very long before I was very sick, first hanging over the edge of the boat and then lying prone on the deck. I was sure I was dying – or so it felt. Dudley thought I may have eaten something bad but I was not so sure. It had been so rough overnight, rolling up and down the quayside, that I was not wholly convinced that it wasn't this that had made me seasick. Our navtex weather had failed to transmit that morning and we were undertaking a long journey with only Dudley able to do anything. As the navigator, and still being of sound mind, I made the decision to change direction and head for Vassiliki on the island of Lefkada. This would mean Dudley could set the sails on a beam reach and sail us single-handed, on one tack, all the way into the harbour.

As we steadily sailed across the relatively open expanse of water, the swell abated a little but I still felt dreadful. We could not decide whether it was seasickness, a bug, or something I had eaten. Either way, my breakfast ended up in the briny. By the time we reached Vassiliki I was feeling very weak but we managed to anchor without mishap and were just settling the boat down when a storm of magnificent proportions broke loose around the bay. Rain pelted down and sheet lightning lit up the whole sky. Some five hours later, the storm still raged around us. It appeared almost trapped within the mountain range that surrounded the harbour of this quaint little Greek village.

Feeling very tired and not at all any better, we decided to take to our bunk for an early night in an attempt to be fresh for the following day. We were both surprised and extremely disappointed to find that our forepeak hatch leaked and our bed was soaking wet from the rains and getting wetter by the minute. We realised that we would have to camp out on the side bunks in the saloon area for the night. That was all I needed after my day of sickness. I told myself that this, after all, was what we were out here for: to live and learn and discover what life on board was all about. Trying to cheer ourselves in our current situation we told ourselves that had we not changed direction due to my sickness, and had continued on the longer journey, we would certainly have been trapped at sea, sailing in a storm, so my navigational rationale had won through in the end. This particular day with its raging storm also taught us another vital lesson: when purchasing a new boat turn a high powered hose onto all the hatches to check for leaks. This way you could make sure all hatches were waterproofed and ready for the first rainfalls crashing down from heaven.

Orpheus fared well under closer inspection. It was only the forepeak hatch that had a minor leak. It was just unfortunate that this was the most serious as this was the bunk we slept in. It would be the foremost important job to get the hatch resealed on our return to Levkas.

Dud was getting good at turning his hand to most things around the boat but some things still evaded him. Although we could barely afford it we made the decision to pay someone to carry out the repair so we could watch this the first time and gain the knowledge to do it ourselves if ever there was a second time. While Dudley was turning his hand to things around the boat, I was trying to vary our meals. I still could not get to grips with how or what to cook on only two rings, one of which was refusing to turn down to the simmer!

The storm continued to rage into the following day so we used the day moored in Vassiliki to re-stock the boat, fill it with water and generally clean up. This was the first of many such days. I soon began to realise that a yacht was much harder to keep clean than a house. Every day I stood and looked at yet another layer of dust and dog hairs which seemed never ending.

The following day there was no wind at all, an extreme contrast, but one you come to understand and accept when sailing around the Ionian. We motored back through the Meganisi Channel and prepared to anchor stern-to on the quayside at Porto Spillia. As we entered the harbour there was a man on a motorcycle waving us into a different anchorage. Dudley and I had forgotten about the 'brothers'. Two brothers ran a taverna with a pontoon directly outside; they enticed people onto the pontoon so they would eat at their taverna. This may sound intimidating but I can assure you, there is no pressure on their part for you to attend their taverna. They are always helpful and in some ways it was very reassuring to have them there.

On this occasion, I had checked the weather forecast before entering the harbour. Although the winds were light at our arrival I was aware that more storms were expected and I explained to Dud that I felt if the wind was to get stronger the pontoon would be untenable and therefore, we should moor stern-to on the quay opposite the floating pontoon. Having had this discussion we enter the harbour, the brother starts waving us over and Dudley is suddenly heading for the pontoon. Without saying a word to me he takes Orpheus to the far side of the pontoon and starts aiming her bow straight at the pontoon!! At this point I am extremely concerned as we have mooring lines set for a stern-to mooring so I say in a very loud, excitable voice that the whole harbour probably could hear, "What are you doing?"

"Mooring," says Dudley. At this point I run around the decks moving the mooring lines from the stern cleats and fairleads to the foredeck and set them for bows to mooring.

Just as I finish this a man on the boat next door to the mooring Dudley was bringing us into, says, "Here is your lazy line."

You will never know the embarrassment and horror I felt standing there at that moment in time. I had rushed around the decks like a woman possessed, whilst Dudley just stood at the helm never communicating one word to me about his insane decision to change our mooring plans. To cap it all I was being handed a line and I didn't have a clue what to do with it. Looking harassed and dumbstruck I said to the man, "What do I want that for and what do I do with it?" He was very kind and did not portray on his face what he must have thought and kindly explained that this was instead of an anchor and I should take it to the stern of the boat, through the fairlead and pull it up tight, securing it to the cleat. Luckily, at this point Dudley came back to the land of the living and dealt with the lazy line whilst I finished securing the bow and taking the mooring lines back from the brother who was standing there patiently, holding our boat off the pontoon.

Any married couple will relate to the following. With the mooring process over and the yacht safe, I erupted. What an idiot he had been! Where was the communication? How could he be so reckless to do such a thing without say a word about it? He knew I had difficulty getting off the bow of the boat without trouble and fear after my accident, and yet he had taken us into the pontoon bows. On and on I went, and I am sure any boat near us at this time would have heard my ranting. I am not ashamed to share this insight into my tantrums and having spoken to many couples it appears this is the honeymoon period of sailing together that most couples live through; it's the period when guidelines, boundaries and routines are formed. Discussing our initial sailing difficulties with people around us, we were told of an occasion when a man, so incensed with his wife's inability, had started beating her with an oar from the dinghy! I did take a moment to wonder if this method would work with uncommunicative husbands!

To bring this whole shamble of events to a head, the wind did get up as forecast and we spent a very rough night rocking up and down in a three to four foot swell. *Orpheus* was chafing the yachts either side of us, both of which were making the same movement as us but not at the same time. It was a dangerous situation that could have been avoided if only the helmsman had listened to the navigator!

The following morning was bright and sunny and, as always, everything looked different with the start of a new day. Harry loved to explore and although his legs were getting tired with age he still liked a healthy walk, so we took him up to the village of Spartachori and learned the meaning of "Beware Greeks bearing gifts." We entered a supermarket simply to purchase butter. The gentleman standing behind the counter, seeing us pick up a particular pack, indicated that the other one was best and much tastier on bread. "You should have this one," he said. Of course we should as it cost us €3.50 for a pack six by four. Our original choice would have been €1.20. We had been had. He had looked like such a friendly chap -all smiles, bad teeth and gums. We should have refused it and changed it for another, but, being very English, we paid the price and walked away. However, we did learn very quickly after this to ask, "Posso cani?" ("How much?")

We returned to *Orpheus* and had a wonderful swim in crystal blue water, surrounded by some of the smaller mountains around the Ionian but green and pretty, still and peaceful. When snorkelling I found that the fish were not only plentiful but of an extensive variety. It was all a good sign as to the cleanliness of the water. This was definitely one of our favourite places to be on Meganisi although some yachties we've met avoid the island, saying they don't want the worry or aggravation of coping with the resident rodents.

After lunch we made the short hop from Porto Spillia to Paleros on the Greek Mainland. As we approached, I dared Dudley to do anything other than what we had agreed and we moored stern-to without mishap. The water here was very murky and certainly did not tempt one to take a swim. We had never been here before, and as we sat drinking a beer at sundown we were struck by the sheer magnificence of the mountain that framed the back of the harbour and village. As the sun set that evening, the sky turned all shades of heavens glow and as the sky changed colour the mountain reflected these changes turning from green to pink, violet and cold, grey white. From this one spectacular evening I decided to name this particular mountain, "Moody Mountain". Following along this particular range northwards, another mountainous peak could be seen. This, I knew from our holidays with Captain Pete who called it, "Mammary Mountain" – I guess I won't need to tell you what shape it is!

We had decided to stay for a day in Paleros and walk around the small village, which had a particularly pretty church tower. As I sat eating breakfast in the sunlight I watched in awe as a spider busily made its web between two of our stanchions. In what seemed a blink of an eye a full web had appeared and the spider sat readying himself for business in the centre of it. God certainly has created a marvellous world. I've said this many times and will probably say it again before my days are ended that the complexities of nature and wildlife are wondrous and will never cease to amaze me. Each insight into its wonders gives me such a joy and happiness inside I just can't explain how special it is. For me to be allowed to see the secrets each creature holds feels like a gift from the Almighty and I feel so very lucky.

As I was sitting, contemplating the web, Dudley thought it was raining since he could see tiny circular movements on the surface of the water. Fearing he was going off on a tangent I looked for myself. Side by side, we stood staring into the water, looking at the tiny circular ripples that did indeed resemble rain, and that was when we saw the fish, thousands of tiny, little silver fish bobbing at the surface of the water. We then noticed a shoal of pipefish swimming by; neither of us had ever seen so many before. I began to reassess my first impressions of the water in the harbour. It was murky but obviously it couldn't be as bad as I'd feared because if it were, the fish wouldn't want to be swimming there. Every now and again we saw a big bubble rise to the surface from the bottom and burst. We couldn't make our minds up if it was due to gases released from the muddy bottom or if it was bigger fish feeding on the bottom. As if all this nature wasn't enough we saw our first of many jelly fish, the size of a plum, white and transparent pulsing its way around the boat in search of food. Having never seen one close enough to be able to study its delicate nature, we were both very excited.

I dampened down some bread and put little pieces on the quay at the back of the boat for the sparrows. There appeared to be quite a large number of them as we walked along the quayside headed for town and they appeared quite healthy. The village was small and pretty and had almost everything you could wish for, which surprised us. We learned that there was quite a large ex-patriot community living here and strangely this was reflected in the village, although I couldn't exactly tell you why I felt that. The building works that had been carried out recently and those still awaiting completion meant that this small little village would not be so small in the coming years and sadly echoed signs similar to those all around the Ionian.

As we walked back to the boat I spotted a kingfisher on the rocks by the water's edge. In my excitement to show Dud the bird I frightened the poor thing away. The sparrows were busy feeding as we reached the yacht and we stood back, watching, not wanting to disturb them. Dudley can be such an understanding partner; he is very patient and accepting of my whimsical ways with birds and animals. As we watched, I thought back on the wonderful day of wildlife I had just had and hoped these creatures would survive the building works being carried out around the village. We had already been told that the numbers of kingfisher were dramatically reduced around the islands due to their natural habitats being taken over.

As I stood, thinking what a wonderful thing nature was, I noticed Harry limping very badly on one front foot. On closer inspection I found he had a rock hard rabbits' currant stuck in his paw. As I removed the offending item I wondered whether I should reassess my recent appraisal of nature being so wonderful !

CHAPTER 10
TROUBLES BY THE SCORE

Following an urgent telephone call from the U.K. we found it necessary to return to Levkas the following day in order to use the internet and sort out some matters concerning the flats. Without my mother there in the U.K. organising matters for us, several outstanding matters could have failed completely. The gas, water and electricity companies were messing us about and were not connecting the services; until this was done we could not legally let the flats. Mother somehow had managed to find a willing tenant to move in at half rent on the promise that services would be connected within the week! Mothers, I think, are really angels in disguise and are a highly under-estimated and under-stated commodity.

We stopped in a bay on our way back to Levkas to finish scrubbing the decks and tidying the boat outside in general. By the time we had finished I had begun to build an affinity with *Orpheus* that I previously had not managed to achieve. She was looking cared for and loved and quite smart. I thought of *Admetus* and somehow felt guilty for caring for *Orpheus* in a way that up until now I had only ever felt for *Admetus*. I still hated the helm wheel, which remained cold, hard and unfeeling; I still had fond and clear memories of a responsive warm wooden tiller.

We snorkelled for some time and Dudley dived below the water in search of more shells. Harry barked as he stood on deck watching us, not enjoying us being in the water at all. I decided to put his life jacket on him and bring him into the water to see if he would take to it. He had never been a dog that liked water and would even walk around puddles when it had been raining. This was to be quite a test for him and us, as it appeared. If we didn't get him used to the water he was never going to let us enjoy it!

At the early age of one year, Harry had ruptured his

cruciate ligament and snapped his knee bone. He was now 11 and the joint was somewhat stiff and arthritic and we were hoping exercise in the water would be good for his legs. Unfortunately when we tried him in the water in his life jacket and looked underwater with our snorkelling gear we found that he didn't use his back legs to swim at all, only his front ones. We were now quite concerned that in a very short space of time his back legs could be lame if they got any worse. As much as we tried and as much as he trusted us to allow us to try, he would not stay in the water to swim; he simply hated it.

On our return to Levkas our mooring was hampered by a cross wind and although we managed to moor safely, I had to point out to Dudley the role reversal that had taken place. Whilst he was just standing at the helm "holding us off the quay on the engine," I was running around the decks like a mad woman dropping the anchor, throwing mooring lines, securing the lines back on board, pulling the anchor up etc. I protested that if we had a stern fender to protect the boat from the quay he could actually let go of the helm and assist in the mooring process. It was a debate left unresolved.

Due to the uncooperative nature of the gas and electricity boards in England our financial situation was far worse than we had anticipated. We had also incurred a far bigger debt whilst building the flats and this had been mainly due to the foundations being piled. We were in serious trouble. I couldn't stand the thought of having to go back to the UK so soon and give up my new life. Dudley had kept the problems to himself and after an initial outburst of anger I tried to become more rational in my thinking to understand why he had done this.

For some time prior to our leaving England, Dudley had been uncommunicative and distanced from me. I had put this down to the pressure of building the flats. Since we had arrived in Greece he still seemed to have the odd day where he seemed to lose all sense of reason and would do unusually silly things that I had found very annoying. I looked at him now and saw for the first time how much weight he had lost, how ill he was looking and how depressed he had become. Looking at it in the cold light of day instead of seeing betrayal, I saw depression. I found it hard to forgive but realised he had wanted to come away as much as I did and he knew that if I had known of our financial plight I would not have come. By some strange sense of logic I realised he had done what he did for me and not to hurt me.

We spent an evening talking about what we were going to do. We had 50 pounds in our account and no money coming in for another month. Mother was holding all our mail and had access to our bank statements. She realised our plight and had raised the alarm. Along with the alarm came money to tide us over until we could pay her back. We consolidated our debts into one loan, thanks to Dudley's daughter, and tried to make a fresh start. We had soul-searching hours discussing whether we should go back or stay, and whether we could survive on nothing and perhaps find work. On and on it went until we both agreed we wanted to stay. We could live on air if we needed to; anything to ensure that this new life would work out. After all, despite everything, we still had each other, and Harry of course.

As if things were not bad enough, at 4 a.m. Harry began barking and showing signs of distress. Five minutes later the wind started to get up very quickly and very badly; Water was smashing up the starboard beam and stern of the boat. We got up and put out a spring and did all we could to help steady the boat but it didn't seem enough. We had anchored on the quayside in Levkas at the end of the canal. The southerly wind that was rising was forcing the water straight at us. Being the end yacht we were taking the full force of the wind and water.

In no time at all it was blowing force 6, gusting 7 and we sat hoping and praying that our anchor would hold. As daylight dawned we were still holding - so far so good - so to take my mind off the weather I took to cleaning the inside of the boat. However, as the wind went on and on and on, we began discussing whether we should pull the bow round to bring Orpheus alongside the quay which meant she would be more bows to the wind and would lessen the affect of the weather on us. This natural instinct was a good one but unfortunately in our ignorance we chose to ignore it, a mistake that we would pay for later.

As dusk drew on, the wind was blowing a constant force 7. We sat watching and wondering just how long the wind could blow. As we sat there a motor cruiser came hurtling down the canal and straight past our bow. He was travelling so fast that the bow wave he caused, added to the already bad swell, and hit our bow with such violence that when the boat lurched up and down the anchor chain jumped off the winch. The result of this was that enough chain came out of the locker to allow *Orpheus* to fly backwards in the wind and come to a stop an inch off the quay wall. Luckily a neighbouring yachtie had watched the events unfold and had jumped ashore to hold us off the quay by our passerelle (boarding ladder). Whilst our fellow yachtsman fended our stern, Dudley and I managed to manually winch up the offending links and brought ourselves back to a safe distance off the wall. We could only hope that this speeding boat had not dislodged our anchor.

Talking to our neighbour, we learned the usefulness of a "snubber". This piece of yachting equipment consisted of a hook secured to a piece of rope. Having laid the anchor the hook would be looped around one of the links on the anchor chain and the rope used to secure the hook to a cleat. This meant that the pressure of the chain was not being taken by the windlass but by the cleat. It also meant that any loose chain in the locker could not be pulled free by speeding idiots who should have known better in such weather conditions. It was a lesson learned the hard way.

We apparently were not the only people to get into trouble, thanks to Mr. I've-Got-a-Big-Motor-Cruiser-But-No-Brains. Dudley and our neighbour ran down the quay to a small wooden yacht with a stern rudder. Their anchor had slipped and their rudder was inches from smashing on the quay. Grabbing fenders and using all their strength, they managed to hold the yacht off the quay as the owner made the decision to cast off the mooring lines and leave the quayside. As he removed his lines he revved the engine and took the boat forward as fast as he could, using the speed and momentum to help him steer the boat across the wind and prevent it from becoming caught on the anchor chain laid downwind. He retrieved his anchor and went further into the middle of the bay and re-laid it there, swinging free and safe.

As I looked on, watching the events unfold, I noticed five charter boats between *Orpheus* and the wooden yacht in trouble. Each charter boat had approximately four people on board and not one of them moved a muscle to help, I was aghast. Talk about generosity of spirit! This was the first time I truly noticed the difference in attitude between those that hire charter boats and those that live aboard. Live aboard yachties understand what it's like to have your home smashed to bits and the months of budgeting to fund the repairs, these charterers just didn't care. It wasn't their boat after all!

We went back to watching and waiting and by 9 p.m. the winds were blowing stronger than ever with no sign of it letting up. It had been blowing for seventeen hours straight and seemed set for another seventeen! I couldn't stand the anxiety of being sat inside the boat, not knowing what was happening outside, not knowing whether we were safe or if we were coming too close to the quay. When I couldn't stand it any longer I put on my wet proofs and went outside to sit a vigil. As I walked out of the companionway, a gust like none before hit the boat, *Orpheus* heaved sideways with a creak and a clunk and I looked to see the stern of the boat almost on top of the quayside. I grabbed a fender and shouted at Dudley, "Get out here quick." I jammed a fender between the stern and the quayside but it wouldn't stay there. With each bob of the water the fender came out. I sat on the stern in the sugar scoop with my foot on top of the fender using my weight to keep it in place. I didn't know it at the time, but this was to be my position for the next hour.

Dud came out in wet proofs, arriving at about the same time as our lovely neighbour, who had also heard my cry for help. Dudley and the neighbour contemplated our situation and it was suggested it would be best for us to come alongside. Oh, why had we not done it earlier in the daytime when we had discussed it? They rounded up a posse of eager and willing liveaboards to come and help. The plan, as it was, was for me to protect the stern with a fender; Dud was going to loosen the anchor chain on command; the neighbour was going to helm and use the engine to keep us off the quay. Once the anchor chain was loosened, the motley crew ashore were going to pull on a line tied to the bow to bring it in to the quayside. We took off the portside stern mooring line and loosened the starboard, a little ready to carry out the manoeuvre.

As the engine started and we were about to do as we planned, the weather decided to rain and howl. The wind was now force 8 gusting 9. Harry began getting very fretful and kept barking and getting in the way. Dudley continually shouted at him, "Shut up, Harry. Be quiet." The neighbour kept giving instructions to everyone and Dudley kept shouting, "Shut up, Harry." All at once, and very quickly, it happened. The fenders had all been placed on the starboard side and we slid to the quayside in a great whoooosh. Luckily the fenders did their job. Dud tightened the anchor to hold us off the quayside and we instantly realised we had gone aground in the mud. Our keel was too deep for the water. The shore crew loosened the line at the bow and the neighbour let out the stern line whilst Dudley pulled up more chain on the anchor and we drifted free of the bottom. Instantly, the boat seemed much quieter and the position she was now in was more suitable to the weather conditions. Dudley shouted out another, "Shut up, Harry," so I went to retrieve him from below and give him a cuddle. As I was administering to our fraught pet I heard Dudley making polite conversation with our neighbour and saviour. "Thank you so much for your help," I heard Dud saying. "Couldn't have done it without your help. I'm Dudley, by the way, and my wife is Bernie."

"Nice to meet you," came the reply. "I'm Harry."

Our neighbour's name was HARRY! We had to laugh. We couldn't believe it. All night long Dud had been shouting, "Shut up, Harry," only to find out this friendly chap had the same name. Had he been wondering at times if it was him Dud had been shouting at? It lightened the moment and in a flash the horrors of what had occurred were forgotten.

We sat on watch until around 3 a.m. when the winds began to decrease and then took to our beds. A full twenty-four hours later, the wind finally showed signs of abating. We spent the next day trying to catch up on sleep and remained alongside as the force 4 wind still looked threatening. We invited our neighbours, Harry and Adele, for coffee to thank them for their help and I knew that I would never forget our hero, Harry. So, here in writing, is a big thank you to Harry and Adele and all those who helped. Without them our life could have turned out to be far dearer. Only those who were there could possibly understand this.

Early the next morning, we awoke to a grinding bang as our keel smashed into the Levkas harbour mud again. We shot out of the boat to see yet another idiot motor boat speeding past us and down the canal. What is this selfish mindlessness these people possess? We quickly let go of the line at the bow and used the anchor to pull *Orpheus* back straight so we were again stern to the quay and the keel in deeper water. Having received a weather forecast indicating that the evening would bring severe storms and a force 7 southwesterly wind, we decided to up anchor and go somewhere safer for the night.

We decided that Little Vathi on the island of Meganisi would be an excellent mooring in a south-westerly wind. At the present time the wind remained northwesterly, so, as soon as we cleared the Levkas Canal we hoisted the sails and were set goose-winged with the wind behind us. It was good to see the sails filled and opened up in glory. This was, and still is, one of my favourite sailing positions. I just loved to look up at the sails and watch them fill and billow in the wind.

I thought of *Admetus*. How beautiful she looked! *Orpheus* looked good, too, but somehow differently. *Orpheus* didn't look graceful and majestic. She looked sturdy, self-assured and solid. She was saying to me, "Trust me. I can do this well." It was a good sign that for the first time I felt as though *Orpheus* was talking to me. *Admetus* had been speaking to me for years through the tiller, letting me know what she wanted. With *Orpheus* this was a first. I guess she appreciated my efforts over the past few days to protect her and a special relationship was building up between us. If you've never owned a yacht you may well think I've taken leave of my senses but it happens. If one day you find yourself sailing a yacht and talking to her, remember me.

We were having a wonderful sail heading straight for Little Vathi. In the blink of an eye the wind turned 180 degrees and began gusting southwesterly. With the storms forecast, I was very worried. The memory of the past few days helped me make up my mind to ask Dudley to take the sails down and motor us as fast as possible to our anchorage for the night. I feared the storms would be on us sooner than we expected. As it turned out I had made a bad judgement call, whether it was the 'jitters' or just inexperience. The wind change had been purely due to the mountainous terrain at that particular spot. I consoled myself with the thought that at least we had played it safe.

We got to Little Vathi and were pleased with our mooring for the night. As the rain pelted down that evening we could hear the storms and noticed across the water in the direction of Vliho and Nidri that they appeared to be getting the worst of the weather. We snuggled down and at last had a very peaceful night's sleep.

The morning brought another weather forecast of storms and southerly winds force 7 and 8, so we decided to stay put and walk around the lovely little village of Vathi, which happened to be the capital of the island of Meganisi. Colourful church towers and beautifully built little temples around the village caught my eye. Restaurants surrounded the quayside and it was obvious that one particular family had a monopoly. Talking to local people, we discovered most of the restaurants provided wonderful food. We walked up the hillside to another village and were surprised to find many houses tucked away in a valley. The walks around the harbour held wonderful views and brought peace as we gazed out at the sea and the mountains in the distance. Moody Mountain was particularly moody on this day and looked as though it was predicting what was to come.

We had just finished having our deck shower later that afternoon when at around 4.30 p.m. a gentleman who went by the name of 'Stan the Catamaran Man' came by to tell us that the forecast on the television had indicated north-easterly winds force 7 gusting 8 and that the anchorage we were in would be very dangerous and we should leave. I couldn't believe that the navtex weather had indicated one thing and the local television another! As quick as a flash we upped anchor and took ourselves just around the corner to a bay called Abeleki.

We got inside the bay only to find that everyone else had had the same idea. Bad weather news travels very fast in the yachting community. We struggled to find a spot and had to make one between two yachts already at anchor. I was a bit concerned that, considering the weather conditions expected, we were a bit too close, but we had no option. We still hadn't managed to buy a dinghy at the right price so poor Dudley had to take a rather cold and late dip in the bay to take our line ashore and tie it to a tree. We laid our anchor at a slight angle, ready for the northeasterly forecast, and felt happy that we had done all we could to make ourselves safe. We had agreed that as we were last to arrive, we would not put the other yachts in jeopardy and if it looked like we were going to hinder them we would let ourselves go.

As darkness fell over the bay of Abeleki an almighty storm raged. The first strong gusts came out of nowhere and from the West. We had set our anchor for a northeasterly wind so from the outset these first strong gusts from the west dislodged our anchor. It remained westerly and as we clamoured around the decks, hoping the anchor would grip in again, we began to drift towards the boat beside us. We left it for another two or three gusts and then decided we were being dangerous and made the decision to abandon the shoreline, pull up our anchor and move off.

By now we were in complete darkness, soaked to the skin and in the middle of a raging storm. We motored up and down the bay for five minutes and I began to get concerned that Dud was planning to do this all night. I forced a plan of action and Dud rose to the challenge coming up with a good idea. Dud helmed us around the bay as we checked the depths all around the clear water. Our depth gauge had no night-light so I had to hold a torch to it and report depths as he motored around in the dark. Standing with my back to Dud I hoped to block the glare from the torch so as not to spoil his night vision.

The storm raged on as we decided on a spot where we could drop our anchor. We dropped in ten metres of water and laid out all our chain, which was some fifty metres. We didn't appear to be holding so Dud put the engine in reverse until the anchor found a positive holding. We kept the engine running whilst we waited to see how she settled on the mooring. We needed to be sure we would not be blown too close to the shore with the gusts. The storm passed through but the gusts remained and thundered on us as per the given weather report, northeasterly! We turned off the engine and took in landmarks with the swing pattern that had developed so we could judge in the darkness if we were dragging the anchor.

One gust would push the boat on a circuit to the right and just before it reached a full circle another gust would push it back again. We began a night on anchor watch, the time now was somewhere around 10.30 p.m. and by 2 a.m. I was feeling very confident that our anchor was going to hold for the remainder of the evening. Dud wanted to continue the watch and our inexperience in such situations meant neither of us could sleep.

Whilst Dud took his turn at trying to sleep, I sat watch in the cockpit as *Orpheus* was shoved this way and that by the wind. We were only thankful that being in a bay we did not have a bad swell to contend with. I watched evil dark shadows crawl their way across the surface of the water with determination until they reached our yacht and sent us spinning. The evil shadows passed through us as though we were not there and raced towards the shore where they appeared to be doing battle with the bright fluorescent surf fairies at the rock edges. The silver surf spray was squirted far into the air and landed again with a gentle hissing sound. There was evil and good, dark and light, wind and whistles as the trees around bent under the forces of the weather. I sat in silent awe of the battle of nature around me but I have to say I did not enjoy one minute of it. My stomach was in a knot and my bottom cheeks were clenched ever so tightly!

Dud took over watch and I lay down, trying to sleep with Harry lying across my chest, trying to calm me and protect me. I must have drifted off into oblivion at around 4.30 a.m. and I awoke with a start at 5.30 a.m. I told Dud to sleep. Daybreak was not far off and I could continue the watch. Just as he was dropping off to sleep I had to wake him. Were my tired eyes playing tricks on me or was there a yacht heading straight for us? I grabbed a torch and started waving it side to side shining it down on the deck. I assumed that the raging wind had finally dragged their anchor, as they seemed to be in some minor distress. They saw my efforts and managed to drop an anchor a safe distance from us.

Dud returned to sleep and I watched in silence as the darkness of night began to brighten. From behind the mountains, the skies turned a deep purple, with them, as always, reflecting the colour. Purple gave way to the deepest red and, silhouetted in the light, I saw birds flying from all directions, congregating in the sky to fly off together for the day. Red turned to an orange halo surrounding mustard coloured mountains, orange to sugar mouse pink and paling to yellows and soft purples and pinks all mixing to create the colours I like to think of as heaven's glow. As the colours disappeared the biggest, brightest sun appeared above the mountaintop turning it lush and green. I felt humbled by the beauty of what I had seen. Even with tired eyes it was hard not to be impressed. Then I remembered the good old saying, "Red sky in the morning, sailors warning." The Navtex report confirmed that there were more storms and strong northerly winds on the way!

When Dudley awoke we took stock of our situation. We had no tender and we had had to abandon our shoreline the previous evening when the weather worsened. Harry was looking to go ashore for his morning constitutional, having missed his evening one because we couldn't get him ashore. We had no netting on our side decks so we couldn't let Harry walk about and it was getting dangerous as he was becoming more and more inquisitive around the boat the more he was getting used to it. I decided that we were too constrained and that we were not sailing safely. I had had enough and I wanted to just settle somewhere for the winter and be done with it for this season. Dudley agreed and it was with a happy heart that I made breakfast.

We managed to raise the attention of the yacht we had been alongside the night before who kindly retrieved our shoreline and brought it back to us in his dinghy. If he had not, poor Dudley would have had a very cold early morning swim to undertake. Harry was crossing his legs and showing signs of distress and this made me very anxious to get him to land as soon as possible. We upped anchor and made our way toward the Levkas Canal. It wasn't until we left the protection of Abeleki bay that we found a rather large swell awaiting us. Dud helmed and I stayed warm and dry below. Poor Dud, he always volunteers for the short straw. He's just such a gentleman, one of the traits that make me love him so much.

As I hugged Harry I tried all the things I could think of to get him to have a wee in the cockpit, including dangling his bits in warm water. I longed to be safe on the mole in Levkas harbour. We returned safely and Harry got his first wee after holding on for twenty-two hours! Two other yachts had returned that morning and we learned that the horror of our night had been repeated all around the Ionian. It had been a freak wind and no matter where you anchored everyone had been hammered by the unforgiving wind. We were told there had been 100 mph winds recorded in the bay of Vliho and a swell that had reached some six feet. On speaking to others and learning of the events experienced by all yachties around the Ionian we felt better knowing that it hadn't been our inexperience but just an experience...

So we found ourselves back in Levkas for the winter. Our finances were so bad we knew we could never afford to go into the marina, so we made the best of a situation and settled on the mole for the coming winter months.

CHAPTER 11
THAT'S WHAT FRIENDS ARE FOR

Now that the initial urge to go sailing was out of our system we began to realise that living on board a boat was not as we had first thought. It was so different from any caravan or house I had ever lived or stayed in. There were certain things that could make life on board easier and those 'tricks of the trade' we had yet to learn. Our learning curve was just about to begin not only about living aboard through a winter but also about those "friends" we had left behind in England.

We found ourselves in the middle of October, some five weeks since leaving England and we had €30 to live on for the next four weeks. The flats were still not let and we still had to find the money to pay the mortgages. It was clear there was the likelihood that we would have no money to live on through the month of November.

Dudley is a kind hearted, generous and giving man who has always been loyal and supportive to his friends. He had, throughout his working life helped many in various monetary ways, only expecting a repayment when, and if, it could be comfortably made. He would recommend his close associates when dealing with his property maintenance business in order to keep them in employment, especially those that were older and considered no longer employable by the bigger companies. Whenever he was asked for work he would understand and respect the pride of the person asking, knowing they needed some income, and he would provide it. When told by one builder he was 'strapped' for cash and needed some income quickly to allow him to provide his bride-to-be with a wedding dress and all the trimmings, Dud promptly referred him for three new contracts, which went a long way to cover the costs. What I'm trying to get across, in a rambling sort of way, is that when we left England, many people still owed Dudley sums of money, which we were now desperate to collect.

Dud set about contacting these people in England, explaining our plight, asking them to please settle their debt so we could afford to live. The response we received was negative, non-committal or disbelieving. One person actually laughed at Dud down the phone saying, "How can you be skint? You're living on a yacht in Greece!" Of all the debts that were owed we received not a penny.

Sadly for us at this time there was, and still is, a common misconception that if you live on a yacht abroad you must be very rich. The mere mention of a yacht is enough to send some people's minds running riot with pound signs.

People never seem to take the time out to consider that we have chosen to live on a simple budget to allow us to travel. We do not actually work and therefore have no income; ergo we cannot be rich.

All those people we had called friends, all those who Dud had helped and supported through the years repaid us not a penny. Over the following months he tried several times to recover the money owed us and some paid under the pressure. We learned a valuable lesson. When starting a new life abroad, recover all outstanding debts and favours whilst you are still in your homeland. It was our experience that once out of sight; you are definitely out of mind. It certainly would not have been viable for us to pay to travel back to England to recover the debts as the total sum owed was not a large amount. However, as we were living on a budge of €7 a day, anything would have been a bonus. This sounds worse than it actually was, as we found by shopping in the right places and eating a simple balanced diet it could be done.

Being people who refuse to feel sorry for ourselves, we went about what was becoming our normal way of life. As we lay having a siesta, still trying to catch up on lost sleep after our sleepless windy night in Abeleki, we heard voices. "I could not hear you," cried a plaintiff high-pitched female voice.

"Don't come back here with your excuses. Just get up there and pull up the anchor," a domineering, loud, pompous male voice said. At this I just couldn't resist a look and I roused Dudley to come and see. We stared through the forepeak hatch as the man continued shouting, in what can only be described as one of the most snobbish upper class English accents I have ever heard "Get back up here and wash the anchor … NICOLA!..."

At this, the skinniest of frames appeared from below decks and went, hands on hips, to stand by the man. She waggled an elegant, nail-varnished finger, uttering words we could not hear. She vanished down below in a flurry of skimpy bikini and bare flesh. Dud growled in appreciation of the view and suggested that the man had just ruined any chances he might have had for the rest of their holiday – if you get my drift.

I found this little interlude hilarious but it reminded me of the many spats we had had when sailing and I decided it was best not to gloat. However, to this day, I still find it a good facial exercise, for a Norfolk girl who doesn't do "posh", to repeat in a supercilious, pompous accent "Nic – co – lar". Try it; you will see what I mean.

The island of Lefkada is a haven of beautiful beaches; not sandy as we know in England, but tiny pebbles, white, clean and edged with clear blue waters. We spent a few lazy days discovering the closest beaches and enjoying them and discovered the meaning of "Lefkada". In Greek "Lefko" means "white". Lefkada meant "the white island", so named because of its wonderful white beaches and white cliffs.

Throughout these days we relaxed and lived on fresh air and sunshine. It was wonderful. We slept and rediscovered what it was like to have a mind free of worry. Bit-by-bit I noticed that the Dudley I had first met and loved was coming back to me and that any signs of his past depressions were fading. With the openness of our situation and the acceptance of it, we found we could still be happy and so much in love, nothing seemed to matter and we were ready to take on the world. The money situation was a problem but even that, during these initial days, didn't cloud our sunshine.

We were determined to stay in touch with our friends and in order to be organised about it we made sure we regularly attended Internet cafés and made a rota of names to ensure that nobody was forgotten. This worked well and those that one would call true friends remained in touch and supported us in our troubled times with encouraging words. Sometimes, a kind word can mean as much as a purse full of money when you are miles away from home, seeking friendship and news.

Dudley and I spent many heart breaking evenings discussing the users and takers of this world and then cheered ourselves by thinking of the givers and supporters. At times we tormented ourselves about how those we had called friends had treated us but soon realised that these people had been acquaintances, not friends. Our true friends were there, still in touch, still caring and still sharing. We forgot the sadness and concentrated on the happiness our friendships brought us.

Slowly we made new friends about the harbour and nearby marina. It was the time of year that live-aboards congregate to enjoy being part of a wintering community. We learnt so much about Levkas town by talking to Jeanette and Vaia. They were always willing to help our transition into this new life by teaching us the Greek language, telling us where to purchase D.I.Y. tools and wood, where to find the local entertainment and such.

We had several projects we wanted to undertake over the winter months, two of which were a new Passerelle board and a drinks holder for the cockpit. As we were planning to spend our winter months using Joe's mooring on the Levkas mole, we felt obliged to give his chandlery our business to show our appreciation. It meant a lot to us in our present situation that we had a safe, inexpensive place to stay.

Towards the end of October the weather started to cool and hand washing clothes on board had become a little uncomfortable, the water during the cooler nights was chilled a little too much. Suffering numb hands was not something I enjoyed, so Dud would boil kettles of hot water to lessen the impact for me. Most places we had visited around the islands had laundries you could take your washing to, the prices varied between six and ten euros a wash. I had made the choice to do my own washing as we were living on such a tight budget but some ladies with a similar view would take their washing into the showers with them to use the hot water there! I simply told myself that this was one of those tasks living on board a yacht you just had to keep in perspective. During the summer I enjoyed sitting on the stern, scrubbing away, sun bathing, watching the fish, looking at the scenery; this particular chore could actually became quite enjoyable. The trick was to stay focused and remember that winter in the Ionian is only for a short time.

As if reading my thoughts the weather worsened very quickly and pelted us with torrents of rain and horrendous winds. We spent several nights sitting up listening, waiting to hear if our lazy lines were going to go "ping". *Orpheus* heaved and heeled with every gust and we sometimes wondered if she could survive such a battering. Finally we decided to secure ourselves to a second lazy line and also, as an extra measure, laid out our anchor and chain. After several more nights of inclement weather we finally felt safe and secure on our mooring and were ready for whatever the winter might throw at us.

We had settled very quickly into a daily routine to ensure our daily chores were evenly distributed. I have always hated shopping so Dudley agreed he would take on this task. We would compose a shopping list each morning and whilst Dud went off to shop I would sweep and tidy the boat. Sweeping floors and wiping work tops seemed essential on a daily basis due to the amount of dust that seemed to accumulate inside the yacht. It became a systematic ritual I carried out without thinking. However, over a period of time this never-ending urge has slowly reduced to once a week. I'm sure the boat gets just as dusty as it ever did but we hardly ever notice it. I guess it's just something you get used to.

As Dud set off shopping one morning I asked him if he could purchase some red peppers, among other things, for a curry I was to make for our immediate neighbour, Kit, who I could only describe as an old fashioned "officer and gentleman". He and Dudley had been chatting for some time, which had resulted in an invite on board for a meal. Dudley returned from his shopping spree and proudly presented everything for my inspection.

"There are no red peppers," I said to him.

"There are," he insisted and promptly grabbed and held aloft a perfectly shaped aubergine! I silently walked over to him, gave him a big kiss and called him a "plonker". He sat dejected with a boyish pout on his face so I had to make him a cup of tea to console him.

As it turned out I put the aubergine in the curry instead of the red peppers and it was one of the tastiest I had ever made. Kit, Dudley and I ate over candlelight and enjoyed amusing conversation. The two men had so much in common and were bonding very quickly, it was clearly going to be a lasting friendship.

I am not a very confident cook and although this evening had been wonderful I warned Dud that unless he did something about the oven I was not prepared to cook for company. The cooker on board still wasn't working correctly; it had become the bane of my life. Dudley would mutter encouraging words whilst standing by trying to support me in my gallant efforts to create food worthy of eating. I had long since given up on the oven section because the flame would extinguish seconds after the door was closed and ended up gassing me. Apart from my health we agreed this was dangerous and so for now I was refusing to use it. Although Dudley's support was gratefully received, all I really needed was either a new cooker or the one we had to be fixed. We couldn't afford a new one and although Dudley had stripped down and cleaned out the one we had, it took only a few days for it to be back to square one.

Having suffered a cooker catastrophe as one of the rings wouldn't turn down, Dud realised it was time for action. No, he didn't fix the oven. He decided to appease me by taking me out for a pizza. We hadn't eaten out at a restaurant since leaving England so this was to be the first opportunity I'd had to dress up in a very long time. It made me realise how un-feminine it can be living on board a boat. I've never been the sort of girl who liked to dress up, put on heels or play with my hair and yet, every now and again, I did like to feel feminine. I was finding this new life strangely void of such opportunities. Since living on board I had made no effort at all with my hair, and make-up just did not exist. Dressing up and such niceties somehow didn't fit into this new lifestyle. It wasn't a requirement, and nobody ever seemed to notice whether your hair was washed or combed anyway! The yachting live-aboard community simply accepts that anything goes ...

As we left *Orpheus* that evening to eat, we were stopped in our tracks, stunned into silence as we admired the evening sky around us. To the starboard side of the yacht was the most brilliant of sunsets. In the skies dark grey storm clouds floated and fused with the deepest fire red backdrop. I thought of the Emperor Nero as he watched his beloved Rome burn to the ground. The sky was on fire dancing with such vibrant energy it was as though you could reach out and touch it. The air was alive; it was tangible and, in a wonderful way, it was somewhat frightening. To the port side raged an electrical storm that was more charged than any we had ever seen. Amongst the jet-black clouds there were continuous flashes of forked lightning. Even when we couldn't see the actual fork the insides of the cloud lit up like a torch under a bed sheet. I thought of childhood games and the sinister faces my brother Tony would make as he pressed a lighted torch to his chin. There was definitely something in the air. It set the hairs on the back of my neck standing on end as we ate our meal sandwiched between the beauty of a sunset and the storm. There was no wind and no rain but the storm remained for the rest of the evening. After sundown the lightning looked even more dramatic across the night sky and created a magnificent display. It was to be the first of many nights that we would never forget.

From a surreal evening to the bright light of day, we were back to sending emails, which had become a constant nightmare for us. The Vodaphone data card we had purchased refused to work and we were being forced to use an Internet café. This was fine for the casual correspondence to friends but not the best environment when trying to deal with personal matters such as banking. My mother had contacted the shop we had purchased it from and several phone calls and correspondence later we still had no satisfactory reply as to why it wouldn't work. After being sent a new sim card from the UK, deleting and reloading the programme, I finally got an engineer to telephone me. After an hour of chatting to him he tried to convince me it was my digital camera programme that was causing problem. I pointed out that this had been installed at the time when I first used the card in England and it had worked perfectly! The £1.50 I had paid for their test message to the card was testimony to this! Following error codes 619, 713, 45 and 617 the engineer went away with the promise of identifying the fault saying he would call me back. To his credit he did call back but only to tell me that they were experiencing severe technical problems with getting the Greek network to speak to the UK network. If I returned the card to England I could get my money back – Hooray.

I would have liked to end this tale of woe on a happy note but unfortunately I cannot. I was refunded the price of the card. However, telephone calls between me in Greece and my mother in England, and the postage and car parking fees she had also incurred meant we remained out of pocket £75. We were informed that any such request for reimbursement would need to be made to the Vodaphone complaints department. A very long and detailed letter was sent to their complaints department requesting a full refund of our out of pocket expenses as none of this had been any fault of ours but their own technical problems. To date, our letter has never been acknowledged and no refund received.

Not holding a grudge and some years later with this system much improved, we gave Vodaphone another chance to prove itself. Sadly, although the local suppliers in Greece were wonderful, Vodaphone were once again advertising something they could not provide. We were told we would receive a 'wand' or "stick" modem free and that they had 3G. This was not the case. We were given a USB attached modem with 2G. Some months later, having been assured 3G was imminent – well done, Vodaphone- we are still waiting but it's good to see that your companies work practices haven't changed over the years!!

At the time, we decided that we would simply use the local Internet cafes, as this was the cheapest option. This problem solved, and gaining impetus from those around us, Dudley decided it was time for us to take our sails down and stow them for winter. We hosed them down and left them to dry in the gentle morning wind. This being our first time undertaking the process, we had taken any advice offered from those around us. We had been told to ensure the sails dried completely. If not, there was a chance they would develop black spot mould whilst stowed over the winter.

When we were sure the sails were dry we slowly released the foresail halyard, dropping the sail to the deck. We then had to try to carry the sail ashore for the folding process. Heavy, huge, cumbersome and awkward were only a few adjectives I thought of as I stood looking down at it lying on the side deck. We managed to roll it into a ball and tie a rope around it to hold it in tight; huffing and heaving we teetered down the side deck, stumbled around the cockpit (with an expletive from Dud as he smashed his head on the boom) and managed to drag it over the passerelle ashore. We then stretched the sail out flat on the quayside ready for folding. We had learned that there were two styles of folding. In general, one method was to concertina the sail and the other was to fold it in reducing halves. We decided on the later and dragged the head of the sail to the toe, keeping it straight along the leading edge. We repeated this action top to bottom, until we finished with a large oblong shape that, once halved sideways, fitted neatly into the sail bag. We carried out the same process with the main sail and by the end of the day both sails were safely stored in the back cabin until spring.

Having carried out this process several times over the years, we have both come to prefer the concertina method of folding. This is achieved by laying the sail out and pulling equal sized sections of the sail down to the foot until the head of the sail sits on top of the pleats. The sail can then be folded sideways to fit into the sail bag. We found that this method leaves the sail in better order ready for hoisting in spring.

Having removed the mainsail it wasn't until the first bad winds that we realised what a noise the mast made now it didn't have the sail tucked inside it. Every motion on the surface of the water that caused our boat to move caused our mast to clunk and clang. It drove us to utter distraction and we knew that we could not live like this for the whole winter. Dudley decided he would go up the mast and try to tie off the runner giving me my first attempt at hoisting him up the mast in a bosun's chair. He was quite confident that I could do it but I asked the owner of a neighbouring yacht to tail the line for me just to be on the safe side. I winched as Dudley climbed up the mast, helping to ease the strain, and in no time at all he had managed to place six ties around the runner inside the mast and secured it tight to one side as best he could.

The job complete, I was ready to let Dudley back down. "Slowly," Dud shouted as I fed the halyard back around the winch. "I said slowly!" he bellowed as he dropped a sudden eight inches all in one go.

"I am doing it slowly," I bellowed back very forcefully. Just as I said it, he dropped another eight inches. I'm too much of a lady to repeat what he shouted down to me this time!

The gentleman who had been tailing the line for me said, "I don't think you realise it but you're letting a whole loop slip off the winch." I had been so busy looking up at Dudley instead of watching the winch I hadn't realised that instead of loosening the line and slipping it around the winch it was bunching and slipping off one whole loop at a time! I apologised and remembered for next time that when winching, watch the winch and not the person in the bosun's chair. I also had it pointed out to me, when Dud was back to earth and feeling manly again, that I should never stand directly underneath the chair as the occupant may drop something. This was a good tip because I tended to get the urge to want to go and stand up on deck and look up at Dud and talk to him, almost in an attempt to protect him in some way but obviously it was safer for both of us if I, the winch person, was to stay clear. Safe back on the deck and the lecture given, I was forgiven for my failings and I put the life insurance away for another day!

Spending our first winter on board and not actually moored in the marina but just outside it, we did not know what to expect of the ex-pat wintering community. We were surprised to find so many British people living on board and staying here for the winter. We had thought that we would be alone through the winter months and had accepted this fact so it was a pleasant surprise to find this was not the case. The Greek people are a very friendly race but their focus is very family orientated; any socialising tends to be contained within family units. Therefore, although we were becoming acquainted with many Greek people on a daily basis, we were never invited into their inner social circles.

Our social life took a turn when we were made aware of the live-aboard "Marina Net". Every morning, at 9 a.m., the "Marina Net", as it was called, invited participation from all listening. We would tune in to the local VHF and listen to announcements of new arrivals and departures within the marina. Also, during these transmissions people offered things for sale or sought assistance from others listening to resolve any problems they might have with either maintenance or health. The best part of the morning "Net" was the update on social activities. Throughout the winter there were car-sharing shopping trips to Preveza, quiz nights, potluck suppers, exercise classes and, of course, Dudley offered a karaoke evening. We were grateful for being included in the marina activities and it felt good to be making new friends at this quiet time of year when it seemed there was little else to do but eat, drink and read books.

During one of the very first transmissions of the 'Net' this winter, Dudley and I listened with some enthusiasm as we were entertained by an exchange between the terribly English controller and a Scottish lady. The lady obviously was seeking advice about something but the controller just couldn't seem to grasp what it was. The exchange had us rolling about in our seats. "I'm lookin' for a wee bill," she said.

"Sorry, repeat the request," came his reply.

"A bill. I'm lookin' for a bill."

"You are seeking a bill, is that correct?" he asked.

"Ach, no, I'm looking for a bill for me bike!" the exasperated lady said.

"So that's Carol and she's asking if anybody knows where she can find a bell for her cycle," the relieved controller invited.

Dudley and I just had to meet this lady and when we did she was as much fun in person as she sounded on the radio. She had a husband to match and over the winter we became firm friends. To us she would always be known as 'Carol with the bill'!

The twenty-eighth of October arrived and we had our first taste of Greek public celebrations. This particular day in history was named "Ohi Day", (No Day), the anniversary of Greece's refusal to join the Italians and be drawn into the Second World War. Nobody seemed sure of what time the celebrations would commence but it was known roughly where. "This is not unusual," others who were also loitering in the streets told us. The only real way to know when something was due to commence was to wait until there was an increase in local Greek people all walking in the right direction!

We duly waited and then walked to the memorial green at the end of Levkas quay. We waited a further three quarters of an hour for something to happen and realised that we were on G.M.T. – Greek Maybe Time. All of a sudden there was a rush of local people who all surged forward to the roadside and the parade began. First came the local Levkas band in black uniforms with red and gold braid, strolling along as though this was just a walk in the park. They ambled around the green closely followed by the military in their slate grey uniforms whose marching technique was a little more professional, but, I have to say, as a person from a Royal Naval family, not a patch on the marching ability of the British military parades I'd witnessed. Suddenly the band reappeared around the corner and we were treated to another circuit of the green by them and the military; then a pause, silence…What, we wondered, was going to happen next?

Out came the school children in classes of ascending ages. We were told the boy and girl who came top of the class of the particular age group led the way carrying the banners, and behind marched the rest of the class. They marched past, all dressed in black skirts or trousers and white tops. A few were parading in national costume but the majority were in normal uniform. They started with the very young, the children getting older and older with each group until there they were, Greece's finest, Greece's future, these surly looking teenagers. Pouting, flouting females wearing short skirts played with their long silky hair whilst the strutting, prancing males swaggered around resembling nothing more than big bundles of testosterone. It was a treat to behold.

It truly was an experience and a brilliant way of bringing the community together. Such a proud moment for both children and parents and we were part of it. The music played and after the last group of parading children had passed, the local people who had crowded around just disappeared. I mean this literally. One moment there was a parade and a crowd of adults clapping and watching and the second the last child finished they all just walked off. It was like watching an ice-cube melt on a fire, one minute a heaving mass, the next, nothing. To watch the structure of Greek celebrations is almost as much fun as the event itself.

Halloween was just around the corner and Dudley was asked to do a karaoke at a private party. It was to be his first proper karaoke since leaving England and he was very keen to please. We had a great night of relaxed singing, the highlight was Pano, a particularly handsome, dark haired and swarthy employee of Joe's who decided to sing and dance. We gathered around and clapped as he danced and sang along to a disc. This is just what we had come for, a community not afraid to sing, not afraid to dance and show their happiness, a relaxed community of friendly people.

Sadly, we heard the following day that Pano had been stopped on the way home from the party and having been breathalysed he had paid a €78 on the spot fine. Anyone who thinks that Greece is a laid back country where you can get away with such offences, think again. "The times they are a changing," and Greece is moving with it. The traffic police, when patrolling, are more visible than those in England and they show no mercy. You have to produce your full original documentation at the time of being stopped, or a copy stamped and signed by the local police to say that the originals had been viewed. If you have committed an offence you will be fined on the spot. As an ex-constabulary employee, I applaud this system. I was glad to see they had a system so simple that it worked. I was also extremely happy to see an officer of the law still with the power to carry out his duty with freedom without fear of complaint and retribution. With this comment, I would have to say that the local Greek community would not dream of arguing or complaining about the stop and fine, unlike England where the community seems to think they can commit a crime and then complain when they get caught. I did feel so sorry for Pano, though. After such a great night, it was a sad ending.

We settled into the winter ahead reading our books and attending quiz nights. We made the most of what we had and were determined to enjoy our new life despite our financial situation and our disappointments.

Birthday an d Anniversary celebrations

Levkas "Keep Fatters" Group

Steve and family

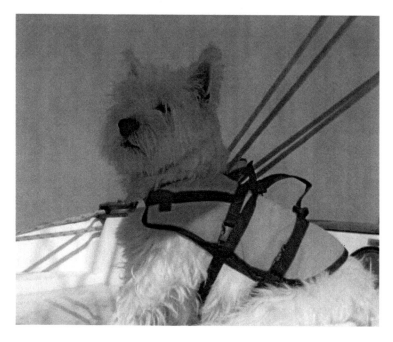

Harry Sailing safely

Monastir cemetery and mosque

Monasir Rabat

"Horace" hitching a lift Northwards

Migrating bird lands on deck

It's a cat's life

Stray dog "Car Park"

When harry met "Moggy"

Orpheus under sail

Bernard and his prize sea bass

Father enjoying a sail

Mother enoying not being ill

South Ionian regatta starting line

Kite surfing, Milos beach

CHAPTER 12
YACHTIE ENCOUNTERS

In our winter lull we were still avidly searching for a dinghy and outboard. Whilst having dinner with Kit, the gentleman who had been alongside for some time, he mentioned that he had one for sale. It was by sheer co-incidence and luck that it was an Avon in good condition and reasonably priced. A lot of dinghies we had looked at would have done the job but for some reason people placed ridiculous prices on their worth. At last we had a dinghy with oars and an outboard bracket. This meant we could anchor off in bays when sailing and still be able to get ashore for Harry's constitutionals.

When telling a friend of our purchase they told us they had an old outboard for sale to go with the dinghy if we wanted it. This was in good condition, and again, reasonably priced, so we purchased it. This meant we were now completely set up, albeit with second hand things, but at the bargain price of two hundred pounds. They were in good working order and were suitable for our requirements. We were not to know it at the time but the purchases were such good ones that we still have them. We were told that of all dinghies Avon's were the best, as they tended not to degrade under the summer sun like most other brands.

Our winter languor meant that we had lazy starts to each day: a leisurely breakfast and an unrushed morning spent deciding what project we should first undertake to make *Orpheus* more homely. One such morning we sat cogitating and a Greek fisherman stood at the back of the boat looking in. It appeared to me that he wanted our attention so I said, "Kalimera." ("Good morning.")

"A Greek boat," the man stated and from there I explained it was an ex-flotilla yacht and we were very happy with her. "A strong boat," he said. I agreed and he loitered further. I could see that he was just itching to come on board so I invited him to come and look at her. His face burst into such delight as he almost ran over the passerelle, into the cockpit and down the companionway. From this moment on I wasn't given an opportunity to speak as he walked around Orpheus slapping his hand on all the wood work repeating again and again what "a strong boat she was- "very beautiful", "well built", "good to sail, a strong Greek boat made to last". I thanked him politely as he continued his banging and slapping of the woodwork and he continued to tell me that Dromor had ceased making yachts but he had heard they were trading under a different name and when he had the money he was going to buy one. After fifteen minutes of caressing and knocking the woodwork he thanked us and left. What a whirlwind! But I guess it was good to know that this country of fishermen and men of the sea approved of our Orpheus!

As the nights became colder and damper I was forced to place all our clothing into bags to stop them becoming damp overnight. We covered our cockpit with a tilt that lay over the boom and tied it to the toe rail. This allowed us to keep the back hatch open to help with air circulation, even during the rainy evenings, and gave us somewhere to hang the linen to dry overnight. We also placed a cover over the forepeak hatch so we could leave that open as we had discovered if we shut the hatch when sleeping, the moisture from our breathing caused droplets on the laminated roofing that would drip on us all night. This was definitely not conducive to a good night's sleep. Both these coverings seemed to keep the damp away from the boat and kept us dry.

November brought a fortnight of sunshine, and whilst lazing and reading books one day, we were disturbed from our languor to be questioned at length by a port policeman. He was wondering why we were flying a British flag and yet the yacht showed a Greek registration on the stern. It had never occurred to us that we had not removed the old lettering and replaced it with new. Luckily we managed to get him to understand that we had only just come out to live on the boat and as yet, had not had the opportunity to change it. We immediately removed the lettering and replaced it with "Orpheus" and underneath the registration, all at the cost of €15. This prompted me to go about the task of cleaning the hull and removing some of the black marks around the cockpit. Another yachtie spotted me rubbing away with domestic cleaner and gave me a tin of proper boat cleaner and polish. This was part of life on board a yacht that had never occurred to me. I was very innocent of the various potions and creams available to help a person keep a boat nice and shiny – I know now! Every single mark was removed and the stern and cockpit were gleaming. I attacked the stainless steel pushpit, pulpit and stanchions with the same cleaner and they shone like new. It was hard work but well worth the results.

In a minor celebration of the hard work and effort I had put into *Orpheus*, we decided to take a drive to the Western side of the island of Levkas to find a place called 'Kathisma' Beach. We had been told that this very long sandy stretch was one of the best beaches Lefkada had to offer. We set off on the main road around the island but soon found that it was blocked and we could not get through due to large rocks and boulders; a result of the August earthquake. We had also been told that we could reach the beach by going over the top of the mountain range and down the other side, so we stopped to purchase a local map of the island to assist us on this alternative route.

We again set off in search of Kathisma. We went up mountains and down mountains. We went round and round the mountains. Never once did we see a sign or a village name that remotely resembled the map I was holding. We went up again and found ourselves driving through a secret army camp! Apparently there is an official map in being that has printed on it an icon indicating where the "secret army camp" is… Well, we drove through it rather quickly without stopping and definitely without taking any photographs. There were signs everywhere indicating no photography and it had not been so long since a group of plane spotters had been treated rather badly so we made sure we kept moving.

Out the other side of the camp and still climbing, we reached an observatory and a dead end. We had not seen another road for miles and miles and I was dreading the thought of having to go back through the army camp. On our reciprocal route along the roadway we saw another track, leading downwards, so we quickly took that and hoped that it was a road. Sometimes it's very hard to tell in Greece what is or is not a road, some of them indicated on my map as 'B' roads had resembled dirt tracks so who was to know what we would find on the lesser roads indicated!

Down the track we went and luckily it did become a very small and narrow road. Alas the road suddenly started to ascend again and as the side railings disappeared my toes started to claw at the soles of my shoes. We were now driving on a road barely the width of the car, with no protection, on a mountainside that was extremely high. To say my bottom cheeks were twitching would be a huge understatement. Suddenly I saw what I thought was dust off the road, coming the other way. I asked Dud to be extra careful because if it was a Greek driver we could be off the road and down the mountainside in no time at all as they all seem to drive like maniacs who think there couldn't possibly be a tomorrow.

As we rounded the peak of the mountain and looked along the road we could see, what I had thought was dust, were actually clouds! We were above the clouds and had to now descend through cloud, on the same road barely a car width, with no side protection... At this point the map was torn to shreds and with a heaving bosom I yelled "This is what I think of this map – get me out of here!" Or words to that effect.

We descended rather slowly and on reaching what I would describe as normal heights, we saw our first sign, it read ,"Nidri." We knew Nidri well and in desperation we headed for it and soon felt relieved, as that is exactly where we came out. We got back to *Orpheus* some three hours later having been to the highest mountain peaks on the island. It felt like we had driven around all of them and still had not laid eyes on the elusive Kathisma Beach. What can I say? It was a hot sunny day and to me it had been wasted; I was not happy. Dudley, who as ever knew what to say at the right time said, "Think of all the lovely scenic photographs you've taken. It was worth the trip, wasn't it?" Bless his little cotton socks, he really is a lovely man and I'll never know where he gets his patience from when I'm throwing one of my tantrums. I guess that's love for you.

Yachties like to settle down for the winter and do so according to their financial situations. Some can afford a full six months in a marina, others just two or three months, and then those like us who couldn't afford anything! The best part about all of it is that nobody seems to care who can afford what. We all become one big happy family, sharing stories and enjoying each other's company until spring. Along the mole, other yachts were joining us so we were looking forward to the winter ahead.

One particular day, another yacht with a family on board, came in to join us on the mole and as is the usual way, it was not long before we were learning their names and nodding as they passed by. On one such occasion they stopped to chat. As the female chatted and chatted, things were starting to fall into place. Dudley was nodding at the appropriate moment and the female was still in full flow. I recognised that voice; I recognised the lady who liked to talk – I recognised the loose lady who flashed all in Kastos! A few pertinent questions slipped into the conversation and I gained confirmation of my thoughts. As it slowly dawned on Dudley who this lady was, I clearly saw his lips sucking inward and his face turn a lighter shade of pale, just before raging into a crimson glow.

I couldn't believe it. More than two years later and the woman who caused me much upset during one of our holidays with Captain Pete was on the end of the mole! I couldn't wait to text and tell him. Captain Pete's reply came back simply stating, "I bet Dudley didn't recognise her with her clothes on!" As always, my Captain Pete was right. Dudley hadn't, but at least he had had the courtesy to look embarrassed.

On getting to know the couple, I learned that they were very nice people and were only staying a short time as they were making their way to Preveza and then travelling back to England for the winter. I must confess, as nice as they were, I was relieved to hear this and to know there was not going to be a repeat performance of her harbour-side striptease.

The couple had a five-year-old son who, apart from being blonde, cute and a character, was what I can only describe as a midget gentleman. They had every reason to be proud of their offspring. During the day he would play and row about in their dinghy. It didn't take him very long to realise that from the mole one had to walk around the fishing boat harbour to get to the marina. From the end of the mole he could row across to the marina in a fraction of the time it took to walk. Being very canny he approached every unsuspecting customer who walked along the mole asking them if they wished to be rowed across to the marina.

Dudley and I were approached one morning and he said, "Will you be going to the marina today?"

"No," Dudley replied. "Well, if you change your mind, I can row you across. It will only be €1."

"Is that there and back?" Dudley asked playing along with the lad. "Oh no!" he exclaimed. "It will be one euro each way and that is only for one person. If you both want to go it will be two euros each way." At that we had to laugh. We were convinced that this young man was going to make it in the big, bad business world.

Women being the fairer sex, mothers, grandmothers and gentle creatures, it was not very long before most of the ladies from the marina came along the mole, for no reason at all and were being rowed across the small expanse of water for the sum of one euro. So it was that this midget man, who even held out his hand to escort you in and out of his dinghy, earned the nickname of "ena evro" – one euro, at the tender age of five years old!

We were once again having a cold spell and we found it necessary to invest in a Tilly lamp to keep us warm at night. With no electricity at all we had only the gas oven to heat the boat. We had progressed into a routine of running our engine late afternoon as the sun went down. This would keep the engine and domestic batteries charged and also warmed the boat a little. Then, whilst cooking the evening meal (I was still battling with on an oven that didn't work) the boat would remain warm. It was around 2030 hours that we started to feel cold and the lamp would be lit.

According to our barometer the cold spell we were having should have been a warm one and we were now totally convinced that it was wrongly set. Dudley went to the Port Police office to ask what their barometer reading was and although they did have one, it read even higher than ours! We then began asking around the community in general if anyone had a barometer that they knew to be accurate. The answer came back: "No." I couldn't believe people didn't seem to bother. On asking why nobody cared they simply said that even if it reads incorrectly it still worked and all most people wanted was an indication of the change in pressure. I could agree with their thinking but I found it sad that this piece of equipment was being neglected.

I had been watching our barometer for weeks, although the reading was wrong, I was getting very close to being able to predict bad winds and weather by the way it rose and fell. It was three weeks later that an announcement was made on the live-aboard network and we were able to set our dial to a true reading. A weather buff named Walter had arrived in the marina and was happy to give us detailed reports and barometer readings. We needed to adjust our barometer by ten millibars and were now confident that it was accurate within one millibar each way.

Before we knew it, it was 20 November. Not that there was anything special about the date but this was the day we realised that fireworks day had been and gone and as yet we had not heard one firework. This was definitely a first. At home we would have been plagued with evenings of noisy, bangs and barks (as they upset Harry) for weeks and weeks before the 5th and weeks and weeks after. This year it had passed and we had not even given it a thought. I am not sure whether that in itself is treason or not. I won't tell anyone if you don't!

Also, having skipped life and time, I am very ashamed to admit we had missed Armistice Day on the eleventh. Coming from a naval family and an upbringing that taught me to respect the memory of those that had given their lives, I was very saddened that we had been so shallow. I had brought with me the wording of the prayers so that we could hold our own service and abide by the two minute silence on board but had been too selfish to remember. I prayed now. I prayed forgiveness from those that died so that we might live and prayed for those that may find themselves fighting for our country in the future. My guilt somewhat assuaged, I promised the dead and myself to do better by their memory next year.

On a lighter note, one of the other reasons I remember the day 20 November is because this was the first day I laid hands on the first Harry Potter book. Dudley had never taken to the idea of these stories and as such I had never had the opportunity to read any of these books. The yachting community are very good at book swapping and I read book one with relish. At the end of this book I was well and truly hooked. I had never understood why these somewhat strange people got carried away and camped outside shops to buy the next book when it was published. To some extent I still don't understand this, but at least now I can understand the attraction. I am, without a doubt, a converted Harry Potter fan.

A week later I got my hands on the second book and as with the first book, at the end I found myself crying. I wondered how it was this talented writer could lead children and adults alike, through a wonderland of intrigue, magic and mystery and still leave this soppy adult crying at the end of it. If I had a single ounce of this literary ability I would be very happy. Needless to say, I was on the hunt for someone who had book three to swap with me.

Dudley and I regularly attended the quiz nights in order to meet other live-aboards. There were many different characters and we really enjoyed getting to know them. I always found the quiz questions much too hard but the social side of the event made up for any disappointment. Sandy and Carol 'with the bill' were great company as were Bruce and Maggie, another couple with strong characters and stories to tell. We had the pleasure one evening to eat with them on board their wonderful boat that was an ex-submarine tender. They managed to get Dudley so drunk that he barked at all the stray dogs in the streets on the way back to the boat! That's the way it was, social evenings of sharing wine and sharing stories of past and present lives.

With some people, we learned, it was best not to drink on board and to only socialise when in the community room. This sounds harsh but we learned quite early on that there were those amongst the yachting community who drank a little bit too much and became something we really did not want to be part of. Amongst the small community there were two alcoholics, a bulimic, an exhibitionist and a violent husband! I don't wish to sound judgemental, as the majority of people within the yachting community are wonderful, but we found ourselves in some awkward situations and realised too late that you simply cannot befriend everyone. Sometimes it was better to stand back and observe prior to inviting people on board. After all, it was and still is our home.

When a huge fifty-two-foot Nauticat joined us on the mole we never realised what impact the owner would have on our lives. For now, he was just another man sailing alone. I couldn't believe how many there were around us. In the space of one month I had met Kit, Gary, Tony, Brian, George, Roger and now Steve; all these single men and no women! The owner of the Nauticat soon became a friend and, as always, I enjoyed feeding these single men. It was good practice after all, and they seemed to appreciate my meagre efforts on my oven of 1.5 rings!

Harry, too, was making many friends and coping very

well with his new life. seemingly loving every minute he was with us. He became more and more demanding with his newfound confidence and freedom and insisted, with great vocal range, on going everywhere with us. He had always suffered from what I refer to as the "Snoopy Syndrome"; he was a dog who thought he was human. Since coming away he had spent so much time with us that he became even more humanised. He simply did everything we did, when we did it. It was like having a small child on board. He loved his morning and evening trips around the marina. He even chose which way he wanted to walk with little care as to whether we followed him! In the evenings he came with us to the community room and whilst we socialised with the humans he went off to socialise with Tara a border collie, Storm a dachshund and three little Chihuahuas Skipper, Taffy and Tess. These were all live-aboard pets.

Harry was living his life to the full, yet we had been concerned for some time that his back legs seemed to be getting worse than ever before. We began to think it was the cold days that were causing him arthritis but he did not seem to be in any pain. It was almost as though he was losing the use of his rear quarters. One day it was like a miracle had happened. I picked him up as we walked into a local chandlers and his back cracked. I thought I had done something terrible to him but instead when we walked back to the yacht he seemed to be walking better. Over the next few days he returned almost to normal and we came to the conclusion that he must have somehow trapped or dislodged something in his spine and I had put it back somehow. It wasn't until much later that we learned Westies, as a breed, are prone to slipped discs.

Harry, being a happy little chappy, continued improving, but the same could not be said for Dudley. As he lay in our bunk one morning, Dudley complained he had a wet pillow and I suggested that perhaps he had been drooling in his sleep. The look he gave in reply was rather threatening and I thought better of repeating the comment. As per our usual routine, Dudley was making a cup of tea to bring me in bed, (I know I'm spoilt, what can I say!) when I caught out of the corner of my eye a rivulet running down the doorframe. On closer inspection I saw water running from behind our cabin light, down to the top of the arched doorframe, down the crack of the frame only to be soaked up by Dudley's pillow! On showing this to Dudley he gave me a knowing look, the unspoken words being, "See? I knew it wasn't me drooling!"

Just another job to add to the list of things that needed to be done! The trouble was, it required money to be able to get on and do them. Not having the spare cash at this time we carried out an emergency repair as an interim measure. The cabin light was taken down and the hole it left filled with tissue paper that needed to be changed after every rainfall. It was hardly a technical solution to the problem but the key thing was, it cost nothing and it did the trick!

As the nights became colder I noticed the side windows in the saloon area becoming very damp when I cooked the evening meals. I decided to tape cling film around the rims to act as double-glazing in the hope it would remedy the problem. It worked a treat until the tape became too damp to remain sticky. Another layer of tape applied and the windows stayed dry and clear alleviating a little more of the damp problem that the worsening winter was bringing.

We had brought with us from England, two fold-up bikes to allow us to sight-see and shop. We had also brought a two-wheel trailer that we could hook to the bikes for Harry. However, before we could use it we needed to build a carriage to sit on the trailer to put Harry in. Dud purchased some wood at an extortionate fee to build the framework. Had we asked around prior to the purchase we would have known we could have obtained it from a nearby wood-yard for a third of the price! We found some appropriate netting to bind to the frame and with a lot of effort on Dudley's part and encouraging words from myself, we ended up with a very pleasing cart that could be taken to pieces and stowed in a locker when not in use.

Our first trip out with Harry was an absolute hoot. The local fishermen had watched our project taking shape and you could see they were all very interested to see what it was to be used for. When they saw us hook it to the bikes and put Harry inside there was much laughter. Other yachties got out their cameras and took pictures as we cycled past and the villagers of Levkas pointed and waved making approving sounds, nods and gestures. It made it worth all the effort just to see their faces.

We enjoyed a cycle ride along the causeway and around the saltwater lagoon that sits at the northern tip of the island. Halfway round we would stop and let Harry have a run along the white stony beach that had a backdrop of mountains and windmills. The trailer was perfect, especially as Harry couldn't walk long distances. Initially, when we first started to use the trailer, Harry would bark but he soon took to riding in it. The trailer gave us a new lease of life as we could now go exploring on our bikes and take him with us.

November came to an end and 1 December arrived. I started to think of the fast approaching Christmas and realised this would be a first time I had not been at home to share it with my family. Mother and Father were finding the thought of Christmas alone quite daunting so decided to break the pattern and booked a holiday to Spain for the entire festive season. I felt better knowing that even if I had gone home they would not be there, but it did little to alleviate my wanting to be with my family and friends around a huge Christmas tree, celebrating the birth of Christ. I wanted to be feeling the presents under the tree and guessing what was inside. Our finances meant that we could not afford presents this year and this was going a long way to make me feel even more depressed. The sun was shining and I was living in my own little paradise and yet I still could not enjoy it.

To take my mind off things, Dudley decided we should take another cycle ride around the lagoon. The sun was shining and it was a glorious day. The hand washing was done and hanging out to dry. We stopped half way around the lagoon and hopped over a sand bank onto the beach. Harry had his usual run, and as it was so warm, we sat down on Harry's blanket to sunbathe for a while. It was then that Dud decided he was going in for a swim. "You don't have your swim suit," I pointed out.

"I don't need one. There's nobody about," he said as he stood there, removing his clothes! He walked down to the waters edge and he was in…

My head was on a pivot. I stood there, watching the roadway behind and looking up and down the beach. I was not happy. The thought of someone coming and catching Dudley with his "pants down" was not my idea of fun. Having had his swim, with no towel to dry on, Dudley sat naked in the sunshine and dried off. Whilst all this nudity was very stressful to me, Dud thought it hilarious; I must admit that for the time of year to be able to do what he had just done made a very pleasant change. You would see only the hardiest of swimmers bathing in

England at this time of year. There never is a dull moment when Seymour is around. Once he was fully clothed, off we went again to finish our cycle ride.

Having succeeded in taking my mind off Christmas that evening, we took ourselves to Greek language classes. We had previously been trying to learn how to speak Greek and now language classes were starting through the network in the Marina Greek. When we attended we learned that the teacher was Georgia who worked for Joe in his chandlery. This was a really pleasant surprise as Georgia is a particularly friendly Greek girl with an excellent sense of humour and a very happy nature. She was definitely the sort of person who radiated beauty from within and filled you with a happiness just to look at her smile. So began our long struggle to battle with a new alphabet and a new language.

The mole, our home for this winter, was a constant hive of activity. People did jobs on their boats on the sunny days and on the windy, rainy days there was a stillness as people hibernated and read their books (Harry Potter three was still being elusive). On one such day we surfaced between rainfalls to notice a catamaran had appeared on the end of the mole. It resembled a floating steptoe's yard with junk tied everywhere on it. "Stan, the catamaran man" had stopped only to do his Christmas shopping before returning to Abeleki on the island of Meganisi, which is where he could usually be found. It had been Stan that had passed on the bad weather report when we had been in Little Vathi but this was the first time we had seen his sailing vessel. The character of man and yacht seemed somehow to compliment each other!

As he left the mole later that day we wished him well and returned the favour of sharing the forecast for later which did not sound good. As predicted, the wind came out of nowhere that night. One minute it was calm and the next, the wind was blowing force 7 from the Northeast, directly on our bows. It reached force 8, gusting 9 and everyone along the mole was out checking their moorings. I was very relieved to say that ours were holding tight. Everyone else appeared okay and so we locked ourselves in for the night. Dudley remained dressed, ready to spring into action if needed and I, although in bed, could not sleep. I wondered whether I would ever be able to sleep in windy conditions or if, forevermore, I would lay awake in these circumstances. Now some years later I need not wonder because I know, when the wind is up I never sleep and if I'm asleep prior to the winds, I awake when they come!

CHAPTER 13
CHRISTMAS ON THE MOLE

The weather around Levkas, we now know from experience, is almost a climate all of its own. We had received reports that there had been bad snow in Athens yet all we had seen around Lefkada were some snow-capped mountains. It was normal for a few days rain and a few cold days to give way to a few hot, sunny days; these were the days that made all the difference to a winter. One little window of the promised weather to come kept spirits high, unlike in England, where it seemed all one could look forward to was never ending cold, rain and wind.

It was on such a sunny weather window on the 5th December that I again donned my shorts and t-shirt and we began to fit netting to the guardrails and stanchions around our side decks. We had worried about Harry walking around the decks ever since we had been on board. We had been frugal enough to afford the netting and Dudley and I set about the task of working out how on earth to fit it!

I had decided to try to get into the Christmas spirit by playing my Christmas cassettes loud enough to sing along to whilst Dudley and I were on our third attempt at starting to fit the netting. We first made sure that the square holes in the netting were running vertical and horizontal and then secured it top and bottom. It was a long and laborious task as we had decided to secure each loop with individual reef knots.

We were halfway down the starboard side, singing along to White Christmas, when another yacht came into moor alongside. We pulled up the lazy line ready to hand to them and just as I was handing it over I recognised who it was. "Harry!" It took him a moment or two to recognise us but then he saw Harry, the dog, and it fell into place. Harry and Adele who had helped rescue us on the Levkas quayside had come to stay for the winter. Things were looking up and at last we had a chance to buy them a drink for what they had done for us.

    I busied myself decorating the boat with tinsel and baubles and put up my one string of Christmas lights that were battery operated. I had been prepared and brought a set out when we came, knowing that I could not possibly have a Christmas without lights. I had also brought a miniature tree with optic fibre lights that was also battery operated. I was trying to make the most of things and use what we had but deep down it wasn't the big tree that I was used to with all the presents wrapped up underneath. I tried not to say too much to Dudley but it was very hard for me to hide my feelings as it just was not the same without Mum, Dad and brother. It certainly would not be the same without the Christmas Eve party at Roy's club when Father Christmas came to give out presents. I missed Roy and all our friends very much. I cheered up somewhat when I finally got my hands on Harry Potter three and four.

    December was rolling on and we both found it rather endearing that the Greeks have the ability to celebrate things at the right time. In England, no sooner had you got back from a summer holiday than the shopkeepers started to display Christmas paraphernalia. By the time December came you had become sick of the sight and sound of Christmas. Here in Levkas it was wonderful. Christmas was not spoken of and did not exist until the beginning of December. Then a transformation started to occur. Little trinket shops and clothes shops emptied their stock and became Christmas shops, selling all things Christmassy. Bit by bit, garlands were strung up around the lampposts the length of the quayside and big displays shone around the local green. In the centre of town, all along the pedestrian parade, there were strings of lights hung from rooftops, and shops transformed themselves into light displays. The highlight for me was walking through the platia (town square), and finding the biggest silver Christmas tree I ever saw right there in the middle, all decked with lights. It was wonderful and it was right; it held a promise that Christ's birth was worth celebrating.

    I began to get the feeling that I would like to attend a midnight mass on Christmas Eve. This was something I had always wanted to do at home but was always too tired to stay up that late. This year I felt I had much to be thankful for and I really wanted it to be special. We asked Jeanette and Vaia in the office if there was such a thing in Greece but unfortunately there was not, not as we knew it in England as the Greek Orthodox churches held different styles of service. My idea was quashed so we would have to be content with our own carols and service on board *Orpheus*.

Coming to the middle of December I began to worry about how we were going to have a shower for the next month. Joe was closing his premises for a month over Christmas and New Year. Up until now he had allowed us to use the shower within his office premises and we had used this as an opportunity to speak to Jeanette and Vaia, increasing our Greek vocabulary by learning words such as "azeme", "avrio", "morea", "cani creo", "kala christouyena" and "xronia polla". In translation these useful words mean "leave me alone", "tomorrow", "idiot", "very cold", "Happy Christmas" and "Happy New Year". In an attempt to see if we could get a shower in the marina I sent Dudley to ask Spiro the manager. The answer was no, we could not use the showers and we could not pay him for the use of them. It wasn't that he wanted to be unfriendly or awkward; this was simply the company rule that he had to abide by.

In my desperation I decided to sneak into the marina and "steal" a shower. Dudley said he would not come, insisting, "You mustn't." All I could think was if I didn't get a shower and wash my long blonde hair soon I'd go mad; the itching was starting to be too much! I put my wash things into my rucksack and off I went, round the fishing harbour, into the marina. Just as I was getting to the first bridge in the marina I was stopped by a security guard "Where is your boat?" he asked.

"Over there," I pointed to the mole. "This is not marina, you must leave."

"Signome," I said, meaning sorry in Greek.

"Please, Miss, just go!" he shouted. So it was with my tail between my legs, still smelling and dirty I slunk back to *Orpheus*. Dudley thought it was hilarious, I don't know why I ever try to be naughty because I've never got away with anything in my whole life. When Dudley finally stopped laughing at me he commiserated, saying he would think of something.

To add to my misery I realised that I was going to have to cook a Christmas dinner on board and I still hadn't got to grips with our oven. I got myself into gear and decided to cook my first roast dinner and happily this turned out quite well. The oven still wasn't burning properly. Once lit, it would only stay alight if you kept its door open for the first five minutes. If you shut it the gas would go out. I was not at all happy with the cooker and was not confident that it wouldn't kill me in the end. Dud remained supportive but still didn't do anything about it!

The nights were now so cold that I had taken to sitting with my feet wrapped around a hot water bottle, which also warmed the cold sheets prior to our slipping between them. Along with the extra cold weather came engine problems for us. Dudley was not able to start the engine and we feared that the problem was going to cost us a lot of money. We had heard horror stories about boat engines being repaired at the cost of 8,000 euros and still not working! Of course this was with disreputable people and the warning there for others and us was to ask other yachties and locals first and get recommendations before committing to having the work done. For us it was simple. Joe was not the cheapest but he got the job done and stood by his work so it gave us the peace of mind we needed.

Dudley managed, with some help, to overhaul the starter motor and then changed the oil and filters. This seemed to do the trick and although the engine smoked a little when it was run, at least it was starting. We didn't have money to spend at this time so were glad that this particular problem had been solved so cheaply. However, Dud felt the injectors might need checking at some stage in the future. We were not to know it then but the injectors lasted us a lot longer than we could ever have anticipated.

Ten days of tying knots and sealing the ends with a gas gun saw the completion of our netting. We were very pleased with our work. It had been a long hard slog but well worth every bit of effort. It was completely solid and we knew that Harry was going to be safe walking around the decks from now on.

A lot of the yachties were starting to drift back to England for Christmas. Some of the best characters we had met were going back to be with their families; I was getting very low but it was silly really because, with Harry, it was almost impossible for us to go back; it hurt none-the-less. For us to go back to England would mean a bus or flight from Levkas to Athens; a flight from Athens to Gatwick and a bus or train ride to Norwich. The problems and cost of such a trip with Harry in tow was too much for us to even contemplate.

To add to my ever increasing depression there was a battle raging between two yachts in the marina as to who could hold the bigger and better Christmas dinner. It was all too much for me at this time of year; money and egos shouldn't be interfering at a time when Christian attitudes should prevail. Dudley and I discussed the matter and decided to stay on our own and eat aboard *Orpheus* and let the wars rage somewhere else. As if this wasn't bad enough, I managed to pick up a cold and sore throat and was really feeling sorry for myself.

Steve, further along the mole, had borrowed our car to collect his mum from Athens; she had flown out to spend Christmas and New Year with him. As I was missing my mum so much he kindly said that I could borrow his mum for Christmas. It was a lovely thought and one of the nicest things for him to say. Christmas day took a turn for us when Steve invited us to go on board his yacht to share Christmas dinner with him and his mother. Other yachts on the mole that were at a loose end were also invited. Dudley and I suddenly began to look forward to spending our Christmas day in the company of, as I had affectionately named us, the 'mole-asses'.

I did not wake with my normal good cheer this Christmas morning. I felt sad because our financial situation had meant that I had not bought a present for Dudley. I love presents, lots of little things to feel around, the excitement of opening them and guessing what they are. This year all I could do was to make promises of what I would give to my loved ones when our financial status changed. One family tradition that we could uphold was to share a morning-time special coffee.

My mother called to wish us Happy Christmas just as we were drinking the coffee and this seemed to be a good sign. An even better one was when Dudley produced a little pile of presents. YES! As always he must have sacrificed something to be able to afford them and he knew just what to get to please. Candles and chocolates, what was this thing with the brick in the end to disguise it? ... A jigsaw puzzle. I felt so happy. Every year at Christmas I would treat myself to a puzzle to entertain myself over the festive season. He had remembered this and chosen one with dolphins leaping in a sea of blue; truly, love is a wonderful thing.

After the unexpected excitement of presents I rallied

round and set about doing the vegetables. It had been agreed amongst all the participating yachties that Steve would cook the meat and we would cook the vegetables. I had already made Christmas pudding so this could now be put to good use. You soon realise when living aboard that no matter how big your yacht is, you still only have limited cooking capability. Sharing the cooking made life much easier for everyone. Lunch turned out to be a huge feast and everyone left Steve's boat with bloated bellies. We had tried to listen to the queen's speech on the world service but it wasn't broadcast; just another small piece of our former life had come to an end.

Being a season of sharing and celebration, Dud decided it was time for a Karaoke. After another monster meal of leftovers and mulled wine we went to the community room to sing our little hearts out. The evening turned out to be a great success with everyone joining in. It appeared that most yachties had a party piece to display at least once a year and this was the night.

The evening became a little tainted the following day when we discovered that following the sing-along one couple decided to have a fight and the local police had to be called out. I thought back to the years, when, as a constabulary employee, I had been called out to provide administrative support to the officers involved in violent crimes that always seemed to be provoked around the Christmas period. I was disappointed at the news as one would hope that at a time of love, celebration and Christianity people could try to behave. After all, policemen deserve to have a Christmas too!

The weather over Christmas and Boxing Day had been gloriously sunny with bright, warm days and cool evenings but now it was about to change; the rain began and the wind howled. Three days later it was still raining with no sign of it letting up and I was very grateful to Dudley for buying me a puzzle which kept me entertained through these rainy days. The weather conditions made things rather awkward as the live aboard community had arranged for a New Year Eve dinner party at a local hotel, the idea being to dress up in all our fineries but it was a good walk from the marina to the hotel!

With the rain still pouring down, we splashed our way to a wonderful meal and afterwards we sloshed in wet shoes to the rhythm of the dance music. Auld Lang Syne came and went and when the time came to leave I don't think either of us cared if it was raining or not. Over-indulgence is a bad thing, especially when there is a passerelle to get across. Needless to say, I spent most of New Year's Day nursing a headache and Dudley sat in the corner tutting at me in disapproval. I was very interested to learn, when I did finally manage to get out of bed, that I can "Cha Cha" very well; which is quite a mystery to me, as when I'm sober I can't do it at all! I should really take this opportunity to discuss the evils of alcohol, but instead I shall quickly move on!

The rain continued day and night through to the 3rd January, which happens to be Dud's birthday. Again, sadness surrounded me like a shroud, as no money again meant no presents for him. Little did we know it but a lovely surprise was forthcoming for both of us, better than any present I could have given Dudley at this time. Mike and Janet, a couple who not only owned a yacht in the marina but owned a house in a nearby village, invited us up to the house for lunch AND A BATH! This may sound like a strange offer but I can assure you if you offered it to most live-aboards ninety-five percent of them would bite your hand off for the chance of a good soak, especially those, like ourselves, who didn't take regular trips home to England. After five days of non-stop rain the idea of a hot bath was absolutely heaven sent to Dudley and me. The excitement and anticipation as I filled the bath with water in itself was a treat. Once the bath was filled, we snuggled together in the hot water and relaxed. Warm and soothed, we reluctantly got out and felt cleaner than we had in a long, long time.

Epiphany arrived celebrating the introduction of Jesus to the Magi; we were told there would be a celebration on the quayside. Getting the hang of the start times of such affairs, we waited until we saw a surge of local Greek people and then took off in pursuit. The weather was not the best-still rainy and windy, but people had turned out in their Sunday best and were milling about everywhere. They all seemed to be carrying bunches of oranges tied together with string, I thought this strange at the time but all became clear in time.

The priest arrived, dressed in black robes and square hat. The raindrops glistened on his long grey hair and beard as he gave prayers and blessed the harbour water. As soon as the blessing had been given, members of the community moved to the waters edge and, whilst dipping their oranges in the water, said prayers. Families were handing around bunches of oranges so that all the members could dip them in the water and pray.

No sooner had the orange dipping stopped than a cross was thrown into the water and two young Adonis dived in after it. One of the two lads reached the cross first and kissing it held it aloft to indicate his triumph. From a religious aspect I was guessing this would mean good luck to the winner; from a local point of view it was rumoured that the winner would have his choice of village girls!

Intrigued by the relevance of the oranges I asked what this meant; I wondered if it was a way of blessing their crops. I was told that it was their way of taking the blessed water away with them into their homes and thus taking the blessing of good with them. To non-believers this may sound all rather silly but the person telling this to me further said, "Every time I've dipped the oranges and taken them home they've never rotted." Make of that what you will. True or not, I think it's a wonderful story to go with a blessed occasion.

Whether it was standing out in the rain or just plain bad luck, the day after Epiphany I went down with the flu and was bedridden for two days. Dudley kept me fed with milk and honey and as much as I loved him I wanted my mummy! Mother's cuddles are so healing when one's not well and I planned to have more than my fair share of mother's and father's cuddles when we were next together.

To keep up our run of illness, no sooner was I better than Dudley came down with a dose of diarrhoea. This may seem like too much information sharing but it's important to understand that illness happens and you have to be prepared for it. Dudley was bedridden for five days. He had taken two packets of pills to stop the diarrhoea and he was still unwell. He couldn't keep water inside and was clearly dehydrating. I became frantic with worry. I felt so alone and worried, I wanted to take him to the hospital but he would not hear of it, so in desperation I contacted his daughter, Helen, a reliable and very sensible consultant radiologist. Having told her our situation and my fears she suggested flat coke as a cure. I was to stir sugar into a normal, full flat coke, which would take the fizz out and get Dud to drink it a little at a time and often. I don't know how it worked, but I was so grateful that it did. He managed to keep the coke inside and within twenty-four hours he could keep in water. Within forty-eight hours I had him eating bread dipped in a hot water marmite drink.

As a result of this illness we made the effort to go and register with a local doctor and obtained an IKA book. This allowed us to go to the doctor if and when required and he would issue us with signed chits out of the book to receive treatment at the hospital. This same system operated throughout Greece at this time so we felt that we would be prepared for when we finally started our travels throughout the Aegean. As is the way of the world this system changed twice in the span of three years and now the doctor signs chits for the service required and it has been linked to the new E111 identity card.

Storms were raging and winds were blowing, I was starting to suffer somewhat with the cold, as I had not come prepared for such bad weather. It may have been ignorance but I had left all my closed in shoes and woolly hat and gloves in England. It never occurred to me that the weather conditions here in Greece could get this cold! Dudley decided to take me to Vonitsa on mainland Greece where they held a Tuesday market; all kinds of things could be found there at reasonable prices and I was after anything warm. Vonitsa, as a place, did not inspire but it had sea frontage with a castle and Dud and I more than once enjoyed the market delights. The stalls of clothes, cloth, shoes, accessories, kitchenware and vegetables made a colourful sight and it was always pleasant to visit.

The sight of the fresh vegetables only reminded me of the ongoing cooker battle albeit my range of meals had increased as I slowly became more used to cooking meals in stages. We were starting to miss certain foods you couldn't buy in Greece, the first of which was an English sausage. All the sausages here were spiced and more like salami. We longed for a low fat sausage dripping in brown sauce and fried onions, surrounded by fresh garden peas. The other meal that both Dudley and I were really yearning for was an Indian curry. We missed going to Ali Tandori in Norwich, our home city. We dreamt of spicy popadoms, onion bhaji, chicken dansak, vindaloo, naan bread, sag aloo and alu gobi. If, and when we managed to get back to England we promised ourselves that this was going to be our first port of call.

At last- a distraction from all the things we were starting

to miss! I laid my hands on Harry Potter number five! Oh no, Voldemorte is back ... I couldn't wait for the next book. During this winter I had read more books than I had in my whole life and I was quickly building a list of favourite authors. Along with J.K. Rowling, John Grisham and Patricia Cornwall were right at the top. Other favourites included Lee Childs, James Patterson and Nora Roberts. Dudley, being a speed-reader, was reading three books to my one so we were more than a little grateful for the wonderful idea of a book swap within the community room in the marina.

Christmas came and went and Steve's mum was returning to England. We went to have one last drink with them, not realising this one drink was to influence the next few months of our lives. Before leaving, Steve's mum intimated that we were going to be invited to crew for Steve and she hoped we would accept. Later on, Steve confirmed this, saying that he would be leaving Levkas the end of February, sailing straight to Tunisia for the month of March and then back again. He invited us to crew for him there and back.

To say that Dudley was cock-a-hoop is an understatement. I had many reservations about taking Harry on such a journey and the fact that I had never experienced open ocean sailing before caused me great concern. After many conversations with Dudley and weighing up all the pros and cons, Dudley got his way and we agreed to go. I did make it clear that I only agreed to do this trip as long as Dudley had completed all of his D.I.Y. tasks around *Orpheus* prior to leaving so that when we returned she would be ready for us to sail through the summer.

Needing no further enticement, Dudley became a man obsessed with D.I.Y. and had the driving force of a buffalo to get things done.

CHAPTER 14
GETTING WINTER BUSY

Many things needed doing with very limited resources so Dudley and I spent the next few weeks managing a very tight budget. It was just as well that we were almost too busy to eat!

I noticed the silicone around the sink and worktop in the galley and heads had become tacky and past its best, so I decided to remove it and re-silicone these areas. Dudley and I set to removing the old silicone and cleaning down, not realising it would take us two days! I then undertook the grisly task of replacing it with the new. "What a mess!" I thought. "My fingers will never look the same again." But the finished job looked ok and after a further three days I had managed to pick the remaining silicone from underneath my fingernails. Whilst basking in the glory of completing our first important task alone we were told it would not last two minutes as we had used ordinary kitchen and bathroom silicone and not marine sikaflex. I certainly wasn't about to take it all off again, so we left it.

The household silicone lasted for two years before it became a little mouldy and needed replacing. At this time we felt as though this justified the difference in cost between household and marine products. However when we did replace the silicone we decided to use marine sikaflex and applied it with greater ease having learned the trick of taping the work surfaces prior to application. As long as the tape was removed immediately after application it left a wonderfully even and smooth edge to the finish. We had further learned that a little bit of fairy liquid on a gloved finger made the application a more pleasant affair with regards to the person applying it. Some two years after this second application, the sikaflex, although yellowing, is still in perfect condition so we would have to recommend that overall the extra costs of the marine product paid dividends after all.

Still having some of the silicone left, Dudley decided to tackle the leak in our bunk. Having already removed the light it was apparent that the leak was coming through the baby stay. Dud unscrewed the baby stay and cleaned out the boltholes and deck surface area. He lightly sanded the surface and then had me squeeze silicone under the deck plate and into the boltholes. Whilst I held the plate and bolts in place on the upper deck Dud went below and tightened the nuts, putting the block and light back in place. Just for good measure, we ran silicone around the base of the plate screwed to the deck and were pleased to find that at the next rainfall we were leak free.

For our journey across Europe we had purchased two foam under-bed rolls for our camping. These bedrolls were not being used so we decided to utilise them by cutting them to shape and placing them on the cockpit seats. They were just enough to give a little cushioning when sailing and it didn't matter if they got wet. For the night time entertaining we had hoped to do we had brought out with us twelve kitchen chair seat cushions. These we tied together to make a seat and back which gave us a comfortable option at a bargain price. To purchase proper cockpit cushions that were hardwearing and weatherproof would have cost us £25 per cushion; our twelve cushions making six seats had cost us £24! Whilst some people may be purists and believe in buying nauticalia I'm afraid I never like to pay over the odds. These cushions were washed each year and lasted so well that they now adorn the cockpit of another yacht as we sold them on four years later when I tackled the task of making my own cushions!

Using borrowed tools, Dudley set about a few woodwork tasks around the boat. There were little jobs, such as fitting the wooden flagstaff to the stern to hold our ensign and cutting a shelf for a stowage locker. Then there was the bigger task of making a drinks holder for the cockpit. I traced a template from the holder in the galley area and adjusted it to allow for bottles and cans. From these Dudley set about making the holder. I felt so proud of him as at home he would never have contemplated taking on such a task. It was a fiddly and time-consuming job but the finished result was as good as any that money could buy. In fact, to me, this drinks holder was better than any other, because Dud had made it for me. Any one can just go out and buy something but to make it yourself is special. To purchase a drink holder would have cost us £80. As it was, this one only cost us Dudley's time as he had made it from scrap pieces of wood he had found. I was so very proud and, from the look on his face, I think he was just as proud of himself.

We next set about making a board to tie to our passerelle. Our passerelle comprises a ladder that is placed ashore to walk across or is dropped down into the water to double as a boarding ladder when swimming. Dudley went to the wood yard and purchased a sheet of marine ply and cut it to shape. Prior to staining the board I decided to draw a motif on it saying, "Welcome," and varnished over it. We then purchased some non-slip strips and placed these at intervals. Once tied, it was obvious to us that it had made the ladder appear more solid. As I was the one who always carried Harry aboard, I was very pleased with the result. As hard as we tried, we never did get Harry to walk across the passerelle himself. The minute he could see the water either side of the plank he simply dug his heels in and refused to move. At least with the improvements made I psychologically felt a lot safer.

For some time we had been annoyed with our passerelle banging on the quayside with the effects of wind and bow waves. The extra weight with the board on top of the ladder made this worse than ever, so I set my mind to designing a system whereby we could lift our passerelle off the quayside. We looked at other yachts and they all seemed to have hoists and pulleys and they all required a halyard from the top of the mast. We did not have a spare halyard at the mast to use and we could not afford to pay for an extra fitting to be added to the mast or the required warp. It took me some time to reach a solution to our problem but I did finally shout, "Eureka" (we were in Greece after all) and I shared my thoughts with Dudley.

Two short lengths of bungee threaded through a shackle that hooked onto either side of the passerelle. The bungee would be attached to marine cord using a Bowline knot and these two lengths of marine cord would go through a wooden batten the width of the passerelle and come together to become one length. This was then passed through a block attached to end of the boom and was tied off on a loop on the base of the boom. The cord was long enough to allow for the lifting and lowering of the passerelle to the height of any quayside. It worked and it didn't hinder anything whilst under sail. We purchased a little fender and tied it on the underside of the passerelle and from that day to this we have not looked back. The bungee allowed for the board to be lifted off the quay and yet the elasticity allowed for it to touch the quay when stepped on. We had tried experiments with all cord and all bungee and it just didn't give the same scope as the combination of both. A bit scientific but we got there in the end at the reasonable price of €20.

Dudley decided he wanted to make a wooden floor for the dinghy. It was okay with human feet but we feared that little sharp dog claws might puncture it, so Dud set about thinking how to do this. Dud is a great people person and net-worker. He loves to meet different people and learn about their lives. Both of us are very open as people and are happy to discuss our lives and projects with others. As a result of such a discussion we found we were talking to a fellow Avon dinghy owner whose dinghy already had a purpose built wooden floor. For the cost of a bottle of wine and a taste of a mean chilli (this was one meal I could make on two rings even if they wouldn't simmer!) we had a template to copy for our own dinghy.

With great patience, and, I might say, a lot of skill for a novice, Dudley cut out the dinghy floor and I stained and varnished it. It looked great and was just what we needed. It fitted perfectly and we felt very proud of our efforts. It was amazing what we were managing to achieve on so little money and, strangely enough, we were enjoying it. The remaining piece of wood was sandwiched together to create an oblong that screwed to our push pit to be used as a base to bracket our outboard to. A simple thing to make at very little expense, but none-the-less, a piece of D.I.Y. that made life on board *Orpheus* that much easier.

Another essential item, for those of us fair maidens that get eaten alive with mosquitoes, was a "mossy" hatch. Our main companionway hatch was made of solid Perspex, approximately an inch thick, which in the summer time would be unbearable. I had suggested that we nail some mossy screening to a wooden frame that could replace the main hatch during the hot summer nights and to further cut a solid half hatch in case it rained. Dudley took this idea a step further and made a very fine job of making my idea a reality. He used the shape of the Perspex hatch to cut out a solid shape; he then cut the centre out covering the hole with mossy netting. He then used picture frame wood to make a frame to cover the inside edge of the netting holding it in place. The solid half hatch was made to slot in at the same time on the outside of the netting to keep the rain out.

It was all going very well and we were feeling pleased with ourselves but I should point out that these items were just another two items we would have to find storage space for when not in use! It was all right having all these handy little things on board to make life comfortable but we had to keep reminding ourselves that we had to be able to store them when not in use.

As Dudley waded his way through carpentry projects and an engine service I turned my hand to more feminine matters. I can hear liberated women everywhere crying out in anguish at my distinction of feminine matters but quite clearly, life on board is about finding out what you are good at and what you are not. The middle ground has to be found and it's essential to identify each other's roles on board. There may be ladies out there who are good at carpentry and D.I.Y.; I am not. These fall very gladly to Dudley along with cleaning and maintaining the engine and getting his hands in the bilges to clean them. This, on board *Orpheus*, is men's work and what I was about to undertake, Dudley considered women's work. Therefore I started some sewing projects.

We had not been able to make room in the car for a sewing machine when we left England. This meant that all my little projects were, unfortunately, going to be done by hand. When we took delivery of the boat, Roy had left bed linen on board that we did not need. I took his pillowcases, stuffed them with foam and sewed them tightly closed. I took the duvet cover and cut the bottom, utilising the snacks, to make two removable covers for the cushions I had just made. This meant I could keep them washed and clean.

I further made, from the duvet cover, a curtain to put across the main hatch in the companionway and one for the doorway into our forepeak bunk. Both of these I weighted at the hem with washed beach stones to help them hang still in the summer breezes. I further used the duvet to make two hanging socks, one for carrier bags to re-cycle as bin bags and the other for the smaller bags that we recycled as Harry's poo bags. (Sorry about that little dose of reality, but we were dog owners that believed in picking up Harry's offerings and not leaving them for the rest of mankind to step in!)

I made the bed sheet into a modesty curtain to pull across the saloon area when this was being used as a bed. This meant if we had someone to stay who wanted to sleep in this area, they could have their privacy when people walked about in the mornings making breakfast and carrying out morning ablutions. It was amazing how far the material went and it worked out brilliantly.

The penultimate job we turned our hands to was a wheel cover. We had long since decided that as I detested the helm wheel and hated the cold harshness of it that we would cover it with something that had some feeling to it. We had decided on natural leather but the cost of a wheel cover kit was 107 euros, far beyond what our current financial status would allow. When we were out shopping in a local D.I.Y. store one day, I noticed a carpenter's apron. I convinced Dudley that I could cut this to shape and as it only cost the bargain price of €7, he decided to give it a try.

I measured the wheel and cut the apron into large sections to sew around the wheel and smaller oblongs to be handholds down each spoke of the helm wheel. Having cut the rough shapes, Dudley used a sharp knife to straighten the edges. I then marked each piece at regular intervals with pen and Dudley began the mammoth task of hammering a nail hole at each of the pen marks I had made. After hammering seven hundred nail holes the air was almost as blue as Dudley's now swelling thumbnail.

Dudley purchased some blue cord (blue being the general colour scheme around *Orpheus*) and, when his thumb had recovered, he set about sewing the wheel cover on. He was somewhat expert at this sort of thing as he used to own a car accessories shop many years before we met and had sewn on several steering wheel covers. This, I agreed, qualified him more than me to take on this sewing task. The finished product was more than gratifying for all the effort we had put in. It was yet another very successful project that we had embarked on and achieved at very little cost.

Just by sheer luck, and not a planned project for this wintertime at all, was our attempt at creating a wind chute. We should have had one as part of our inventory but it had been missing; the cost of a new one at the time was €40, which, again, was way outside our budget. Whilst we were food shopping at a local discount store I saw a set of light plastic suit covers and had a cunning plan.

For €2.99 we purchased two suit covers and one under bed storage case. I sliced the bottom off one of the suit covers and made a hem, I had to be very careful, as the plastic didn't appear to be that strong. I then threaded through the bottom, with Dudley's help, a length of bungee and cord (one part cord to two parts bungee). We had first tried it with all bungee but, as with the passerelle support, it made it too flexible and the wind managed to blow it off the hatch, but once it was adjusted to part cord it worked well. We simply placed a coat hanger in the suit cover and tied it up to our genoa sheets; this allowed it to swing loosely in the wind. We placed the bungee around the hatch so the opening was facing the wind and hooked back the top corners of the suit cover over the hanger to create the right shape for a wind chute. I know this sounds like something that could qualify us for a Blue Peter badge but it really did work and it kept us cool all summer. It was only after one very windy night in September that it finally gave up and had to be thrown away. At the price we had paid we had lost nothing besides we still had the other suit cover left which we made into a chute for the following summer.

As the decision had been made that we would be going to Tunisia for the month of March, crewing for Steve, we felt we should have some input into the preparation of the yacht. Steve had arranged for a lift out and the yacht was propped "on the hard". Dud and I went along to help with the task of scraping off the bottom removing all the barnacles and weed. With three of us doing this, bearing in mind the yacht was fifty-two feet, it took us a good three hours. We had been advised that doing the scraping whilst it was still wet was quicker than if we had left it to dry. Apparently if weed and barnacles are left to dry out prior to removal they are much harder to remove.

Following a good scrape down she was left to stand for a few weeks to dry. Mother Earth shone down on us with lots of sunshine to dry the hull and one such day, the 6th of February, it was warm enough for me to put on a bikini for a touch of sunbathing! The following day was just as beautiful, only much more meaningful as it was my birthday and our wedding anniversary. We had been married six years. We had a great day and an even better evening when we had a romantic meal out in a wonderful Greek restaurant. We ate out so little that when the opportunity arose it was a very welcome treat and this particular treat was a gift from Mother and Father.

Back to reality round-and-round we went with the antifoul until three coats had been applied and our home for the month of March was re-launched back into the water for final checks to be made by her captain prior to us leaving for Tunisia. With so little time left before our departure Dudley set about doing the odd jobs of maintenance around *Orpheus*.

We checked our navigation lights and found that the port side light didn't work. When Dudley tried to check the bulb he couldn't get the cover off the housing. A battle of wills ensued as Dudley tried to prize the plastic from the surround to allow him to see what the problem was. As always with these situations, you struggle for ages and then with a sudden slip, slap and a whoosh the plastic flies off in your hands and you stumble backwards not knowing whether to laugh or cry because you've just dropped the screwdriver in the water! Dudley cleaned off the connections, which were showing signs of corrosion, and once all was put back together again, it worked perfectly. To try to prevent the corrosion re-occurring we sealed around the light with insulating tape hoping to keep some of the damp salt air out.

Having previously checked the sea-cocks we knew one or two of them were somewhat stiff. Obviously, whilst in the water, we were not keen on the idea of forcing them in case they broke and we started to flood. With this in mind we set about finding all our sea cocks – of which there were many. Most of them moved and a few of them needed a little gentle encouragement but two remained stubborn and would have to wait until we came out of the water in a year's time. We had only budgeted for lifting out to anti-foul every two years so until then they remained unmoved. We added regular moving of the sea cocks to our rota of "things not to forget" to ensure those currently moving would stay that way.

We wanted to clean out our very shallow bilges, as they seemed to have oil in them. This meant that there was a slight musty smell about the boat and I was not happy to leave it this way. Having lifted the relevant section of floor to clean out the bilge we discovered underneath a thick layer of insulating dog hair! Completely diverted from our now empty and dried out bilge we lifted all the flooring, washed it top and underside and swept up approximately ten dustpans full of dog hairs. We had only been on board for five months and it seemed as though there was half a dog lying in our bilge! This gave me something else to stow at the back of my mind and worry about - if we didn't do this regularly the hair would pile up underneath the flooring and if ever we found ourselves in a situation requiring the use of the bilge pump, would the hair clog the bilge pump filter and render it ineffective? Regular cleaning under the floorboards was another task added to our rota of things not to forget to do.

As we were lifting the floorboards in the port rear cabin I smelt diesel. We had filled the tank the previous day and I was somewhat concerned at the sudden appearance of the smell. Out everything came, karaoke equipment, sleeping bags, camping equipment, chairs, bowls, hatches, it was the garden shed after all! We had things strewn everywhere around the boat only to discover the fuel tank situated under the bunk had developed a leak and diesel had seeped everywhere.

We soaked up the surplus diesel and washed everything down with soapy water. It took us quite some time and at the end of it we both felt quite queasy as the fumes had been awful. We removed the top plate from the top of the diesel tank and discovered that the seal between the plate and the tank had worn and clearly wasn't doing the job it should. Hoping that this was the only problem, we cleaned down the top of the tank with alcohol and prepared it to take a new seal. We shied away from the cost of a made to measure marine seal and went to a local garage asking for a twelve-inch square sheet of thick rubber. This was purchased at a snip of a price and we used the old rubber as a template to cut the middle out. We then used silicone as an extra seal as we laid the rubber onto the tank and again more silicone between the plate and the seal as it was screwed back into place. A simple job after all and it cured the leak well enough that it never returned.

The last little job was for Dud to fit a block of wood to the side of the grab rail in front of the oven as it was loose and moved about. This secured, there was little else to do to *Orpheus* until our return from Tunisia. I still had many reservations about the trip that lay ahead but as I lay in bed, one morning, staring at my cup of tea, watching the steam rise in a thick dancing ribbon and every breath I exhaled made me look like puff the magic dragon as steam flared from my nostrils, the thought of warmer climes was becoming more attractive.

    The middle of February was upon us and one particular morning, having been used to rising to a very damp boat with sodden windows, I noticed something strange. There was no damp, no little droplets falling on my head from the hatch as I stood carrying out my morning ablutions. On closer inspection the reason became very clear; there were no droplets because they were still frozen in an icy film over the inside of the hatches! I couldn't believe it, I was now going to bed in socks, vest, pyjamas, hot water bottle, husband and dog and still feeling cold! Was it any wonder Tunisia was definitely looking good to me?

    Dudley and I took Harry out for his usual morning walk on this frosty day and came across an ice garden. Somebody must have left a fire hydrant dripping or it had a leak. This leak had flooded the surrounding ground and through the cold night, as it froze, it had continued to build and spread. In the morning we found instead of a patch of weeds, plants and grass covering four square feet there was a complete mass of crystal icicles. Strong tall fingers of ice rose off the ground some twelve to twenty inches then branched off into icy spines that finished with the smallest of ice needles covering each branch like hairs on the stem of a cactus. It was the most spectacular display I have ever seen. I rushed back to the boat to grab my camera but by the time I had run back the scene was fading fast. As with most frosty mornings, once the sun rose, all evidence of the evening cold disappeared and all that remained in the ten minutes I had been gone were the fat, icy fingers that had been the base of this wonderful display of nature.

    Very many times I've said to Dudley that chances in this life last but a second and if you are not there ready to enjoy that moment it will be lost to you forever. We were hoping that this new life would afford us the chance to be there and not to miss anything. God's creations, without a doubt, are some of the finest.

    With so little time left before our departure we turned our minds to preparing ourselves for our getaway at the end of February.

CHAPTER 15
SEA SWELLS AND SICKNESS

The most important thing for us to consider during our sail across to Tunisia was what Harry's life on board was going to be like. He would be required to stay on board a full four days with no land in sight so he would need to be trained to do his toiletries on deck. This was something we had not achieved thus far, so I didn't hold out much hope for success but for everyone's sake I was prepared to try and we began a ritual that the local Greeks must have thought very odd. Usually every morning when Harry did his "jobbies" we cleared it away and disposed of it. Now we were keeping it in the bag on the transom of the boat trying to encourage him to realise that this was a good place to go. We also started soaking up his other offerings in a towel to leave on the back of the boat. Obviously we were hoping all these smells would invoke a response and when he wished to relieve himself he would find it too tantalising not to renew the scent on board. The response we invoked could not have been predicted. If a dog could ever talk we knew, in no uncertain terms, what Harry was saying to us. We would encourage him out to the back of the boat and point to the nicely maturing heap and Harry would look at it, then at us, sniff the pile and look back at us with a look that clearly said, "You two have lost the plot and need locking up. If you think I'm going there you can think again. It absolutely stinks." After glaring at us he would walk away from the pile with total disgust and determination, clearly thinking to himself that he could wait until we took him ashore. With just under two weeks left to the set sail date we persevered but there was absolutely no sign of Harry giving in to the temptation.

It occurred to us that there might be the need for some kind of protective injection prior to taking Harry to Tunisia and a trip to the local vet confirmed this was the case. Harry required an injection to protect him from a virus local to Tunisia that attacked the chest and lungs. This was administered and whilst looking through his papers the vet pointed out that he required his rabies booster. I queried this, as according to the U.K. vet's date in his documents this was not required for another year. The local vet pointed out, very firmly, that whilst in Greece the requirements were for the booster to be given EVERY year. It is very important to note that if I had done, as indicated in England, Harry would no longer be allowed a renewal of his PETS certificate by the local vet as I would not have complied with the local rules. We would advise any pet owner to check on arrival at any country the local situation to avoid any problems in the future. Harry returned two days later to have his rabies booster jab and he was proclaimed fit for the journey.

We tidied *Orpheus*, ready to leave, and following our last cycle ride around the lagoon Dudley dismantled Harry's trailer and stowed it in the back locker. We removed all the winter covers, ready for our return, and left one middle hatch open with plastic covering over to ensure air circulation whilst we were away. The weather had not settled enough that we felt confident leaving the boat uncovered. We had gone from one sunny day to a very bad windy and rainy day where waves were rolling past level with the galley hatches. The weather was changing so quickly that we were leaving *Orpheus* safe for all eventualities. The promise of Tunisian sun, t-shirts, shorts and cooling beers was just around the corner.

As if to spite our organisation thus far my body decided to have "one of those days". As far back as I can remember every once in a while I have "clumsy days". As a child when shopping with my mother on such days I would be told to "touch nothing; don't move; just hold onto the cart." This day was definitely one of those days as in the space of two seconds I had snapped the handle off my hairbrush, banged my head, broken the bilge pump and the fridge handle. Dudley had gone shopping and when he returned he thought a tornado had passed through the boat. Having been married for some time he was used to these days and luckily for me, as always, he went about fixing things with a steady patience.

I was so glad our departure was arranged for later in the month because that meant that Dudley and I were still in Levkas for CARNIVALI. The Sunday before "Clean Monday" in the Greek Orthodox calendar the local people have a carnival procession along the pedestrian parade through the town centre of Levkas. Neither of us knew what to expect and, as usual, nobody seemed to know what time it would commence. We waited for that telltale surge of Greek people moving in one direction and followed along. Just like a bank holiday celebration in England, it had to be raining just hard enough to make everyone in the waiting crowd wet and uncomfortable.

Dudley and I huddled under a shop veranda and waited for some sign of what was to come. All along the main pedestrian street people huddled together under cover of the shops. Those who arrived later created an inner rainbow of umbrellas as the bobbing colours danced about in anticipation. The music began and the majorettes came dancing past, throwing their batons, smiling and enjoying the event. They looked so proud to be there and to be involved. If they noticed the rain they certainly were not showing it. These young girls, or should I say, near adult ladies, were closely followed by more pretty little faces that were made up as a group of Draculas. I found this quite strange but soon forgot it as boys and girls paraded in groups as clowns and gnomes and various other characters.

When all the children had passed by there was a lull and nothing happened. It was quiet except for the rain and the chatter around the crowd. Dudley was about to leave, thinking that the end had come, and I promptly stopped him moving off, indicating that normally the crowd would just disperse at the end of an event but they were still standing around. Surely there was going to be more. I thought my logic was quite good but Dudley didn't seem too convinced until the music struck up again and the first float came into view. It truly was magnificent. A great deal of effort must have gone into making these works of art. It appeared to me that each float was sponsored by a local business and took some very strange forms. There were thin men, fat ladies, bats, oysters and windmills. These displays were the size of lorries and were very professional. Compared to the Lord Mayor's procession in our local city of Norwich, what the Greeks had achieved was marvellous. The last few floats to come past were rather risqué in that one was a bar full of drunks throwing drink over the crowd; the next was full of Greek men dressed as French cancan girls wearing no underwear and the very last float was a gigantic pirate ship holding a damsel in distress. Apart from the rain, which never stopped, it was a fantastic display that was to be followed by fireworks. Unfortunately for us, this would upset Harry so we took ourselves back to the boat and had to watch what we could see from inside *Orpheus*.

Clean Monday arrived heralding the beginning of Lent. As with the tradition of the day, I cleaned out all the cupboards and made sure any signs of food were gone to ensure that we would not get overrun with pests and insects whilst we were gone. I packed our clothes, ready to take, and the rest were stowed to ensure they would be kept damp free. I cleaned and tidied all day and felt happy that we were leaving a ship-shape Orpheus. Steve, Dudley and I stocked his boat for our forthcoming journey and, apart from some last minute fresh food shopping, we had enough to feed an army for a week.

The 27 February was upon us and Steve asked us to move on board to make sure we made ourselves comfortable before setting sail. Whilst I moved our bedding, clothes and chattels on board Dudley secured things on board *Orpheus*. The outboard was fixed to the bar in front of the oven, the life raft was taken inside the boat along with the bicycles and anything else that may be attractive to the resident gypsy community that were camping on the car park just opposite the mole. At the end of the day we locked the hatches and left *Orpheus* secured under the watchful eye of friends. It was amazing how sad I felt and just how close I had become to our little yacht. I was really going to miss living on board her.

The day of departure arrived and whilst Dudley went to purchase the last minute things like meat and vegetables Steve readied the outside of the boat to sail. I cast a quick look around the living quarters and galley to make sure everything was stowed to sail and by 0930 hours we were ready for the take off. As we were making ready to go and were removing some of the mooring lines, the wind started to blow us a bit close to the quayside. Steve started the engine to help hold us off, putting her into forward gear. As quick as a flash he pulled it back into neutral again, tried a quick burst of astern and back to neutral. What none of us had noticed was the wind had somehow carried the boat over the port side lazy line; this meant the line had gone underneath the boat and out the starboard side. Once the engine was put into forward gear the obvious happened and the line got wrapped around the propeller.

The engine was turned off again and whilst I watched the stern ensuring we didn't get pushed onto the quay, Dudley helped Steve get into his diving gear, ready to dive and release the line from the propeller. The plan had been for him to dive in clearer, cleaner waters prior to leaving the island of Levkada to cover the bow thrusters with custom made shields. As he was already in the water he took the opportunity of bolting these shields over the thrusters' holes to make for a faster sailing motion. As Steve would now have no bow thrusters to control the boat as we left, we rigged up a slip-line to a neighbouring yacht and we were ready to go. As we slipped the mooring lines at 1100 hours I watched Harry and Adele waving us off along with Gary, Jerry, Janet and Mike and felt so very sad to be leaving and felt even worse on Harry's behalf as he had just had his last wee ashore for four days.

We motored down the Levkas canal and headed for the Meganisi Channel. At the end of the channel we headed towards the southern point of Lefkada. Once past here there would be no more land for some time. Just as we were drawing level with the village of Sivota, southeast of the island we noticed the engine cooling water no longer squirted its thin fountain of water out of the side outlet. A check of the instrument panel showed that the main bilge pump light was on; Steve went to investigate and came back saying there was a leak in the engine room and we would need to stop for repairs. We changed our course to head into Sivota where we anchored off for Steve to consider the repairs.

The actual problem was identified as the cooling hose that had blown off the oil cooler. The hose had perished and was of no use. This meant Steve was going to try to fix it using a length of tubing from an inner tube and we would not be sailing anywhere this evening. With this in mind I set about cooking a chicken dinner whilst trying to appease Harry who could see and smell land and couldn't get to it!

We ate our dinner and drank wine and were sitting in the dark of the night feeling rosy, thinking it would not be long before bedtime, when Steve decided he wanted to set to sea and get going! Snapped out of our languor we set about making the galley ready to sail. Once the anchor was up Steve helmed whilst Dudley and I shone a powerful torch at the water's edge to help navigate through the winding, rocky entrance to Sivota. Out into clear water, I heaved a sigh of relief and then realised the true weather conditions into which we were about to be sailing. The wind was blowing southerly force 6 which meant it was almost directly on the bows and the swell and sea state was choppy. We were just nearing Vassiliki when the cooling water stopped running and the bilge light came on again. A quick check by Steve resulted in us turning back to Sivota as the repairs he had undertaken had not been man enough for the job and the same problem had recurred. Having re-navigated the rocky entrance again by shining a torch on the rock face we anchored in the same spot we had just left and were forced to await the morning before any further repairs could be carried out. We decided a small glass of wine was in order to ease our nerves and a quick prayer of thanks for the delay. Then Dudley and I went to bed.

In the morning, as Dudley and I surfaced from our bed, Steve indicated he had been up all night and had made some refinements to his repair, the difficulty being the original hose was tapered and without another identical hose any replacement would need to taper in the same way. These repairs done we again set off and yes, again, as we drew level with Vassiliki the same problem occurred. As the wind had been blowing strongly all night the sea state was even worse than before and the swell was now quite bad. I was the only one on board that was feeling somewhat queasy and I was very happy when the sails went up and we headed back to Sivota for more repair work.

The only hiccup we had to face now was we needed repairs and it was Sunday. We knew of no chandlery in Sivota and on a Sunday the chances of anything being open were very slim. Steve had previously become acquainted with a yacht mechanic who lived in Sivota and had decided to seek out his help. This meant when we came into Sivota for the third time we moored alongside the quay, much to the joy of Harry as this meant he could go ashore. He had already been nearly twenty-four hours without a chance to do his toiletries and he was showing no signs of relenting until he got ashore. I had known this was going to be an awkward situation for Harry and I and this had now been reinforced. It was going to be a very stressful trip for the two of us under the circumstances that were beginning to arise.

Steve, with assistance, felt sure he had made a strong and secure fitment to remedy the problem we had been experiencing. With this in mind we were all getting ready to finally slip our mooring lines knowing this time we would not be coming back. We ate our evening meal and just before sundown we motored out of Sivota. Just outside Sivota the engine failed, the sails were hoisted and Dudley and I slowly sailed around the open water whilst Steve identified yet another fault requiring him to change the diesel filter. Twenty minutes later this task had been completed and this time we truly were off.

As we passed Vassiliki at the southern point the swell became worse, the wind was still blowing a force 5/6 on the bow and the boat began a brisk corkscrewing motion in a three-metre sea. The dark of the night surrounded us and tiredness kicked in but the minute I lay down to sleep I was lost. A short while later I was being ill over the side deck; half an hour after that I was being ill into a bucket; stomach empty, I was still being ill until, finally freezing cold, shaking and too tired to care I fell asleep with my head in Dudley's lap. Steve was sleeping and Dudley was on watch as we all stretched out around the side seating area in the wheelhouse saloon of the heaving Nauticat. Dudley comforted me as he kept his watch and was able to warm me up a little when he asked Steve to take a watch at 3 a.m. When I awoke around 7 a.m. the next day, feeling somewhat ragged around the edges, Steve went back to sleep and I kept a watch until everyone woke for breakfast.

So this had been my first night on the open ocean, I certainly had not enjoyed one minute of it and I was sincerely hoping I was not going to suffer the same fate all day long. The wind continued to blow force 6 gusting 7 straight on the bow. The motion of the boat had not improved in the slightest and I certainly feared the worst. There was no land in sight and I really didn't know what to expect, I had never in my life imagined ever doing anything like this and I was starting to regret letting Dudley talk me into it. The day was a very quiet one with Steve cat napping and Dudley doing the majority of the watches in between fussing over me. I began to feel a little better by midday and again took a watch so Dudley could sleep. Instead of the swell lessening it was definitely getting worse but luckily I appeared to be getting over the sickness and was feeling well enough at dinner time to eat a chicken sandwich with the rest of the crew.

Feeling a bit better for the food, I took the first watch

and tried to get Dudley to sleep. However, he was still worrying about me. Rest for him was fitful; Steve on the other hand was snoring like a trooper! Dudley took over from me around 2300 hours and he handed over to Steve at 0300 who stayed on watch until I awoke in the morning around 0700 to take over. This system seemed to work for all of us and that was the way we remained for the trip. During the day the men would sleep, if they wanted to, and I would keep watch. I knew I would find impossible to stay awake all night so I was happy to do as much as I could during the daytime.

The weather conditions had not changed at all over the last two days and the sea had increased to a 4/5 metre swell. It was during the morning of the second day at sea that there seemed to be a lull and the sea state seemed to calm a little. We all decided to take this opportunity to have a shower and fry up an egg and bacon butty. Now I was definitely feeling better and ready for anything. Harry still had not been to the toilet at all and I was beginning to feel very stressed about the cruelty of the situation for him. It was only after he had eaten and I managed to squeeze a little pee out of him that he finally relented and ran around the whole deck peeing and pooing as he went. What a relief for the pair of us!

Steve was concerned that we were having to motor all the way so far instead of sail but the weather conditions were such that the wind was still directly on the bow, blowing 6/7 and if he wanted to sail he was going to have to come off course and sail a further distance in the long run. As the day progressed the wind turned to our rear quarter, but no sooner did Steve put the sails up than the wind changed again. The wind began gusting at us from all directions and the cutter sail banged from side to side as we motor sailed. The wind gradually died down somewhat and the cutter was left to slide as darkness again closed around us.

After our evening meal I took the watch and as the men slept I was starting to feel somewhat anxious. We were heading for a headland at Syracuse on Sicily and once we had reached this we were to change course. Looking at the charts we had, it did not indicate what light combinations marked the headland and the island just offshore. All I could see were lights ashore and two flashing combinations but I couldn't be sure which was what. As we were getting closer and I was getting more and more tense both Dudley and Steve awoke and took over the watch. Boy, was I relieved! Of course, to Steve this all meant nothing, as he had sailed this route before and knew exactly what he was looking at and where he was going to go. My inexperience was definitely showing and I felt I had very little confidence in my ability on board. Dudley was comforting and I knew this was all good experience but I still worried.

With the autopilot set and radar programmed to alarm with a range of 2 miles, it was an easy task of keeping watch on such a big boat. Warm inside the wheelhouse, on comfortable seating, and warm air heating blasting out, it was a far cry from Orpheus. If we had wanted to do the same journey with her things definitely would have been different. I had all sorts of thoughts running through my head as the wind started to pick up and the cutter slapped and banged back and forth. I decided that even though the weather conditions were still quite rough I was desperate for a night's sleep in a bunk. I took to bed with Harry, and just as I did, Harry decided that it was time to let his bladder work and did it all over the duvet cover!

Things cleared up, I took Harry and settled down for sleep. I held on to him as the boat pounded through the swell, seesawing up and down whilst the cutter banged about. I spent half of the night lying on the bunk and the other half floating two inches above the bunk but at least I slept. I was aware in the distance of Dudley waking Steve to take his shift around 0300 hours and then I drifted back to sleep until there was an almighty bang and the boat lurched on its side. I leapt out of bed shouting to Dudley to see what had happened. Steve had decided that, with the change of course and the increased wind, we were now in a position to sail. The banging had been the crack of the wind in the genoa as it opened and the lurch had been the lift of the hull as she started to sail at a 35 degree heel in a force 7 wind. Poor Dudley had only just finished his watch and so far hadn't had the opportunity to sleep; it didn't look like he was going to get any at all this night with the heel of the boat and the sailing conditions.

Our third day at sea came and promised little change at first but the wind appeared to be easing a little and changing direction to come more off the bow and to the forward quarter. This meant that we had a better sailing position and were more on course. The sun was shining and after a quick shower and breakfast it seemed like it was going to be a good day. We sat on deck enjoying the sailing, and appreciated what it could have been like had the weather conditions been different.

What an eventful morning it had turned out to be! As we sat on the top decks enjoying the sun, I noticed some miles away a big black mass of cloud appeared to be developing two funnels. I drew this to the attention of Steve and Dudley and we all sat watching as the funnels developed and gradually stretched out their long spindly tendrils to the water. One funnel seemed to just disappear and the other grew larger and looked to reach down to the water but we were just too far away to see the effects it was having. I think we were all disappointed and very glad at the same time that the weather system that had created such a wonder was a long way away.

The wind direction had changed, and now that we were managing to sail, the motion of the boat was much more enjoyable although the sea state was still approximately a four metre swell. As Dudley and I sat cuddling with Harry in the cockpit, music appeared from the speakers. Steve had set playing one of our favourite songs, Calypso by John Denver. We were very touched by the tenderness of the thought and for a short time we all relaxed and were having a really good time.

In the relaxed atmosphere Steve and Dudley thought it was time to see if they could catch any fish for dinner. Out came the fishing line, hooks and lures and the pair of them sat there loving every second, waiting for some poor unsuspecting fish to come along. I may as well share with you right now that I hate and detest fishing. I fail to see the enjoyment of luring an innocent fish to its death by spearing it in the gullet with a hook, then taking it out of the water letting it suffocate and thrash about whilst you torture it by tearing half its mouth out whilst removing the hook. I guess you realise I was not happy about the fishing situation.

A short distraction from the fishing was a pod of dolphins that came up to the boat and began playing with the bows. I was trying my hardest to see them but with such a big boat it was impossible to be able to see them clearly. I was very disappointed as this was the biggest number of dolphins I had ever seen together. The dolphins having left, we set to preparing dinner. It was at this time that the swell seemed to be increasing again and the winds picked up. As we ate dinner I realised that this was the biggest swell I had ever been in and tried to take some video footage but my batteries failed. My disappointment was nothing compared to that experienced over the next 24 hours. If I had managed to capture it on videotape I could have used it to put people off sailing forever.

After we had eaten the wind kept coming and coming. Luckily for us we had managed to clear away all of the crockery and everything was stowed. The wind increased to a gale force 9 and gusting more as the seas built to a good six metres. We were taking the wind on the starboard quarter fore of the beam and had only a handkerchief of a genoa out with the cutter and were making seven knots. The sea state now was very rough and as the waves came across the bow the boat lifted and heaved over the top and surfed down the other side. Occasionally the waves were already breaking when they hit the boat and would smack into it with a thunderous crush making the boat lurch; the waves covered from bow to aft of the wheelhouse.

To say that I was not a happy person would be an understatement. Poor Harry couldn't stand up at all. The moment he tried to move anywhere he just slithered about on his stomach. As for us, we were now moving around the boat with extreme difficulty and were having to hold on at all times as the heel and roll of the boat in the water must have reached 45 degrees. This, on my part, is all guesswork. I will leave it to the technical people to work out that if the toe rail of a Nauticat 52 is in the water, with the amount of free board it has, what sort of heel we had. As I was standing in the wheelhouse, sandwiched between the seating and the chart table, I watched each set of waves pounding into the boat. The height of the waves coming towards us was higher than the grab rail around the decking. The whole situation had become extremely stressful. I was way out of my league and I just wanted the whole dreadful experience to come to an end.

As we couldn't allow Harry out on deck in these conditions I tried to get him to have a pee inside. The sea state, as already described, was too rough for him to be able to stand, let alone be still long enough to contemplate a pee. In an attempt to get him to go to the toilet I spread our already pee covered duvet over the flooring of the wheelhouse and laid Harry down. I sat there trying to convince him to go but he just sat looking at me with such a helpless expression. This really was the cruellest thing I had ever done to an animal in all my life and I promised Harry there and then that I would never do this to him again as long as he lived. It was just as bad when I tried to go to the toilet myself. It is not an easy thing trying to hold on so as not to fall over, keep the toilet lid up, get your trousers down and manage to sit on the toilet seat before the lid falls down again!

Just as my own dilemma was taking place Steve realised that he had left the fishing line out over the side and in the fun of sailing and wind and swell he had forgotten to bring it in. Dudley went to help him, as this was proving no easy task with the speed we were sailing through the water. Nevertheless together they managed to reel it in and came back down below with a rolled up mass of line and hooks. Just as we all stood there in the middle of the wheelhouse the boat gave an almighty lurch and shudder as another crashing wave hit us. Like something from a cartoon sketch, Dudley who was to my left, whilst still standing perfectly vertical, slid across the floor on the spread out duvet and crashed full weight into the dining table to the right of me. As he had his hands full of hooks he took the full weight of the table on his stomach and literally lifted the table off the floor.

After a quick moment of confusion and a few screams of protest from me, Steve showed himself to be a great captain and calmed us. He clearly communicated to us how to set about putting the table back. We placed mattresses around its base to secure it in place for the rest of the journey. I again spread out the duvet cover and this time Harry, whilst I held him, let go his bladder for, hopefully, the last time at sea. All this mess cleared up and the excitement of the day over, we settled down for the evening in a rough and tumultuous sea. The cutter and genoa were out and we were continuing to sail on the auto-helm. During the day Steve had also fitted his latest purchase, a wind vane steering system. This had been his first opportunity to fit it and set it up correctly and it seemed to be working very well but it made the helm very heavy to steer.

Settling into our normal routine, Steve had gone to sleep and I was to be on watch but Dudley was still awake. He became very anxious when he noticed a rather large container ship holding its course and bearing down on us. He felt it was getting a little too close for comfort so he woke Steve from his sleep. When the ship came within one nautical mile range of us and the radar alarm was bleeping, Steve decided he would call the ship up. Nothing was heard on his first attempt but on the second he was successful in raising the captain of the vessel on our port aft quarter. Steve explained we were under sail and, in the weather conditions, requested that the captain of the container ship change his course as at the present time he was on a collision course. Without any further explanation necessary the captain notified that he was changing course, which made us feel a whole lot better, and he passed behind us at some distance. Steve thanked him and asked if he had an update on the current weather conditions. It was with a heavy heart that I listened as the captain said that the current gale force 9 gusting 10 wind conditions would continue for the next twenty-four hours.

We all settled down again and I tried my hardest to sleep. With the heel we currently had, all of the contents of the boat not screwed down had crashed to one side. Every time a rogue wave hit us everything would crash back and forth. I could hear the glasses smashing and the plates crashing; everything in the cupboards was heaving; the tins were banging and bottles rattling. Sleep was not going to come that evening. All I could think to myself as I lay there was, "I'm so glad that the things I can hear smashing aren't mine." Had they been, I would have been devastated.

Dud sat watch until 3 a.m. when he let Steve take over. One minute we were sleeping wedged in for the heavy port side heel we had and the next we were flying off the seating in a bang and a crash along with the rest of the contents of the boat. Everything smashed from port to starboard. "What the (bleep) heck was that?" Steve had decided, whilst we slept, to tweak the wind vane steering and had brought the boat the wrong side of the wind and thus the sails had crashed across and we were now sailing in the wrong direction. Dudley jumped up from his very short spell of sleep and helped Steve put the boat back on course.

This excitement over and the boat back on course with the wind vane steering re-set, and the auto-helm working, Dud lay down again to try to get some sleep. No sooner did he manage to drift off to sleep than we were both shaken to the core with an almighty smash and a crack; the boat heaved down and then up and the contents again smashed in all directions. One of the cupboard doors flew open as a bottle flew across the galley and smashed to the floor. Dud jumped up to shut the cupboard door and went to see what had happened. Steve had decided that we were not sailing quick enough and so had put the engine on to help drive the boat through the swell.

Every wave that came at our bow cracked at the hull and I sat there, holding Harry in the darkness, listening. The wind howled, the sea roared and crashed around us and with every wave hitting the hull I was waiting for the boat to just split open. It was deafening and frightening. To say I was not having a good time would be a lie. I was having the worst time of my life. Dud realising my distress and that of Harry suggested that if Steve pulled back on the power maybe we wouldn't crash through the waves quite so much. After an hour of hell the power was brought back and Dudley managed to actually lie down and get some sleep just as daylight was dawning.

During the morning I insisted that Dudley sleep as he was now looking very tired indeed. He had had the least sleep of all of us and I was concerned about him. The wind started to reduce somewhat to around force 7/8 but the swell continued. When land was spotted at 10.30 a.m. the relief I felt was great. Perked up by the appearance of Monastir coming into view I rallied round, had a bit of a tidy up and prepared for the arrival. Steve went up on deck to change the flag and hoist the customs Q flag. By 11.30 a.m. we were in waters that were a little more protected by the land mass but were still steep and choppy. However, we were assured over the radio that we would find protection from the wind once inside the breakwaters and inside Monastir harbour.

Steve and Dudley prepared the mooring lines and we readied the boat to come alongside at the fuel quay. All fenders were on the starboard side and the plan was to go into the harbour, collect ourselves and then come alongside on Steve's command to throw the lines. Even though the harbour waters were calmer the wind still howled inside. Steve went into the harbour, turned the boat around and came up to the quay. The wind was so strong that he was afraid it would take the boat with a crash into the quay if he approached on an angle. Although all the men ashore were screaming for us to throw the lines, we awaited Steve's command.

Steve went around again and still did not feel happy with the approach. He wanted to reach the quay directly abeam so when the wind caught the boat it would push it sideways onto the quay and hopefully the fenders would do their job. Still lots of shouting and jibing from the quayside by four men standing there, and still we held our ground and awaited Steve's order. Without the bow thrusters to help control the boat, because of her size, she was going to be at the mercy of the wind when he reduced engine power to stop her.

    The plan was for Dudley to throw the stern line and Steve would go forward to do the bowline. I was to run the side decks with a roving fender to protect the hull when the wind took her. Steve lined up again and this time came perfectly beam to the quay. The minute he took the power off the engine the wind took control of the boat and it all happened so fast I couldn't really say what happened. I heard Steve shout, "This time, throw your line." By the time the next thought came to me, the boat had moved with much speed straight at the quay. I ran to the beam and managed to jam a fender against the beam just as it crashed hard into a set of steps running down the quay wall into the water. There was a rush of shouting and a blast of white dusty smoke as we hit. I looked up to see Dudley watching as his line was ashore and Steve on the bow also watching and his line ashore. We all exchanged a glance and then a huge, big smile. We were here, we were safe and there were no more six-metre waves. After four nights and almost four days we had done it, we were tied up and ready for a month of sunshine in Monastir, Tunisia.

CHAPTER 16
TESTING TUNISIA

At last we were finally in Tunisia and, much to Harry's delight, the first thing Dudley and I did was to take him ashore for a walk. With the new smells and bushes to investigate it seemed only a very short space of time before Harry appeared to have forgotten the horrors of the previous few days.

My first impressions of Tunisia were a little unnerving. The booking-in procedure was very strict; two men appeared on board and Steve had to sign a declaration confirming the contents of the boat. All equipment had to be logged including cameras, video cameras, number of radios and number of bottles of alcohol and computer equipment. These formalities having been completed, we were allowed ashore. Steve had to take our passports and clear customs and arrange for our marina space for the next month.

The only thing that rivalled the severity of this procedure was the appearance of Arab men watching from behind facemasks who followed us as we walked Harry around the marina complex. It all made me very uneasy. It seemed to me that every corner we turned there were at least two pairs of suspicious eyes watching us, watching what we were doing, leering. It was not a good start to our arrival.

We were allowed to remain on the fuel quay for that evening and we unanimously agreed what we all needed more than anything else was an early night. The next day we all awoke refreshed and ready to start the process of putting the boat back together again. As Dudley and Steve went about the task of re-screwing the table to the floor, I tidied and cleaned the galley and was pleasantly surprised to find that although there had been a great deal of smashing coming from the galley there were very few breakages. Apart from one glass and a few chips out of the plates, everything in the galley area had survived very well.

As the men sawed and sanded and re-housed the table in

a way that would prevent the same thing happening again, I followed behind with the Hoover and duster and tried to make the boat home again, ready for the arrival of Steve's mother, Enid. Having spent Christmas and New Year with her, I was very much looking forward to the arrival of "Mother", especially as she was a particularly good cook. Originating from Dorset, "Mother" was what I would describe as a typical farm lady, a cuddly mass of motherhood in an apron.

Steve had a further project to carry out on board. We had awoken that morning to find one of the side windows into the wheelhouse smashed. We didn't know whether this was foul play or just coincidence, but either way it needed to be secured. Dudley and I took this opportunity to take our first walk into town to see what delights Tunisia had to offer.

As we walked from the Marina complex I felt those eyes following us. As we made our way into town I began to have mixed feelings. The huge, red, sandstone ribat was the nucleus of all the shops and housed several stalls and shops within its walls. As we walked through the shop-lined streets, every single stall owner jumped out in front of us trying to get us to buy something. Shop owners would bar our pathway and stare straight into our eyes, saying with such fierceness, "You come into my shop." The tone was not a friendly one as if to say, "Please, you come in and look." It was spoken with such menace and in such a threatening way, it said, "If you do not come in and look, wait and see what you get." There was only so much of this I could take before I was starting to get very annoyed and somewhat frightened so we moved from the ribat out into the general shopping area.

There were shops and shops and shops; I was amazed how the old and tatty mixed right in with the new. Banks, car sales and garages; I'm not sure what I expected but I did not expect it to be quite so modern. There was no sign of ladies dressed in black yashmaks with their faces covered; most of them were wearing modern westernised clothing. This was a huge surprise to me indeed. Never did I expect it to be so liberal. The image I had of it was that women were still very subservient here but I guess, as with other countries, 'the times they are a-changing'.

In a relatively out of the way location, we stumbled across the railway station and, more importantly, a huge, covered market. As we walked around it there appeared to be every sort of produce you could wish for: fruit, vegetables, meat, grains, spices and to Dudley's delight and my absolute horror, the biggest fish stall I had ever seen. As Dudley stood there, drooling over the fish lying there with their dead little eyes staring at me, I ran out to get some fresh air.

We made our way back to the boat and found Steve in company of the gentlemen who had first come on board on our arrival. They were indicating that we could not stay at our present mooring and that we must move as soon as possible into the marina. They obviously did not like us being too near the fuel tanks for too long. I wondered whether this was the reason we always appeared to be being watched. Did they fear we were going to steal something or maybe blow something up? Whatever the reason, they definitely were not taking their eyes off us.

Another restful night with good food and wine was had. It was good to be relaxed again. In the morning Dudley helped Steve remove the dinghy from the davits and put it back into the water to enable the passerelle to be dropped. We were preparing to take up our position in the marina but prior to doing this Steve wanted to remove the covers from the bow thrusters to give him better control of the boat when we moved. Once again, kitted out in his diving gear, it was necessary for him to be in the water for only a very short time. He surfaced with a very serious look on his face and told us that there was no visible sign of the bow thruster covers at all. They were both gone completely, bolts and all! Dudley and I were not surprised to hear this as the boat had taken such a pounding on the journey over. The only thing that occurred to all of us and made us laugh was remembering the difficulty we had experienced whilst coming into moor. We had thought the bow thrusters were covered and could not be used. The fact is, we could have used them and had a much easier mooring in the bad wind conditions. There is nothing in the world like a good dose of hindsight!

The boat ready, we made the move into the marina and once settled, had our first taste of the local music. Steve had picked a spot in the marina near to the shops and facilities, as 'Mother' following a hip operation wasn't so good on her legs. Unfortunately, a restaurant not far from where we were, insisted on playing its music at full blast. It wasn't a gentle rhythmic kind of music but an Arab wailing type that was only really enjoyable in small doses. It was not long before I found myself threatening to do things involving inserting the musical cassette into one of the orifices around the restaurant owner's body.

To get away from the music for a while Dudley and I went for a walk into town again and this time discovered the most wonderful mosque I have ever seen. The pathway leading up to the actual mosque was ornately decorated and lined by gardens with seats that allowed you to sit and contemplate life. The iron gateway into the mosque itself was a work of art and the mosque truly was a temple worthy of Allah. On this visit we could not enter as Harry was with us and I did not wish to appear disrespectful by taking him into their grounds. There would be another visit later.

Leaving the mosque, we walked back to the boat through the shops and, feeling it only right to give it a second chance, we walked through the ribat. Once again, we were accosted at every stall and shop in the same threatening manner. We just kept walking, hoping they would get out of the way or just go away. One of them shouted after us, "Hey, you. You look at me when I talk to you." The rudeness and arrogance of these people was beyond me and I really had taken a dislike to them. If this was a taste of what the whole population was like I was in no hurry to come back.

The following day brought glorious sunshine and we cleaned the windows and hovered in shorts and t-shirt. Mother and Aunt Doreen were arriving that evening and we wanted the boat to be especially nice for them when they finally got here. We had never met Doreen but were looking forward to the company and catching up with news of England.

With the kiss of sunlight on our skin we happily went about our individual tasks and, coming together for lunch, sat out in the warming sun. Then, after a beer we sat back and did a spot of people watching and enjoyed the view around the marina. It was good to just be still and feel warm and relaxed after such a tiring trip. That afternoon the wind blew up out of nowhere and a band of dark cloud seemed to appear within seconds. Before our very eyes the cloud was building faster than anything I had ever seen before. I looked around the marina and shopkeepers everywhere were running around collecting up their goods and taking them back inside their shops. Others were covering their goods with plastic and without a doubt they knew what they were doing, so we removed our deck seating and started closing some hatches. Within five minutes the heavens opened and the whole mass of black cloud was emptied onto the earth below. Just as quick as it came, once empty, the cloud was gone and in the warm wind the dampness that had laid the dust dried up and disappeared.

After eating a homemade pizza, Steve took off to collect his mother and aunt from the airport. Dudley and I eagerly awaited their return and by 8 p.m. we were all together drinking wine and hearing all the news. We told our stories about our sailing trip across and they told us stories about 'jolly old England', which apparently was not so "jolly".

The days that followed were wonderful, relaxing in the warm climate and enjoying the company of Mother and Doreen very much. I made my mind up there and then that when I got old I wanted to be just like Doreen. What a character she was! We laughed and joked and played cards. She liked a drink and knew how to live life to its fullest. Mother, more subdued because of recent surgery to her hip, kept us all in line by telling us off if we giggled too much and kept a motherly control over all of us. What a joy it all was! It was just a shame about the attitude of the "locals".

We tried to give Steve private space and time to spend with his family and often he would go off shopping and walking around the town, coming back with tales to tell of what he had found and places of interest. It worked so well because this meant we knew where to go and what to see and we could leave Harry on board with Steve whilst we went. By now Harry was totally in love with the luxury of Steve's boat and I was starting to doubt that he would want to go back onto Orpheus. To be honest between Steve's lovely cooker, microwave and bread machine – not to mention washing machine – I was beginning to seriously doubt whether I would ever want to go back onto *Orpheus* myself!

One day, Steve came back explaining how he and the family had stopped for coffee in a restaurant and when it came to paying for the drinks the man serving asked for four dinars. Steve queried this as he had noted the price of a coffee when ordering and enquired if this amount was correct. With a cough and a splutter the man said, "Um, oh, yes, sorry. I make mistake, two dinars." Well now, this was my second big disappointment. Not only had we been bullied and accosted by the shop keepers but now we realised we needed to check prices and our change because the restaurants would charge whatever they thought they could get away with!

During the sail across, the cutter sail had lost its sacrificial strip (a canvass strip along the outer edge of a sail that protects it from UV deterioration when furled). As well as this, there were some ripped stitches on the genoa and Steve was keen to repair these before making the trip back to the Ionian. Mother and Doreen went off to "shop till they dropped" and we set about getting the sails down ready to sew.

The quayside in the marina was quite large so Steve decided to lay the sails out on the quayside and sew them there. The trouble was we didn't have a table strong enough to take the sewing machine and portable enough to take ashore. Improvising in the best way possible Steve went to one of the tavernas in the marina and asked to borrow a table and chair for the task, which they gave willingly. One could say this clawed back a little favour in my negative thinking of the people around me.

All equipped and ready to go Dud took the weight of the sail. I fed the sail through the machine and Steve turned the wheel of the machine. System in place, we found that we needed to take it at a running start and once going not to stop, as once we stopped the cotton would foul. The machine was doing a good job but we were asking very much of it so we found what worked and tried to stick to it, as there was quite a lot that needed to be stitched. During the three hours we were doing this we attracted much attention. People passing by would stand and stare like they had never seen a sewing machine before. Others were amazed that we were managing to sew a sail at all. Then came past Mr. I-Know-It-All, who felt it necessary to tell us that it wouldn't last, and that we shouldn't really be doing it. He told us there was someone in town that might be able to help us out for a fee and we should be using them. It was not our place to say anything so we stayed quiet and Steve remained very polite. To be completely honest I would have liked to say, "What's it got to do with you?" I always find it rude and very annoying when people feel they have the right to interfere in something that is quite obviously none of their business.

When we had first come out to live on board we had

found the first few weeks quite strange in that our life was on display. Only a handful of activities on board take place inside the yacht; the majority such as washing, eating and working take place outside and as such can be observed by others at all times. Even when those niggling moments and arguments take place that all couples experience, the walls are never thick enough; everyone can hear. Yachtsmen tend to accept these conditions and there is an unspoken code that one 'turns a blind eye' at certain times. Of course, there are always those that do not have the decency to merely observe but rather judge and interfere. We had experienced it in Greece and now we had experienced it in Tunisia by the intervention of Mr I-Know-It-All.

We did manage to sew the majority of the sails but couldn't get the needle through the many layers at the clew of the sail. Steve found the 'man in town who could help' and left it to his industrial machine, operated by a tailor, to fix the clew. We discovered there were very few sail makers to be found but the local tailors were very helpful with their industrial machines and, with a little direction, were more than willing to assist in any way they could. Although they were being paid for the work this kind of generosity again helped to lift my view of the local people and, keeping an open mind, I tried to forget the bad things and feelings I had experienced thus far.

Having walked around the shops a few times Dudley and I had seen many decorative tiles and had decided that if we could buy six picture tiles we could fit these over the top of an ill-placed mirror in our heads (toilet) aboard *Orpheus*. This would mean instead of sitting on the toilet seeing my own face staring back at me I could look at something more scenic! We both agreed this was a good idea so we dared to run the gauntlet of shopkeepers. Without Harry with us this was easier as we could walk faster and just keep moving. We got to the Yasmina Centre and found it wonderful. They had absolutely everything you could want and all very good quality. Store attendants politely asked if they could help, which was a refreshing change but it did become a little tiresome, as they seemed to have one person asking this question for every single stand with the shop. Every time we stopped and looked if only for a second we were approached but at least this wasn't as bad as the rude and threatening manner of the street sellers. Unfortunately, they did not have a picture tile collection that Dudley and I liked, so we were forced to take to the streets.

After stopping and looking at a few shops and going through the aggravation of explaining we were 'just looking', we finally found a shop that had some picture tiles we liked. The shopkeeper's eyes lit up as we entered the shop and all of a sudden nothing was too much trouble. The minute we looked at anything it was whipped down off the shelf and presented before us. In no time at all the whole floor of the shop was covered in six tile picture sets all being dusted and paraded before us. We had two or three we liked and we had to choose one so we started to ask prices. This was when the real fun started.

The tiles in the Yasmina Centre had been 24 dinars; the opening gambit of this gentleman was 40 dinars! Both Dudley and I hate to barter and are no good at it at all. We like to pay the asking price and expect that price to be fair so we said, "Too much. We will leave it."

The man instantly went to one of the other two sets and said, "This one here is only 32 dinars."

"Still too much," we said.

"This one here is the cheapest. It is only 28 dinars," said the shopkeeper with the biggest smile as if to say, "How can you resist that?"

Both Dudley and I said, "No," and made to leave. Just as we stood up, he ran to block the door way and said, "Look, look, which do you like the best? I make you a very good price, just for you."

At this we nearly burst out laughing, not because of what this gentleman had just said but what every shopkeeper had kept saying to us, which was, "For you very, very cheap price, Asda Price".

From our memory, this was a very old saying from an advertisement on TV for a particular supermarket chain. How on earth had it made its way to Tunisia? "How much for this one?" Dudley asked and the man said, "24 Dinas especially for the lady as she likes it so much."

"We can buy it for that in another shop," Dudley said with such daring I could hardly believe my ears.

"Oh you rob my family," complained the man "but just for you I will take 22 dinars." We paid the price and left the shop with our tiles. In all probability we had still been robbed at this price but at least it was the cheapest we had seen anywhere.

What an experience! I was very impressed with Dudley as I've never seen him stand up and question or barter in such a way before. I was starting to realise that living in this environment would never be an easy or restful one. I constantly felt like I was being watched, cheated, robbed or harassed. Dudley didn't feel quite as strongly as I did but once we left the marina environment I felt I was struggling to relax doing anything. I understood this was the culture of the local people and I accepted they had to make a living but this was definitely a place that I would never like to be for an extended period of time. It was wonderful to experience and see. I enjoyed the chance to observe the different way of living but it simply wasn't for me. Steve simply embraced the new culture and accepted it although he could understand a woman's point of view and how it may all seem different. However, Doreen and Mother enjoyed it very much and didn't seem to attract the threatening manner when they went shopping. Maybe it was because of their age and the locals were showing some kind of respect.

Having settled into the marina and with the wind still blowing, Steve decided not to sail further along the coastline so we decided to take the local train to visit Sousse. We again forgot how difficult it could be trying to do something when you have a little dog in tow. Not thinking, Steve bought us all return tickets for the train ride to Sousse. As Dudley and I took our tickets we asked if he had checked if it was okay for Harry to board the train. He hadn't. We all approached the ticket box and asked if it was okay to take Harry on the train. The reply came, "No, no dogs." We then had to explain that we wanted a refund as the tickets had already been purchased. This seemed to cause him even more of a problem than simply letting the dog go, so he gave in and said, "Ok, no matter. You take the dog." The first hurdle over, we hoped that would be it for the day.

We settled into the train ride, keeping Harry on my lap and he got some nervous stares from the local people. It wasn't until we set off and Harry started to puff and pant and get somewhat upset and nervous that I realised that this was the first time he had ever been on a train. Every time it stopped and the doors hissed open and shut he would let out a whimper, which I tried to muffle. The locals hadn't looked too keen before and did not look any happier when he started to bark. He could obviously hear something we couldn't and I found it hard to chastise him; I could only do my best and hoped we would get there soon.

In no time at all we arrived at Sousse and were immediately struck by how similar it was to Monastir: the same colour buildings and surroundings, the medina and souk enclosed behind the old city walls and the people in the shops all looking keen to sell. As we walked around I noticed the people were not quite as aggressive in their manner when trying to sell something to us and, all in all, Harry was the star attraction of the day. Every person who had a child with them stopped and wanted the child to pat Harry. It was almost as though this was the first and probably only dog they would see in their lifetime. We had more than one offer through the day to buy him; the highest price being 10 dinars, that I guess, to some would be an awful lot of money. They didn't indicate whether this was to keep as a pet or eat so I just glossed over the whole thing and tried not to think about it!

The shops were all much the same as in Monastir selling sandals, dresses, bags, wooden craft and crockery. We walked up alongside the city wall and around the houses of the village and then down again finding ourselves in an absolute warren of tiny paths and alleys all lined with shops and cafes. The more corners we turned the more secluded alleys we found and I couldn't help but think of Ali Baba and his forty thieves. Needless to say, with the seclusion and the closeness of contact with the shopkeepers, the hassle was relentless and by the time we surfaced my nerves were in tatters.

We met up with Steve, Mother and Doreen and decided to have a drink before heading back to the train. During this rest and refreshment I tried to regain some composure and made light conversation with the others. As I was looking around and starting to relax I noticed an old man in the corner of the café. He had a turban around his head with the end scarf hanging loose around his neck. His clothes were quite tatty but clean and as he put a cigarette to his mouth I could see that every one of his fingernails was black. "Quick," I thought, "Look away. You're being rude in the extreme." No matter how much I chastised myself my eyes kept being drawn back to the man and I noticed that he had an unshaven face, which sported a rough greying beard and moustache; his eyes were sunken and seemed to have no colour just a pool of black. His skin, tanned and leathered, was hinting heavily at his apparent old age. Then he looked at me. His smile was quick and it displayed a few teeth that were black, brown or missing. I nodded in reply and quickly looked away, "That will teach you for staring," I told myself.

I just couldn't help it. My eyes kept drifting back to him and each time they did, I began to notice something else about this man smoking in the corner. He was eyeing up Doreen! A few more looks definitely confirmed it; he was trying to catch her attention and was clearly enjoying the view more than a man of his years should have been. I told Doreen of my suspicion and the minute she looked at him his face burst into one of the biggest, and obviously what he thought sexiest of smiles. Of course, completely contagious, now I had alerted Doreen to the man she felt compelled to keep looking at him and every time she did he would smile. I laughed until my sides hurt all the way back to the train station. Without a doubt, Doreen had "pulled". I'm absolutely positive if she had shown the least bit of encouragement we would have been leaving Sousse without auntie but probably with a few camels in tow to take back to the Ionian!

We got back onto the train without any problems until the doors opened and on came a group of three men in very smart uniforms. The way they walked through the train spoke of authority and the amount of gold braid on the shoulders of one of them told us that he was in charge and the other two were his bagmen. They began checking tickets and asking questions and I gained the impression that they must be carrying out an on-the-spot inspection to ensure that everyone was doing their job correctly. As he was getting closer to our seats I noticed the man looking at Harry and indicated to Dudley that there may be trouble ahead. Steve was sat some seats away from us and he indicated to Dudley that he would deal with it.

As the man came to me he spoke in French. I am ashamed to say that my French is only limited (having been told I was useless at the age of twelve and not allowed to take it as an option). What I had learned was sufficient for me to say hello and indicate that Steve had our tickets. This officious man moved over to Steve, puffing himself up and standing to his full height and I could see that something was wrong. This man who was seriously overweight and appeared to have high blood pressure from the colour of his cheeks said to Steve that Harry should be muzzled and in a cage. He then asked to see Harry's ticket and Steve had to explain we had not been required to pay for the dog. There then followed a rather heated exchange between Steve and this man, which we sat and watched from a distance. It culminated in Steve standing up (a tall man at six foot two inches) and tearing up the tickets he held in his hands and throwing the pieces at the man's feet. At this the braided man stomped off closely followed by his two assistants and if I hadn't been so worried I would have laughed because he reminded me of the "Fat Controller", a character in a famous children's book about trains. Only, this controller had a really bad attitude and the train wasn't called Thomas!

Once we were off the train we managed to ask Steve what it had all been about. The "Fat Controller" had asked Steve to pay three times the price for a ticket for Harry, which he had naturally refused to do explaining we had bought return tickets and if they had required the dog to be paid for it should have been done in Monastir and not on leaving Sousse. He had insisted that he be caged but Steve had explained he was sitting on my lap, not annoying anyone or running loose and that we didn't have one. The controller again insisted on payment, which was when Steve pointed out that our tickets were return tickets from Monastir to Sousse and back again and he would not pay another penny and ripped the tickets up. It obviously did the trick and Steve, my new hero, was right in every respect and both Harry and I were very glad he had won the day. Safe back on the boat we laughed about it and put it all down to experience, whilst raising our glasses to the 'Fat Controller'.

We took a day's rest after all the excitement of Sousse and the train ride. We discovered there was to be a Saturday Market/Souk in Monastir but were told it was too far for us to walk. Dudley asked the price for a taxi ride to the market and was quoted 1.5 dinars. When the taxi driver saw Harry this increased to 5 dinars, so we took another taxi who charged us 3 dinars. I swear they just made it up as they went along and if you looked like an unsuspecting person they charged you double. As it turned out, the market had been close enough for us to walk to so the whole thing, for me, had already started badly. Situations like these leave a very bad taste in my mouth.

All the way through the market we got hassled. If we dared to stop and look at anything we were pounced upon. We looked at a leather pouf, which was very nice and to us because we were English only 135 dinars. If we had been American it would have cost 160 dinars. We moved on past all the 'very cheap Asda price' stalls and found the vegetable and livestock. This was definitely not for the faint hearted with its cages of chickens running around, being bought and slaughtered before my very eyes. GET ME OUT OF HERE!

I was totally unimpressed with all the in-your-face murder, and on top of everything else I felt I had suffered, I was convinced that this was not the place for me. Dudley took me out of the market and down a side street where we found a second market – second hand clothes, shoes and toys. Along with these were some of the best stalls I liked to be near, the dried pulses and spices. The colours and the smells of the spices and dried beans were wonderful. This was what I had come to see and enjoy, I tried to forget what had been and enjoyed what was now. Later we learned that most of the clothing and shoes would be aid donations. What other countries had given freely were not being distributed free of charge but taken to market to be purchased! "Can this be true?" I wondered, as this was not how, when we donate, we perceived it to be. Not wanting to get into anything political and certainly not wanting to darken my view of this society any more than it was, I decided to leave well alone.

The experience of the market over, we all went out for a lovely meal to celebrate Steve's fiftieth birthday. We went to one of the restaurants on the marina complex and were greeted by the most pleasant man who introduced himself and his wife and guided us to a table welcoming us to Tunisia and his restaurant. Taking the time to look around I was surprised, yet amusingly content, to see an avocado colour Jacuzzi bath in the centre of the restaurant masquerading as a goldfish pond. A nice little fountain and rockery around the edge meant that most people would never know the difference but I am of the generation when the avocado and aubergine bathroom suites were all the fashion so it was hard for them to try and disguise it from me.

The meal was spectacular and the company was great. We laughed, talked and sang Happy Birthday before returning to the boat to sleep off the food and wine. Alas, the next day, both Steve and his mother had taken to their beds with very bad sickness and diarrhoea. Hoping that this was going to be a short term situation, we went out to leave them in peace and quiet to hopefully get well.

We took Doreen into town and walked around the magnificent mosque. From start to finish the whole building, walkways and gardens were perfect in every way. On the approach to the building the paving was laid out in a decorative manner that almost seemed to draw you into the gateway made of iron welded in a complex design. Through the gates and well-maintained gardens more tiled pathways led to the building itself. Wow! That's the only way I can describe it. Golden domes and marble pillars, mosaics and paintings. WOW!

As we were leaving there were groups of children of varying ages milling around everywhere, giving the appearance of a school trip. One group of teenagers broke out into song which became wailing in banshee fashion whilst the boys beat drums – an outward display of celebration of their religion or a lack of respect – I didn't know what to think of the situation, but as we passed by they certainly looked like they were having a good time. A walk back along the seafront of beautiful white sand and blue sea forced me see what a beautiful place this really was. It had so much to offer in the way of things to see and do and everything was so interesting and eye-catching. Even their huge cemetery stopped us in our tracks and we just stared and took time to pay respects and catch our breath. Why, oh why, did the people have to be so threatening and untrustworthy?

Two days later Mother and Steve were still unwell and we were starting to get worried, especially as Mother was so pale and frail and losing weight fast. Neither of them could get out of bed and even drinks of water were going straight through. Doreen went to the chemist to purchase some medication and for the first time I felt, with them being so ill, that Dudley and I were truly intruding into what was a very personal and family affair. All that could be done had been done and we took Doreen out for a walk.

We had decided to try to get into the fort museum but this meant taking Harry along. When we got there he was not allowed to enter, even if I carried him the whole way round. Doreen and I sat outside with Harry in the gardens opposite whilst Dudley took a walk around and shot some video footage and photographs for us to see back on the boat. Steve's boat having a TV built in made this quite easy and this was just another luxury that I was becoming quite fond of.

Another two days saw Steve almost back to normal and Mother starting to improve but still not quite right although she would not go to a doctor and would brook no argument. We took ourselves off for another battle around town and witnessed a funeral. At first it was hard to tell if it was a political meeting, riot or anything else that comes to mind when you see a large group of men gathered around the back of a tatty old transit van. The van had a microphone on the top and it just looked like they were about to commence a protest march. Not thinking anything more, we crossed the road to avoid the bedlam just as the van started to pull away. We stood still with Harry to let it pass, and as it did we saw the wooden coffin draped in a green cloth inside the van and watched as the men walked behind in silence. Once the realisation that this was a funeral parade sunk in we bowed our heads as they passed and were amazed to see that we were the only people around the streets who were paying it any heed whatsoever. It could have been that the coffin was empty or that the person inside was not popular. Either way, it all seemed a bit cold and unfeeling to me; just another difference in culture that slapped me in the face, and left a bad feeling.

By now the local music was starting to drive Dudley mad and I was on the verge of insanity. The restaurant at the back of the boat in the marina insisted on playing VERY loud music which was not to our taste at all, all day and night. Every now and again the Tunisian equivalent to the Lambada would play and I'd get up and dance just to annoy Dudley even more. The music would then turn back to what I affectionately called the Fred Titmus song, as all the way through there was a lady singing, "Fway, hay hay hay!"

Needless to say, I was starting to miss the Ionian very much and was looking forward to being in the peace and quiet of *Orpheus*; to be in a place where people didn't stare at me when they thought I wasn't looking; to be with people who gave the right change and didn't overcharge; a place where smiles were out of friendship and pleasantness was given freely, not just because you were spending money. I missed the Greek people and their easy culture. I definitely did not feel at home in this country.

Sensing my mood, Dudley took me for a soothing walk along the sea front and we had only just exited the marina when I was screaming out in pain. Not looking where I had been walking, too busy looking out to sea trying to forget where I was, I had stepped wrongly on uneven paving and badly sprained my ankle. Dud had to carry me back to the boat giving me a piggyback, which attracted the attention of just about everybody we passed. Was this my punishment for being so judgemental and ignorant in the ways of these people or was it just stupidity? Either way I paid the price and my ankle was bandaged as it began to swell and turned a nice shade of black.

Mother, still not well, but well enough to travel came to the end of her holiday. She and Doreen were packed and ready to leave and it was a rather sad time. We had had such a good time together but it had been marred by the illness and we all hoped once home Mother would soon get back to normal health. Hugs and kisses, and Steve made the trip to the airport to wave goodbye to his family.

The purpose for the trip over, I tried to clean the boat as best I could with one foot and sorted the washing. Dudley and Steve made sure the broken window repair was watertight and Dudley went up the mast to untangle the lazy jacks on the mainsail. With the boat ship-shape, Steve went out with Dudley to stock the food cupboards for the return journey and I sat and wondered about what this journey would entail.

Steve had indicated the return journey would be done in dayhops so it would be a bit friendlier for Harry and his need for trips ashore. I had looked at the weather closely and it had been showing Gale Force 8 all through the afternoon and evening and into the next day. The plan was to leave the following day at 5 p.m., which meant that the sea state would be pretty much the same as when we came in and I was not looking forward to that at all. We discussed the weather that night and Steve seemed to think that it would be alright to leave the next day – I was not convinced in the slightest and I knew exactly what was going to happen.

CHAPTER 17
HOMEWARD BOUND

The day to leave arrived and as the fuel prices in Tunisia were very reasonable, Steve filled the tanks prior to our departure. We left our mooring in the marina in a force 6 wind and came alongside the fuel quay. This hadn't been the easiest of manoeuvres but this was the least of my worries. The wind had been relentless all afternoon and I was convinced we should not leave in such conditions. Later that afternoon when Steve booked us out with the customs office my heart sank. We were going to be sailing off in the dusk of the evening into an already angry sea. I knew the inevitable was going to happen. However, it did seem fitting that my parting view of Monastir was three angry, unsmiling customs men.

We left in near gale 7 winds with choppy two/three metre seas. We hadn't even lost sight of Monastir before I was asking for the bucket and I spent the whole night heaving and shivering and wishing Steve some serious harm. Whilst being ill I had to try to jam myself into the seating as the sea state meant I was slipping all over the place. This was not the easiest of things to do with a sprained ankle and every now and again the pain was unbearable. I eventually lost consciousness and fell into a fitful sleep that was only eased by the ever-constant presence of Dudley who obviously just wanted it to be over for my sake.

As with the previous journey, the next morning I was feeling better and by the time we arrived at Lampedusa (a small Italian island), I was ready for a shower and something to eat. Steve had called up the harbour master as we arrived into the port at Lampedusa and we had been told to come alongside some of the fishing fleet vessels. As we came alongside and tied up I had great reservations, as after a night of sickness the last thing I needed was a mooring next to a stinking, smelly, fishing boat. Luckily for us the wind must have been blowing in the right direction and I didn't have to suffer a single whiff of fish.

Steve and Dudley took a walk around town but I just couldn't get off the boat with my ankle as it involved climbing over two other boats to get ashore. During the afternoon, as we rested, I had heard lots of "cooing" and "kiss kiss" noises but didn't really think anything of it. Later, when I went out on deck, the chef of the fishing boat "Archangel Raphael" brought some meat and bones, presenting them to me. "For the bambino," he said and pointed at Harry. Is there no heart that this dog will not melt? Grown men, big ugly hard faced fishermen were falling to pieces and cooing over Harry offering him the remnants of their meal! I couldn't fail to be touched by their manner and I added them to a growing list of local fishermen for whom I had much fondness. No matter how hard and angry they looked on the outside I was fast learning that inside there was a pool of cuddliness. I had found the same with the fishermen in Levkas harbour and I was now taken with this Italian crew.

Having got over the sickness, we settled into the same watch system whereby I stayed up until 11 p.m.; Dud would take over and then wake Steve about 3 a.m. We set sail for Malta in a Force 4/5 wind and were doing 7 knots speed. All went well and we arrived at Malta at 9 a.m. the next morning. We were asked to come alongside another yacht with engine problems to book in through customs.

Steve went ashore with Dudley as we had been warned that there would be problems taking Harry into Malta. On the approach to the harbour Steve had called up, explaining that we had a dog on board and they had said it would be no problem as long as they could inspect his documentation before he left the boat. Dudley went off with the appropriate papers and came back saying they may wish for a vet to come and examine Harry. We sat and waited for the outcome and no answer came so Dudley went to enquire if there was a problem and was told that we were free to take Harry ashore. Out of curiosity, Dud asked what the problem was with dogs and that we had been told they were shot on sight. The man very affronted said this was not true and this had never been the case in Malta. Other sailors may have experienced a different approach but as far as we were concerned, our animal's papers and vaccinations were in order and we had not one problem. The vet had been happy with the papers and did not want to see Harry in person and we were free to take him anywhere and enjoy the delights of Malta.

As yachties do when alongside each other, we got chatting to the skipper of the Hong Kong registered yacht next to us. It transpired that the skipper was delivering the boat from the U.K. to Hong Kong. It was an ex-racing yacht that had been donated for use under the "Outward Bound" scheme that provided holidays and outings for under privileged and deprived children. I congratulated the charity and was heartened that there was still some good to be found in the world. Well-done, "Spirit of Hong Kong". I hoped that all who went on board her would enjoy the experience and gain benefit from the fun it would surely give them. If it hadn't been for the generosity of our Captain Pete I would never have known the fun of sailing and would never have had the opportunity to be where we were at that time. Maybe this boat was going to open up others lives the way Admetus had done for us.

Unbeknown to Dudley and I, we were supposed to have moved off the customs quay once we had registered. Steve had stayed and wanted to stay for the night so when the annoyed man from the customs office came calling we wondered what on earth it was all about. Steve told him we would move in the morning and he left looking none too pleased. However, as promised, the boat was moved and we were at anchor in Msida Creek the following day before I had even got out of bed! Steve and Dudley had moved the boat and laid the anchor in the creek without my even knowing. I really must have slept well. This was something I hadn't done for some time as I had found it almost impossible to get my ankle comfortable. I hoped this was a good sign and that it was healing.

Steve took the dinghy ashore and did not return until later that evening. Dudley and I had a lazy day alone on board and realised it was the first time we had been alone for a very long time and it felt good. The closer we got to *Orpheus* and Levkas, the more I wanted to be alone with just our little family unit of Harry, Dudley and me. Without a doubt I was going to find the transition very hard. The thought of going back to life with a cooker that didn't work and no washing machine made me feel quite sad.

When Steve returned that evening he took Dudley ashore with Harry for his last visit ashore before bedtime. The weather being quite cold, Dud had pulled his black woolly hat on and zipped up tight his black thick overcoat. When they returned they were giggling like naughty conspiratorial children as they explained to me that what they had thought to be just an island inside the creek was actually military property. Whilst walking about in the dark, with dark clothing and hat pulled well down, Dud had been stopped by the Maltese Navy and asked what he was doing. Just as well he was only walking a little west highland white and not a Rottweiler!

The following day the wind was blowing hard, a "gregale" had been forecast; this being the name given to the local strong winds. Normally this wind was known to last three to five days at a stretch so I thought perhaps we would sit this bad weather out until it passed.

Steve and Dudley decided to go ashore sightseeing and shopping, but I couldn't go because of my ankle. Harry couldn't walk too far so we were left behind to guard the boat. The minute Dudley left I began to get the familiar, sinking feeling I always get whenever I am not with him. I always feel as though something vital to my existence has been taken away and I find it hard to concentrate on or enjoy anything until he is back with me. Silly, I know. Some might say where's your own self-confidence? It's just the way it is and always has been since the day we met. I just simply love to be with him.

When they finally came back and the hugs and kisses were over, it felt as though he'd been gone a month, instead of a few hours. It appeared he must have missed me too, as he had brought presents!! I had been treated to an Easter egg, a watch, a pastel drawing of Malta and a HARRY POTTER DVD! Had he missed me or what? In addition to this, he and Steve happily announced that, knowing I couldn't walk far, they had found somewhere to moor the dinghy that was only a few steps from a bar and we were going ashore for a pint! Well, you would have thought it was my birthday! It was with great glee I downed three halves in a local pub and then went back to the boat for a hot chilli and to watch the DVD.

We had had three days at anchor and my sights of Malta had been very limited. However, I had looked through the binoculars at the buildings and streets and remembered my visit of many years before. How things had changed over the twenty-three years in between visits! I took video footage to show my parents as they had lived here for three years between 1959 and 1961. They had never been back and I was betting they would have some strong views on how things had built up. Both Dudley and I thought the buildings and history surrounding this place was wonderful and agreed that if our travels brought us back this way, Malta would be a great place to winter, as there were so many things to see and do.

The following day, Steve wanted to move to the quayside so we could fill with water, prior to leaving the following day. As Dud was pulling up the anchor it became obvious we had a problem, so Steve went to see what it was. They struggled for some considerable time as a big, heavy hawser had snagged on the anchor and they needed to clear it before we could fully lift the anchor and leave. After a long struggle and a lot of effort we were at the quayside and making ready to sail the following morning. As the "gregale" was still blowing I suspected the sea state after three days of wind would be rough. I could only hope that as we had sat still for three days I would not have to go through the sickness stage all over again.

Most people along the quay were saying they were going to wait another day when the forecast indicated the wind would die down. Steve, ready to depart, left at 11 a.m. that morning in the "gregale". The sea state was rough and the wind was directly on the bows so we were ploughing through the waves. I was so glad when I found I didn't feel sick and I knew I was going to be all right. We were now headed for Syracuse on Sicily where we arrived at 1 p.m. the following day having motored through the night. The minute we arrived, Dudley helped me hobble to a telephone, as it was my father's birthday. The fact that it was raining and I couldn't walk very quickly didn't leave me in a good temper when I found that there was nobody at home. Back at the boat, showered and fed, I felt more human and hoped that my father had had a better day than I had.

April Fools Day was upon us and we knew that we would be leaving that afternoon for the final leg back to Levkas. We took the opportunity to have a short walk around town as my ankle was still playing me up. Fantastic buildings and friendly people made this a great place to visit and again a place that we definitely would like to come back to.

You may have noticed my mentioning my bad ankle at every opportunity. This should portray my state of mind at the time as my life seemed ruled by it and I should like to justify this with a quick tale of woe about living on board with an ankle that doesn't work. For several days I had to hop, not being able to bear putting my foot on the floor. When I could finally rest some toes to the ground it still took many days before I could stand with my full weight on it. Trying to move around a boat, even as big as Steve's, was very difficult. I found myself climbing upstairs on my knees and moving around the furniture one-leg, one knee at a time. The worst was trying to get over the lip at the bottom of the doors that were just too high for me to hop over. I managed by putting the knee of my bad leg on the floor over the lip and squeezing the good leg through. I tried not to complain too much but I can assure you it was no bed of roses and was very, very tiring. I am not the smallest of ladies around the thigh region and to take the weight of my legs on my arms was a very uneven contest. In short, living on board a boat with a bad leg was almost impossible. It was uncomfortable and made me darn right miserable.

During our time sailing we have met physically impaired sailors, sight impaired sailors and sailors that are wheelchair bound and they love it, never seeming to complain. Looking back on those days of my self-absorbed woe, I feel ashamed.

Back at the boat after our lunch, we all tried to get some sleep, as we would have to be at sea for two days and thus sailing through the night again. Just as well we did because although the swell was moderate and the winds kind we were sailing close-hauled all through the night, which made the sleeping arrangements somewhat difficult.

We had one minor hiccup as we left Syracuse. We set the sails and began to sail close-hauled and as the boat heeled I noticed the dinghy drop to one side. As quick as a flash, Steve went to the stern only to find that the davits (metal arms at the stern used to hold the weight of the dinghy) had bent in badly. The combination of the weight of the outboard, which Steve had left on the dinghy instead of bringing back on board, the weight of water inside the dinghy following a recent rainfall and the heel of the boat, which concentrated the weight into one spot, resulted in the davits giving way. Steve secured the dinghy with rope supports and we were soon on our way home sailing through the night.

The next day proved to me how enjoyable the whole experience could have been if it had not been for the terrible winds and swells we had experienced on the way there. We now appreciate that this was a bad time of year to be taking a journey across the Ionian Sea and Sicilian Strait and if we tried it alone we would pick a different time of year to undertake the trip. However, today the sun was shining and we were sitting on the top deck, still sailing close-hauled, in force 4 winds. I listened to the waves foaming up the hull as we ploughed through the water and reflected on what had been. Without a doubt, this Nauticat had been tried and tested during this journey and it had proved itself throughout no matter what weather and man had thrown at it. I was very impressed with it on the whole and although I had been nervous about the conditions, I had never once felt nervous about the boat and its ability. Sadly, I think the cost and up-keep of such a yacht would always be out of our reach as our budget was a small one.

It had been a wonderful day's sail, peaceful and trouble free and my only worry was when and where Harry would deposit his last night's meal! Sitting out on the deck, trying to encourage him to do his bit, Dudley noticed a bird fly down and land on the deck next to me. Looking round slowly and keeping a tight hold of Harry I saw a tiny brown bird with black and white markings and a long curved beak. It seemed to want something but was very nervous indeed and it flew off the minute it realised we were looking. It tried to come back on board and almost made it but couldn't keep the speed up to get to us. It was with much regret and sadness that we realised it was so tired, it needed to rest and eat but had been just too nervous to trust us and let us help. It was gone from sight and we could only hope that it would live. Sometimes nature shows us a black side to the beauty but I guess this is what the scientists would call natural selection and what keeps a species strong, as only the fittest survive.

My sadness for this little bird was soon forgotten as we celebrated Harry doing his business on deck. Now we could all relax! Whilst washing down the deck we almost missed a little yellow bird, sitting watching us. It appeared to be a cross between a finch and a tit. It flew inside the boat and out again as though it was just taking a look. It then circled the boat in the air and then decided to check out the inside again coming out to settle on the guardrail. None of us dared move, as we didn't want to scare it away. We sat watching the bird as thrice more it checked out the inside of the boat and came outside again. On the fourth trip inside it settled on top of the fruit bowl. It sat preening and sunbathing so Dudley got a small dish of water and a crumbled up biscuit to see if it would eat and drink.

Very slowly and gently Dudley placed our offerings beside the fruit bowl and the bird did not move. Then, after a few more minutes of preening he hopped down and took a drink of water, ate some biscuit, more water and then hopped back up onto the fruit bowl and went to sleep in the sunshine. I would never have believed a wild bird could be so intelligent and so trusting as to check us out, find us suitable and then make himself at home. Steve told us he had had this before on open ocean journeys and that by late afternoon more may come in the hope of finding somewhere to spend the night. Come sunrise, he said, the bird would leave and fly on its way.

After studying the bird for some time I had decided it was a male. It was very pretty and in the avian world males are usually the prettier. This decided, I named him "Horace" as he was making himself well and truly at home. He hopped around the wheelhouse checking everything out and taking a drink and eating as he pleased. The trouble we found though, for every mouthful in there was a little present out and it wasn't long before we had a nice little trail of bird poo everywhere! In an effort to keep the boat in some kind of hygienic order I followed behind cleaning it up. I had seen what it could do to car paint so I didn't want the same thing to happen to Steve's varnish and woodwork; besides I wanted Horace to stay.

Towards dusk Horace commenced a thorough inspection of the whole boat. We sat watching as he went into the galley and walked around the worktops, then into the dinette where he looked around and sat on one of the soft seats. Obviously not what he was looking for, he went into the heads and came straight out and then into what had been Mother's cabin. He landed on the bucket shelving, took a look and hopped down into the shelf, snuggled into the corner and tucked his head under his wing. The cheeky little thing had been trying to find himself a bed for the night. We left him there and that was where he stayed all night.

As dusk approached Steve had been right and we found ourselves suddenly invaded by swallows trying to get on board. Steve asked us to shoo them away because one bird was more than enough inside the boat. We stood in the companionway waving our arms as four birds tried their hardest to get in. They were not nervous at all. One managed to get past us and poor Dudley had to catch it, scoop it up and throw it out again. It was a hard thing to do because we wanted to help them but I hated to imagine what I would have to clear up in the morning!! Realising that they were not going to get in, they nestled underneath the dinghy on the stern platform making themselves comfortable there for the night.

Amongst all the excitement of the birds, Steve had forgotten he was trailing a fishing line and went to check it. Dudley went along to help and suddenly there were excited calls from the deck as they landed a five-pound Tuna. Whilst they both stood there, taking photos and murdering the fish, Harry and I stayed below with me muttering great objection and shouting the odd word like 'murderers'. With bloodthirsty grins they asked for a plastic tub and within a short space of time a tub full of blood red tuna steaks had been loaded into the fridge. Just in case I didn't shout it loud enough in protest at the time, I say it again now, "MURDERERS!"

As the men sat gorging on fresh tuna that night, I glared at them in disgust and ate cheese. Harry glared at all three of us in the hope he might get some cheese and tuna for himself. Through the evening the sea state got a little bumpy and I wondered how Horace was faring so I went by torchlight to check on him. I was about to panic when I found he wasn't on the shelf but I need not have worried. He had taken himself down onto the pillow and nestled in so he didn't slide about as the boat heaved. I had to laugh at the barefaced cheek and intelligence of the bird. I stopped laughing when I saw the little trail of bird pooh he was leaving behind him but didn't have the heart to move him. After all, I could wash the pillow in the morning.

Having closed the boat up for the night I began to worry that in the morning Horace would want to escape the confines of his cabin and would not be able to get out. Early in the morning when we awoke I was very pleased to see him still happily sleeping on mother's pillow and making no attempt to leave. We sat having breakfast and he came flying out and went straight to the fruit bowl to have a drink and some biscuit. We all thought he would leave so we opened up the hatch only to be greeted by one of the swallows sat on the top step and not moving. Horace went out for a fly around and we thought he would be on his way but no, he came straight back to sit on the fruit bowl quite clearly not wishing to leave just yet!!

As the morning wore on, the swallow, now known as Bertie, moved inch by inch onto the top step, then the arm of the seat, then the table until he found himself a nest on the top of the helm instruments in the wheelhouse. He looked thin and would not drink and really looked quite sorry for himself. Apart from bugs I had no knowledge of what swallows ate and I tried to tempt him with some suet fat but he really wasn't interested. He just sat and slept. Horace by now was completely confident and didn't look too happy about the intrusion but Bertie stayed well away and we went about our day's sailing.

The wind had dropped considerably and we were now motoring so we sat out on deck enjoying the fresh air. Every now and then Bertie would come outside and fly a lap around the boat as if he was checking we were still going in the right direction. On one of his laps, rather than go back inside the boat, he chose to nestle on a cushion beside me. As usual, when I feel a strong emotion, I find an appropriate song to sing. As I sat singing, "Oh, what a beautiful morning; oh, what a beautiful day …" I noticed that Bertie appeared to be enjoying it. It sounds silly but he really did seem to be looking at me and appeared to relax. Enjoying my new audience I changed songs to, "All things bright and beautiful, all creatures great and small…". As I sang, two more swallows came down and sat on the deck. Now I had a full house and was totally in my element. It was totally amazing. As I sang, one of the new comers sat on top of my head! I've never experienced such a moving moment. These wild creatures actually wanted to be with me and were apparently enjoying my singing. It was a very special moment, a God given moment, a time to be thankful for. Even Dudley couldn't believe it.

With all the chirping and cheeping from the birds Harry was definitely keeping a close eye on events. Whilst we had always taught him not to chase the birds in the garden at home, the attention they were receiving was almost too much for him and every now and again I caught him just sitting and staring at them, working out his strategy for attack. He had already been tested to his limits as we sat eating lunch. Harry was by my side and Horace decided Harry's feet needed a clean so he landed on the chair next to him. He then promptly started picking at the grit between Harry's toes. I held on to Harry for all my might as he went rigid with the want to have our feathered friend for dinner.

With all this excitement it felt as though we arrived back to the island of Lefkada in no time at all and Vassiliki was in view. We were nearly home, and as Bertie took a look around on a fly past, we were sure he would leave. Land was in sight but neither of them looked ready to leave. It was when we drew level with Sivota that they took their last fly round and decided it was time to go. They headed off towards the land and that was the last we saw of them. The whole episode with the birds had been too magical for words. I simply cannot describe what joy they had given.

We arrived at Tranquil Bay near Nidri back at Lefkada and anchored off for the evening, ready for our big arrival back at Levkas quayside the following morning. Following a relaxed evening meal we had a nice, quiet night's sleep and our journey was all but done. We could not believe it. What an experience! We had been so far and it had passed so quickly, and now we were back at Lefkada we had mixed feelings. It was good to be back, yet we were sad it was over. Our month away had passed so quickly; we had dealt with rough seas, new cultures and wild creatures; so many firsts for both of us. There can only be one person to thank for the chance to take such a journey and for the gift of the whole experience, so Steve – we truly thank you.

We awoke well rested the following morning, and whilst Steve and Dud ate the rest of the murdered Tuna I sat, making suitable noises, eating my cornflakes. Whilst they later set about making minor repairs to the stern making ready for our arrival in Levkas I started to clean the boat and made it presentable to the friends that awaited us on the mole. I had received a welcome back text message and the promise of a greeting as we came in to moor. The anticipation was great and it gave us all a big lift and a surge of energy to get this final lap of our journey finished.

As I helmed approaching the Levkas Canal I saw another yacht heading towards us so I altered course to pass them port-to-port. The other yacht seemed to have a bit of a death wish, being much smaller than us, and kept heading straight for us so I made Steve aware of the situation and he took the helm. It was then that we noticed it was a red-hulled yacht. There are so few red yachts that we knew instantly who this must be. Their faces came into view and we cheered and waved as we recognised

Mike and Janet. They were going out for a days sail and had wanted to welcome us back.

We carried on up the canal and as we passed the end of the marina there were a few of the people we had spent winter with, standing, waving and blowing air horns to announce our arrival home. To us this was our home for now and it felt so good to be back. We turned into the harbour and saw more people there to welcome us back and I could hardly contain myself. The minute the mooring lines were secured I jumped ashore and kisses and hugs were shared all round.

We had arrived at around midday but it wasn't until around 3 p.m. that we sat down with Steve to eat our lunch. There had been a constant flow of friends and acquaintances from the marina coming to welcome us back and to ask how we got on, wanting to hear tales of our journey. We were told that word had got back that I had hated the journey so much that I had left Dud and taken a ferry from Italy to get back home!!! Where do these rumours come from? Having worked in an office environment for many years I knew that rumour and gossip could spread rather quickly but to think we had travelled just under a thousand nautical miles, had crossed the Ionian Sea and the Sicilian Strait twice and these rumours had flown all the way back ahead of us!

It was nothing further from the truth. In reality the journey had brought us closer together and when Dud went on board and came back reporting that *Orpheus* was clean and dry, and her engine had started the first time I kissed him long and hard. I tentatively went on board myself and was relieved to find her just as we had left, not damp, not smelling but wonderful and looking more like home than ever. We enjoyed the moment and looked at each other wondering if it had really all happened. Were we really back and ready to start our summer sailing?

Rather than just rush off and leave Steve alone, we had all decided that it would be nice to spend one last night together. We cooked, we ate, we laughed and we recounted the adventure we had just undertaken together. The memories we hold of this journey are still as wonderful today. No one was ever going to take this experience away from us and, hopefully, in many years to come we would all look back on the adventure with fondness.

The next day we found ourselves very busy indeed. Dud was putting the boat back together again, moving the life raft back on deck and re-fixing the outboard to its mounting. I started the task of moving everything from Steve's boat back onto *Orpheus* and in doing so I realised how much I had missed her. Steve's hospitality had included many luxuries such as hard firm beds, microwaves, washing machines, a cooker that worked and a big cold fridge but when all was said and done *Orpheus* was my home. I was taken by surprise and quite shocked to find myself so strongly attached to her.

It was with some guilt that I looked across at *Admetus*, standing lonely, on the hard opposite the mole. Surrounded by other yachts her blue hull blended with the blue sky filled with fluffy, white, summer clouds. I felt suddenly sad. She was a beautiful yacht and Dudley, Captain Pete and I had had some wonderful times with her and yet it now seemed my affections lay more heavily with *Orpheus*. This realisation gave me a jolt as I never thought I would have any affection for a yacht with such an unforgiving helm. Maybe there would be a chance for me yet.

CHAPTER 18
MIRACLES, MONEY AND BOATS

The weather was beginning to warm up again and both Dudley and I were looking forward to the summer ahead as it would be our first real summer of non-stop sunshine. England, in the main, was either overcast or rainy with the odd day of sunshine. We were being told that here in Greece once the weather settled we could look forward to sunshine for months.

To enable us to enjoy this summer sailing we had decided we were in need of new mooring lines and genoa sheets so we took a drive to Nidri in search of some cheap lines.

We had heard of a company selling off old stock cheap. The drive made me feel good about life. Everything was bursting with energy and colour as it began to come alive. All along the roadside, wild flowers and weeds waved in the breeze, bobbing their pretty, flowered heads. The summer birds were returning, seeking out partners for their spring fling. Lefkada is a very pretty island with fantastic mountainous views and we got to enjoy it all as we drove along the coast road. We could see the first of the white sails belonging to the flotilla boats as they returned from their winter moorings. This was a sure sign that summer was on the approach.

Whilst we were in the area we took the chance to visit a particular butcher's that sold frozen sausages, but not just any old sausage; these were ENGLISH sausages. This is something you just cannot find in Greece so we were very happy to find this rare source. It had been so long since we ate a good old-fashioned English sausage full of everything but meat and spilling oodles of fat into the frying pan that it had become quite a fantasy.

As well as the sausages, we found some cheap lines and sheets, and although not exactly what we would have wanted, we had little choice on the budget we had. This now gave us the opportunity to put the sails back on *Orpheus* and to ready ourselves for the first sail of the season. Buying cheap lines really is not something we would recommend unless, like us, you were on a very tight budget. It really was a false economy. It took only one year for these lines to wear and we had to replace them. It has been our experience that when buying warps, sheets and halyard you are better paying the extra and buying good quality as it really is a case of "You get what you pay for."

There was only a moment's hesitation when we unfolded the sails and I asked Dud, "Can you remember how these go back on?" He gave me a stare filled with wisdom that told me to be quiet and we managed to hoist and furl the mainsail and the genoa with very little trouble and were ready for action. We used Steve's body weight on the halyards to ensure they were hoisted as tightly as possible, which we later found to be a very wise thing. The following year we had no such luxury and struggled with a main that would furl easily but bulged on the haul out. We finally discovered this was due to the upward tension not being tight enough.

As we shared a meal with Steve we realised it was only seven days since our return from the journey together and already it was feeling as though it had been months ago. The whole trip had, in such a short time, become almost surreal and none of us could believe that it was over; but over it was and we had our own lives to move on with. Steve was already making plans to leave, heading eastwards, and we carried on with our summer preparations in the hope of enjoying a summer in the Ionian.

Dud inflated the dinghy and used it to get around the boat and scraped all the winter growth and barnacles off the hull at the waterline. I followed behind to scrub off the green algae and then commenced the very tiring job of polishing the whole hull by hand from the dinghy. This would normally be done with the boat out of the water but we had no plans to lift out this winter due to financial constraints so it had to be done the hard way. I was totally exhausted by the time I had finished. It hadn't simply been a matter of polishing the hull. As I polished, the dinghy moved away from the boat, so to prevent this from happening I had to hold on with the other hand to keep the dinghy close enough to the boat to be able to polish it. A long and tiring job but in the end it looked so much better. The sun shone down and was reflected from the water creating a dazzling dance of ripples on the freshly polished hull. I was proud. She had never looked better; she looked loved and cared for and she was ours.

As I started to polish the upper decks and clean the stainless steel Dud set about the task of finding some Perspex. Unfortunately we could not find any thin enough to be able to replace the Perspex sliders that fronted the cupboards in the galley. Not to be thwarted in his task Dud settled on some veneer covered hardboard. Once cut and in place the wood effect didn't seem too out of place and I actually preferred it as not being transparent I could have my cupboards as messy as I liked and nobody visiting would be able to see in them. Perspex cupboard sliders meant that the contents were always on display to anyone and everyone. Not anymore; that problem was solved.

With just the fenders and warps to wash and clean we were ready. Orpheus was ready. Let the summer time commence...

Alas, this happy frame of mind was not to last and as we sat contemplating our financial status, things looked grim. The flats that had been let for only six months were now due for renewal and two of the three had indicated that they would be moving out. This meant that unless we found replacements quickly we would be incurring a £900 overspend each month. We could reduce this to £500 if we didn't take any money out of our account to live on. This in effect meant that we had nothing to live on at all and we were still going to be getting into debt every month the flats were empty.

We had spent seven months with so little money and had managed to keep our morale up and live within these means. This latest turn of events pushed me into an abyss and I screamed in anger and pain at our situation. I couldn't believe I was going to have to live this way forever, constantly struggling and never being able to afford anything. I couldn't cope. I didn't want to cope. I recalled many conversations before we had left England when, being very self-righteous, I would say, "We will never be rich but how much can a person eat and drink? We will enjoy a good, simple life on what little we will have. Living simply and being close to nature is all we need." If I could eat those words, I would. It all sounded very romantic and honourable but it was an absolute crock of you know what. I hated living under these circumstances, wondering which way to turn, wondering if we could eat today, tomorrow, next week. I didn't want to go back to England but I just could not face living this way too much longer and I really didn't know what to do for the best. I prayed. I prayed hard. I prayed for forgiveness for blaming it all on Dudley. I prayed for a better life for both of us and I prayed for help.

Our monetary situation as well as the anticlimax of having returned from our adventure left me depressed and flat. Dudley and I held each other night after night and wondered how we were going to be able to get through this. Mother called to say one flat had been re-let so this meant if we could just manage to live somehow, without taking any money from our account, we could break even. Whether you are a believer or not, for us it was like a miracle and it came in the form of work.

I was approached to see if I would consider cleaning boats for the summer and Dudley was asked if he would help to prepare boats by putting the sails, spray hoods and biminis on. The pay was not much but we were not proud and anything was better than nothing. "Never look a gift horse in the mouth," they say. We both launched ourselves into this invitation with great willingness and verve and thanked God, our lucky stars, angels and all things mighty for the chance we had just been given.

For the first few days I felt so tired I didn't know what to do with myself but at the end of the week, when we both sat down and put our money on the table, the tiredness just disappeared. Being a complete boat-cleaning novice, apart from what I had done to our own boat, I was shown the best products to use for washing down and polishing. I was also shown how to remove rust stains and how best to get a teak deck looking like new. Dud was learning very quickly the tricks of the trade on how best to put sails on, fitting the varying designs of spray hoods and biminis and also some other handy hints on carrying out repairs.

Paired with another lady, I spent happy days in the spring sunshine washing down decks with sponge and brush and polishing stainless and smooth decking. I found it a wonderful way to spend a day and was further encouraged by the fact that I was getting paid. Some of the time it was very hard work, especially teak decks, which I found a particular nightmare to clean, but at the same time it was trouble and hassle free. I thought back to my previous life, working in an office with phones ringing and people shouting whilst sitting in a false climate controlled atmosphere. I thought of the need to wake up each morning and wonder what on earth to wear, how best to impress those around the workplace and how best to behave to encourage bosses to think you worthy of promotion. I remembered the pressures and responsibility of the work I had carried out and the demands of the everyday workload. None of this existed in boat cleaning, and as hard and back aching as it could be, I was left wondering why I had not thought to do it many years before.

We would sit over our meal in the evening, swapping boat stories and it seemed that the financial injection had given us the zest to take life on again. At first we found the size and beauty of some of the boats we had access to unbelievable. The initial shock of walking into a yacht longer than twelve metres was always pleasing. Each yacht we entered had its own wow factor and we were fast learning about the different layouts, woods and upholstery. Some appeared so luxurious with their huge cabins and shower rooms that we almost lost the sense of what a boat should be about. Little by little, the more yachts we saw, the more layouts we compared, and between us we started to gain a very clear idea of what we would like in another yacht should we ever decide to sell *Orpheus* and buy something else.

It didn't take very long for the initial 'wow' factor to wear off and for me to begin being very critical of some of the more luxurious boats. Looking at it sensibly with a clear mind and with the mind of a person who planned to live on board 12 months of the year, suddenly these big beauties became monsters. During the winter months, when the rains come, there is very little to do on board apart from socialising within the community and reading books. We didn't have the luxury of electricity over the previous winter so we had no television or heat. These bigger yachts had more space, more cabins and more hatches and at this time all I could think was, "How would I keep this warm in winter?" I now know that my mind was blinkered by our financial constraints but it is something to bear in mind.

My first criticism of all these fine yachts from a live aboard perspective would be the waste of space. On descending the companionway steps I would be faced with a wonderful big empty space. Set to one side you could usually find a magnificent table surrounded by chairs and on the other side either two soft seats or nothing at all. We had spent the majority of our winter sprawled on the side seats within *Orpheus* and we had been very comfortable and the collapsible table had not seemed intrusive. On these bigger yachts with their unyielding tables and circular seats I could not envisage a relaxed environment where you could put your feet up. *Orpheus* had a liveability that these modern luxury yachts didn't seem to have. They were functional and created a wonderful seating area to sit at a table and eat but once the meal was over, where could one relax? Even without electricity we had played music and sung to each other and sometimes Dud played his harmonica whilst I sang. Relaxation in many forms could be enjoyed on *Orpheus*; it just seemed to me that the bigger yachts were taking this ability away. The seating didn't seem to take winter relaxation into account unless lying horizontal on one of the bunks.

Moving to the bunks brings me to a second criticism of these bigger yachts. At first you look at the huge beds and go green with envy. Dudley and I had had many spats during the night about whose feet belonged on whose half of the bed; we definitely needed an extra metre in length and width to make the forepeak cabin completely comfortable. This envy gave way to puzzlement. Why were there plush seats at the edges of the bed? What function did they have? Why can't people sit on the end of the bed? Why could they not be replaced with extra storage, a dressing table with mirror or even better, reduce the size of the cabin to make more space elsewhere? And this was just the master cabin.

When we looked at the other cabins we found, depending on the size of the yacht, these cabins looked as though they were never used or alternatively they were filled with possessions and were being used as open storage space. Every live aboard we've met utilises one cabin as the "garden shed". On *Orpheus* the port side rear cabin was filled with all sorts, so I question why designers insist on having all available space filled with beds, why could they not leave one space neutral. This would allow for it to be adapted to whatever the owner required of it i.e. a dressing room, a wardrobe, shelving, a computer room, garden shed or tool storage. I could think of many things and many different layouts for our port side cabin that would better suit us other than a bunk. No matter what size a yacht was, it appeared makers were determined to fill every single spare piece of space with a seat or bed that really wasn't needed. Why would you take up all this space and still stint on the shower cubicle?

Whether the heads and shower were en-suite or shared, they were all too small. No matter what size the yacht the shower was still guaranteed to cause you to bang your elbow at some point or other. I couldn't understand why designers didn't remove the big plush seating and extra beds and simply make the heads and showers bigger. I wondered whether it was because they simply didn't consider the live aboard community when they made them. I gained the impression that yachts in general were designed for people who use them for sailing holidays or summer breaks. Of course, at vacation time, meals are taken outside, days spent swimming, evenings spent exploring and deck showers are the norm. As a person living aboard we were looking at yachts with the merit of offering all year round comfort and maximum storage and we decided that Orpheus, although not perfect, was quite near the mark.

The only area on these bigger yachts that we really could not fault was the galley. Normally these were laid out in a similar fashion the only variable being the amount of space to move about in and the area of worktop. Taking *Admetus* at ten metres, *Orpheus* at twelve metres right up to a fifteen-metre luxury yacht you would still find only the basics. There would be one oven, one fridge (sometimes bigger), one sink (sometimes double) cupboard space and worktop. What do you need more than that? The only other point I considered was the cooking at sea situation. *Orpheus'* galley was "L" shaped which created an area I could wedge myself into and in addition there was a grab rail fitted to the oven front. Some of the bigger yachts had long straight galleys with nothing to stop the chef sliding everywhere with nothing to hold onto. Again, for shorter trips and summer sailing this was fine, but for a long-term lifestyle a grab rail was a practicality that to me seemed essential.

Some of the yachts we saw had microwaves and washing machines, and one even had a freezer but I consider these things non-essential. We were buying fresh food daily and had no need for a freezer and we certainly did not require a microwave. I had never used the one we had whilst living in a house, although I did miss the ability to make great jacket potatoes! I don't deny that a washing machine would have been nice but there are several smaller machines on the market we could purchase for use on *Orpheus* that wouldn't need to be plumbed in.

All these electrical items require mains power so to use them outside of the marina environment you would need a generator. We have spent many idyllic evenings having the peace ruined by yachts running generators. Unless they are fitted correctly, the noise pollution itself is a very good reason not to have these appliances on board. We have debated the pros and cons of all these electrical items and still consider them non-essential to a comfortable living environment on board.

The more we thought about it and the more we discussed it, we failed to see the benefits of a bigger yacht with the exception of having a bigger bed! It would have been nice to have a bunk wide enough for four human feet instead of only three. I personally felt the ultimate size yacht would be around the twelve- to thirteen-metre mark; anything bigger was a waste of space. Dud was of a different opinion. He would have liked to go to 13/14 metres but I argued the extra expense in the upkeep of the yacht and the higher marina fees did not equate to the extra benefits gained from the bigger boat for all the aforementioned reasons.

For me, as a person living aboard, I wanted an area to relax in, a comfortable bed, a functional shower and galley with space to store food. *Admetus* had fitted this bill and so had *Orpheus* with some minor changes. All in all, in amongst the hard work and cleaning, Dudley and I had gained a very clear picture of what we would like from the inside of another yacht. It was just a matter of whether we would ever be able to find such a boat with the layout we required. Until such time as we did, *Orpheus* remained a very comfortable boat for us to live on and we are proud to say that everybody who has visited us uses one adjective to describe her: homely.

A quick word on the exteriors of yachts. From my own experience trying to clean them and from what Dudley told me in relation to various fitments, it became clear that this too was a minefield of choices. Having cleaned teak decks I knew I certainly never wanted to own one, unless one day I found myself rich enough to pay someone else to clean it. We both thought teak decks were beautiful to look at but we also found them VERY hot in the summer time and VERY, VERY hard to keep clean. There are various forms of non-slip decking and these have to be tried and tested as not all of them, when wet, remain non-slip.

I found some decks relatively easy to walk around and others made it impossible to do so without stubbing a toe or other appendage. English yachtsmen insist on wearing shoes around the decks at all times and of course this is the best practice. However, life in the Mediterranean normally means bare feet, especially when the decks are being cleaned so to us this was still something to be considered should we ever change yacht. I simply put forward the question, "Would you ever consider buying a house that required you to constantly wear shoes?" It's just a matter of perspective and ours is one of living aboard and not weekend sailing. It should also be noted that yachting etiquette usually required the removal of shoes prior to boarding another yacht. This practice not only prevents damage to decking but is said to prevent the carrying on of cockroach eggs. I personally have never heard of this being the case, but I am perfectly willing to understand the theory of it.

Surprisingly, we found it did not necessarily follow that bigger yachts meant more deck space to walk around. I found some of them, having a lot more deck equipment, rigging, sails and big booms just waiting to injure, were just as bad as the smaller yachts and sometimes even worse. Dudley found many ill placed spray hoods and biminis whose only use seemed to be to bang your head against. Some of the biminis were placed to keep the cockpit in shade but left the helm open to full sunshine. I found this a particularly strange phenomenon, as each member of the crew is free to move around, barring one- the person at the helm. Why would a yacht have a shade that covered everything except the one area it was essential to shade, the helm?

To draw my personal ramblings of discovery to a close, we concluded that the purchase of a yacht and its size boils down to 'horses for courses'. If you have the money and can afford the marina fees, repairs and cleaning bills then I guess you don't care about wasted space and teak decks. On the other hand, if you have chosen to live aboard and have a tight budget to keep to, every little bit of space that can make your lifestyle more comfortable is at premium. Neither Dudley nor I had thought about any of these things up until the point of taking on this work.

When we had bought *Orpheus* our only criteria had been a double cabin and heads forward and aft, to allow privacy when visitors came and for the anchor windlass to be electric, so poor Dud didn't have to break his back pulling it up all the time. In addition, we knew we wanted roller-reefing genoa and in-mast furling for the mainsail so we didn't have to worry about walking around the decks and manually putting in reefs in rough weather. Having lived on board through a winter we now knew just how lucky we had been with our first purchase but would add a few additional wishes to this list.

Our work slowed and suddenly summer was upon us. Our lives looked slightly better than it did in spring and we began to look forward to the first visits by family and friends.

Ligia Lefkada winter sunrise

My baby Harry

The Olympic flame

Rescued swallow "Bertie"

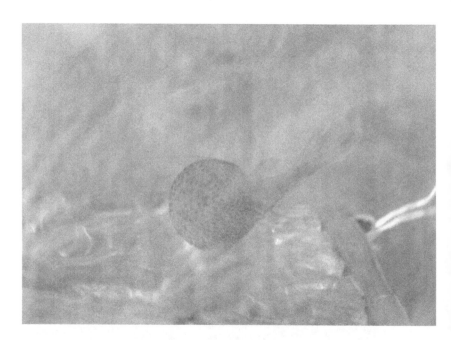

Purple jelly fish

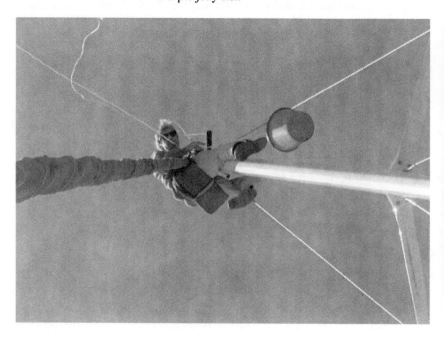

Norfolk friend "Neil"

Local "Red Fsiherman" Lefkas mole

Dud and I scraping *Orpheus* hull

Harry at home on board

Nidri waterfalls, Lefkada

Harry and I at Nidri Falls

View across Athens

Family of three set sail

CHAPTER 19
MAY AND JUNE!

The sun was shining and Dudley and I were on the way to the airport at Preveza to collect Captain Pete who was coming out to start his summer sailing. It was going to be the first time we had seen any of our friends or family since leaving England, which had been nearly eight months ago. Dud, Harry and I stood at the Arrivals door waiting for Peter to come through and it was with great excitement and glee that I hugged and kissed him. It's rude to stare but when you've missed someone very much when you first get to meet them again it's a natural thing to do.

It was so strange; it was the same Captain Pete yet he looked so pale. It had always been the other way around before and he would be collecting us and we had been the pale faces. It never occurred to me that as Dudley and I had been working in the sunshine we had gained golden tans. Well, mine was golden; Dudley's was more a deeper, darker brown. Anyway after the initial shock we spent a great evening hearing all the news from England about our friends, acquaintances, road changes and buildings erected in our home city of Norwich and caught up on all the gossip.

We only had a few days with Peter before my mother, June, and father, Bernard, were due to arrive and we were going to take them out sailing. I was somewhat apprehensive about this, as, busy working, we hadn't had a chance to get back into the swing of sailing after our winter. It really felt as though we had never sailed before. I struggled to remember knots and all the things we had practiced. I only hoped, once under way, that our sailing together would go a little better than before, because neither Mother nor Father knew how to sail. Father would be quick to learn being an ex-matelot, but Mother was a different kettle of fish.

We had had some wonderful spring weather and it was 'sod's law' that the day my parents were due to arrive we had some horrendous rainfall and a thunderstorm. I had visions of them coming into land in the middle of the storm and thought about my mother's white knuckles, as the blood supply would surely be cut off by my father gripping her hand too tightly. He was not a very good air traveller and coming into land in such weather conditions might just finish him off.

I should not have worried, as by midday the storm had passed and by 1400 hours the sun was out and had dried up all the rain and the itsy-bitsy spider climbed up the spout again! As all this was going on, Dudley and I were on the way to the airport in the car and were eagerly looking forward to seeing my parents. It was absolute torture waiting for them to collect their luggage. I stood with my faced pressed to the glass panels lining the walls at the arrivals lounge. I could see them but could not hear or touch them. At last they came through the doors and, shaking with excitement and crying tears for joy, I hugged and kissed them both. I had missed them more than I had realised and I seemed unwilling to let go of them for a very long time.

Although we had been in touch almost every day via text message or email it obviously wasn't enough. It was good to see them looking well, even if they did seem to have this very sallow pallor that all the English people arriving seemed to have. I was beginning to understand that we had become so used to looking at Mediterranean skin types that remained tanned and olive all year round that these pale creatures arriving on these first flights from the U.K. really did look quite ill.

We were soon in the car on the way to *Orpheus* and Mother was telling me all her news. I had spent all morning frantically cleaning the inside and outside of the boat as this was going to be the first time they would see her and I wanted them to be impressed with my new home. I wanted them to be able to understand why we had chosen to leave a big house in England and live in a tiny boat in Greece. For some strange, childish reason I was seeking their approval of my new life and wanted them to enjoy it too. By the time we had reached the boat it was starting to feel like we had never been apart.

Once on board, the beers were broken out and the cottage pie was put to heat in the oven. My culinary skills were about to be fully tested as my father is one of the fussiest to feed and the oven was still not working very well! The sun was shining, birds were singing and father was beginning to relax. He got his very pale, hairy chest out and reclined. Mother was looking a little more apprehensive and was obviously already trying to combat the psychological warfare of seasickness.

After a day of rest to recover from the travelling from the U.K. we made ready to go for our first sail of the season. Alas, the forecasted wind did not appear which meant we arrived under power at Spartachori. As always the brothers came out to greet us and help with the mooring process. Mother and Father must have thought we did really well as they seemed rather impressed. We were both rather humble with our efforts as we were very aware of our inability and inexperience. This could not be said about the flotilla sailors we were meeting along the way.

It was still relatively quiet being the start of the season but we found it then, and still do now, very strange why people hiring a completely strange boat, sail off with little or no tuition, create havoc and then seem to be very proud of their sailing prowess. We had now been living on board for some time, knew our boat inside out and had some experience sailing together, more than the average holidaymaker. Still, we were hesitant about our abilities. If only I knew where they got their arrogance and confidence from I would go and buy a big bag of it to keep for myself.

A short trip the following day took us to a reunion barbecue at a little bay around the corner called Abeleki. This had been arranged so that all the yachties who had wintered together in Levkas could meet up again to celebrate the start of the sailing season. We thought it would be a lovely idea for us to attend as my parents could then meet some of the people we had spent our time with since leaving England.

Just as we arrived in the bay Dud suggested I helm, saying he would lay the anchor. I was not too keen on this idea for two reasons: one I still didn't like the helm wheel, and second, we had never done it this way before and now I was going to have my first attempt in front of my parents and a harbour full of seasoned yachties. I felt the pressure of many pairs of eyes watching me. Getting very hot under the collar and taking a couple of goes at getting used to reversing, I became very angry when I did it perfectly and Dud had been so busy watching me that he had forgotten he was supposed to be laying the anchor. Out we went again and this time managed to drop the anchor and reverse up to the shore. The anchor dug in well but the wind was on our aft quarter, so until Dud and Dad managed to get a shoreline secured, our stern was drifting quite close to the boat next door. Luckily it was a very nice chap named Tony who we had met through the winter, and, understanding our plight, he kindly kept a watchful eye.

Dad and Dud took to the dinghy taking our shoreline with them. Dud climbed out onto the rocky shore, avoiding the sea urchins' spikes and the pretty looking, purple jellyfish that seemed to be infesting the spring waters in the bay. Once Dud had tied the warp to a tree and was back in the dinghy, my father thought it would be a good idea to pull himself along the rope back to the boat as opposed to rowing. This would have been a good idea apart from two things: one was that I had not tightened the rope on board and thus, although it looked quite tight, it was not, and second he decided to stand up!

As he stood and took hold of the rope, the rope gave way with his weight and the upward motion caused the dinghy to move away from him. The result of this left my father hanging on the rope with his hands, his body completely horizontal to the water and his toenails clinging onto the dinghy. Below him was nothing but the cold spring seawater and all that it held. Mother and I watched and waited for the splash but it never came. I didn't know my father could be so agile. He somehow managed to claw the dinghy back with his toes whilst holding the rope and got his backside on the edge. At this point Dud's reactions kicked in and he pulled him back into the dinghy. This had all happened in a split second and as we looked on, being the kind hearted and caring people my mother and I are, we burst out laughing which, for some reason, continued for quite some time.

After the excitement of the near early swim we went to the barbecue. Mike and Janet being a couple that always made you feel comfortable, soon broke the ice. What they said to us this day I shall never forget and shall always be eternally grateful for. As complete strangers to the yachting community it was always going to be very difficult for my parents to fit in and hold conversations with people with whom they have nothing in common. Janet stood in welcome and said very proudly, "Come and take a seat. Please, don't worry about us. We're the grotty yachties not the snotty yachties!" In other words we are just like you, not like the hooray henries that cock little pinkies over cocktails on the aft deck and look down their noses at the peasants as they pass. From that moment on my parents and I relaxed and enjoyed the afternoon.

It was nice to see Bill and Laurel Cooper, renowned authors and fellow East coast people from Norfolk, there. Mother liked the look of their barge named Hosanna and it took me a long time to explain that it needed experience, time and money to be able to handle such a big beast. "All in good time," I said. "Let us get used to this one first!" Being as generous as they always were, the Coopers opened their boat to everyone present for drinks on board that evening, but unfortunately we had other plans.

The following morning we had to motor to Vassiliki as the wind remained elusive. Father was disappointed as he was really looking forward to a sail but I believe Mother was grateful for the gentle easing into the motion of the boat. Back to our normal routine whereby Dudley takes the helm and I drop the anchor, we came into the harbour for a stern-to approach. Usually Dud made a good call as to the distance off the quay but this time he laid it offset over the top of a neighbouring yacht. As if this was not bad enough when we came to tie up to the quayside the result of the ill-placed anchor resulted in us not being at right angles to the quay. This was something that, for some reason, annoyed me immensely.

Just as we were trying to straighten ourselves out and get ourselves secured, a young couple of holidaymakers started asking questions and wanted to get Harry ashore so they could make a fuss of him. Unfortunately, Mother started to bask in the glory of the cooing over Harry and started making moves to get off the boat before we had even tied up. She just stepped off the passerelle not even looking to see if it was on the quay. Luckily it was! I was already angry at Dud for not mooring correctly and now Mother was getting Harry into very bad habits by insisting on taking him straight ashore and not making him wait. We would pay for that when they were gone as he would still be expecting the same treatment and wouldn't get it. Things were not going well and the situation had not improved when I pointed out that the forecasted wind of NW 5, expected later that evening, would create a problem. As we had dropped the anchor too far to the East it would be rendered useless when the wind came. We immediately put a spring out to try to keep us straight and safe but in hindsight what we should have done was upped anchor and started the process again, preferably laying the anchor upwind so it would have a good hold when the winds came. We all love hindsight. Shame we don't have it in advance!

That evening the wind got up badly and as our anchor did nothing to help hold the boat off the quay, we were not safe at all. When the following morning arrived a yacht left from beside us. The forecast indicated bad winds all day, so we made the decision to pull up the anchor and come alongside bows into the wind. The first attempt was aborted as the wind proved too much for Dud to control the helm. He went round again and this time we managed to get the bow line on, but instead of immediately throwing the stern line to Father, Dud would not let go of the helm. The upshot was the wind took the bow with great force and smashed it into the quayside. A secure stern line would have prevented this, so once again I was shouting at Dud and pointing out that once alongside with a line ashore, he could let go of the helm and help.

Poor Dud. I have such strong ideas about what should happen that if something goes wrong I get quite upset. My parents must have wondered what on earth was going on as I was throwing a tantrum for the second time. I was again grateful that we had invested in an over-engineered strong boat and one that did not cost thousands of pounds. Accidents will happen and the bigger and more luxurious the boat, the more money it costs to repair. One little scratch to *Orpheus* wouldn't devalue her much but had it been a new shining example, the re-sale price would have dropped, not to mention the extra worry factor involved. At least we were now safe and we managed to spend a nice day on the beach, watching the wind surfers' skimming up and down beside the cliff face.

The following day the wind had dropped enough for us to consider going sailing but we found it near impossible to get ourselves off the quay wall as other yachts had come alongside and moored too close to us. Having made one attempt, the yacht in front realising our dilemma, came to our assistance. Using a big ball fender on our stern quarter, Father released the bowline and Dud used the engine to steer away from the wall. As the stern line was still secured, the bow came out and the boat rolled against the fender. The stern line was quickly released and we were clear to go forwards. I felt somewhat useless about all this and was confused as to what was happening, as I had never seen a manoeuvre like this before. Sailors who are experienced in coming alongside learn these tricks very quickly but the only sailing I had experienced involved stern-to mooring. There was obviously much to learn. One thing was certain in my mind-when our financial situation improved we would invest in one if not two of the big ball fenders.

We had decided to set sail for our little bay at Frikes on the island of Ithaca but I had given little thought to the wind of the previous days. The winds had left but the swell remained and the direction of travel meant that this was on the beam giving a rolling motion. If I had given it some thought we could have headed in a different direction, but as it was, poor Mother started to feel a little jaded.

We arrived and anchored in the bay around lunchtime with Mother not feeling too good. We dropped the anchor, ensuring it was dug in correctly, and were very conscious of a dinghy on shore and three men standing and watching us. They never said a word to us but just stared. This is not very unusual as, for some reason, people like to watch a yacht coming into moor so we thought nothing of it. It was only once we turned our engine off and were making ready to take a shoreline that they shouted at us to move somewhere else as they were about to retrieve their anchor which had been fouled and abandoned! Now why didn't they say something before? Why had they waited until we had finished mooring and turned our engine off? Some people can be really perverse.

I shouted back that we were staying the night and that they were welcome to dive underneath. Dud at this point became more interested in what these gentlemen were doing instead of finishing securing *Orpheus*. In the afternoon wind a seesaw motion began and I was not happy. It had been our experience that this motion tended to wriggle loose the anchor on a sandy bottom, yet Dud seemed to be making no effort to make us safe. I started to complain and he ignored me so I complained louder, "*Orpheus* is more important. First we secure our boat then you can show an interest in other people's". I was clearly talking to myself as Dud had rowed ashore to watch these chaps retrieve an anchor from the seabed that wasn't even theirs and then he decided to take our shoreline. By this time I knew it was going to be too late. He had left us yawing side to side for much too long.

Within ten minutes of the shoreline being put on I noticed we were getting closer to the shore. The wind started to pick up quite quickly and I started the engine just in time to stop us going aground. We pulled up the anchor and Dud went ashore to get our line as I motored in circles waiting to retrieve him. We tried to head towards the harbour at Frikes but soon realised that the wind was too much and that trying to moor there was going to be very difficult. I doubted our abilities as I found our inexperience and lack of knowledge worrying. Had we been experienced we probably would have headed for the harbour and taken everything in our stride, but as it was, I looked in the pilot book for the nearest safe anchorage for the wind conditions and this took us back to Sivota on Lefkada.

As navigator I made the decision to turn back the way we had come, take the wind on our aft quarter and get to the very protected little bay at Sivota. Of course what this also meant was that Mother, who had survived the trip across by the skin of her teeth, was now going to have to relive it. This time she was aware of the sea conditions out there so she was already losing the psychological battle and was settling herself down to be sick before we had even left. To her credit, she held on very bravely as we crossed. She turned all shades of colour from white to grey to green and back again but actually wasn't ill at all.

We arrived at Sivota with a savage crosswind; more than I had anticipated in this bay, but there was quay space and we were going to have to get the anchor laid and get quayside. We followed our normal routine of dropping the anchor, digging it in and then, as Father was there to throw the shore lines for me, I could stay with the anchor and lock it off to hold us when Dud gave the order. Dud helmed us in against the cross wind, keeping the bow slightly into the wind for better steerage and everything went so smoothly I couldn't believe it; we were even square on to the quay! After the last two days of such bad helming and things going wrong, I was very relieved.

My relief was soon overtaken with anger, however, as Dud turned round to us all and said, "Well done crew that was very well done!" I know he was only saying this to cheer us and in some kind of relief that all had gone well but I couldn't help but feel congratulations were condescending. It was at this moment I realised that the role of Captain had still not been clarified aboard *Orpheus* and Dudley was vying for position. Well, I wasn't too happy about that. He would have to prove himself to me first.

We spent a restful day in Sivota, allowing Mother a day's respite from the sailing. We took the opportunity of a quick boat clean whilst my parents took a long walk around the bay. All was quiet and peaceful until approximately three o'clock that afternoon. As we sat contemplating having a deck shower a flotilla of four boats, sporting huge big yellow flags, came in. The lead yacht made to drop his anchor two boats up from us when a man standing on the bow of his boat bellowed, "You can't drop your anchor there idiot. Can't you see? Can't you ***** see where you are going? You're over my anchor." The abuse was such that the anchoring yacht left the spot and anchored further down the quay.

The rest of the flotilla moored their boats and the final one made ready to come alongside us. The lady at the helm told us that this was the first time she was bringing a yacht in astern and as such we tried to encourage her as much as possible. This was still something that I had not tried. She eventually brought the yacht close enough to us and I called for the man standing on the deck to throw me the mooring line so we could walk them in. The first throw missed, so my father shouted, "Harder!"

With that the line was re-thrown and this time it hit my father directly in the face. There was a gasp and a grunt from him and a profuse apology from the man throwing the line who said, "Sorry your voice sounded further away than that." It was at this point I realised that the man was sight impaired.

After all the flotilla yachts were moored, the chap who had received the verbal abuse came to introduce himself and thanked us for assisting the yacht next door. It transpired that that ignorant and very drunk "rotty yachtie" had been shouting, "Can't you see?" at a flotilla of Guide Dogs for the Blind yachts. All crew members except the skippers were partially sighted and sight impaired, I wondered how this yachtie felt now and I hoped he felt very small indeed. There are ways and mean of communicating displeasure and we had just witnessed one of the worst examples, I tried to learn from his mistake and promised myself next time we had a sailing debate on board *Orpheus* I would try to remain a little calmer.

Whilst Mother was treated to the delights of her first deck shower the yacht alongside took its crew swimming in pairs and washed down the boats. If we hadn't known any different we could have been forgiven for thinking they could all see perfectly. They walked with perfect confidence around the decks and looked far more professional at what they were doing than we did. What we felt cannot be described without fear of sounding condescending but on board *Orpheus* we were humbled and felt great admiration for these fellow sailors.

The following day we were off again, heading towards Little Vathi on the island of Meganisi. Captain Pete had been in touch to say that Liz had arrived in Levkas and they would be heading towards Vathi so we were hoping to meet up. Again, there was very little wind and most of the day's travel had been by motor. We arrived without mishap at Little Vathi even though the stern of the boat was at 25 degrees to the quay instead of 90! Being grateful for small mercies I said nothing, thought of my new resolve and bit my tongue.

As the day wore on, I started to think that Peter and Liz were not going to be able to get to Vathi but late afternoon Admetus appeared in the harbour. By this time there was no room left at the quay but due to our jaunty angle we managed to pull ourselves across which made just enough room for Captain Pete to squeeze *Admetus* in. Together again at last, *Admetus* with *Orpheus*, my parents, Dud and I with Liz and Peter, the evening was looking to be a very good one.

We decided prior to our evening meal to take a walk from the harbour up the mountainous valley to a village (Xora) at the top. Harry made a valiant effort of walking with us but his legs held him back badly these days. The walk back down was better for him as his legs freewheeled underneath him. As we walked and talked we made a plan to set sail for Paleros the following day and in a moment of madness I decided to challenge Captain Peter to a race across. At this his face lit up and a gleam came to his eye as it glinted at the challenge. Pleased at the reaction I had incited, I fuelled it further by saying, "I'll whup your butt."

The body language changed, his feet parted, his hands went to his hips and the glint in the eye had a little flash of red in it as his reply came, "Right. You're on." His head gave a determined nod and the tight-lipped smile only hinted at the thoughts he was having.

Anybody who knew Captain Pete also knew never to throw down a gauntlet unless you were able to go through with the duel. Admetus was first to leave the mooring and Peter and Liz waited in the entrance to the harbour as *Orpheus* joined her. "Ready to race?" he called across.

"You bet," I answered.

Our captain gave us room, as he made ready to hoist up his mainsail and unfurl his genoa. Then he was off in no time at all. Dudley was at our helm as my father pulled out our genoa which should have given us a port tack that would take us all the way to Paleros, so why were we moving so quickly towards the rocks? I checked the helm and found that Dud had been too busy watching what everyone else was doing instead of paying attention to his responsibilities and he had left the engine in forward drive! This meant we were now not sailing in the direction we should have been headed and had put ourselves too close to the wind to be able to take the trip on one tack.

We put in two quick tacks, brought ourselves into a better position and settled for the long haul across. We had decided to use only the genoa, as we didn't want to heel too much and risk upsetting Mother's stomach. After our shaky start and the halved sail power it seemed as though *Admetus* was already miles away from us but I was determined we were going to catch up. The sun was shining and the wind was just right. It was a perfect day for a sail; not too much wind but just enough to make it fun. We appeared to be gaining some ground. I started getting excited and then we gained some more ground and I looked through the binoculars to see what our captain was doing wrong that we should be gaining on him. Not a thing was going wrong, I noticed that he had let his sails out a little and that *Admetus* was sitting flat in the water with very little heel. He had taken the speed out of his sails and was gently cruising along at half speed and we still couldn't catch him!

As we were getting closer he pulled the sails in again and off he went. Half way across the stretch of water that lies between Lefkada, Meganisi and the mainland I noticed that Captain Pete put in a tack, "What on earth for?" I was questioning as he was heading straight for where we were going. Then I realised, as he put in another tack that we were lagging so far behind again that he was now sailing back towards us with the wind on his aft quarter! Now talk about rubbing salt in the wound! He sailed up to us with a smile on his face that definitely made him look like the cat that not only ate this morning's cream but had also managed to find the milkman and had eaten tomorrow's as well.

"You don't need to give me a chance," I shouted over. "We're still gonna get there first."

There was absolutely no chance we were ever going to beat *Admetus*. She was a perfect sailing boat, thirty-two feet, light and had a very experienced captain at the helm. *Orpheus* was also a perfect sailing boat but she was forty feet, heavy and had Dudley and I to contend with! A deep guttural laugh was intermingled with the sound of flapping sails as Captain Pete tacked again and was just in front of us heading in the right direction again. I was sure that I could hear Liz telling Peter off for being so competitive and saying, "Take your hands off your hips."

Admetus disappeared and we kept heading up into the wind until we finally got to Paleros. When we arrived *Admetus* was already moored at the quayside and I was all of a sudden very nervous. This would be the first time Peter had seen us come into moor. I wanted everything to be right and I hoped that Dudley was not going to do anything silly.

He didn't. In fact he could not have done it more perfectly if he tried. Dudley began reversing and called for me to drop the anchor. I dropped twenty metres and dug it in. Father threw the mooring lines and the next thing I knew we were tied up, square to the quay, the anchor secured and it had all gone so well. I can't explain the relief and pleasure it gave me to have it all come together so well and in front of my Captain Pete. I was feeling so proud that I almost forgot that he had well and truly "whupped" us at the race. Not that I will ever admit to it in public or during conversation but my Captain and *Admetus* could have gone to Paleros and back twice and still beaten us into the mooring! Maybe next time I shall keep my gauntlet tight in my hand where it belongs and put all thoughts of bravado behind me.

The following day we took our towels and spent the day lying on the beach. It was a small, sandy beach, partly used for boat maintenance by the local fishermen. Still early in the season, the water was cool, but we had been expecting this as we had already experienced the skin numbing experience whilst we were in Vathi. Being a wimp this time, I had come prepared with a wetsuit jacket to keep me warm.

Having had my exercise, I took Harry down to the water in an ongoing attempt to get him to take to swimming. Once his front paws were in the water he soon turned around and made back towards the towels. I lifted him up whilst holding him tight to me and walked out into the water. As soon as he could see water underneath him his front legs started to paddle as if he was in the water so when I actually bent down to let him loose he was already swimming at full pelt! As I was doing this, two gentlemen came to the water's edge with a little black and tan wire coated Dachshund. The minute this little dog saw the water it ran across the sand and dived straight in. *This was just what I needed*, I thought. Harry loves other dogs and I hoped he would see this all happening and would want to go and be with the other dog and play. No such luck. He just ran up and down the sand, barking and waiting for the other dog to get out.

Watching the Dachshund, I was amazed by how much it enjoyed the water. It swam straight out to sea with no fear and was obviously enjoying every second. As he approached the little waves he would open his mouth and bite each wave as it passed and then swim straight on. Dudley and I stood laughing when we noticed the gentlemen had the dog on a very, very, very long length of rope. Once at the end of the rope the men started to pull the dog back in to shore but as they were doing it the dog was still swimming out to sea. We asked why they had the dog on a line and they explained the dog loved to swim so much that unless they pulled it back on the line it would just keep swimming straight out! They landed the dog like most men would a fish and even as its feet were touching sand it was still trying its hardest to swim back out to sea. Seeing us laughing, they let the dog have a little slack on the line and it was straight back in swimming hard out towards Meganisi. As if this hadn't been the cutest thing we had ever seen when we went back to the boat, we saw the gentlemen rig up a hose and shower head to a water tap and the dog walked over to stand underneath the shower to be rinsed off. It all seemed so natural that I would not have been surprised to see it lift a paw and clean under its armpits!

Dudley lit a barbecue on the quayside that evening and

we spent a starlit night eating and drinking. Special friendships are so hard to find and this evening, in my mellow mood induced by red wine, I realised that I had three special friendships all around me, all of them different. There was Peter and Liz who were true friends and people that I never wanted to be without. I found their company a great joy and as people they were caring and sharing and very lovable. Then there was Dudley, not just a husband but also a very special friend who shared my whole life, thoughts and soul. Finally there were my parents, no longer just mediums of authority and learning, but friends. There was certainly a big bubble of love surrounding the quayside over *Admetus* and *Orpheus* that evening.

The following morning we said our goodbyes. We had to head back to Levkas as a cleaning job waited for me and Liz had the remainder of her holiday to enjoy. On the short trip from Paleros to Levkas, Father took the helm. Dudley decided it was time to tack and my father looked at me with a look of horror on his face saying, "I can't do that you had better take the wheel."

Well, little did he know that I still found it difficult to helm with a wheel and had little confidence in doing this myself but I did not let this show and I dug deep into my memory banks and in a clear, confident voice, just as Captain Pete had said to me, I told him verbatim what I had been told some five years before.

"You are on a port tack with the wind just fore of the beam. To tack you bring the bow through the wind until the wind is on the starboard side. To know where to aim for, look over your left shoulder and take a landmark on what you see. When you turn the wheel, aim directly for the landmark. Dudley will pull the sails across and you will be sailing on the other tack."

"Tell me when," said Father.

"No," I said, "You tell us as you are at the helm. When you are ready say, "Ready about" and as you turn the wheel you call, "Leeward ho."

It was wonderful. Father called his first "Lee ho"; Dudley pulled the sail across and we were sailing off on a starboard tack just like that. It was perfect and Father's smile matched his obvious satisfaction. I knew that feeling, I could see in his face the joy and excitement that I had felt when I first managed it on *Admetus* and I wondered if Captain Pete had felt as proud of me as I did of my father.

We made three more tacks on the journey towards the Levkas canal and all went well even when Father over steered and missed his land mark; he was quick to bring it back. I knew I must have got my sailing genes from somewhere and he definitely had the hands for it. The disappointment in his face was undisguised when the sails had to come down and we were motoring up the canal. In a blink of an eye we were back on Joe's mole securely moored with a lazy line and twelve days of my parent's holiday had passed.

After a day of thunderstorms, cleaning and a car trip to Nidri, the weather cleared up somewhat and we took a drive to Kathisma beach. We had an empty beach all to ourselves with golden sand, blue seas and scenery to take your breath away. Being with my parents on a beach brought back lots of memories from my childhood and my father nearly choked on a cherry when I asked him to help me dig a hole. Any parent reading will understand that this is something that just has to be done when visiting the beach with a child. After all, I was still their baby. After hole digging, Dud burying, stone skimming and chasing Harry, I was ready to sit down for a minute or two.

I found it hard to believe that my parents would have to return home the following day. After months of anticipation and waiting to see them they had now been, seen and conquered, soon to be packing to leave. It had all gone so quickly and the thought that we would not see each other again for a long time was a sad one. The next morning arrived all too quickly and before we knew it we were saying goodbye at the airport. Hugs, kisses and tears were in abundance and it was with a heavy heart that went back to a very empty boat.

It was lucky for us that things had been planned for a quick turn round. As we waved goodbye to my parents, we knew we had two good friends, John and Diane, coming to stay with us for a fortnight and we only had two days to get up to Corfu to collect them. This gave Dudley and me lots to think about and little time to sit and mope, which was good for both of us. I set about cleaning the boat inside and out and Dud checked the engine and equipment making sure we would be safe for the 60 mile journey north.

CHAPTER 20
ANEMOSTROVILOS

Still having a few things we needed to do, we left Levkas later than we had anticipated. We had originally planned to pass through the ten o'clock opening of the Levkas bridge but due to the port police keeping Dudley waiting for so long whilst he booked us out we missed this bridge and had to wait another hour until eleven o'clock when we managed to make it through.

In no time at all we were out of the shelter of land and there was sufficient wind for us to sail. At first we were making good headway but the wind dropped a little as midday approached and we were only making four knots speed. The feeling of being out sailing and in such good conditions lulled us into a false sense of security. We were so enjoying the sailing that we lost sight of the distance we had to cover that day.

We had planned to stop half way at Gaios on the island of Paxos, which was approximately thirty miles, and then head for Corfu the following day. But as I did the navigation that afternoon at around 1600 hours, I realised that for the hours of daylight left we were still a long way from our destination. It only took a quick calculation to work out that if we did not stop sailing, put the engine on and motor into our mooring, we were going to be out sailing in the dark- something which neither of us was very keen on doing. We agreed the sensible thing to do was to increase our speed under motor and get ourselves to Gaios. This we managed just as it was getting dusk, but all was not going to go well for us.

As usual Dudley set the anchor ready for me to drop and I had put out the fenders and prepared the mooring lines. We were all ready for our mooring procedure but were having trouble finding a space along the quayside. We were somewhat perturbed because Gaios, although well protected and a very beautiful little place, was very narrow and if we couldn't find any space at the quay there was no room to anchor off.

We motored along the length of the quay and saw no room. However Dud had noticed that a particular yacht had moored rather badly and was actually taking up two spaces. He decided this was going to be the spot we would moor in and we would "make some room" between these two moored yachts. He brought *Orpheus* round, minding the shallows ahead of us, and lined up to come into reverse. As he did this there was a strange revving and his face set in a serious look. He looked me straight in the eyes and said in one of the calmest voices I have ever heard, "We have no reverse gear."

I didn't know what to think. Was he joking? Was he serious? "What?" was all I could manage to say in reply.

As he fiddled with the gear lever he said, "We don't have any forward gear either."

"What?" I said again with a little more feeling and a sense of doom setting in.

More fiddling with the helm and, still very calm and collected, he announced, "In fact we don't have any drive at all."

"WHAT!" At this my heart rate increased tenfold and my legs were thinking about turning into jelly.

No time to panic with Dudley in charge. "Just take the helm a minute," he said and disappeared down below to the engine, which is situated behind the companionway steps. I stood at the helm watching *Orpheus* drift nearer the shallows and although I was trying to helm it was having little effect without any engine power. No engine, adrift in a narrow channel and Dud cheerfully called up, "The gear cable has snapped. You'll have to bring us into an alongside mooring whilst I pull on the cable from down here."

"WHAT... NO WAY."

After a second of explanation Dud showed me where to press when he told me to and he would helm. We had spotted a tripper boat just ahead of us and he thought he could bring *Orpheus* alongside it. I had dipped out of helming in preference to sticking my hands inside a red hot and oily engine with cogs, wheels and cables. I only hoped I would still have all my fingers by the time we had finished. "Now," Dud shouted and I pressed the lever connected to the cable. "Enough... a little more...nearly there." At this I looked up and saw that we were very close to the tripper boat and that I could catch it with a lasso. I quickly shut the companionway door and ran up the stairs and to the bow. I picked up the mooring line just as Dud had brought us level with the bow of the tripper boat. As quick as a flash, I threw the line and managed to lasso a raised wooden cleat and secured us to it. I ran back to the stern and did the same there and let out a sigh of relief. We were safe.

It was now almost completely dark and I was very conscious that we were tied up to a tripper boat and the owner was nowhere in sight. We had done this without asking permission and the ethics of this was all wrong. Dud set about looking at the engine and I went ashore and started asking where the owner of the boat was. I located him having a nice cold beer in the front of a taverna right by his boat; he had sat and watched the whole thing! I explained we had engine problems and asked if it was okay for us to stay alongside him overnight and that we would be gone first thing in the morning. He agreed to this and seemed pleased that we had made the effort to ask.

I went back to tell Dudley who reported that the cable was snapped, completely irreparable and that we needed another. He went out in search of a yacht repair service and came back with a rather plump, elderly chap who agreed with Dudley's diagnosis and said that he would be back at 0900 hours the following day to fix the problem. We couldn't believe our luck and, for the first time in many hours, we relaxed with a glass of wine and realised it was almost 2300 hours and time for bed.

0900 hours arrived the following day and there was no sign of the mechanic. I guess he must have forgotten to warn us that he was working in G.M.T. (Greek Maybe Time). I noticed that people were starting to congregate by the side of the tripper boat and panic was beginning to set in. The tripper obviously was going out; we were still tied alongside and the owner would want us to be gone. We asked what time the trip was and he indicated 1030 hours but we were not to worry. What did he know that we didn't?

No sign of the mechanic and 1030 arrived. By now I was cleaning everything in sight; polishing, washing and scrubbing anything rather that think about the fact that the time had arrived for us to be gone and we still had no engine. Then another thought occurred to me: if we were not fixed and gone by 12 midday we would not be able to get to Corfu in time to meet

John and Diane's flight. Worse still, if we couldn't get the part and get it fixed we may have to stay until the following day which meant that John and Diane would have to book into a hotel for the night. I warned Dud about what all this meant and he sent a text to John letting him know what had happened.

As we waited and I worked around the boat I noticed that a local policeman arrived to move a car that had been parked along the quayside. I asked a man sitting by the tripper boat what this was all about and he explained that the quayside was a no parking area. I voiced my amazement that the Greek police bothered with such things as I had always been given the impression that they would let such things slip by. He explained that this may have been the case five or six years previously but now they were very strict with road violations and did not tolerate drunk driving. I was glad to see and hear it and hoped that the RTA (Road Traffic Accident) statistics might be improved in the future.

As we spoke, I explained to the man that the last time I had come to Gaios I had fallen and smashed my face requiring a trip to the local Doctor Kostas. It had been just over a year since I had taken this fall and now in the same place our gear cable had snapped. I suggested to the man that this must be my cursed place and he said, "No, this is a beautiful place and I think the next time you come, the third time, maybe things will be better." Obviously they have a similar saying in Greece as we have in England: "Third time lucky!" I couldn't disagree with his comments though. It was a beautiful place and even though we had had some awful things happen there we had always met some wonderful people and been treated with great courtesy.

As we talked the people booked for the day trip all stood and started to walk towards the boat and then, to my relief, walked past it and to the next boat. As there were only a few people the tripper man was taking out his smaller boat, which meant that we were safe to stay where we were. Just as this relief was setting in, a young man named Dimitrios appeared to say that he was the son of the man we had seen yesterday. He was the engineer and he had come to fix the cable.

By 1100 hours Dudley was up to his armpits in the engine and back cabin and the young man was in the cockpit taking apart the gear lever. I made myself busy and got ready to sail, as the minute the repair was finished we would be off. By

1215 hours the cable had been replaced and I started putting all our things back in the rear cabin ready to leave. Dud paid the bill and we left a thank you note and a bottle of wine for the tripper boat captain. By 1230 hours the engine was roaring into life and we were off.

Because of the lateness of the day we dared not risk sailing to Corfu. The winds were light and we did not have the time to spare. We were looking at six hours motoring at 5 knots or longer if we chose to sail. We kept the motor running and were determined we would get there in time to meet John and Diane when they arrived. We came into Garitsas Bay in good time and laid our anchor close to some steps up the quayside. We were conscious that there would be suitcases to load into the dinghy and it seemed the sensible thing to be as close to some stairs as we could manage.

There was a rolling swell into the bay as it was quite open but the anchor was holding well and from the height of the aircraft coming overhead we knew that we were very close to the airfield. After a quick shower Dudley went off to find the airport and to meet John and Diane's flight, which, luckily, was on time. Suitcases and friends on board, we settled down to a drink and a chat. I laughed and reminded John of his text message about us camping in Belgium on the way out to Greece. After a few more drinks I was treated to the best rendition, with actions, of "There was a dog, a little dog, who cocked his leg so high; he cocked his leg, he cocked his leg, so high it reached the sky!" We had missed them more than we thought and were looking forward to the following fortnight with them both.

In the morning, after a relaxed breakfast, we started our reciprocal journey. This time we had decided to stop at Parga on mainland Greece which was an approximate half way mark. There was little to no wind, which disappointed us as John and Diane really loved to sail and we wanted John's opinion on how best to set our mainsail. We had not been able to stop the leech flapping, no matter what we did, and we valued his opinion. Having completed the navigation we all took it in turns to helm and it was only as we neared our destination and there was nothing in sight that I began to worry. I desperately did not want to embarrass myself in front of John as his experience far outweighed ours and I did not want him to think he had come on holiday with an idiot.

All we had in front of us was a rock face and nothing else to be seen. The more I checked our position with the GPS and plotted where we were the more I knew there must be something there as we were in the right place. There was still nothing evident and I was starting to get a little unnerved when suddenly a gap appeared. As if by magic, a gap opened up in the middle of the rock face, and as we drew level we could see a large bay tucked inside. We motored in and were amazed at the beauty which was unfolding before us. Bit by bit it opened up to reveal a wonderfully protected bay with crystal blue waters. Mountains surrounded us on all sides and a hotel backed a long, sandy beach with a few shops. It all appeared relatively unspoilt and it appeared to be an excellent choice for our overnight stay.

We tried to moor in the small harbour but there had been no room and manoeuvring inside it made me a little nervous. The depth was only two metres and we had a draft of 1.8 metres! I hoped the harbour hadn't silted up during the winter months as if it had we would surely go aground. Being a very experienced sailor in England and France, John suggested we nudged into the sand and mud on the opposite side of the harbour and spend the night there. I'm sure this is something that he has done a hundred times before but the sound of voluntarily grounding myself went against every bone in my body. We went just outside the harbour and dropped our anchor there.

Just as we had secured ourselves, a water taxi buzzed past asking us if we would like to go ashore. We thanked the gentleman but indicated we were staying on board and if we needed to get ashore we had a dinghy. As he motored away we heard a high-pitched dog bark in the distance. Being a dog lover, my ears are attuned to barks and I recognised immediately the three little Chihuahuas we had spent winter with. A quick look through the binoculars confirmed that Janet and David were indeed anchored next door. We've found over the years that during the winter we make friends and during the summer you will be forever bumping into old and new friends in anchorages when you least expect to see them.

The following day we were making our way back to Levkas and Dud thought it might be fun to trail a fishing line. Not wishing to make a fuss about murder again I sat very quiet until that blood curdling sound of a bell rang out heralding a fish had been caught. I took the opportunity to go below and stay out of sight until the men had killed, cleaned and sliced the fish up and it was dead in the fridge.

We just missed the four o'clock bridge so we heaved to and John and Dud went in for a swim. A warming coffee and a quick trip through the five o'clock bridge saw us back on the mole at Levkas. For the first time since they had arrived, John and Diane were free to walk ashore any time they wished. It had been a very tiring four days for us and I vowed that I would never do it again. The days had been long and tiring and it was such a long way to go to collect visitors. Dud and I agreed that these circumstances had been special to us as we had so wanted to see our friends but in the future it would be a ferry and a coach trip for anyone who flew out to Corfu.

With the worst of our journey over, Dud and I relaxed with our friends and looked at the charts to make a plan for the rest of their holiday. After a fried Tuna breakfast the following day we left Levkas and made our way out of the canal heading south towards Spartachori. The wind was blowing gently and it was exactly what we needed for John to get the sails out and give us an opinion on what was wrong. The genoa was lying slightly on the pulpit and the mainsail was loose in the middle. He tinkered for some time and could not make the main sail fly without luffing but he did not retire defeated. He said he would try again when there was slightly more wind.

We came into Spartachori with the help of the brothers and it was the first time that Dudley and I really considered the difference between sailing in Greece and that in England and France. When Dudley brought us into moor stern to the pontoon John told us that he had never done this before. Small differences in sailing technique were emerging such as tying on fenders. Usually, in England, a yacht would come alongside a pontoon and hence fenders would need to be low. In Greece the protection was needed higher up and amidships as the fenders were needed against the yachts we were mooring next to.

At this time Dudley and I were still going through the initial stages of deciding which of us should be captain. We've found it usual for the males on board to always be the captain but I refused to stand down on the basis of gender. Even when we had attended the Port Police Office on arrival we had faced this problem. A female officer had taken our details and written them on our newly acquired transit log. She looked at me saying,

"You are the owner of the boat?" I had replied in the affirmative. Then she looked at me with a stern glare that warned me not to argue as she said aloud, "Okay, but I say he must be the captain." Well, she could say what she liked as long as I got the paper work but that didn't necessarily mean that I agreed with her sentiments.

Dudley and I were equally qualified and I had enjoyed and wanted to take on the navigation. I knew that I couldn't possibly take on all roles but although Dud said he wanted to take charge he always seemed more interested in other people's yachts than his own. As we sat having a beer in the brothers' taverna our passerelle was banging the quayside, when I pointed this out to Dudley. He simply said, "It doesn't matter." I always seemed to be the one caring for our boat and keeping a watch. Surely this was a role for the captain. I would see and react to things preventing damage and accident but Dud either didn't see or didn't want to see these things. This was an ongoing debate and one I felt would continue for some time into the future.

Captain Pete (now there's a real captain) and Liz came into moor to join us for the last night of her holiday before returning to England. Sensing my frustrations with Dud Liz took me aside and calmed me down. I was going to miss her very much. I missed our chats in the club on Friday nights and I missed the guidance she gave. I missed the sense she made of my thoughts and I missed my girlfriend.

Although a joy, I found the next few days, very testing. Dud being such good friends with John and in awe of his experience found it impossible to assert himself as the captain. I took Dud aside and tried to explain that he was not doing anyone any favours. He knew these waters and had sailed here for many years and he needed to be the captain. It was his yacht and his responsibility. I would have been happy to take on this role but I, too, was respectful of John's experience and I thought taking instruction from a female who had only just passed her Day Skipper Course would be a considerable insult. I tried to encourage Dud by pointing out that the crew on all ships, including us when we had crewed for Steve, looked to the captain for instruction. If it wasn't given, the crew wouldn't know what was expected of them.

We sailed to Vassiliki and spent a lazy day there. John had noticed a fray in the topping lift, which he and Dud cut out, and they replaced the main haul-out. They then quietly took themselves off as John showed Dud how to make an ocean weave mat out of the spare warps. Enjoying themselves immensely, we stayed for a second day and the men hoisted the genoa so that it no longer lay on the pulpit and all the runners and blocks were oiled to allow the sheets to be pulled more freely.

Diane and I chatted and read and enjoyed the sunshine as the male bonding took place. It had been a long time for Dud and he was clearly enjoying having his mate with him and being busy. He says very little about how he misses his friends from home but seeing him together with John spoke volumes; he missed them a lot.

From Vassiliki we sailed to Frikes where we intended staying the night at anchor and having a barbecue ashore. The last time we had been here it was with my parents and we had dragged anchor. Not wishing to repeat the experience, I asked Dud to concentrate and to ensure our boat was safely secured with a shoreline before doing anything else. Anchor dug in and shore line secured, we were as safe as could be.

I decided to go in for a snorkel but could not enjoy it as in the warming shallow water there were swarms of purple jellyfish the size of plums. Dud went into the water to check the bottom of the hull and remove any weed that might have grown and I kept guard, batting any jellyfish away with a broom if they got too close. As we were getting out for lunch and I was helping John out of the water, he swiped at the water in an erratic manner. I looked and saw that he had been stung by one of the jellyfish and it was about to have a second go. I grabbed the broom and shoved it away as John climbed back onboard. I immediately went to the first aid box and gave him two Piriton tablets. I then quickly grabbed the pilot book to see if this particular jellyfish was going to send him into spasm. Luckily it wasn't as its sting was said to be non-life threatening and resembled that of a very bad wasp sting. Within seconds there were big red weals coming up on John's neck, arms and chest. He didn't complain and never even once said, "Ouch". He was my hero. If it had been me I would have been screaming.

At the setting of the sun the wind started to get rather strong so, instead of staying at anchor, we pulled up and went alongside the quay wall in the harbour. By the time we had finished our mooring and settled down with a beer the wind died away again and a peaceful night was had. By this I mean it was peaceful in the sense that there was no wind or swell, not in the number of people and boats. Dudley and I had not been into the harbour at Frikes since we were last with Captain Pete on *Admetus*, which was approximately three years ago, and oh, how it had changed! There were now flotilla boats rafted up four and five boats deep all along the quay. We had never seen it so busy. John told us of his adventures in France when sailing there the previous year with Diane. "This is nothing," he said. "You should see how they raft up there." The thought of this type of rafting and the tidal height changes made me almost cringe. I don't think I could ever cope with this mooring process. I would definitely end up being one of those yachts hanging half way up a quay wall by my mooring lines, waiting for the tide to rise again!

Twenty-four hours of Piriton and John still had big red weals in evidence but felt only a little pain so we set sail for Little Vathi. John set the genoa and it was looking better than it ever had but the mainsail was a different story and on closer inspection he said that the middle had been patched. It was an old sail that had stretched and there was nothing to be done apart from invest in a new one. We were in no financial position to consider doing this so we accepted that we were just going to have to live with the one we had "luff and all".

We arrived at Vathi and the mooring went extremely well for the first time since John and Diane arrived. I had been hinting at Dud about things for days and I was starting to get a complex about what our friends would think of me by the time they got back to England. I liked things to be done in the correct manner and I was trying my hardest to instil this same quality into Dud, but he just didn't seem to care or take charge the way Captain Pete did. I realised the comparison left Dudley with a lot to live up to but I knew deep down he could do it if only he would try. After all, he had proved himself capable during our little drama and crisis in Gaios.

We had arranged to meet up with Captain Pete in Sivota the following day but on the way there the wind blew stronger and stronger and the rains began. When we eventually arrived we decided it would be best to anchor off rather than try to get a mooring on the quay, as the gusts were particularly bad. We motored around the bay, working out where best to lay our anchor in relation to the other yachts and checking depths. I asked Dud to drop it well forward between two yachts and, as if I had not spoken, he started asking John's opinion. John had already explained that he had never anchored off like this and would never dream of doing it in this depth of water in his own yacht. Dud almost seemed like he was trying to make John responsible for a decision that he was actually more qualified to make. He really had not grasped the concept of what being a captain meant and clearly was not getting to grips with his responsibilities. What was worse was he appeared to be totally discounting anything I had to contribute.

With the anchor set, we awaited the arrival of Captain Pete who rowed out to share a beer with us. Just as he was leaving, amidst the blowing wind, we were laughing and joking about him having to row back to *Admetus* when a gust flipped our dinghy over. Dud and John immediately went to right the dinghy and another extremely strong gust of wind from the opposite direction made all the yachts in the bay turn 180 degrees in the blink of an eye. John immediately started the engine and as he did another gust drew my attention to a small yacht in front of our bow. I noticed it moving strangely in the water, a further gust brought it too close to our bow for my liking so I ran up the side-deck shouting, "WATER!"

The chap on board the yacht ran to his bow and said, "We are holding fast."

"No," I shouted back. "We are holding fast and you are moving into us. Pull up your anchor." As he did this he moved away, but his delay whilst arguing had left the recovery too late and the string around his life buoy snagged our anchor roller as he pulled his boat forward away from us. Luckily I had been watching and had managed to fend off whilst he had been messing about. If I had not raised his awareness to the fact he was dragging, his yacht would have hit us hard on the bow.

I shouted to him to make sure that the string on the buoy was still secure to ensure he didn't lose it. He checked it over and nodded it was okay and I went back to watching the other boats that were around us. As I stood on the side deck watching, I saw a couple running along a pathway, ice cream in hand, watching a boat moving backwards. Dud drew my attention to the water as a whirlwind passed over the water between us and the smaller boat. As the whirlwind passed between us it was lifting water straight up into the air about a metre high and then it passed directly through the stern of the small yacht sending it spiralling in a circle. I swear to this day the man on this yacht did not have a clue what happened either to his yacht or to any other around him.

As quickly as it came, the wind died away and returned to its original direction, and gradually and gently all the boats in the harbour returned to their original positions. We checked our landmarks ashore from the bow and stern to make sure we hadn't moved from our original position and were very pleased to find that our anchor had held and had passed its first real test in bad weather conditions.

Just as everything calmed I saw the couple, who had been running along the shore when the whirlwind hit, rowing out to their boat in their dinghy. I spoke to them and assured them their anchor had held, as they seemed to think it had dragged. Their yacht had appeared to move in the water as it was lying in a different position but when they tested it under engine it was holding. During our conversation I found out they had laid 50 metres of chain in ten metres of depth. From the shore they must have seen the wind stretch their chain out laying it on the bottom giving the appearance they were dragging.

All the excitement over, we set about cooking our evening meal when there was a tap on the hull. It was the man from the yacht that had almost hit us. Dud went to speak to him and as I listened from below I could hear the man accusing Dudley of being at fault and he was going to call the port police. In a matter of seconds I went from being Labrador calm to Rottweiler protecting her puppies. I almost flew up the companionway steps and looked this man in the eyes as I shouted, "Good, call the port police and I can tell them how irresponsible you are and that thanks to ME shouting a warning at YOU a collision was avoided." He went on to insist that he had been at the anchorage first so that meant we must have impeded his swing circle. His manner left me in no doubt that he thought I knew nothing about sailing and he could clearly win his point by trying to confuse me with his knowledge. How mistaken he was! I calmly pointed out the sea rules of how much chain to lay and given swing circles and forcefully told him what happens to set swinging circles when one of the yachts is dragging an anchor. By the time I had finished giving him a sailing lesson I had escalated to the point of angry and my body language dared him to argue further. He looked at me and then at Dudley and whilst he sloped away he said, "Hey man, you have the right attitude. The lady there needs to calm down." Maybe he was right, and hopefully God will forgive my temper, but there are two things that make me angrier than anything else in the world: one is people who tell lies and the other is injustice, and he was trying his hand at both.

Just before bedtime there was another knock on the hull and a very drunken sounding man announced that we would have to report to the port police in Nidri the following day and report the accident. He obviously thought he could have the last word but I was more than prepared to stand up and tell the truth against this blackguard. The bit between my teeth, I was certain I was going to be prepared the following morning so that I could get my point across to the port police. I grabbed my dictionary and began writing down the pertinent words to explain what had happened in Greek; the most important two were "Aftos Lathos" (It is his fault) and "Anemostrovilos" (whirlwind).

The following morning we took a leisurely sail to Nidri and reported to the port police that afternoon. Completely uninterested in the event they sent us away saying they were expecting a visit from the president and we could come back tomorrow. We forgot the whole thing for the day and went for a swim. The following day Dud, John and I went to the port police who told us the captain would be half an hour and to come back later. We went back to the boat to find that Diane had had a visit from the captain who had come out to the yacht in our absence! By now I was becoming very annoyed and Dud decided it was probably best that I stay on the boat with Diane when they went back for a third time.

On their return, Dud reported that the port police were not going to get involved at all. They had indicated they could neither prove nor disprove the true version of events, as they were not there. They had sent them away saying the matter should be dealt with through our insurance companies. Well, an unsatisfactory result but one that could not be argued with. They were right. Why should they believe either story? The fact that this man was claiming that we had managed to drag our anchor forwards and hit his stern with our bow didn't seem to make any difference with the port police. If we had a yacht that could achieve what we were being accused of we could make a lot of money.

Needless to say, months later when the insurance forms had been filled out it transpired the offending yacht was claiming for a badly damaged wind generator. I knew for certain that this yacht did not own a wind generator as, if it had, my hands would have been sliced to bits as I fended it off our bow! It all became clear. We had obviously become the latest victim of a dishonest person trying to make a quick buck out of an unfortunate natural phenomenon. I do believe that such people are called opportunists and luckily there are not too many of these amongst the yachting community. Needless to say we did not back down and his claim against us was mysteriously dropped some ten months later. The unjust part is that due to him making the unsubstantiated claim we still lost our no-claim bonus!

The excitement of the port police visit over, we set sail for Paleros and had a wonderful trip across. One of the best sails we had had in a long time. *Orpheus* glided well through the water with the wind on her beam. Both sails filled nicely and a natural rhythm emerged as she parted the water. We spotted a few flying fish passing by us in quite a hurry as we all relaxed and it seemed that we were arriving at Paleros all too soon.

We began our mooring process and were about to lay our anchor when Dudley noticed that the yacht we were about to come alongside had mooring lines tied in all directions. It had obviously been left over winter and the owner had not been out to remove his wintering lines. He had three lines from his bow, one of which was tied to the opposite side of the harbour and another that was tied to a mooring that was obviously going to foul our anchor and maybe our propeller. As we were deciding what to do a familiar face appeared ashore and he offered to go on board the yacht and drop the mooring line that was about to foul us.

Once safely moored, we learned that this selfish owner had left his yacht like this all winter. His lines had fouled several propellers and yachts already this season and when people complained to the person who appeared to be minding the yacht the reply came back, "Hard luck". This one yacht, with all its lines, actually took up three spaces and the owner/minder didn't seem to care that it was causing damage to other yachts. Most yachtsmen abide by the unspoken etiquette of not taking up too much room at a quay but obviously there will always be an exception. This exception just joined the section of yachties that I like to call the "Rotty Yachties".

The following day we returned to Levkas and as I was busy cleaning the men made themselves busy about the boat. They had the floorboards up and levelled them to stop a couple of them creaking. The electric windlass down button had not worked all season and this was taken apart, rebuilt and made to work. The boom vang that had proved to be useless was found to be broken and was removed and replaced with warp. All in all the men had had a very busy day and that evening they were looking very proud of what they had achieved. Dud, enjoying the male company and being able to share the responsibilities, was like a dog with six tails. It was very obvious he was going to miss John very much when he and Diane returned to Corfu by ferry the following day.

Dudley took John and Diane in the car up to Igoumenitsa to catch the ferry back to Corfu from where they would fly back to the U.K. After they left I sat reflecting on the past fortnight with affection. They were a lovely couple, so easy to be with and live with on a boat. Their knowledge and experience had been invaluable. I just wished that Dudley and I could have been surer of ourselves so we had not constantly disagreed about things. Our own inexperience had led to some difficult situations and I hoped that one day we would get past this and that Dud would feel able enough to be a strong captain.

I would miss John and Diane very much. Diane had been a motherly, calming influence whose relaxed air had kept us all on an even keel. John has a character the size of King Kong and it would be a long time before I forgot him and his colourful descriptions of everyday items and activities. A few of his favourite sayings are, "bum nuts" which to you and I are eggs, "mystery bags" which are sausages, and "brick sniffing" meaning visiting an archaeological site.

CHAPTER 21
U.V.W (Us, Vets and Work!)

The summer lay ahead of us and as there were no more planned visits from family and friends we settled down into a routine of swimming, cycling, sunbathing, working and saving as much money as we could to help our ever struggling finances. Due to our property being empty we were once again in the situation of having no income and a lot of outgoings.

Besides our cleaning work we were offered the chance to re-organise a store in a chandlery and help with their stock-taking. Being very grateful for the offer to earn a little extra money, Dudley and I grabbed the chance with both hands. In between this work we continued to do little maintenance jobs around *Orpheus* one of which was to replace the foam in our bunk.

We had been sleeping onboard for nearly ten months and both of us were developing bad backs. The old foam had not only gone soft but was slightly sloping to the centre of the bunk. This meant that I spent all night trying to cling to the left hand side and Dud was doing the same to the right. We had both developed the same back problem but on opposite sides. This spoke volumes and as soon as we had a little extra cash we invested in some foam.

We purchased one sheet of foam measuring seven feet by four feet; it was four inches deep and cost £70. Dud used the old foam as a template and cut the new foam using a very long and sharp kitchen knife. Once we had worked out how to get all pieces cut out of the one sheet of foam, the cutting out was quite painless and the new pieces fitted into the covers a treat. That evening we lay on a hard, flat, foam surface and slept very soundly indeed.

Realising that we were not going to be sailing for a while we decided to deflate and pack away the dinghy. In a very short space of time the dinghy had acquired a weed covered bottom so we made the decision to pack it away until later in the summer when we hoped to be able to enjoy some sailing. For the present we were committed to finding as much work as possible.

Dudley was asked if he would fit netting around the guardrails of another yacht the same as we had on *Orpheus*. He agreed to do this with my help but forgot to ask me first whether I wanted to do it!! I wasn't very happy when I found out about it as I had had raw fingers for days after fitting our netting and now he had volunteered me to go through it all over again. I knew we needed the extra money but I would be the one that paid for it later on. However, having fallen into the pitfalls whilst applying netting to *Orpheus* most of the new netting went on almost painlessly, apart from the thousands of reef knots I had tied resulting in red, sore fingers. By the time we had finished we were very pleased with the result. In fact when I compared the finished result with our own netting, our second attempt had the benefit of our experience and looked very smart indeed; even though I say so myself. We had the opportunity some years later to again admire our handiwork as we came across the yacht and on close inspection found it had lasted very well.

A very unexpected and also unpaid job seemed to have fallen into the remit of my life. Having had my half an hour tuition with Dudley's barber on how to cut his hair, it now appeared I was cutting others. I had already cut Steve's hair when we had been in Monastir and was very flattered by the compliment when he came back for a second cut. Seeing this, Captain Pete was getting ready to go back home before the weather got too hot and asked me if I would give him a quick short back and sides. I was rather more nervous cutting his hair because I knew if it wasn't up to scratch that Liz would be very angry. With a shaky hand and a prayer asking for the clipper battery not to run out I set about his trim. There had been many a holiday with him that I had shaved his neck so I don't know why I was so worried about a little haircut. I kept this in mind and the result was an okay hairstyle and one that wasn't too short for Liz.

Having seen all this hairdressing activity on the mole one of Joe's employees asked if I would cut his hair too!! I really didn't know what to think. The responsibility and worry of having their heads in my hands was too much for me. It was definitely time for me to hang up my clippers and stick to doing only Dudley's hair. I don't know how hairdressers have the confidence to take people's hair and snip it into various designer cuts. They must either have nerves of steel or be very competent. I take my hat off to hairdressers everywhere.

A lull appeared in our busy summer and we took the opportunity to spend some time on the lovely beaches around Levkas. It was suggested that we might like to try the pool at a local hotel that we liked to call the, 'One onion'. It was at this time that we learned that most hotels around Greece allowed outside visitors to use their pools with the proviso that a drink was purchased. Dudley and I very much enjoyed swimming in the pool but the summer was passing us by in a haze of work which snatched our moments of fun. This was not quite what we had planned for our first year on board, but nevertheless it was all pleasant up until the middle of June when we had to take Harry to the vet.

Harry had developed a tiny growth on the left side of his muzzle. This had not previously caused him any concern but with the heat of the summer I had noticed him scratching at it and it had become quite angry looking. A trip to the vet resulted in the need to have the mole removed. The vet, a very attractive and gentle woman, gave Harry an injection and then sent us out into the waiting room. Somewhat confused, I sat with Harry on my lap and wondered what on earth was going on. It was only when Harry started to go limp in my arms that I realised she had given him a sedative and I was to cradle him until it had fully taken affect.

Unlike the vets in England, where you take, leave and collect your animal later, in Greece you actually become the surgery assistant. I held Harry until he was almost sleeping and then carried him to the table within the surgery. I laid him down and reassured him as the vet administered further injections around the area of the growth. The pain numbing injection worked instantly and she quickly removed the lump; I held a swab to the wound whilst she placed the offending object in a test tube. No stitches were required as there was only a minor wound and we were told it would heal in no time at all. The only after care needed was to keep the wound clean with antiseptic spray. Tests were carried out on the removed growth that concluded it had been cancerous but benign.

Harry had taken this visit to the vet in his stride as always but I really didn't know what to think. I had been so closely involved with the operation that my emotions had been in conflict the whole time. I had wanted to protect him from pain and yet I knew the cuts had to be made. I certainly was not going to break down in front of the vet! I remembered previous visits to the vets in England. Harry used to get so upset when I left him there and cried the whole time. At least I can wholeheartedly say that he found this surgery stress-free and much more bearable as I was there to hold and comfort him. He knew I would care for him; I was his "mum". It must be better for the animal having the owner around rather than a room full of complete strangers. As my help negated the need for a surgery assistant the costs were minimised and the whole procedure including consultation, operation, analysis and after-care only cost €143, the equivalent to £100 at that time. My only frustration, if asked, would be to say that at the outset it was presumed I understood what was happening and what was expected of me. Living in a different society with different methods can be confusing. The hardest thing for us was that, although the costs had been reasonable, the way our finances were at that time, we could ill afford to be paying such a bill.

Our work continued and our finances struggled on. I was becoming increasingly depressed by the financial rollercoaster our life seemed to be on. I had wanted little and ended up with nothing. I had wanted to be closer to nature but didn't want to feel like I was being forced to live as a woman from the Dark Ages. I tried to be optimistic but the sadness and the constant worry were starting to erode our relationship and for me this was the worst thing that could possibly happen. This was not the rosy dream I had thought it would be and living without money was not the idyllic life I had imagined. We were in no way missing England; we were not homesick at all, but we did miss our friends especially in times of trouble.

In amongst our troubles, life brought us pockets of happiness in the form of people around us. We met characters from all walks of life and the pleasure they gave was endless. Friendships were built and stories were swapped over glasses of wine and bowls of olives. Some of the characters were unforgettable and whether they were politicians or refuse collectors you would never know from their appearance; they simply became just another yachtie, the same as anyone else. This is the true beauty about the yachting lifestyle: there is no pretence, no façade, just ordinary people with something in common enjoying each other's friendship; always there to help, always willing to give and never failing. This is the live-aboard community around the Mediterranean as we found it.

    We met a ninety-year-old gentleman who had been an ex-Australian Naval commander and one time chairman of the Burmah Oil group. He was sailing in the company of a lady in her early seventies who had once been a Royal Navy WREN. Another owner turned out to be a professor of immunology at a Scottish University whose wife was a highly regarded professor and microbiologist. Yet another had been the family chairman of a well-known highland-distilling group. One retired gent in his 50s revealed that he had been a sidecar racer lying prone and kneeling in the cart often at speeds of over 180 mph. Another pleasant chap had been the leader of a services free-fall parachute team. An elegant lady and gent moored next to us invited us for coffee and turned out to be a Peer of the Realm! We met several people who had worked for the various services such as Army, Navy, Air Force, Fire Brigade, Police and Ambulance Services all of whom were still enjoying the thrills of life through their sailing and cruising. We met many people like ourselves who had everyday jobs and a life they constantly strove to improve, until one day the decision was made to simply opt out of the 'rat race' and live a simple life, being free to travel where they wished on their limited budget. Many we spoke to said their lives had become unbearable with the increasing weight of red tape and regime forced upon them by local and national governments. They had decided their lives would only become more blighted as time passed and had decided to call it a day and sail away.

    After spending many evenings with new friends I was starting to realise that most people had managed to get to grips with their ovens and could cook quite nourishing meals. I plucked up the courage to try my hand at baking some cheese scones and shortcakes but forgot to take into account the time of year. I had been so focused on remaining calm and trying not to panic over my decision to bake that I hadn't realised that it was the hottest time of the year! An hour and a half later I stood with hair, wet with sweat, stuck to my forehead and neck, and my clothes damp and clinging to every crevice, but my smile was the biggest you ever saw. I had done it. I had baked my first cheese scones and shortcakes and they weren't burnt. In fact, they tasted quite good and for the first time it was thanks to me and not Deliah!

Euphoria over the cooking passed and we were back to working on the boats. It was as we were walking along the quay one morning, that I noticed something flapping in the harbour water. It was a tiny little bird in obvious trouble. In a flash, Dud got into a dinghy and rowed round to the bird managing to pick it out of the water. By this time I had jumped from the quay onto a local fisherman's boat so that Dud could hand the bird to me to wrap in a towel. I took the bird back to our boat and immediately rinsed him in some fresh water, placed him on a towel in a bowl and left him in the sunshine to calm down and dry out. I made regular checks to see if the little bird was okay but he lay so still I wasn't sure if he would make it. Being a swallow the natural thing for us to do was name him Bertie 2 after the swallow that had joined us on the return trip from Tunisia. We both made regular checks on the bird, trying to be as quiet as possible as he seemed so frightened by the whole affair. Before sundown we placed fresh water in the bowl and covered the bird to keep the cold out. All we could do was pray we had done enough to keep him alive to see another day.

First thing the next morning, whilst I was still lying in bed, I heard Dud go outside and check on Bertie 2 and he came back reporting him alive and drinking fresh water. I was touched at Dud's tenderness and caring and was reminded that I was married to one of the kindest men in the world, I was very lucky indeed. Throughout the day Bertie 2 began a preening process and continued to drink and, although he made no effort to leave the bowl, we were now certain he was going to survive. After another night with us I wondered if I sat the bird in the open, on top of our bimini, he may fly away. It took him only a short while of sitting on the open bimini before he showed interest in his surroundings and with a quick flick took off into the skies. It was a very satisfying feeling, watching him flap into the distance.

Just two days later, another bird was rescued by one of the local men named Pano. Having seen me with the other bird he brought it to our boat for me to look after! So we had Bertie 3 with us for two days, and using the same process of washing and watering, we successfully released another swallow into the sky. We came to the conclusion that there must have been a nest nearby and that the little birds were fledglings and their first attempts at flying had ended badly.

If only we had it within our power to heal humans as well as we had managed with the birds. Janet, our dear friend, had been ill for some time and was now facing open-heart surgery. The emotions we faced were extreme. We were frustrated and angry that we were not in a position to fly home and be with her. We felt useless and impotent. There was nothing we could do to help her and we were constantly tearful in anticipation of news of how things had gone. It was the first time we felt real regret at not being in the U.K. and found it very heart-wrenching that we didn't have the finances to get home. It was almost more than we could bear. We were informed that Janet's operation had gone well and that a good friend would be staying with her to aid recovery. Apart from 'phone calls and well wishes there was nothing more we could do but pray for a painless and speedy recovery.

Still battling with what nature was throwing at us we were informed that "Car Park", Harry's wild Labrador friend, had been found poisoned under a bush. A local fisherman who used to feed him every morning with a loud call of "Oi!" came to see him and thought by slapping him round the face with a large slice of pork he could bring him out of his stupor. In best pigeon Greek-English it was explained he had been poisoned and could not eat. He was taken to the local vet who flushed him out but it was touch-and-go as to whether he would survive. In no time at all word spread around the fisherman the length of the harbour and in even less time the poor vet was faced with lots of worried fishermen demanding that she made sure he lived. It may be difficult to picture these big, rough-and-ready men of the sea being concerned, but I can assure you the care and love that they showed for this one dog was very touching. The Greek people in general have a bad image when it comes to dogs and animals but what I witnessed that day was quite different.

Happily, with a few days tender loving care, Car Park made a full recovery and was soon lying on the mole being fussed over, loved and fed better than ever before. In fact there was so much food being produced for him all of a sudden that all the bitches in town thought he was wonderful. Being the best provider of the moment, Car Park suddenly had his own harem of followers. The fishermen continued this loving care until he was back to full health and then it was left to the one fisherman with his morning visit. Wherever we were at the time we could hear the old fisherman shout "Oi," and Car Park would run from his hiding place to be fed big slabs of meat and cheese. Whilst eating the food he would get a lump on top of his head by a big heavy hand; the fisherman showing his affection the only way he knew how.

The summer was passing us by very quickly; August was upon us and we awaited what is locally called the Italian invasion. Apparently the Italians all like to get away during the month of August and this results in a high volume of Italians being on holiday in the Ionian at the same time. In fact, over a period of years, this one month invasion has become two, July and August. Our work was coming to an end so we were hoping to enjoy some sailing but the down side of this was, not only would we not be getting extra income but we would also be out in the mêlée of Italians!

We were glad that we delayed our sailing for a few days as we were told the Olympic flame was due to be run through Levkas town. I never would have believed that I was going to have the opportunity of seeing the Olympic flame but this year the games were being hosted in Athens and we were going to get to see it. The port police emptied the harbour of boats and blocked the bridge and canal entrances so there would be no movement of yachts during the run past with the flame. All the cars and traffic were diverted and those normally parked along the harbour were moved. If not moved by the owners, they were removed by the local tow truck. The street was quite deserted; we had never seen it so empty. Police guarded the roads and the local Greeks gradually appeared to line each side of the street.

A small parade of brightly costumed people passed before our eyes and in a flash we spied a portly man, who looked a tad unfit, walking past, carrying what appeared to be a golden candle stick with a flame at the top. He managed to increase his walking speed to a trot just as he passed us and waddled out of sight.

"Was that it?" I asked Dudley.

"I think so," he said.

Five minutes, a blink of the eye and one photograph and we were walking back to the boat completely deflated. I'm not sure what I expected but I had visions of a stallion fit athlete jogging past holding up a big golden torch flaming for all to see. "Never mind," we thought. "We were here. We saw it and it was another occasion in our life that nobody can ever take away." Shame about the lack of a stallion in skimpy shorts though – oh well!

The walks along the beach at Levkas had been an absolute delight for us since the beginning of spring. All types of heathers, flowers and brightly coloured weeds had appeared to blossom and reproduce. However, the best was yet to come and during August I could not believe the beauty of the lilies that appeared. Giant white lilies lined the dunes at the back of the beach; their perfume resembled that of lily of the valley and could be very pungent first thing in the morning. I could not believe that such beauty would be possible in England. I thought about the demise of wild bluebells due to people digging them up and felt that these lilies would have gone the same way had this been the U.K.

During one such walk of admiration for the natural wonders of Levkas, Dudley and I spotted a particularly elegant and beautiful girl learning to windsurf. We stopped and watched for a while as she struggled to stand on the board but kept falling off. One hour later she seemed to be improving and we told her so as she walked up the beach. This attractive waif was covered head to toe in bruises from constantly falling off and climbing back on the board but she did not appear deterred.

Curious, we went back the next day and the next and watched as she improved not only to be able to stand but surf up and down the coastline. Her tutor explained about turning on the board to change direction and she eagerly went back into the water, trying it out. It was at this point that we had our first taste of the Italian selfishness we had often heard about but never witnessed.

Three dinghies with outboards running, roared up to the beach and one of them sent the surfer girl spinning in the air and falling into the water. Her tutor recovered her and the board as the three boats ignored the accident they had caused and roared up onto the beach. Levkas beach is one of the biggest beaches with so much room you would think you could never be crowded out. Wrong! Even though there was an expanse of beach to the left of us they chose to come and sit right in front of us, all six adults and eight children, who commenced shouting and screaming and running around what had, up till then, been a very peaceful beach.

An argument ensued between the surfer's tutor and the Italians who dismissed the whole thing. They didn't care they had nearly drowned this girl and they didn't care that they had invaded other people's personal space. They didn't care they were making so much noise and spoiling everyone else's enjoyment. They didn't care full stop. Just for the record, in case you find yourself being half drowned by Italians, the rules of the sea say that if using your dinghies on the sea, all outboards should be turned off and lifted out of the water if approaching a beach to prevent the blades causing injury to any person who may be swimming in the area you approach. The whole scene was completely unnecessary and could simply have been avoided if they had made the decision to go a hundred yards further down the beach that remained empty!

With a bad taste in our mouths we made the decision to pack up and leave the beach. I felt like we were giving in to their bullying attitudes but at the same time I felt like I needed to display my displeasure. I knew if I had stayed I would have said something I might have regretted later, so it was best all round for us to leave.

This display of idiotic behaviour was so alien to the island of Lefkada that I had truly fallen in love with during this past year. The villages were quaint and the locals always had a nod and a good morning to give. The town of Levkas was a glorious place to shop, surrounded by beaches and mountains; the skies were clear blue all summer and we couldn't believe we had just experienced a summer without rain. There had been only fine weather since the beginning of May, which meant for the first time in our lives we had been three months rain free.

Some people find the Greek people rude and unapproachable but we never found this to be the case. All the local shops had warmed to us, especially Dudley, as he usually did our shopping. Whilst Dud won the hearts of the ladies working in the shops I continued my practice of the Greek language on the local fishermen. Everyone seemed to enjoy the effort both of us made to speak the local language and we made friends with local taverna owners to the extent that if they saw us out they would buy us pastries from the bakery. On the odd day that I would accompany Dud to the supermarket, I found the checkout girls an absolute treat to behold. We placed our items on the conveyor belt and stood back to watch the mystery of the staff training unfold. Standing at the end of the food catch I felt like Gordon Banks, a famous goalkeeper from days gone by. The checkout ladies grab at the food, giving it a good hard squeeze to bruise anything soft and then throw it as hard as they can down the slip to crash into the food catch at the bottom. It didn't matter what it was, tinned goods or eggs they were all treated to the same handling as they hurtled down the slide at a great rate of knots; I discovered the best way to handle damage limitation was to catch the item before it landed!

We were once out shopping and waiting our turn to be served in a queue at the till when what we saw made us laugh so much that we still talk about it today. The till girl did a really good job of hurtling the food down the slide and towards a Greek lady who, in turn, picked the item up and dropped it from a height of one metre above her trolley to land with a crash in the bottom of it. Again it didn't matter if the item was crisps, eggs or tins. They were all dropped from a heady height to crash to the bottom of her trolley. We looked at each other and back at the trolley as the next item was dropped and on it went until all her groceries were nicely crushed and ruined. Dud and I agreed there could be only one solution to the mystery of what we had witnessed. She surely must have been an off duty checkout girl!

The weather was now wonderfully warm and we stayed cool by spraying Harry and ourselves with a garden water spray. We were leading a simple and beautiful life and I couldn't think of a better place to be. Dud kept trying to remind me that it was only for this summer and that next year we would be moving on to pastures new but I was oh so in love with Levkas I did not miss my home city of Norwich at all. Sensing my growing attachment to Levkas and its local people, Dudley decided that it was time to go sailing for a while. I was happy at the thought of sailing again and as we had been told the Italian invasion did not extend North of Levkas, we decided that was where we would go. Over the years we had visited the Ionian with Captain Pete. It had become increasingly difficult to find moorings as the flotilla companies had increased and during the peak season it really was a battle to find quayside space. During July, and especially August, it was almost impossible, so we agreed on another route and northwards we went.

CHAPTER 22
SAILING WITH PRIDE

We made a mad dash through the Levkas Bridge at eleven o'clock. Dud had been held up at the Port Police office again and we were delayed getting away. Not allowing this to dampen our enthusiasm, we headed towards the Preveza Channel. We had never negotiated this channel before and had been advised to be watchful as there were strong currents running through it at times.

A little wary, and yet still excited, we had a great sail across the short distance of five nautical miles to the entrance of the buoyed channel. There was only a slight current as we motored along the two miles past Preveza and into the Gulf of Amvrakikos. The wind was in a more favourable direction as we entered the Gulf and we had a beam reach that allowed us sail all the way to Vonitsa.

We had driven to Vonitsa previously to visit the Tuesday market but had never sailed into the harbour and didn't know what to expect. As we arrived we noted all the yachts were alongside so I readied the boat by putting out fenders and setting lines. I then looked at the spot Dud was going to bring us into and I thought to myself, "No way." I said nothing and grabbed a fender ready to dab between the boat, the quay and the boat that was going to be in front of us. I was totally convinced the space was much too small for us to get into but I must confess I can't park a car either! Dud slid *Orpheus* into this spot with such ease I could not fail to be impressed. The bow came a little too tight to the quay but I was ready and she just slid in and came to a perfect halt. I couldn't believe he had managed it just like that!

Apart from the Tuesday market, Vonitsa had so much to offer in the way of an excellent view, a castle, and an abundance of shops and tavernas. We settled into our mooring and had a wonderfully peaceful evening until around 1 a.m. when loud disco music started and continued until 4 a.m.! We discovered that they had a disco in the castle just above the harbour at least once a week during the summer.

We made the most of the next day, taking a walk around town and enjoying the benefits of the hard work that had been undertaken in improving paths and walkways around the castle. They had not only improved the paths but also the rockery gardens that ran alongside them. Various plants and bushes had been dug in around the walkways, creating a restful and flower filled scene. It all looked very tidy and attractive and much more eye-catching than we remembered from our very first visits here by car.

After spending a few days and a few sleepless nights in Vonitsa, we decided it was time to move on. Having bumped into friends we learned that the Italian invasion had lessened so we decided to go back southwards and head for Meganisi. As we left Vonitsa, the admiration for Dud's wonderful helming coming into the mooring wore off as he now decided he could do everything on his own. Without any communication he let off lines, was holding fenders and was trying to helm all at the same time. The upshot of this was that our take off from the quay was almost disastrous and the parting view of *Orpheus* leaving the harbour was me screaming at Dud, "You cannot do it all by yourself. One thing at a time. Speak to me and tell me what it is you are planning to do."

The journey back did not get any better for, as we were coming into moor at the quayside in Levkas, we prepared to drop anchor when Harry decided to be unwell. He ran all around the seating and cockpit leaving a trail of thick, green slimy pooh as he went! Standing off, I had to clear it up before we could come into moor. This in itself would not have been embarrassing. Only there was someone standing on the quayside, waiting to take our lines. They must have thought we were complete idiots and it didn't help matters when, instead of sticking to our normal routine, Dud decided he was again going to try to helm, throw lines and forget to indicate when he wanted me to drop the anchor.

All in all, that night I gave Dud a hard time and the speech about doing one thing at a time, communication and being a good captain came back resounding in my ears the following day as my pride came before a fall.

The next day we headed for Abeleki Bay on the island of

Meganisi. We had been there several times before and knew where we were going. As navigator, I knew exactly where I was going and felt no need to check charts and pilot book for any information that may have been useful to me. I know now that this is the most stupid attitude a navigator can take. Yes, pride comes before a fall and I learnt the lesson big time. Not checking charts and reading all available information, even if you know where you are going, is not just a big mistake but a huge one that can turn out to be a costly one.

As we approached the island of Meganisi and Abeleki Bay we were sailing between it and a smaller raised rock. Dud asked if I was sure we could sail between the two as he could see blue water ahead (pale blue water indicating shallow depth). He went below to check the chart and I took the helm. We had already started the engine and as I slowly brought the boat through the gap I noticed the depth gauge drop from 20 metres, 7 metres (at which time I put the boat into reverse) and 1.5 metres. BANG!

In the blink of an eye the depth had dropped to nothing and even though I had reacted quickly it was too late to recover because of our forward momentum. We had run aground on a reef between the raised rock and the island of Meganisi. I immediately started to rev the engine in reverse and waggle the rudder as I had seen others do when aground. I wasn't sure what I was supposed to do but at this stage I was willing to try anything. I then turned the helm in the hope that the wind would help us somehow, by which time Dud had come running to the rescue. Just as he took the helm, the bow drifted round and he managed to get us off and away to safety.

I sat down feeling totally sick. My legs were shaking and my ego was bruised. I couldn't believe I had been such an arrogant idiot to think that I knew best; that I knew where I was and didn't need to consult charts. WHAT AN IDIOT! Trying to make myself feel better, I looked at the chart, which did not actually indicate the reef. But looking at the pilot book I noticed there was a big clear inlay chart giving very clear instruction to avoid the reef. If I had bothered to look, the whole incident could quite easily have been avoided. I felt terrible as I gave myself a lecture on navigation but at least I had learned a very valuable lesson: you can never know too much. Consult every single piece of information available to you before every passage and never become complacent.

Luckily, once anchored with a line taken ashore, Dud took a swim and said there had been no damage to the keel. We had only just nudged onto the rock as I had already put the engine into reverse but things could have been very serious if we had just continued along our way and Dud had not first asked the question "Can we get through?" After all my nagging about his abilities and skills I was now feeling a total and utter useless imbecile and to make matters worse, instead of Dud shouting at me, telling me what a fool I'd been, he was actually being nice. I took this as a double insult, which made me feel even worse. When he did something wrong I told him off. Here I did something wrong and he was being nice. Needless to say, I felt terrible and concluded that I was being reminded by my maker that to err is human and I, like Dudley, was human after all.

Just as a point of note, we have since discovered the Greek laws in relation to running aground. The law states that should a yacht run aground in Greek waters it will be required to lift out of the water and be inspected by a recognised surveyor. Only after the inspection finds the vessel seaworthy can it be re-launched. If you are ever aground and call out the coast guard for assistance or tow they will insist on the lift out. The way our finances were there was no way we could have afforded to pay for a lift out or a surveyor so I was very glad that we managed to free ourselves without damage.

The following day we swam and enjoyed the peace that the bay offered us. Cicadas, birds and fish all provided nature's music in a green mountainous surrounding. We were reading books and enjoying the sunshine when a big motorboat further down the bay launched a little speedboat and started towing a water skier. We did not think anything of this and quite enjoyed watching the girl until the speed boat started towing her across our anchor chain and much too close to our boat for our liking. As they came past, *Orpheus* was straining up and down in the wash they were creating and I was uneasy that the motion might contribute to our anchor being pulled out.

Everything calmed down as the skier and driver got back onto their motorboat but as I sat reading I looked down to see that we had crossed our shoreline and our anchor had indeed been pulled out and we were drifting. Dud immediately started the engine and took to the dinghy to release the short line. We discussed whether to relay the anchor but decided that as we had started up we may as well travel the short two mile journey along the shore to Little Vathi and spend the evening there. We arrived and moored up, for the first time ever, without any assistance whatsoever and were very pleased with our efforts. Usually there would always be someone willing to take shorelines for you but on this occasion we had had to manage it all by ourselves and, happily, everything had gone smoothly. Why couldn't it be like that every time we moored?

Vathi was one of our favourite places and we stayed the day here, enjoying a walk up into the village and trying to keep Harry out of the grass as the last time we had taken him walking there I had picked fifty ticks out of his fur. During the day we saw a tripper boat come in and drop off many tourists. Never before had we seen this and we feared that it was going to be a sign of the times and this quiet little bay was on its way to ruin. We witnessed the arrival of the flotilla boats and their anchoring ability at the end of which our egos were boosted quite considerably. I like to do all things in a correct manner and as such am very hard on both Dudley and myself in an attempt to be proficient at sailing but these people were atrocious and didn't seem to care. That evening when we ate out at a restaurant we had been to several times before we found the prices had nearly doubled and were well above the normal price of meals. This sleepy little place was waking up fast and was going to be spoilt in no time at all.

As we left our mooring the following morning, we had the delights of discovering along with three other yachts, that one of the flotilla boats had laid their anchor across four others!! I must give the company their due; their flotilla leader took to the dinghy, dived for the anchor, lifted it and cleared all four without much effort at all. We followed our normal routine for leaving a mooring and as we did so I heard someone on the yacht next door say, "Now they've got good team work." I couldn't believe they were actually talking about us. Maybe I needed a good dose of confidence and then I would stop worrying and nagging quite so much, which would probably be a good thing for Dudley! This little episode over, we made for a little bay in the Meganisi Channel, dropped anchor and had a cooling swim.

We backtracked to Spartachori where we took another swim and I spotted an octopus under a rock, several fish, sponges and coral. It was some of the cleanest and healthiest water I had swum in for a long time. We stayed another day and treated ourselves to a relaxing meal at the brothers' restaurant and enjoyed more swimming and snorkelling. Unfortunately the lady I had been cleaning with was due to travel home to England for a holiday and I had promised to go back to cover any cleaning jobs until she returned. So, very reluctantly, we left Spartachori to sail back to Levkas.

As we arrived in Levkas once more, we had a nice surprise in the shape of Steve, our captain, from our Tunisian trip. He had left early July to sail to Turkey and here it was September and he was back. Needless to say, we spent the evening catching up on all his news. It's one of the best parts of yachting: as you travel around sailing and wintering, you make friends; these friends will be found anchored in a bay when you least expect it and you then get to swap stories, catch up on news and make friends all over again.

The strong southerly winds had started to blow and we were having a rough anchorage on the quay but we were holding well. The saddest thing was that Liz had come out for a holiday with Peter and had been trapped on the mole for three days as the winds blew force 5 and above. This meant I had Liz's company for a few days, and, being selfish, it was great. The winds did die and Captain Pete and Liz were at last able to sail away for a few romantic days together on *Admetus*.

No such romance on *Orpheus* as in-between cleaning I had discovered a puffy sack on Harry's ear that had continued to increase in size. A trip to the vet resulted in another sedation and treatment. Dudley and I held and comforted Harry as he lay on the stainless steel table. The vet took a scalpel to his ear and made a short incision releasing the blood from the sac. Another small incision was made and a drainage tube inserted vertically down the ear through the two small cuts. This tube was stitched in place and the ear cleaned with antiseptic spray. The vet recommended anti-inflammatory, antibiotics and a hood to stop him scratching at his ear. The entire treatment cost 145 euros. We obviously followed the vet's recommendations but found that the recommendation of the hood and tablets turned out to be a waste of money.

Once the sedation had worn off, Harry started shaking his head to get the hood off from around his neck. He was in more danger of hurting his ear by trying to get the hood off than if it wasn't there, so I removed it. He lay down and went to sleep! The first lot of pills made him violently ill so we decided not to give him any more. As it turned out he accepted the tube in his ear and paid it no attention at all. Although the ear looked very sore he acted as though nothing had happened to him. It's amazing what dogs can accept and put up with.

The following day Donald, a friend who had been anchored in Paleros with his wife Caroline, approached Dudley. They had abandoned their anchor on leaving the harbour as they had found it to be fouled when they tried to lift it. Dudley took the car and offered to dive for the anchor with Donald whilst I tended to the needs of a demanding dog with a tube in his ear. Dudley came back later that day very proud and very pleased that he had managed to dive down the four metres to retrieve the unmarked anchor. Donald and Caroline were so appreciative of his efforts that they insisted taking us out for a meal. The only downside to this little tale is that it started Dudley on his still ongoing request to purchase dive equipment. I keep telling him if he can find somewhere to store it on board he can have it, but until then he can't!

A quick trip to the vet to have Harry's stitches removed at no extra cost and we were off again in the yacht heading towards Nidri. We had decided to take part in the South Ionian Regatta. We had competed in the regatta twice before on board *Admetus* with Captain Pete, but I was unsure whether we were competent enough to do this on our own. As always, the Regatta was the talk of the sailing community around the Ionian and everyone seemed to be taking part. It seemed impolite not to join in the fun so we made our way to the Meganisi Channel to have a test sail prior to going to Nidri ready for the pre-race briefing the following day.

We timed our arrival at the Meganisi Channel to coincide with the time the race would start so we could see what the wind pattern was for that time of day. We then hoisted sails at the start line and began a practice run. Just at that moment I spied another yacht doing exactly the same thing. It had a pale blue hull, and it was *Admetus*. I grabbed the binoculars and confirmed my suspicion. Captain Pete had visitors on board and he was putting them through their paces ready for the race the same way he had done with us. *Orpheus* chased *Admetus* down the Channel and was keeping pace but not making ground. We decided to turn back and anchor off in a bay so we could scrape the slime off the bottom of the boat in the hope we would go faster the following day.

As there were three other yachts already moored in the bay we took our time deciding where to drop our anchor. Just as we were doing this, a flotilla boat came racing into the bay to the spot where we were considering anchoring. It is common practice for ill-mannered people to race you to a mooring just to pinch your spot so I stood tall on the bow and glared at the male at the helm. It was then I noticed a silly blonde bimbo on the bow of his boat wearing no bikini top and very little at the bottom. My glare deepened to such an extent that the man shouted across, "We are just turning around you. We are now leaving." I watched as he slowly paraded his bare chested tart to the whole bay and left. I created yet another section of the yachting community for those young and not so young who like to parade their private bits in front of others. These I named 'totty yachties'.

Dudley and I put on our wet suits, grabbed brushes and started diving under the boat to clean off the weed and slime that had accumulated through the summer. The hull needed to be anti-fouled and we planned to lift it out this coming winter but for now all we could do was brush off the unwanted plant life and hope it made a difference. As we were busy rubbing away I heard a female voice say, "Ahh, look. Look at that lovely little dog swimming in the water." At that I dropped my brush and turned 180 degrees in less than a second to see Harry desperately trying to swim towards me. I gave a couple of strong flipper kicks and grabbed him. Harry still hated the water and would get upset if Dud and I swam together. I knew there was no way he could be in the water voluntarily. All I could think was he had slipped off the back step onto the sugar scoop and fallen in. He looked so afraid and the minute I grabbed him he clung to me so tightly I couldn't prise him off to get him back on board again. We made the conscious decision never to leave the back netting gate open if we went into the water together. Harry was never a good swimmer no matter how much we tried to get him into the water, and if it had not been for the attention he had attracted we could have lost him prematurely.

All this excitement over and the bottom of the hull clean,

we motored into Nidri for a nail biting evening, awaiting the following race day.

Thursday, 16 September: a day I shall never forget and I am not sure a day that I want to ever repeat. I awoke with a churning stomach and feeling very sick. It was worse than any pre-night nerves I had experienced as a child when I used to take part in dance shows or as an adult when singing in Norwich Cathedral for the Chief Constable with the constabulary choir. Dudley and I went to the pre-race briefing and sat with Captain Pete who was looking relaxed, tanned and very confident. I, on the other hand, felt pale, shaky and very nervous indeed. We purchased the obligatory t-shirt, listened to the weather report and the rules of the race and went back to the boat. Captain Pete had the same look on his face that he had worn when I challenged him to a race from Vathi to Paleros, and Liz would not have been happy with him as he had his hands on his hips. I could almost hear her saying to him, "Oh Peter ... and take your hands off your hips!"

We left Nidri at approximately 1245 to steadily head for the Meganisi Channel. Our timing of the previous day worked perfectly and we approached the start line with ten minutes to spare. Not wishing to get involved with the yachts already sailing and vying for a lead position we motored at the back until there was just two minutes to the gun. We then pulled out the sails and cut the engine. BANG! The start gun!

Adrenaline was pumping with all the excitement, but the wind only offered us four knots which was barely enough for us to keep our sails filled. We were in the third row of boats but we were all closely sat together and I spied *Admetus* just two boat lengths in front of us. *Orpheus* was moving very slowly through the water and actually passed thirty boats that were becalmed to the port side. Everywhere yachts were either bobbing helplessly or creeping slowly along. To our starboard the smaller, lighter boats had managed to pull away a little, but, being a big, heavy, live-aboard boat, we stood little chance if the wind didn't pick up. Suddenly it was our turn and we were totally becalmed. Ten minutes later we were facing backwards and a further twenty minutes later I was so dejected we decided to give up and put the engine on. Just one hour and twenty minutes, and we were motoring to Sivota where the race would end. We saw *Admetus* bobbing with sails flapping as we motored past and wondered what on earth all my anxiety had been about. I felt half a stone lighter in worry and for what? The race day fun we had had with Captain Pete on our holidays somehow did not take on the same meaning when the boat being raced was actually your home. I didn't want to throw it around and "hooliganise" as Peter called it and I most certainly did not want to take any risks. I decided there and then this was my first and last regatta on *Orpheus*. She was my home and not my plaything.

We moored at the quayside in Sivota and awaited the arrival of the keen sailors who had stuck it out. We learned that they had sat with no wind for a further forty minutes after we left until it finally began to pick up, and then when it did, it became quite strong. It was so strong in fact that one yacht had flooded and would have sunk had it not been for another yacht that had a crew of holidaying RNLI lifeboat men on it. Hearing the distress call they abandoned their place in the race to go and assist. Talk about a busmen's holiday!

Finally all the yachts were back in harbour, no thanks to a super yacht that had tried to anchor across the mouth of the bay, right on the finishing line, and had almost totally blocked off the entrance and run down two yachts in the process. Getting the drift that they were hindering an important event they took off again and left the sailing yachts in peace. Rafted two deep at the quayside, the stories started about the race, with everyone swapping tales and basking in defeats and glories. We had been here before and had no shame in saying we gave up as anyone who knew us well enough would have known there was no way I would ever have the patience to sit and wait forty minutes for the wind to get up!

The usual stage was set up on the concrete courtyard on the Sivota quayside and the night's activities commenced with live music and jokes. The trophy presentation came later, followed by more dancing. We sat on the back of the boat, slowly getting inebriated, cuddling Harry, when a couple stopped by our boat and the gentleman asked if he could come on board and hold Harry for a while. Surprised, but only too glad to share Harry with him, we invited them on board. We learned that he was a vet on holiday and was missing the animals so much he just wanted to have a little cuddle. Now that is the sort of vet I had looked far and wide for in England and never could find. Yet another lovely couple we got to meet thanks to the cutest little dog in the whole world – my Harry.

We had a fantastic night despite the lack of our participation in the race and as we went to bed that evening, we realised that it was a year to the day that we had arrived in Greece to start our new life on board *Orpheus*.

In the morning we met up with Captain Pete and his crew for coffee and found out that he had come nineteenth overall in the race. He had done extremely well as there had been over a hundred boats involved. What else could anyone expect of my Captain Pete? I wondered if I should learn this hand on hip thing to see if it could make my sailing any better.

Our goodbyes said, we left for Paleros to fill with water prior to making our way back to Levkas in some high winds, ready for the arrival of my brother and parents. I had not seen my brother since leaving England and I was looking forward to his visit. They had booked apartments in Ligia and we had tried to get a mooring there but it had been too full of fishing boats (it is a fishing harbour after all), so we went through to Levkas. As we finished mooring I realised the last time anything had gone wrong for us sailing, mooring or leaving a mooring had been when I had run us aground. This, I calculated, had been three weeks ago and all our sailing since had been perfect. Dare I start to believe that we were finally getting it together as a team and doing it correctly? I certainly knew that I was enjoying this stress-free sailing a lot better than before.

CHAPTER 23
SUN, SAND AND SEA BASS

Once again in Levkas, we washed down the boat and prepared it for the arrival of my family. We had previously checked out the apartments they were to stay in, situated in the village of Ligia up a small hill overlooking the mountains of the mainland. They were quiet, clean and very suitable for my parents but I was wondering whether my social animal of a brother would find it a little too quiet.

We purchased some essential food items and placed them in the refrigerator within their apartments and sat by the pool, awaiting their arrival. The winds had been blowing very hard from the south when we left Levkas, and whilst waiting we could not help but worry about *Orpheus* being left on the town quay. Strong, southerly winds could make certain parts of the Levkas town quay untenable and damage could be caused in the blink of an eye. As soon as they arrived and the kisses, tears and hugs were over, we left them to settle in and returned to check that everything was okay with the boat.

As we arrived we immediately knew something was amiss as our passerelle that normally only just reaches the quay, was pushed back so that our stern was nearly on the quay. We quickly got on board and pulled ourselves off by winching up the anchor a few links. Although the anchor felt like it was holding, could we really be sure? You could never tell if it was the wind stretching out the chain or if the anchor was working loose. Either way, it meant that I would be worrying myself sick until the wind dropped.

Later, the wind decreased enough to make us feel more at ease and we enjoyed an evening meal at one of Ligia's best fish restaurants. The following days went by in a flash as we showed our family around the various shops around Levkas and the beautiful white-pebbled beaches that lined its coast.

The winds continued to blow strongly from the south

and so we decided that taking Mother sailing would not be such a good idea. Instead, we managed to squeeze all six of us into the car and drove to Nidri and Sivota. Both places were just as charming approaching from land instead of the sea and there had been no sickness to worry about.

The following day being overcast, we had a lazy day of chatting and catching up on news. A siesta was needed to recover from all the travelling and eating out. Dudley and I were now so used to a quiet easy life that all this excitement was wearing us out! We were just awaking from our sleep when there was a bang and a crash and we could hear voices shouting everywhere.

Dudley and I scrambled out of bed in time to get the gist of what had happened. There had been one really strong gust of southerly wind that had caused the yacht on our starboard side to drag their anchor. This meant we had the full weight of their yacht and the wind on our anchor and she was not going to hold much longer. We had already been pushed back to such a degree that I donned my boots and took up my usual position in these circumstances and sat on the stern pushing a fender between *Orpheus* and the quayside. This was starting to feel like an old routine as we had been through this so many times in bad winds and we both knew what needed to be done.

As the wind continued to blow, Dad and Dudley went ashore to try to get the yacht alongside us off the quay and away ready to re-lay. Until they stopped laying on us we were trapped and couldn't move anywhere. The force of the wind was compounding the situation and the yacht pushing on us was making the yacht on our port side strain at its anchor. If something was not done quickly we were all in danger of smashing our sterns on the quay.

By this time the quayside was abuzz with people from everywhere. Those sailors who know Levkas well knew that if the winds became strong enough from the south there would definitely be sailors in need. People from the marina and further along the quay all came running round to offer assistance, doing anything and everything to help to ensure that any damage to the yachts was minimised.

Neil, a fellow Norfolk man living in Greece and a very good friend of ours, appeared out of nowhere and took charge of the situation with great ease and expertise, having seen the very same thing a thousand times before. They cast off the yacht alongside us and then Neil, Dudley and Dad came back on board and got ready to cast us off. I was at the anchor with the instruction to winch it up as fast as possible and not to stop for anything. Neil took the helm and was preparing, at full revs, to take us straight out into the wind and off the quay. Dud and Dad were in charge of the mooring lines and Mother was in charge of keeping Harry out from under everyone's feet, a highly understated but important job.

I am very happy to report we left the quay like 'streaked lightening'. We shot away from the quay and the anchor came straight up. Once in relative safety, we prepared ourselves to come alongside the quay further down where the wind would be more on the bow and less dangerous to our yacht. Dudley asked Neil to take the helm as, without a doubt, he was the more experienced person to be negotiating the winds and we prepared to step ashore and secure lines. Needless to say, we came alongside without a hiccup with Neil's help, and were again safely moored at the quayside.

We had tried to explain to our family when they arrived why we had been so nervous about leaving the yacht on the quay in the bad winds but I do not think they really understood the full potential of the wind and damage that could be caused. It was just another experience for us, but I believe, an eye-opener for them.

The winds remained relentless throughout the next day so it was a trip to Vassiliki in the car and the men decided they would like to go fishing off the rocks. Mother and I lay on the beach watching the windsurfers and enjoying the sunshine. Our summer had been unbelievable. The last rain we could remember was early in May and we were now at the end of September. Never before had we known such good weather for such a prolonged period of time and, even better, been able to enjoy it. The winters in Greece can be cold and wet but I think most people would agree that it's easier living with a short period of bad weather knowing there is four months of non-stop sunshine to follow.

My optimism of the weather was shattered the following day when we took the boat to Ligia and picked up the family. We had decided the weather looked calm enough to do the usual sightseeing circuit of the Onassis' island of Scorpios. Just as we were approaching the island on a windless grey day, the skies opened and it started to drizzle, then shower and then rain very heavily. A quick lap of the island and we were soon back in Levkas.

The following day, the weather broke out into the usual sunshine and we motored to a bay that had many names attributed to it by yachties. We called it St. Nicks as on the charts it is shown as Agios Nicholias but others called it 50 degree bay and one tree bay – for obvious reasons. On the way to the bay my brother and father decided they would like to trawl a fishing line to see if they could catch something edible. In a very short space of time my brother raised the alarm indicating he had a bite. Very slowly and carefully, he pulled in the line, as he didn't want the fish to get free from the lure. What happened next was totally unbelievable.

As Tony reeled in the fish we all looked at the water behind the boat, waiting to see the size of what he had caught. As he slowly pulled the one hooked fish the whole shoal followed behind. We had a shoal of approximately a hundred fish swimming behind our boat following the doomed member of their clan. I couldn't believe the other fish didn't recognise or sense the distress of the hooked fish. Surely they could tell he was about to meet his doom? Why didn't they save themselves and swim away? It was only as Tony lifted the fish from the water that the others realised they were in danger and darted away from the boat.

The fish having been murdered and filleted by Tony, a trained chef, we were on our way again. Father now had the bit between his teeth and had a very determined look on his face. He wanted to land a fish like Tony's, only bigger, and he wanted it very badly. Alas, it wasn't going to happen for him that day as we motored on, watching huge orange and white jellyfish float past the boat. Their big frilled edges and long tendrils did nothing to entice a person to want to swim in the waters, which was what we were heading to the bay to do.

We entered a bay of crystal blue waters, surrounded by velvet green slopes and white beaches. The swim was cooling and such great fun as my brother discovered the benefits of a buoyant wetsuit. The wind gradually increased as we ate lunch and by the time the galley had been cleared, we had twenty knots of wind and were able to have an exciting sail back to Levkas.

Father was at the helm, calling, "Lee ho," as Dudley pulled the genoa across.

A little voice from the top step of the companionway said, "Should there be water on the floor down here?" Jayne, my brother's partner, had noticed water running over the wooden floor below. I ran below and immediately put on the bilge pump I then asked Dudley to come and investigate what had happened as I went topside put the engine on and started to put the sails away. I immediately set a heading to the nearest port, which luckily was Ligia just 1.5 miles away.

Dudley appeared from below, announcing that all was under control. The bilge had been emptied and no more water had appeared. It was a mystery as to where the water had come from and so discussions trying a process of elimination were started. In a very short space of time we reached the conclusion that the small leak we had previously found in our calorifier must have become a big leak. The water from the tank must have been held under the bunk in the stern, there being no drainage to the bilge. This pool of water had been tipped over into the engine housing as we heeled over with the sailing and from there had drained through and filled the bilge. I felt relieved that this was all it was and added the removal of the calorifier to our 'winter jobs' list.

The following day we motored to Little Vathi and Spartachori and had lunch at the brothers'. Again, my brother caught a Sea Bass and my father caught nothing. I won't tell you of the expletives my father used to describe the extremely lucky nature of my brother. Jealousy was soon forgotten when the wind finally arrived for the day giving us 19 knots and he took the helm. Close-hauled, we raced through the water back to Ligia.

The next day we sailed from Ligia across to Paleros, and, of course, Father was even more determined that he was going to land a whale sized fish to beat anything caught before. The lines were out trawling when suddenly my father, getting very excited, said, "I've got one. It's a big one I can feel it." All eyes were on the water waiting to get a glimpse of what he had caught. Dudley was hoping it would be a tuna but it was another sea bass. It was the biggest bass we had seen so far and probably measured half a metre long but as with all good fishermen's tales, this one did get away!

Poor Father just couldn't believe his bad luck and was spitting fur as he let the lure out again, hoping to re-catch the fish. In a blink he got another bite, successfully landing it this time. It wasn't quite as big as the previous fish so his elation was somewhat subdued but once everything settled down and the briny was missing one more fish, Father sat back with a very satisfied and smug look on his face. At last he had caught a fish!

We were told by a local fish restaurateur that it was the season for sea bass. With the first strong southerly winds in October the sea bass flood into the stretch of water that lay between Levkas, the mainland and Meganisi. This was the reason why there were so many fish to be caught and so many fishermen out on the waters, fishing. We had wondered why we had found it so difficult to find room to moor in the small fishing harbour of Ligia. Now we understood; it was a busy time of year for them.

To give the sea bass a break we decided to spend the day on Milos Beach, my favourite of all the beaches around Lefkada. We lay watching the kite surfers and enjoying the sound of the rolling surf crashing up the beach. My father loves to dive between the waves of rolling surf as he had been born in Caister a seaside town in Norfolk and had the sea in his blood. That evening we enjoyed watching a colourful display as the sun set and we made a barbecue on the beach. Eating, drinking and watching bonfire flames dance and kiss the darkened sky, we agreed this place truly was a paradise and I began to covet the fantasy of owning a little villa overlooking the beach and mountains.

Market day in Vonitsa arrived, so we took the family to see what it had to offer and then on to Preveza for a shopping spree and lunch there. The only trouble with Preveza for a lunchtime treat was the prevalent smell of sewage, which spoiled the harbour restaurant's ambiance. Not deterred, we enjoyed the shops in Preveza and then went back for a quick change and the last night of the family holiday. We chose to eat in the excellent fish restaurant in Ligia harbour and wondered when we would all be together again. Dudley and I were very lucky to enjoy such a wonderful life but sometimes the pain of missing family and friends was great and the freedom to travel home when we wanted would have made a world of difference. We both loved Harry dearly, but whilst he lived it was almost impossible for us to travel anywhere with any amount of freedom.

We waved goodbye the following day and went back to a very quiet and empty boat. We felt like we needed a long rest after all the travelling and excitement but this was not to be had as we had been invited on board another yacht to celebrate a 70th birthday and then to eat out with Captain Pete. A fellow writer who had discovered the Greek Paradise of her dreams many years before, joined us. Lizzie could only be described as a "Luvvie". This is not meant as an insult but the only description I have to fully describe her larger than life personality. During conversations there would be copious amounts of 'Darling!' and, on greeting and parting, two cheek kisses just would not do. She was yet another colourful person, with a colourful life, and a character that touched our lives briefly but in such a way that we will never forget her.

After the boat was cleaned, re-stocked and filled with water, we decided we should take off for the last sail of the season. We were now in the second week of October and thinking back to the previous year this was about the time seriously bad winds started. We hoped they would hold off long enough for us to enjoy just a little more sailing.

CHAPTER 24
NATURE'S WONDERS AND LIGIA

We headed for Paleros and a few days' quiet recuperation prior to going sailing. As with most places these days, we would bump into people we had met before and there would be daytime coffees and chats or evening sundowners to share. On this trip to Paleros we met Sid and Anne who, unfortunately for me, had a windsurfer for sale.

Dudley, having watched the young lady learning in Levkas, was harbouring an increasing urge to try the sport. He had tried it many years before when he was a young man and now thought it might be fun to try it again. Our financial state was not improving and we were only just holding our heads above water so I pointed out to him that if he wanted to purchase the wind surfer he was going to have to pick what other item he did not want; for example the diving equipment he continued to hanker after.

It took only ten minutes of sales talk and a quick look at the wind surfer for Dudley to part with our badly needed cash to purchase the offending board. From the moment he brought it on board I hated the silly thing. He tied its mast, which happened to be fibreglass and very prickly to our shrouds. It always seemed to be me who grabbed hold of it and itched for the rest of the day. He tied the board to our stanchions on the starboard side, which made my lovely *Orpheus* look not only untidy but also very cluttered. I was not happy with the situation at all and was made even more morose by Dud thinking this was a good sport to be trying at his age. I immediately began hinting at my displeasure and nagging that we could ill afford to buy such a thing.

From Paleros on to Spartachori where we met up with Captain Pete and his all male crew. I hated to think of the fun and mischief they were getting up to and was very glad that

Dudley was not sailing off with them the following day. In the morning the forecast indicated a southerly force 7 gusting 8 with storms so we decided not to go sailing and to stay safe in harbour. We asked Babis, one of the brothers owning the pontoon, if they had heard the forecast and he indicated that the wind we had at present would change and if there was a need for us to move the boat he would let us know. The local fishermen had said the wind would come from the north and not south as the Navtex forecast had indicated.

The day followed its usual path until suddenly Babis came and said. "Captain, the wind change. You must move now to the quay the opposite side of the harbour." We did not question what he said, we had been to this idyllic spot many times before and the brothers had always given the utmost help. We re-moored on the quay opposite along with the other 10 boats that had been on their pontoon. They helped each and every one of us into a safe mooring just as the wind changed in one violent gust and what had been a southerly 6 was now a northerly 8.

We had been told whilst sailing around Greece that if you wanted to know what the weather was going to be to ask a fisherman; now I knew exactly why. The fisherman had been right and all the forecasts had been wrong.

These winds continued for three days but we were safely moored in Spartachori with great company from other yachties and the brothers. We decided to take the opportunity to sort out some of the summer things on the boat to store for winter and commence my "Father Christmas" clean. Visitors bedding was aired and stored in bags, cockpit cushions were washed and stored and summer clothing packed away and replaced with long sleeved woollies.

We were not to know this but the packing away was premature. The winds stopped and the weather brightened for what was to continue into a week of sheer bliss and warm sunshine. We left Spartachori and travelled to Sivota where a real treat awaited us. Last time we had visited this enclosed harbour it had been full of yachts and flotillas. This time there were only three yachts to be seen and we were one of them. It was quiet and peaceful and picturesque. It reminded us of the early days when we had first started to sail these waters with Captain Pete. The frightening thing was that those early days were not that long ago and things were changing so fast that the Ionian was in real danger of being spoilt forever.

As we sat drinking sundowners I spotted a cobalt blue kingfisher sitting on top of a lamppost. As if it understood my delight at seeing it, it flew down and landed on our stern anchor and sat looking at me. The kingfisher made a quick study of me and decided that I had nothing to offer and took off to land on the next boat. Loving birds and all wildlife I looked around the quiet harbour and noticed wagtails and blue-tits everywhere. All the times we had previously visited Sivota I had never noticed there were so many birds. I could only guess that when the harbour was busy and full of people the birds became shy and took to the hills.

We left Sivota the following day, sailing towards Big Vathi on the Island of Ithaca. As we rounded the Northern end of Arkoudhi, an uninhabited raised rock/island, we were treated to a display by flying fish. Obviously something big was after them as time and time again they flew from the water and glided across the top surface before re-entering a great distance away from where they had first surfaced.

With Vathi almost in sight, Dud suggested we visit Kioni instead. Kioni was a small harbour that neither of us could remember visiting before. This was the beauty of sailing. We had the ability to change our minds, set the sails and simply go. Making the most of what time we had left this year, we altered course only by a few degrees to take us to this new location. We entered the harbour with an intake of breath. It was small, quaint and very pretty. Some might say, "We've seen it all before," as the harbour was surrounded by colourful buildings, but somehow Kioni had managed to bring the best of Greece together in one, small, delicate and very pleasing parcel.

We spent a pleasant evening here that was only spoiled by the huge surge that came heaving into the harbour around 1830 hours. Apparently this happened every evening and was caused by a super-fast ferry passing by the entrance. It was unfortunate for the yacht moored next to us. They had forgotten to tighten their anchor chain on mooring and when the surge hit their yacht it hit the quay. Dud was off the boat like a shot, assisting in fending the yacht from the quayside whilst the owners managed to tighten their anchor and very quickly peace fell upon Kioni once again.

The following morning, whilst taking Harry ashore, I saw a crowd gathering at the end of the quay, and being curious, I went along to take a look to see what was entertaining them. As I approached I saw a huge octopus slowly crawling towards the harbour wall across the rocks. I shouted for Dud to grab the camera and come quickly but he didn't understand the concept of quickly! The octopus slithered over the rocks completely out of the water. There was obviously something it wanted badly enough to be taking this risk. It came to a rock, picked it up with a tentacle, wrapped it underneath itself and shot back into the depths of the water as fast as it could.

Just as it was taking off again Dudley obviously decided that quickly did mean quickly after all and started to run towards the crowd. One of the women in the gathered group shouted out, "Oh no, please, please don't kill him." She obviously thought Dudley had a weapon and was planning to spear the poor Octopus. It was with a devilish grin that Dudley showed the lady the camera. He was clearly enjoying the scare he had given.

The upshot of Dud's languor was that I missed a perfect picture opportunity with the octopus out of the water and had to console myself with a shot of a huge red sea-centipede. My disappointment at missing one magic moment was assuaged a little later as we sailed towards Poros on the island of Cephalonia. I managed to capture a photo of a dolphin as it played with the bows of *Orpheus*. We were just rounding the southern tip of Ithaca when we saw three dolphins approaching the yacht. Holding the course steady to allow them to come to us we enjoyed watching them swim underneath the boat. One of them went to the bow and I managed, on shaking jelly legs, to stand on the bow and capture what I consider to be the best photograph I've ever taken. I don't know how I managed it as I was so excited and my legs were so unsteady.

Two dolphins were standing off, just swimming alongside *Orpheus* and one gave a nod and swam away as if it had said, "That's enough now. Come along." At this command the little dolphin playing with the bow simply swam away with the others. My excitement was such that half an hour later, when I was trying to make lunch, I kept breaking the crackers in my shaking hands. What a special treat the day had turned out to be! There were so many beautiful things that nature had to offer. The world is such a wonderful place with treasures hidden everywhere for ungrateful humans to find.

We had not been to Poros since our first holiday with Captain Pete. We were looking forward to it very much as we remembered our Karaoke evening with Peter winning the booby prize! We remembered a long golden beach backed by tavernas and a picturesque walk along the road to the harbour that was backed by gardens. Sometimes it pays not to go back to places that you have fallen in love with, as I would rather have held onto the memory I had prior to this one of our second visit.

We arrived at Poros and were instantly made aware of a huge ferry berth and mooring buoy placed in the middle of the harbour. Because of the time of year we were able to easily find a mooring alongside the quay but we were blissfully unaware of what was to come. Flotilla boats began to arrive and it was quite clear they didn't have a clue what they were doing. Dud had to assist every one of them into a mooring at the quay. Once this was done he learned they had just picked the boats up and were delivering them for the company to their wintering destination. They were doing this in exchange for a free holiday, which was fine until we realised they had no qualifications, not even an ICC which was a basic requirement to sail most European waters!

The last of the flotilla boats to come into the harbour messed about lining up in the harbour right in front of one of the biggest ferries I had ever seen. Dud shouted for him to stand off and to clear the path for the ferry but he was totally oblivious to what was happening as he continued his mooring. Dud helped him in to speed his process and asked him what he thought he was doing and questioned why he hadn't stood off and waited for the ferry to come in ahead of him. His reply was that he simply had not seen the ferry behind him! A boat the size of a hotel approaching close to the stern of his yacht and he hadn't seen it! Now I was really worried!

Unfortunately this was not the end of my disappointment. The ferry came in to berth, as did a second, and their mooring lines were tied to the buoy in the centre of the harbour, which in effect closed off the entrance and exit unless you were a very shallow draught fishing boat. I became distressed at the sight of many tiny dead fish surrounding the ferries. Either they had put something into the water or it had been the sheer force of their thrusters that caused this killing. As if this waste and pollution wasn't enough these ferries commenced to run their generators all night long, resulting in a very noisy and sleepless night for all in the harbour.

Trying to make the most of the visit, we took a walk along the road from the harbour to the village of Poros. The roadway had now been paved which was a positive step forward for the yachtie walking about in the dark on the trip home. As we rounded a corner and commenced our walk down to the beach my heart sank. Where was the long golden beach of before? It somehow seemed to have shrunk and the clean, golden sand was no more. It was now dark brown and stained with oil. Obviously the ferries were taking a toll on the cleanliness of the beach and the whole place seemed dirty, run down and spoiled. What in our memories had been one of the best places we had ever been to had turned into one of the worst.

The brightest moment of our visit to Poros was our trip to the port police to book in. Captain Pete had experienced much trouble with the port police here and we were expecting a surly reception. When we arrived we were met at the door by a young lad who was pleased to see us and, in fact, turned and ran ahead of us saying, "Please come this way." We walked slowly behind him and entered the office as he switched the television off. We did not think anything of this and went about our booking in process. It was Dud who noticed that on the blank TV screen, in the bottom right-hand corner, it read Eroticas FM!! Maybe it wasn't our stunning looks and friendly personality that had made the port police man so happy to see us.

The following morning we watched with interest as the flotilla yachts fumbled out of the harbour, one of them pushing almost raw oil out of his exhaust as he revved his engine so hard. We left disappointed but not deterred as the sun was still shining and the winds were still blowing. The days' winds were light so we decided to make our way up the channel between Cephalonia and Ithaca heading for Eufemia. As the flights to the local airport at Preveza had stopped we found another empty harbour. The village was empty of tourists and not one flotilla was in sight as most of these had finished with the last of the flights. The only yachts left around the Ionian at this time were either private yachts or live-aboards enjoying the last of the summer sailing prior to settling down for winter.

Eufemia is a large harbour with much to see and do but it was clear that the shops and restaurants were closing down for the winter. There was a stillness that did not seem to sit right for the place as we knew it. A bustling busy place, like a grizzly bear full of life and energy was going into hibernation. At least this meant we were going to get a good night's sleep.

The following day, Dudley, in his wisdom, decided that we were getting quite proficient with our sailing routine and thought perhaps it was time for me to take the helm. I had been enjoying sailing without arguments and mistakes and I was very loath to upset the apple cart but I did understand his point of view. I really did need to get used to helming *Orpheus* into a mooring. The next half hour was very gruelling as Dudley made me bring the yacht alongside first starboard side, then port side, time and time again. Then he moved on to reversing up to the quay several times as well. This was all well and good but Eufemia was a large harbour and at this time there were no other yachts around. I knew that if there had been a full harbour and a crosswind my performance would have left a lot to be desired but I wasn't letting on. Happy that I could bring the boat into moor if I had to, Dudley allowed us to go sailing further north to Fiskado. Could it be that with the extra sailing confidence Dudley was gaining he was becoming more confident as a captain and more aware of his responsibilities? I hoped so.

This trip was proving to be full of surprises. We remembered Fiskado as a busy, noisy and over crowded place. We had never anchored in the harbour with Captain Pete, but in a neighbouring bay just to avoid the clamour. We were very pleased to find the harbour relatively empty and the waters very clear, blue and clean. Obviously somebody had noticed a decline in previous years and had turned this place around. Buildings were cared for, the streets were clean and gardens well-kept. The pontoons were well tended and the waters were not in the slightest bit polluted. It was one of the few harbours around Greece that I would have been happy to swim in. Either our memories were playing tricks on us, or Fiskado had regained its beauty like a Phoenix arising from the ashes.

It was time for us to be making our way back towards Levkas to settle for the winter and we decided one more visit to the brothers at Spartachori was in order to wish them a good winter. Storms had been forecast for the following day and we could think of nowhere we would rather be hauled up for a few days. It turned out we were there for three days before we could make our way to Paleros where we spent a week alongside the quay. During the summer months, with so many yachts in the Ionian, it was usual to moor stern or bows to. At this time of year with so few yachts out sailing and such unpredictable weather it seemed the norm was to moor alongside.

During our time in Paleros we were lucky enough to see the "Ohi Day" celebrations that were rather downbeat this time compared to those we had seen the previous year in Levkas, although the ethos was the same with proud parents and confident children parading the streets. Knowing the weather was due to change to bad northerly winds we decided to leave Paleros, but were unsure where to head for.

Contacting friends we had left behind in Levkas, we found out the whole town quay had been dug up and was completely untenable to any yacht. This was also the case in Nidri and Vassiliki. We discovered that the government had released funds to the villages to repair the earthquake damage to the quays and what better time to carry out this work than through the winter when there were no tourists? Alas, this meant that our options of mooring had been reduced quite considerably so we trusted to luck and headed to the fishing harbour of Ligia.

We came alongside the harbour wall mooring at the very end and asked the local fishermen if we were going to be in their way. Their response was very gracious and they welcomed us to their community with open arms saying we could stay as long as we liked and that they were happy to see us there. It was now the end of October and it was going to be a whole month before we could afford to go into the Levkas Marina for the winter. Our budget was still so strained that we dare not risk booking into the Marina before the beginning of December so we hoped that the Ligia fishermen would extend their hospitality to us for the month of November.

Dud collected the car from Levkas and brought it to Ligia so we had transport and the ability to go shopping in town. It also gave him the freedom to take himself off and help continue renovating a Spiti in the hills with a friend. Whilst he was away working I began to put the boat in order and continued the "Father Christmas clean" I had already started. I stripped all the cupboards and sorted contents. I cleaned and dusted everything in sight to ensure that when Father Christmas came he would see I deserved a present. You may think what you wish but in my heart he does still exist and I like it that way just fine.

Being in Ligia with no shower facilities available made washing my long blonde hair a very cold and miserable affair. We had to take strip washes instead of showers as the sun wasn't strong enough to heat the water and the cockpit was too cold to be getting undressed in. Dud was away a lot of the time and I was getting a little depressed with my lot in life. There was no money, no shower, cold water, the weather cooling and I was alone most of the time. My only companions were the fishermen and I tried not to socialise with them too much because they were Egyptian crews away from their families and I was not sure what their culture was in this respect. So it was that I gained the nickname "Lil Lonely in Ligia"!

Dud and I enjoyed walks along the beach and never failed to be pleased by the mountainous scenery and views of the sea. Lefkada is a beautiful island and I was sure I would be happy never to leave it. As we sat in the winter sunshine one day we watched as a little elderly fisherman sat baiting hooks on a long line. He sat there for what seemed hours without a drink so I went and offered him a coffee. This was a very daring thing for me to do and I was certain he would politely refuse. I knew the Greeks liked to drink their coffee in a completely different way from the English and rather than be rude they would simply refuse the offer. You can imagine my shock when he said, "Yes, please."

With a shaking hand I served coffee to the gentleman accompanied by a glass of water. He seemed delighted that I had made the effort to serve the coffee in the Greek way and began telling Dudley about his family. It transpired his home was in the village we had walked to several times above the harbour at Little Vathi on the island of Meganisi. He came to Ligia to bait his lines and fish for a few days at a time to make money. He would then return to the bosom of his family for a few days before repeating the whole process again.

He finished baiting his lines and as it was getting late in the day, I offered him a beer. He declined, saying he was to fish early the next morning and when he returned he would have fish for me. I always knew that my chatting to fishermen would get me into trouble and now it had – he wanted to repay my kindness by giving me some of the fish he would catch during his dawn raid. Dud thought the whole thing hilarious. I knew I couldn't refuse his offer, as he would be offended. I also knew that I would have to taste the fish so when I told him how lovely they were I would not be lying to him completely. Oh, what a dilemma I was in! I hate the taste of fish and I hate the thought of killing fish and now I was going to be made to cook them.

The following morning there was a tap on the boat and I went out to see this lovely, weather beaten, gentle fisherman standing beside the boat with his hands full of fish. "I had a very good night fishing," he said and held his hands out for me to take the fish.

"Dudley!" I called, "Bring me a plate, please." I handed the plate to the fisherman to place the fish on so I didn't have to touch them and thanked him for his kindness. It seemed to me it was some two hours later that Dudley was still laughing at the expression on my face as he cleaned the fish ready to eat.

Normally, I would refuse to cook the fish, but as this man had been so kind to give them to us I couldn't bear to think of the waste of their lives if Dudley didn't eat them. I relented and grilled the fish and then dared to have a taste of a piece. I'm sorry I just do not like fish and I was very grateful that I did not have to tell this to the fisherman, as when we awoke the following, day he had gone.

I have a very fond affection for the Greek fishermen. They all look so craggy, serious and angry but once you get talking to them and get beyond the outer appearance they are some of the most caring, gentle and friendly people amongst the Greek community. I hold a particular affection for my "red fisherman" and his friend "Kyriakos" in Levkas and now for this little man who at the age of seventy-six was still working for his family. He had touched my heart.

Another moment that gave us hours of fun and delight that we can enjoy even now, is the memory and innocence of a conversation we overheard outside our yacht one evening on the Ligia quay. We had noticed during the daytime that there seemed to be a lot of English people walking about and presumed they must be part of some last minute end-of-summer holiday group. That evening, whilst enjoying some music and a glass of wine by candlelight, we heard the voices of a couple outside *Orpheus*.

A strong male Cornish or Devonshire accent proclaimed right outside our boat, "That's a private yacht, that is. Look there. That's Greek on the front there; that's the name of the boat, so it's Greek then I reckon." As we were alongside, the gentleman could not see that most yachts in Greece have the name on the bow one side in English and in Greek on the other side, and he obviously was looking at "_____" the Greek version of "Orpheus".

A gentle version of the same accent said, "Oh yeah, I see that."

The man continued with excitement, "See there, that's a pukka job that is. I'd love to go sailing around the harbour in that." Now Dud and I, still listening, were positively basking in the glory of owning the yacht that this man had called "the pukka job". We were almost tempted to go outside and invite them in as we had with many others, always happy to share *Orpheus* with anyone.

Before we could move, the gentleman carried on, "See that there; that's a life raft that is."

"Oh yeah," came the echoing reply.

"It's stupid I reckon. They reckon if that big boat there is sinking then that little old thing there is gonna save them. They'd be better off sailing that little old thing and towing the big one behind." At this point I am ashamed to say Dudley and I were rolling around in our seats laughing. The innocence of the comment was touching. He clearly knew nothing but would dearly have loved to. We were inside, sitting in candlelight, and found it hard to believe they couldn't see the light from outside. It was even more unbelievable that they didn't know someone was listening; so, as we cowered below trying to suppress laughter, the couple outside continued.

"What's that there then? Do they use that?" The question from Mrs. Unknown had made me very curious. What were they looking at now?

"Oh no, they won't use that," said Mr Unknown. "That's matting that is. That'll be screwed down to the deck, that will." We then realised that they were talking about a rope mat Dud had made that we placed on the side deck to step onto when coming aboard. "No," continued the man "That's matting and that'll be screwed down."

"No it's not," said the lady. "No. Look. There aren't any screws. No, it's not. You lift it up and see." As we sat below we watched through the side windows as the man bent over the top of our guardrail and picked up the rope mat.

"Oh no! You're right. It's not screwed down but they won't use it because they'd have to make the mat up like that every night, wouldn't they?"

"I suppose so; I suppose you're right," she replied. With that they walked away into the night and Dudley and I spent the next hour reliving the whole unbelievable conversation we had just been witness to. I felt as though we had been really naughty in not making our presence known but on the other hand it was really encouraging for me to witness such innocence, an innocence that I thought had disappeared in this world and I was heartened to know it still existed.

The following evening we had a treat to listen to a different couple, bearing the same accent, give a great detailed account about how we would "Use those black bags to shower. They fill them with water; the sun heats the water and then they shower with those bags."

"No, do they?"

"Yes, I tell you they are shower bags."

The fact that on the black plastic, written in big white letters it said "SOLAR SHOWER BAG" just didn't seem to convince the young lady that that's what they were!

The middle of November came and so did the rains, almost non-stop for three days. We decided to re-visit the waterfalls at Nidri, as on our previous visit during the summer they had been dry. We felt certain that after all the rain there would be something for us to see, but as it was the first flood of water it brought with it all the loose earth. The waters, instead of being clear and pretty, were pretty muddy. Friends told us later that with the continued rain the waters had cleared and were much prettier for it.

Being "lonely in Ligia" I had a whim to try to play Dudley's Ukulele, which we had brought out with us from England. I started to strum along and teach myself 'When I'm cleaning windows' and Dud thought it was hilarious. For some unknown reason I seemed to just pick it up and thoroughly enjoyed playing it too. My rather fat fingers found some of the chords difficult but nonetheless I persevered and soon was giving a performance that sounded something like the actual tune!

During this lonely month I also filled my days with cooking. Slowly I began to bake cakes, buns and bread, anything really, just to see if the oven would cook it, how long it took and judge what would need to be cooked on high and what required low. By the end of my time in Ligia I had lost my fear of the oven and began to feel a little more confident about trying to bake other things.

Alas, our fun in Ligia came to an end all too soon as they began to dig up the quayside there as well. We stayed as long as we could but we still had ten days before we could go into the marina. It seemed there was no quayside space left anywhere that hadn't been dug up. We contacted Joe in Levkas and he allowed us to moor on his mole until the first of December when we moved *Orpheus* for the first time in fifteen months into a marina.

CHAPTER 25
LOVELY LEVKAS 'LECTRICTY

We booked into the port police to announce our arrival for winter and secured our mooring on the mole for the short time we were to be there. I was touched by the big hairy grin the 'Red Fisherman' and his friend gave us as they noticed we were back in Levkas.

As we settled on the mole, live-aboard yachties came and went, all looking for somewhere safe to spend their winter. One of these yachties stayed on the mole next to us and over a period of time we got to know Jonathon, a very friendly ex-ambulance driver who, throughout the winter, became known to everyone for his catch phrase, "Did I ever tell you I had a boat on the Thames?" Jonathon was such a big part of our winter that year that I want to mention him so that we can always remember him and so those reading who might have known him can smile in his memory.

Things were all moving along very quickly. The beautiful Baia who worked in Joe's office was getting married, a new hardware store was opening, Christmas was fast approaching and Dud was pre-occupied in re-laminating our life raft cover and getting it serviced ready for next year's sailing. In amongst all of this one of Jonathon's two cats decided to go walk about.

Before taking to our beds we had tried to help find the cat. Even the Red Fisherman had looked for it and appeared as concerned as the rest of us. In the middle of the night as we lay there we could hear Jonathon calling out for the missing cat. It was heartbreaking to hear him walking the length of the town quay calling out in desperation. The next morning I tried to explain what I understood about cat behaviour and kept insisting the cat would not stray outside of its territory until such time as it knew where it was and knew how to get home again. I suggested he tried looking at all the other boats along the mole to see if it was trapped. Later that afternoon he came to tell me that he had found 'Puddy' trapped inside a yacht at the end of the mole. He had airlifted him through an open hatch to his freedom and returned him to his playmate "Tom Tom". Jonathon was naturally very happy to have found the cat safe and sound and when he told the Red Fisherman about it he responded by giving him one of his best toothy grins.

I tried to settle into the winter discipline of exercise and study. I was desperately trying to learn Greek but Dud showed little interest so I spent fleeting moments trying to hold conversations with the Levkas fishermen. The live-aboard community within the marina was starting to grow and activities were commencing. Dudley and I went along to the exercise classes and Dudley was very keen to become involved in the music group as he had a five-string banjo on board and was eager to play it. He went along for the first session and came back perky as a pig in spring. There would clearly be no need for me to wonder where he was every Saturday morning of the winter!

Neil, a fellow Norfolk man, was fast becoming a close friend and a great source of knowledge. He came to visit us frequently to chat, drink coffee and enjoy my culinary offerings that no doubt reminded him of the delicious things his mother used to bake for him when he was a young man living in England. On one such visit he asked Dudley if he would go with him to collect a boat from Nidri and sail it back to Levkas. Without hesitation Dud agreed and the two men were gone. I tried to take my mind off things by baking a Christmas cake and pickling some onions but couldn't help but worry. I was sensing there was something not quite right. The boat appeared late afternoon with Neil and Dud safe on board and I was told a tale of being stranded in the canal with engine problems. It was best I didn't mull over the worst-case scenario of what could happen and simply be grateful Dud was back.

Being back on the mole meant that Car Park "Parkie", the stray Labrador, had taken to our daily routine with Harry, and seemed to want to come for an evening and morning walk with us. We didn't mind; in fact we enjoyed it. I just had to battle with myself on the rainy days not to take him on board and try to make him mine. He was a stray dog and had always had his freedom. As much as I loved him, so did many others and to try to tame him and restrict his freedom seemed almost as cruel as leaving him out in the rain. Dudley had told me in no uncertain terms that he WAS NOT coming on board and I WAS NOT going to have another dog. We loved Harry dearly but when he finally left this world there would be no others. The constraints being placed on our lives on board were many and some were not easily overcome, especially when we wanted to travel home to visit family. Once again, Christmas time was coming and I would have liked to visit our family and friends, but because of Harry we found this impossible.

At last the first of December arrived and Dud announced it was time to move the boat into the marina and plug into ELECTRICITY! The evenings and mornings had become increasingly cold and damp and Dud knew how strongly I felt about not wanting to spend another damp winter on board. We had invested in an oil filled radiator in preparation for our arrival in the marina and that evening, for the first time since leaving England, I had radiated heat.

It's strange how much a little thing like electricity can change your life. At first I had not missed having it at all and could not see what all the fuss was about. I had managed very well with 12v for music, reading books, battery lighting, gas heating and hand washing. I didn't think I needed electricity for anything other than ensuring we stay warm and damp free through the winter. Oh how gullible and wrong I was! I had a whale of a time with lovely Levkas 'lectricity.

First we plugged in the radiator and then the television and to our delight we found a local television channel showing English films. I then went about putting up my Christmas decorations and realised that I could have real Christmas lights this year as opposed to one string of six lights being battery operated. I sent Dud to the local shop to buy two sets immediately. I was having an excellent time with all this electricity and it finally dawned on me just how much I had missed by not having it.

The community life within the marina was now in full swing with exercise classes twice a week, pot luck suppers, pool nights, first aid seminars, quiz nights and a music group; to which Dud kept trying to get me to attend with the Ukulele, but being the shy and retiring type I wouldn't... I'll pause here because those who know me now would never believe that statement!

The yachties living aboard this year were all different from the previous year, but having witnessed the deterioration in relationships the year before, Dudley and I agreed not to become too involved in anything or with anyone. Little did we know how close and how good a yachting community could be.

Once settled in the marina, Dud began his winter jobs, the first of which was to take the oven apart and make an attempt at fixing the rings so they would turn down without popping out and to find out why the oven would not stay alight properly. After some hours of rubbing and screwing, sanding and huffing he put the oven burners back together and lit the oven. THEY WORKED! I finally had an oven that worked and Dud had fixed it so I could turn the rings down to a simmer! He still couldn't see a reason for the oven not to burn evenly but we had already learned the trick of leaving the oven door open when first lighting it for a few minutes. Once the oven had warmed a little the door could be shut and it would work in a normal way. To this day it remains the same but having cooked many a gourmet meal in it, it no longer holds the fear and dread that it used to.

With the introduction of electricity into my life I began to relax and thoroughly enjoy life on board. As we sat watching television one evening, a question occurred to me, "What didn't we have at that present time that we had when we were living in a house?" Safely moored in Levkas Marina we had wonderful showers, a laundry at the cost of €10 a wash, a local bar with a pool table and regularly cleaned quaysides with bins being emptied every day. We had a local doctor, dentist, hospital and vet, not to mention fresh bakeries and vegetable markets. Thinking about it we had more now than we'd ever had before. The only thing missing from on board *Orpheus* was a bath!

I was very happy indeed and very content. If we could only keep the flats let in England to enable us to get our finances straight we were sure we could lead a very happy life on a relatively small amount of money. At that moment we were struggling to achieve that because of the troubles we were experiencing at home with the properties.

In spite of our contentment, just to keep us on our toes, we hit a run of bad luck that resulted in the need for the engine alternator to be overhauled and a major repair to the galley foot pump for fresh water. Dud took the pump out onto the pontoon to fix it and met a man that was to change our outlook on the rest of the winter. We had kept ourselves to ourselves as we had agreed and only attended a few social gatherings. As Dud was working away, Kevan, a chap from a yacht further along our pontoon, stopped and offered his help. Dud is definitely a man that works better with some moral support and so he gladly took the help offered. A wonderful sunny December day, warm and bright passed by in a haze of chit-chat and work. By sunset a friendship had been struck that would not only keep us amused through this winter but for years to come.

It's strange how people pass through your life affecting you in different ways. Some become passing acquaintances and others friends or soul mates. We've met so many people from so many different walks of life and for every one of them I give thanks for the opportunity we had to meet them. Dudley and I felt very lucky in having the chance to live this life with such wonderful people and in an attempt to give something back to the friends we made that winter, we thought it was time again for the "Cuddly Dudley Karaoke Road Show". Dud enjoys the pleasure of having and giving the chance to hear people enjoy themselves. Yachties all seem to live by the ethos of giving which seems endless and the more you give the more you seem to receive in return. Despite ourselves, we were becoming more and more involved with the community and becoming closer to all of them.

The nights began getting colder and Parkie, our stray Labrador friend, had gone missing. We didn't know it then but we would never see him again. However this was not a time of year for sadness. Christmas Eve was here at last. We enjoyed mulled wine in the candlelit community room and sang carols and my excitement grew. I couldn't wait for Christmas morning to come because, unbeknown to Dudley, I had asked a friend to bring some Woods Rum back from England. This was Dudley's favourite drink and as he was going to be 65 years old in the New Year I wanted him to have a special surprise. It had been a very hard job to keep it hidden on board, as there are not too many places that are not in daily use. I figured he wouldn't be using his wet suit for a while so had hidden the surprise bottle there.

We had decided that we did not want to have our

Christmas lunch with the community in a local hotel. With the lovely Levkas electricity we were happy to have the day to ourselves and eat alone on board *Orpheus*. We woke to partake of the Page family ritual of special coffee after breakfast and I presented Dud with the first of four clues to solve to lead him to his ultimate present. He had not failed me either. The fact we had little to no money had not deterred him from buying me several little presents to open. I just love those silly little things that I can guess and feel and tear open; chocolates, candles and an electric toaster! Without a grill on our oven I had been unable to make cheese on toast in a satisfactory way. I can't ever remember being so excited about electricity or cheese toasties in my whole life. I LOVE LEVKAS 'LECTRICITY.

We had a very nice Christmas day that ran into a Christmas week. We had a social life with great people and had so much fun that I really didn't have time to miss family or friends at home. It sounds a really shallow thing to say but the truth of it is, it appeared with the introduction of electricity. We had become so busy doing things that we simply didn't have time to miss our families. This winter other yachties had been our family and we couldn't have wished for a better replacement; we had much to be thankful for.

Dud's birthday arrived and I wanted him to enjoy his day but didn't know what to do to make it special for him. I have always hated using any method of voice recording or loudspeaker as my Norfolk accent makes me cringe. Whenever I hear it played back I conjure a picture in my mind of a floppy hat, white smock and a long piece of straw between teeth being sucked on. Putting all these fears aside I used the VHF radio for the first time to invite everyone round for drinks. From mid morning to mid afternoon there was a constant flow of people coming to celebrate Dudley' birthday. The first of the visitors was a Norwegian family – Kristian, Jane, Martin and Marie. They came knocking on the hull in their dinghy and as Dudley went out in response to the knocking they began waving their national flag and singing the Norwegian version of Happy Birthday. This family had touched our hearts in a very big way and, like so many special people we've met, we shall always stay in touch.

Just after Christmas the lady who had been providing exercises classes for the wintering community left the marina.

Dudley, knowing I had been a qualified aerobic instructor, put my name forward to take over the keep fit classes when she left. Once I got over the shock of having to remember what to do I knuckled down to making up a routine and recording some music. I had taken classes before Dudley and I met but this had been many years before and my nerves were getting the better of me as I stood before the first massed group. I need not have worried as everyone encouraged me and helped me to relax and let my latent training come to the fore. I had always liked to keep my classes light and fun and with this group of people it was made very easy. We chatted, we shared jokes and we gelled as a unit of people. Jonathon did his own thing in the corner at double time until his head steamed and Chris could be heard to say, "Are you sure?" every time I shouted, "Twenty more!" We all had such fun together and the dynamics between the different ages, sexes and abilities simply made it all the better. By the end of the winter our little group had become known as the "Keep Fatters".

As we still had a car for transport we decided to assist a member of the community with a lift to Ioannina. We made the seventy-kilometre journey through snow-covered mountains that provided us with some breathtaking scenery. The lake and town of Ioannina were certainly bigger than we imagined they would be and we could be forgiven for thinking we had left the country of Greece. As we stood looking across a lake with a mountainous backdrop and turrets it put us in mind of Switzerland or Austria. It was a very pretty and busy little place with a hospital that provided cancer treatment. On the way back we stopped at a fresh trout farm. This was definitely not the best bit of the journey for me. "Fresh" meant very fresh, as they were still swimming around. One minute they were happily swimming around a freshwater tank and the next they were dead, gutted and wrapped up in paper!

Having visited the hospital in Ioannina it made us feel very grateful that since leaving England we had been in the best of health and not needed any kind of treatment. Many fellow cruisers had not been as lucky and had required treatments in both Ioannina and Levkas town. We were encouraged by what they had to say about the hospital treatment in both places. There did not seem to be any waiting lists for major or minor surgery. Blood and ECG tests were carried out and results were available within the hour. They really seemed to have their system together. Individuals were made responsible for their own health records and the results of tests and x-rays were given to the patient to keep. In Greece it is the individual's responsibility to keep their records in order and to bring them to the hospital when next attending or requiring treatment. If a prolonged stay in hospital was required it was usual for a family member to feed the patient, as the hospital food was limited. However the visiting rules were not so strict – 9 a.m. to noon and 2 p.m. to 10 p.m. Even these times were flexible as family members are encouraged to bathe, wash and feed the patients. I thought then and still think now that the Greeks have a perfect system: adults being responsible for their own records and lots of family contact when you need it most. It was a comfort to know that good treatment was available if we should need it but for now we were just enjoying our winter.

    Unbeknown to me Dudley had asked a fellow yachtie if I could borrow her classical guitar so I could go along to the music group. Dud was thoroughly enjoying it and he wanted me to join in the fun. I felt rather nervous about this as I had never played a guitar before and I hated the thought that I might damage what was almost an heirloom. Dudley talked me round into trying it out, as he always does, coercing me into trying different things and so I went along for my first lesson with Pete and the music group.

    In a short space of time I began to enjoy the sessions and found myself practising almost every day, trying to remember the chords. For some strange reason I found the guitar, as with the Ukulele, quite easy to learn and so when my birthday came around Dudley treated me to a guitar of my own. It had been a special birthday for me. I had just turned forty and with the money I had received from family and friends in England Dud made up the difference to buy me a steel string acoustic guitar. By the end of March I was feeling confident enough to join Peter playing for a sing-along with the rest of the yachties in the community room. I couldn't believe I had learned so much in such a short space of time. The trouble was, now I was hooked on playing, I wanted to learn more about picking and strumming to improve the sound I was making.

    Winter times always seem to be about fun, frolic, keeping fit and trips home. This winter was no different and we had volunteered to drive a couple to the airport so we could take the opportunity to do some sightseeing around Athens. Luckily, another couple offered to baby-sit Harry whilst we had our day away, which was a huge bonus because this meant we didn't have to worry about leaving him in the car. We awoke at 0430 hours and dropped Harry round to Steve and Shelagh, his mum and dad for the day. We arrived in Athens by lunchtime and said our goodbyes to our friends. We parked the car in the airport car park and caught a bus into the centre of Athens to visit the sights. As we drove through on the bus and saw all the traffic hooting, swerving and nearly hitting each other, we were very glad we had decided not to drive ourselves into the centre.

Once there, we did a whirlwind tour of the National Park, Zappelion, and Temple of Zeus and then headed for the Acropolis. We obviously approached the Acropolis from the wrong side because we ended up nearly circumnavigating the whole structure before we could find a gate that would allow us entry. As we arrived at the ticket booth I looked at my watch and realised that we had only twenty minutes to walk around the site and from the look of the stairs it was going to take us that long to get to the top. Better judgement told me that €27 was a high price to pay for twenty minutes so we walked away, disappointed that the four other gates we had passed had been locked.

Athens was huge. I really cannot put into words the vastness of it as we stood on the Acropolis hillside overlooking a valley full of buildings and structures. It almost seemed as though they would go on forever if it were not for another mountain stopping the spread. Walking around the town, there was almost a physical buzz about the place. It was manic, frenzied, busy, and smoggy with traffic everywhere. I couldn't believe the atmosphere that hung in the air; everyone in this place meant business. It was well worth the trip and the effort to see, feel and smell the very being of Athens. Sadly there was a bus waiting to take us back to the airport and the car. We needed to be on the road back to Levkas so as not to be too late to pick up Harry.

It has to be stressed that this is the reality of life on board with a dog. We had come to live this life to enable us to see something of the world but we were definitely being held back by the love we had for our little dog. We were back in

Levkas by 2130 hours in order to pick Harry up from the kind sitters. We didn't realise it then but it was to be the start of a lasting friendship with Steve and Shelagh and they would remain Harry's second Mum and Dad for two years. What a busy and tiring day we had had! At least we three were all back together again in our yacht enjoying a quiet half hour before flopping, exhausted, into bed.

We had missed an opportunity to offer our services as crew on a delivery returning from the Seychelles because we felt this would be unfair on Harry. He was certainly curtailing our activities but we loved him so much. Being together twenty-four hours a day had somehow made him even more special. He was now eleven years old and we had noticed him drinking more water than usual. I was aware that older dogs sometimes developed diabetes or kidney problems so we took him to the vet for urine and blood tests.

The result was a great shock when we were told that his kidneys were fine but his liver count was ten times higher than it should be. The implications of this were that he had liver cancer and the vet recommended we took him to Athens to have more scans and biopsies to confirm the diagnosis. When we asked what could be done for him if this was the case, the reply came back, "Nothing." We discussed what we should do at length. Should we have further tests to be a hundred percent sure of the diagnosis knowing that nothing could be done for him or did we leave him in peace? After many tears and much debate we decided the best thing for Harry was to leave him alone and not put him through the miseries of further tests and operations. The best thing for me was to not know what was wrong with him as this way I could live my life in blissful ignorance and pretend he was well. Who was I cheating? When the realisation sank in that we didn't know for sure how much longer Harry would be with us we were determined to ensure that he had the best of everything.

More sadness hung over us this winter, which again hinged on our inability to get home when we wanted. Our dear friend, Janet, who we had been told had made a reasonable recovery from open-heart surgery, was found dead. We received an urgent email message to say that she had been found in her home having passed away peacefully reading a book. We had desperately wanted to go home to the funeral but couldn't because of Harry. Janet was special, one of a kind and we had loved her dearly. Dudley's relationship with her and her late husband had been very special for years before we met and neither of us could comprehend that she was gone and we had been denied the chance to see her one more time. This was the worst part of being away from home, friends and family. The feeling of helplessness is a heart wrenching burden and the inability to change circumstances led to many sleepless nights.

Back to lighter topics. Spring was just around the corner and we were, for once, in the right place at the right time for yachting purchases. We were told of a forthcoming sale at a village named Vounaki where a reputable flotilla company had a base. They were selling off surplus stock and we knew we needed a new mainsail and couldn't afford to buy a new one. Could this be the answer to our prayers?

The weather, which had been raining for what seemed an eternity, had brightened and it was a warm spring day when we took to the roads for Vounaki. Locals told us that it had rained consistently for sixty days and we believed them as we had been trying to anti-foul *Orpheus* and had been delayed time and time again. We enjoyed a drive with the windows down and smiles on our faces and everything seemed to be coming to life with buds and blossoms everywhere. We were in such a light mood that even the sight of an ostrich pen holding four birds didn't faze us. Never in our wildest dreams was this something we thought we would ever see in Greece!

We easily found the sailing base and after a quick look around and friendly negotiations we left Vounaki with a nearly new mainsail at the cost of €100, two boom tents at a cost of €40, two cruising chutes and four life-jackets free of charge! The chutes had minor tears and holes and were being thrown out. I took two chutes, one to cut up for patches and the other to use as a sail on *Orpheus*. We were in need of a boom tent to shade the companionway during the summer months. The other I cut up and used to make spray dodgers, lifebuoy cover, outboard cover, life raft cover, helm and binnacle covers. The life jackets were nearly new with built in harnesses but due to regulations the flotilla company could not use them. It is stipulated that the life jackets have to be self-inflating and be fitted with flotation devices. These were manually inflated. Dudley and I left the campus feeling as though we had just had the luckiest day of our lives.

Our winter had turned out to be one of the busiest of times for us. It was the first time we had ever hauled the boat out of the water and the fun, games and hard work we had with this is the subject of a following chapter. Apart from the sewing, cooking and socialising, our lives were pretty much dominated by the weather conditions and the need to get *Orpheus* back in the water.

Four months had passed and it did so in a haze of happiness. This was all thanks to the crews of eleven yachts. I was very sad to be leaving their company as we had all got along so well. We had been one big happy family and it is with much happiness and thanks that we remember Kevan and Linda, Kristian, Jane, Martin and Marie, Ray and Jan, Steve and Shelagh, Jonathon, Chris, Tony, Eddy and Aneka, Janet and David, Peter and Sue, Paul and Sue, Geoff and Jenny and last, but not least, Mike and Janet.

CHAPTER 26
IT'S A "HARD" LIFE

My first experience of the yacht being hauled out came on the fourteenth of January and I was feeling very anxious indeed. Inexperience led me to worry about every single thing. Questions such as where do they put the strops (straps put around the hull to lift the boat out of the water) and how on earth we take the forestay down if required concerned me. I was worried sick about what would happen and what we would find underneath.

Dudley and I had already been to the port police and purchased our three-euro permit to haul out. This had not been a necessity the previous year but with a new head of port police came the re-introduction of certain old laws that previously only related to merchant ships. The new boss thought this law appropriate for private yachts and Dudley and I were not about to argue over such a small sum of money. We paid our money and produced our permit to the marina yard and were given the time of 10 a.m. Of course, 10 a.m. came and went and this did nothing to settle my already rattled nerves.

It was nearing lunchtime when Dudley finally went to investigate why there was a delay as even for G.M.T. (Greek Maybe Time) this was a little unusual. A Greek charter company had decided to lift their boats and so the marina were taking them first as there were so many of them. As long as there was nothing else for me to worry about I was happy for the delay.

At 1500 hours the call came for us to bring the yacht round to the lifting bay. A friend went on board with Dudley to show him what to do and I walked round to the haul out with Harry, who was sensing there was something not quite right. They positioned the lift and asked us where we would like the strops to be placed. Little did we know most yachts have marks on their hulls indicating where to position the strops. *Orpheus* had none of these and we certainly didn't have a clue but our friend Kevan came to the rescue and from the dockside indicated an approximate position either side of the keel.

The lift revved into action and began tightening the strops around the hull, gradually lifting *Orpheus* from the water. I was extremely nervous as she looked very vulnerable sitting there all alone. If she started to sway during the lift they halted momentarily, waiting for her to steady, then would continue on until she was clear of the water and the quay. The lift then manoeuvred away from the slipway and took her the short distance to the washing area.

We paid €50 for one of the haul out crew to jet wash the hull. At first we had thought this a lot of money and had considered doing it ourselves. After all we were on a budget. Someone had advised us not to do this and to take the offer of a jet wash and we were very glad we had listened to this advice. The hull had only a small amount of weed growth but there was an abundance of slime and barnacles. The jet wash took only half an hour and by the time it was finished the hull was as clean as a whistle. Apart from the odd rogue barnacle there was nothing left for us to clean off by hand. We couldn't recommend it highly enough to anybody. Lifting it out was worth every penny of the fifty euros we paid.

I held my breath as they moved off with *Orpheus* again. She wobbled and teetered in the strops until they brought her to her winter resting place and sat her in two prop cradles. All secured and a ladder provided, we set about re-connecting to electricity and sorting the boat out for being on dry land.

We flushed fresh water through the sea toilet, catching it on the outside in a bucket and also the holding tank toilet. Normally hoses would be fitted to the sink outlets to allow for the water to be taken by hose to the nearest drain but we had been positioned nowhere near a drain and were told it would be okay to let it drain onto the ground beneath the boat where it would soak away. At this time, in our innocence, whatever the yard said was fine by us, but having lived three months like this the ground beneath the boat became sodden and the earth washed away to leave a crater. It was not the most ideal of situations but we tried to make the most of what we had.

We were completely unaware that it is recommended to put a fresh water hose to the engine and flush fresh water through the engine. Somebody asked us if we had done this but we had already been out of the water nearly two months and it was far too late to worry. Apparently the seawater evaporates leaving salt crystals and these in turn will corrode and damage any metal work or plastic. I must stress that this is only what we were told. There will always be somebody to share some pearls of wisdom or rumour to give you food for thought no matter what task you undertake.

The best part of lifting out is the yachting custom that comes with this activity. Amongst the yachting community everybody understands what the first night of lift out is like. All day is spent messing about with the boat trying to get it salt free, flushed and connected. The last thing anybody needs to be worried about on the first day is shopping for food and cooking that evening. Like an unspoken code of honour and support when any boat is lifted, there will always be somebody offering to cook you an evening meal. I certainly know that I was so tired at the end of the day I would not have been able to stand and cook a meal for Dudley. We were and still are very grateful for the delicious "Killer Kev Curry" that we enjoyed that evening.

Yachties have many strange little habits and rituals when it comes to various activities concerning boats and one of them is that every man, and I do mean every man, in the marina will visit the boat that's just been hauled out to have a look at the bottom and comment on its cleanliness, worthiness and state of well being. Don't ask me why they do it. I'm a woman; I didn't see any of the other women showing so much interest either.

I'm not the best person in the world when it comes to ladders, so being out of the water and having to climb a ladder up and down several times a day with a dog in my arms took a lot of getting used to. It took me several weeks to get in the swing of holding Harry in my left arm whilst holding the ladder with the right hand. The worst part was once at the top of the ladder there was nothing to hold onto for the last step on-board. Dudley fixed a grab rope to the push pit, which made life a little easier, but it didn't help with getting to grips with the height. I never did get used to the horrible way the boat moved and swayed in the high winds. At times the boat would judder in such a way I could be completely convinced we were suffering an earthquake but Dud would assure me that this was normal! We did have it suggested to us that maybe we should ask for a third support; *Orpheus* is twelve metres long and had two double supports but when looking at others around the yard we noticed that they had three or four double props.

We didn't like to make a fuss or question the work of the yard but we were wrong not to. Most of the weight inside *Orpheus* was in the stern cabin and this meant that the majority of the weight was behind the prop. After being re-launched we noticed tiny little things around the boat that had not been there before and could quite easily be attributed to over-stressing the hull as a result of not being supported sufficiently. We would not be so polite again and we would insist on at least three props around the hull to ensure even distribution of weight and extra support for the stern.

As this was our first lift out we didn't know if these things would always happen but following our launch we found tiny drips from water seals around the base of the toilets. A small leak had developed from around the frame of a window, which was showing signs of a hairline crack. On the decking there were hairline cracks that were not there before. These may just be natural occurrences but when they all came, or were noticed, at roughly the same time it became too much of a coincidence.

Our good friend Neil came by, like the other men in the marina, to take a look at our hull. We valued his opinion very much and were disheartened when he said, "The anti-foul on the hull is getting to the stage where it is really too thick, I would recommend you take it back to gel coat." The gel coat is a laminate layer of protection that forms outside of the hull when built which is then further covered to prevent osmosis and weed growth. Not really realising the magnitude of what Neil was saying, having never done it before, we happily agreed that this was the best thing to do and purchased the necessary tools.

Angle headed scrapers, similar to paint scrapers, were used to scrape the anti-foul off the hull. As previously mentioned we had many comments and suggestions over the month it took us to clear the hull. Yes, a whole month. At first we found the work so tiring we could only do half hour stretches, take a break, and then do another half an hour. Dud ended up doing much more than I as he seemed to have more upper body strength and determination. The weather wasn't helping our situation at all as it started to rain and just seemed to continue on and on.

The other options offered for removing the layers of anti-foul were to sand it off or to purchase the equivalent of a paint stripper; a fluid that could be painted on, left to dissolve the anti-foul and then scraped off. Taking advice from Kevan and Neil, both of whom had tried various methods of carrying out this job, they recommended we stuck to the scrapers. Sanding was just as demanding and would result in buying numerous discs as they needed to be changed approximately every 10 minutes. The paint stripper was very expensive and would not always remove the anti-foul on the first application. All in all the cheapest and what appeared the easiest option was to scrape it off. It was just so time consuming and exhausting, not to mention very messy.

We finally settled into a routine and managed to stick at it for two hour stretches. Dud got up the ladder and started from the waterline down and I got underneath the hull and started bottom up. Face masks had to be used and rubber gloves worn. Eye protection would have been in order but Dud couldn't get on with them and I wore glasses anyway. We were advised that this level of protection was necessary due to anti-foul possessing poisonous properties. Over-exposure over a period of time could make a person seriously ill, as the poisonous properties could be absorbed into the body through the skin and by inhalation. One of these substances we were told was arsenic!

After approximately one month's worth of hard work and dodging rain showers the hull had been scraped clean of anti-foul. However, there were still the blue remnants left that needed to be removed and this was a one man job with a sander. I would like to be able to say that meant I got to take a rest but it didn't. As Dudley took to the sander and cleared the hull back to pure whiteness he began his list of jobs for me to do.

The propeller blade was removed and I spent three days non-stop scraping and sanding with rough grade paper, then medium, fine and finishing with wet and dry. What was a filthy mess became a shining work of art. The idea was for me to polish it as highly as I could and make it as smooth as I could, as the smoother it was, the fewer barnacles it would attract. Unfortunately our propeller turned out to be quite pitted and although it shone it was never going to be completely smooth.

We had the option of leaving the brass, pitted but shiny and hope for the best or paint it with a special anti-foul. This last option was not the one I wanted as I had just spent three days cleaning it but it was the one we finally chose. Other ideas put forward for keeping the propeller clean were to coat it in egg whites or lanolin. I didn't fancy sticking my fingers in sheep's fat and just how many egg whites does it take to coat a three bladed prop? I was put out by painting anti-foul on thinking that my hard work had been wasted but this wasn't the case as when we lifted out again two years later all the anti-foul was gone. It was as though it had never been painted on in the first place.

Dud continued to sand "ligo ligo", (slowly slowly) but when we tested the hull with a damp meter, the hull was not drying out. The wet weather was so against us and the trouble was if the hull did not dry out completely we would not be able to apply a coat of epoxy and all the hard work would have been for nothing. Epoxy is a resin based protective shield that prevents the transference of water into the hull (osmosis). If applied to a wet hull it would have trapped the dampness in and would cause internal problems.

By the beginning of March Dud had sanded the whole hull but it still did not seem to be drying out properly. We were treated to two pearls of wisdom from Neil one of which was to soak the hull in fresh water as many times a day as we wanted but certainly at least once. This sounded somewhat contrary that we should soak the hull to help it dry, but apparently washing the salt water out of the hull would help it to dry quicker. It made sense as we knew salt attracted moisture. The second was to drill a tiny hole in the base of our rudder to let the retained water drip free. We were told that every rudder takes in and retains water but by making a small hole in the bottom any trapped water would be able to drain out. After draining, the hole would simply be filled with epoxy filler and painted over prior to re-launching. Had we known these two things earlier we could have saved ourselves a few stressful weeks.

We had to leave the marina by the end of March and this meant we would need to be re-launched on the twenty-ninth at the latest. The date was now the third and the hull was still much too wet to even contemplate starting to paint with epoxy. We took the decision to keep waiting in the hope that the weather would improve and the spring sunshine would give us the dry we needed.

Dud started to fibreglass some damage to the keel. We had not seen the boat out of the water before and being an ex-flotilla boat it had one or two chips out of the front and rear of the keel. Layer on layer he gradually built up and moulded the keel back to its original lump free shape and then sanded its surface to make it nice and smooth. Whilst he was doing this I had the onerous task of wire brushing the last twenty metres of our anchor chain, as it was particularly rusty.

We were advised that an anchor chain should be turned around every year to give even wear of the chain. This would mean that the end tied to the hull would become shackled to the anchor and vice versa. As I cleaned the chain reaching the end of the rusty section I noticed a flattened link and a marked difference in the quality of chain that followed. I initially thought that this link had corroded and we were in fear of it snapping. On seeking advice it was explained that this was a joining link. Our fifty-metre chain had been made up of a twenty and a thirty joined together and we had been completely unaware of this fact, as we hadn't checked the entire chain out before. This was not an ideal situation, as a joined chain would never withstand the same amount of pressure as one solid strand. The saying "a chain is only as strong as its weakest link" is completely true.

There was little we could do about this now as we did not have the funds to purchase a new chain and we knew when we did we wanted to increase its length to seventy metres. We were already making plans for the new sailing season and it was our intention to leave the Ionian and head for the Aegean. People with much more experience than ourselves whom we had spoken to told us that fifty metres was barely enough for the winds in the Aegean. We were going to have to trust to faith and luck that our chain would hold out another year until our finances looked a little rosier.

Next came a saga of immense proportions with our cutlass bearing. For those like myself, who knew nothing of these things, I should briefly explain. The propeller is held and connected to the gearbox by the shaft and this shaft is supported by the p-bracket. Inside the p-bracket is a tubular piece of metal with a cushioned inside that supports and protects the shaft within the p-bracket and this is called the cutlass bearing.

I know this all sounds rather like a song you sang as youngsters about the foot bone being connected to the leg bone but this was "the way of the lord"! Needless to say to be able to remove the cutlass bearing we first had to remove the shaft. We found that our shaft was in straight alignment with the rudder and as such could not be pulled straight backwards. This meant we either had to dig a huge hole and drop the rudder or, with the help of Ray, take the gearbox off the engine so the shaft could be pushed further into the boat and clear off the cutlass bearing.

I need to point out at this stage that neither Dudley nor I knew anything about such things. Dud was keen to learn and willing to do things but before you can start to tackle jobs of such magnitude you first need to know what it is you're doing. It was a frustrating time for all of us that was eased by Ray with his quiet helping guidance as he patiently guided Dudley through a steep learning curve.

This is the beauty of being a live-a-aboard yachtie. Everyone understands you are living on a budget and can't afford to pay for workmen to carry out jobs that are possible to do yourselves. There is a fountain of knowledge to be tapped into in a marina during the wintertime and when these jobs are being carried out there is always someone willing to help and advise. Word obviously echoed around the marina that there was a big job on and, as is the case, all the men came filtering past the boat that day to stand and stare, offer helpful words and generally try to learn an extra helpful titbit that may be useful to themselves one day.

Having got the shaft clear of the cutlass bearing the following day, the task was to remove the cutlass bearing from inside the p-bracket. This should have been a relatively easy task but it turned out not to be so. Dudley, Ray and Neil banged and bumped and shoved and heaved and all the men in the marina came past again with another string of ideas to get it out but none of them worked. Ray rigged up a push-me pull-you system and millimetre-by-millimetre it came sliding half way out and then stuck. We were forced to cut the proud piece off in order to push the remaining piece back through the way it had come. With the extra leverage to push, the second half came out relatively easily.

We discovered the reason this task had proved so difficult and offered so much resistance was the person fitting this particular cutlass bearing had fitted one too small and had padded it out by using a copper shim between the cutlass bearing and the p-bracket. The copper had reacted with the brass and had started to weld itself together with the p-bracket. The chemistry of the whole thing was beyond me. All I can advise is: DON'T DO IT.

Using wet and dry I cleaned up the p-bracket inside and out, ready for the new cutlass bearing to be fitted when we discovered a crack! "How bad is a crack in the p-bracket?" we asked. Back came all the men and the comments ranged from, "Oh, that's nothing to worry about," to, "You'll have to open up the hull, dig it out and re-laminate." We decided it was time to consult somebody who really knew what they were doing and Neil collected a local Greek engineer who looked at the p-bracket, looked at us as though we were mad, spoke to Neil in Greek and with a shrug simply walked away. The upshot of this display of local body language was he couldn't understand what all the fuss was about. It was a tiny, hairline crack that did not go all the way through and he couldn't work out why we had wasted his time.

That was all good news but knowing there was a crack there at all was a little unsettling so Dudley covered the p-bracket in fibreglass to give it extra support and to prevent the crack becoming anything other than hairline. The new cutlass was fitted without mishap and this monster job was completed. Of course our knowledge had been increased ten-fold and should we need to do it again in the future it won't seem quite so frightening.

The hull was still not drying and we were seriously worried that we were not going to be able to epoxy as we only had a fortnight left in the marina. The good thing was the sunshine had come out and we were washing down the hull regularly whilst polishing the upper hull, washing lines and cleaning fenders. The upper decks were washed and polished and the stripe along the side had been cleaned and taped, ready to patch. At amidships there had been some parts of the stick-on stripes lifted off and we had ordered strips to patch it rather than replace the whole stripe.

The day arrived for a further damp metre test on the hull and with hopes high it was announced *Orpheus* was dry enough to paint. The only patches of slightly high reading were located where the water and fuel tanks were situated. We were told this was normal as good quality damp metres could actually detect the moisture level through the hull. I was so glad all our hard work and effort had not been a waste of time and that we were finally going to be able to apply the epoxy.

With the weather quite warm all of a sudden, we

managed to get two coats of epoxy on in one day. Epoxy should be allowed to dry until it is 'green' which means touch dry but still a little bit tacky. The following day we applied another coat of epoxy and the first coat of anti-foul and were grateful that the rain had stayed away long enough. When applying epoxy it should be kept dry and not allowed to get too wet. If it had rained during these last two days it could have spoiled everything, so for once we had been lucky.

The next stage was to apply a half coat of anti-foul. This covered the waterline and down the hull approximately half a metre, around the bow, front of the keel and rudder. Next we gave it another full coat of anti-foul and our hull was complete, but not quite... ...

The props were covering squares on the hull that each measured a quarter metre square. There was no way we could leave the hull as it was, as it would have raised lumps. We approached the marina and asked if we could be lifted to enable us to work underneath the pads. To do this the marina were asking for another lift and chocking fee, which we could not afford to pay. The compromise came that they were prepared to hoist us last thing at night and let us stay in the strops overnight ready to be launched the next day at 0930 hours. This meant that we had approximately seventeen hours to scrape back, sand, clean down and dry the four squares; then to epoxy and anti-foul the same number of coats ready to re-launch.

Time had run out for our ordered stripes so I asked Dud to go and see why they hadn't arrived. It transpired that the red and blue stripes were no longer available, only white and black but we couldn't leave the boat with only half a stripe! We were leaving the marina within the next two days so we would no longer have the use of electricity. Removing the stripes from a dinghy when back in the water would be almost impossible, so within the next 17 hours we knew we had to remove completely the remainder of our stripes.

It was absolutely manic and very stressful to say the least. Each coat of epoxy had to dry to its 'green' state. How was this going to happen overnight? Neil to the rescue again: "Use a hairdryer you silly, Norfolk woman," he said. Now why hadn't I thought of that!! Using a hairdryer, we managed to get each layer dry and all coats applied by 0900 the following day. The only thing left to do was to remove the remainder of the stripe, which

Dud was still doing at 0930 when the men arrived to re-launch us.

I couldn't believe we had done it. The underneath looked smooth and the upper hull was clean and shiny. The only thing that spoilt the look of her was where the stripes had been removed, as for some reason she didn't look so sporty without them. There was no way we could do anything about it until we lifted out again, which would be in two years time, so we would have to accept her new look for some time.

Never mind. She was clean and she was gently nestled back into the water. It was with a sigh of relief that Dud and I stepped on board. All that remained was to see if her engine would start. Even Harry seemed to be a little excited and appeared very pleased when he realised he no longer had to be carried up a ladder. The work had been long and hard but it had all been worth it.

CHAPTER 27
GOING, GOING, GONE

Dud went below to check around the boat and to make sure all the seacocks were still water tight and then went to start the engine. As usual, the customary two pumps of the kill switch were given for a cold start but as Dud pulled the handle of the kill switch I heard a muffled grunt, a fumbling and an expletive I couldn't possibly repeat. As I looked round to see what the problem was I saw him kneeling on the cockpit floor with the kill switch handle and a long length of cable in his hand! Obviously it had snapped inside along the cable somewhere and had pulled through with his effort. Luckily the engine started without mishap and Dud assured me as we motored round to our mooring for our remaining two days in the marina that there would not be a problem stopping the engine or repairing the cable.

Being on the hard ashore had not been an easy time at all for apart from the hard work we had carried out, living in these conditions had been considerably messy. As we scraped the boat the blue anti-foul had spread everywhere and usually, as we worked, Harry would sit under the boat watching us. Of course this meant that my white dog was actually sitting in blue anti-foul and over a period of time had turned a pleasant turquoise colour. This earned him the nickname 'blue rinse' but luckily it did finally wash out without causing him any skin irritation.

Constantly washing the boat down to dry the hull had made the ground around the boat very muddy. Naturally, as we worked and walked around the yard we picked up the mud and anti-foul and carried it up onto the boat. In a very short space of time we had gathered bits of anti-foul, mud and grit everywhere especially in the grooves between the teak panel strips in the cock-pit. We took the opportunity of our remaining two days in the marina to ensure that the upper decks were returned to their normal clean state and were glad that this was only going to be an experience to suffer every two years.

We left the marina and moored alongside the town quay as we had anticipated getting some casual cleaning work prior to sailing towards the Aegean. A little extra money to boost the coffers was needed as we had spent a lot on the boat and we were unsure what the cost of living and mooring charges would be once through into the Aegean. Unfortunately, not only did the cleaning work we anticipated not come to fruition, but we also found out that one of the flats we owned in England had tenants living in it who were refusing to pay their rent. Even worse, the agent had only just informed us that the situation had been on going for three months! This meant we had been spending money we thought was in our account but were now being told it wasn't. The result was that we were short a considerable sum of money and were going overdrawn at the bank.

I began to wonder if our lives would ever get any easier. I had almost convinced myself that there would never be a time that I wouldn't constantly worry about our finances. Would I ever be able to say yes to a purchase of something that was non-essential? We had lines that were showing signs of wear, we needed a longer anchor chain and we needed extra living funds. We were just not going to be able to afford to go sailing. This was not how we had planned our departure from England or our life in the Ionian. What would we do?

A stroke of luck or a helping hand from above, whatever you call it, came in the form of passing friends who were looking for help sanding down and anti-fouling their boats prior to their Springtime re-launch. Knowing we had just completed extensive work on our own yacht they asked us if we would assist in doing theirs. "No problem," we said and began a regime of work that just seemed to fall our way. We helped to polish hulls and painted on stripes for other boats, I thought it a shame we had not been able to do one on *Orpheus* as once I was shown a few tricks of the trade it really did seem quite simple. It was all manual labour and hard, dirty work but we were not proud and we needed the money. I was grateful for being given the chance to earn and definitely felt that someone up there was looking after us.

The weather began to slowly improve but it was still too unsettled to go sailing and also still too cold for deck showers. It worked to our advantage that we were working on the yachts in the marina as we were allowed to use the facilities. After experiencing the luxury of electricity, I planned never again to be without it through wintertime. I intended to save a little money each month to ensure the following year we would be able to be in a marina from November to April. These were and still are my two worst months onboard outside the marina environment as deck showers are just too cold.

We worked throughout the month of April whilst completing sewing jobs and making plans to be on our way. We wanted to try to be here for the return of our good friends Kevan and Linda who had been away for some time on a delivery trip. We wanted one last meal and pleasant evening with them prior to leaving, as it would be quite some time before we would all be together again.

We had set 11 May as our leaving date. This would allowed us time with our friends and we could enjoy another Levkas Carnival. Dud had wanted a spinnaker pole and we had been told there was one in Vounaki for €20. We decided our first day out from Levkas would be a short one by way of a test sail, and if everything was okay we would be ready to take on the Aegean. We would make Vounaki our first port of call but in the meantime we were determined to enjoy our last few days here in the Ionian.

Easter saw an influx of people arrive at Levkas and, sadly, not all of them the same as the well natured people who live on this wonderful island. This Easter in Greece happened to be a whole month later than in England and big polystyrene rabbits appeared all around the town, which was great for the children and bigger kids such as myself. The trouble was that with the influx of strangers came crime. Each morning we noticed something else had been torn from these beautiful statues and thrown into the bushes. It was mindless destruction of things that were put there to please everyone. Why do people think they have the right to take these pleasures away from others?

These holidaymakers also thought it fun to throw stones at yachts as they were walking past late at night. Four young lads thought it would be a laugh to try to take our bikes from the back of our boat one night, but they didn't find it so amusing when they were faced with a very angry Dud. We had been in Greece now for some years and had never known anything like this. Greece had always been a place where, if you left something lying somewhere, it would still be there two weeks later. I guess the times really were changing in Levkas. I began to wonder whether this lovely island of Lefkada would still be so friendly and trouble-free when we made our way back in two years' time.

Having decided that we were definitely taking off to pastures new we began to prepare the boat and stock it with provisions. We just didn't know what to expect. I did know that I had already had enough of staring at this huge surfboard tied to the deck and insisted that Dud sell it. I was not happy sailing with this hindrance tied along the side deck for me to stub my toe and trip on every time we were laying our anchor. Lucky for me, Dud agreed to the sale and this gave us extra cash to make sure our forthcoming journey was going to be trouble-free with regard to weather forecasts.

Our old Navtex, that was the size of a miniature television, hardly ever received weather transmissions and we agreed that it was important for us to be able to receive regular weather reports and also to have a VHF radio that had good reception. One never knew when a mayday was going to be required and I wanted to know that if such an occasion arose we had the capability.

We purchased a new Navtex that Dudley fitted with relative ease but that they had not made the cable quite long enough so we had to purchase extra. He checked our aerial cable and found it to be full of verdigris so a further €70 was paid out to purchase a new one and Neil agreed to go up the mast for us to fit it. Dud also extended the windlass wiring, so, instead of standing on the bow to drop the anchor I could drop it, dig it in and then come back to the cockpit and activate it up and down from there. This allowed us the luxury of being able to talk to each other instead of shouting. This, we hoped, would work better as it gave me greater flexibility and allowed me to come back to the stern to help with the mooring lines whilst still being able to control the anchor windlass.

All these little bits of work were still to be completed so we were kept very busy for these last few weeks in Levkas. Kevan and Linda returned and we loved hearing their news about their exciting journey all the way from the Seychelles, across the Equator, through the Red Sea, Suez Canal and the leap across the Mediterranean to Turkey. What a trip that would have been for us to take part in! But I did not want to leave Levkas and found the thought of tearing myself away increasingly harder as D-day drew nearer.

Soon Dud had completed all of his jobs and was keen to leave. I had one last cleaning job to do before we could take off. It was warm and sunny again and the summertime clock had begun. For a week the weather had remained settled and the sun consistent. I left the boat to start work, leaving Dud to clean our boat down ready for our departure. As I returned from my morning toil I noted that nothing had been done around the boat and questioned as to why this was. "I just didn't have time," came the reply.

"I had to do this and that and I did a little shopping and the day has just gone." The response sounded a little too guilty for my liking. I stood looking, my eyes taking in all the information that was available to me. I saw a cushion on the seating, I saw a book, I saw a bleary eyed husband who had on his chest, appearing before my very eyes, a perfect imprint of an arm that had been folded across his chest with a hand tucked under the armpit. He had obviously left his thumb out over his arm, as the imprint was very distinctive in amongst the increasingly red skin that had been exposed to the sun. All these things combined did not give me the impression of a man who had been busy working all day. It was more likely he had fallen asleep in the sunshine whilst reading a book. When asked if this was the case, a long period of denial followed until I made him take a look in the mirror so he could see what I could see!!

All our work finished, the boat cleaned, stocked and ready to go, the fateful day arrived. We visited all our friends who were still in the marina to say goodbye and our closest friends came to see us off at the quayside. Hugs and kisses and the lines were off. We were underway. I couldn't believe that Dudley was making me leave this wonderful place. I had become so attached to Levkas and I truly didn't want to leave, no matter what excitement awaited us. I cried with all my heart as we left, I loved Levkas and didn't feel ready to leave it behind. It had been our home for a year and a half and I was really going to miss it.

As we motored down the Levkas Canal the mobile phone rang and it was Neil, my fellow Norfolk mate wishing us well. I cried the whole length of the Canal that day and then some more as we headed to Paleros and Vounaki to collect the spinnaker pole. Through the tears some logic began to make sense. It was our first true adventure into the unknown together and we were very much in love with each other and apart from Dud and Harry I had three other special things in my life that nobody else had - I was forty years old, I was absolutely free and *Orpheus* was on the move.

APPENDIX 1
BERNIE'S BUNS AND BOLO'

Having spent quite some time complaining about the lack of an oven, now that it had been fixed I tried to get to grips with culinary things, although I am not a very good cook by a very long chalk. I struggled to produce anything edible for a very long time as cooking on a boat oven is completely different to any other. The actual oven only afforded high or low settings and the two rings on top were the same with absolutely no indication as to what level of heat you could expect in between. Most recipes indicate dishes are to be cooked on a certain gas/electricity mark. When you don't know what you are doing and have no idea what mark your oven is, things can be very frustrating.

I would have liked to change the cooker on board but a replacement would have cost almost three times as much as a household oven. This made no sense to me at all as it had only a fraction of the usefulness, but I guess that's boating. The only useful tip somebody passed to me was, if I wanted a new oven, to ensure I purchased one with a crescent shaped burner that snaked around the bottom of the oven and not a straight burner that sat at the back. Apparently the back burner only heats enough to cook one side of the food and regular turning is required. The crescent burner produced more of an all-round heat.

Over the years of trial and error I've found one really useful piece of information that, to some, may be obvious but for many months kept getting me caught out. This handy tip is to be completely organised. There is so little space in a yacht's galley that the chef needs to prepare in advance to save last minute panic. More often than not I would find myself halfway through cooking a meal and needing something out of the fridge, a fridge I had just buried in all my other ingredients! My only real workspace, when using the oven, is the top of the fridge or to cover the sinks with boards and use these as a surface. I've found covering both sinks annoying as quite often you need to drop things into the sink to clear the work space or you need water to mix things and wash hands. I guess I'm lucky that I have two sinks and have found a happy medium in leaving one sink open and one covered. On *Orpheus*, when the oven is not in use there is a board that pulls over the top to provide another work space. However, I've found over the years that my acceptance of the smaller work area means that I hardly ever use it. The only time it is really put to good use is when I have prepared a buffet salad lunch, as it's a great place to lay the food out for people to help themselves.

In general I have very few cooking utensils on board and have found that my pastry and cake baking can be achieved with the smallest of kitchen scales, a rolling pin the size of a large tube of smarties and a set of pastry cutters.

Whatever I'm cooking, as per my handy tip, I check all the ingredients and make sure they are either placed out on the worktop or are accessible before I start doing anything. Take some time to sit and consider what you are going to cook and the best order in which to do it – BE ORGANISED. For example, if you wish to cook a fried breakfast with eggs, bacon, beans, fritters, mushrooms and tomatoes all on two rings, where do you start? Some yachties are really good cooks and for them this may sound like a silly question but I am an utter idiot in the kitchen and it took me several fraught filled attempts at such a fry up before I worked out the best order in which to cook these so that all of the items got to the plate still hot and edible.

I do not own a pressure cooker. Although many yachting cooks I've spoken to swear by them I'd rather use the space to store my big, beautiful wok. Before leaving England I purchased a set of saucepans with little side handles that have served my purpose very well. The smallest is approximately six inches across and sits inside the next biggest all the way up to Big Bertha, as I like to call her, which is fourteen inches in diameter. Bertha only tends to see the light of day when we are having winter celebrations with friends and I make a huge pot of steaming hot chilli or a big batch of mulled wine to warm the cockles of a Norfolk heart!

Talking of wine, Greek wines are wonderful and when

decanted straight from the barrel can be very cheap. The local vintner in Levkas had four different kinds of wine in barrels and, when presented with clean empty water bottles, would fill them with ruby red nectar for only €1.75. Since we first came to Greece this price has risen over four years to €2.25. Bottled wines are also available and used to be a little more expensive, around 4 euros a bottle, but with the introduction of several discount supermarkets to the islands these are now available from 2 euros upwards. All types of alcoholic drinks can be found and purchased but you can expect to pay a little more for the imported ones. Locally, the Metaxa, a tasty brandy, can be purchased in three different grades, all at reasonable prices and Ouzo (a local aniseed drink) can be bought for as little as 2.50 euros a 70cl bottle.

We used to find eating out very cheap as one of our favourite meals was a giros. A chicken giros consists of a flour pancake filled with chicken bits, Tzatizi, salad and chips. These used to cost only €1.50 but have since increased to €2. Dudley enjoys a meal of liver or lamb, which used to cost €4.50 but for which now we pay €7.50. Such is the exchange rate at the time of writing that eating out in Greece has become almost as expensive in some places as it is in England. This, obviously, is a fluctuating affair but I do fear for the future of a cheap Greece. It seems that there has been a steady increase since our time here and it does not look like it will drop.

Despite the costs, there are many local restaurants to enjoy around the Ionian with varying atmospheres to enjoy and different characters to meet. Some of the best evenings we've had have been spent sitting on uncomfortable chairs and eating off rickety tables, listening to the husband and wife team cooking, serving and shouting at each other. If the customer is really lucky you will be treated to music and dancing at the end of the evening.

There are some wonderful foods to find in Greece but they do lack the type of butchery that provides the customer with a decent beefsteak. We are told it is to do with the way they butcher and hang the meat that makes most cuts of beef tough. Even beating before eating doesn't always make it tender. We have purchased fillet steak, hammered it until nearly flat and still sat chewing hours later. Some restaurants manage to serve a nearly nice steak, though. I guess they get first choice of the cuts of meat from the local butchers but most people we meet say they have not managed to find a good steak. Nor have we managed to ever find a gammon steak.

On the other hand, the pork is some of the most tender and fresh Dud has ever had and the chicken really tasty. It wasn't until he brought home our first breast of chicken that I realised when purchasing a breast you got the whole chest including ribs. I was initially a tad squeamish about this but have slowly got used to it and now find it better this way, as the meat seems so much fresher. Most meat used to be good value for money but, as with other areas of living in Greece, the costs are rising.

Our local butcher in Levkas loved the fact that Dudley ordered in Greek and would boast to his other Greek customers, "He is learning". With each new word added he would tease and nod approval and by the end of the first winter was guiding Dud in the right direction. Whenever we buy beef for a stew we ask for 'Stiffado' beef and this has never failed to be tender and tasty but this might have something to do with the fact that it has been cooked slowly on a low heat for at least two hours!

The fruit and vegetables are always fresh and all year round there is something very tasty to be had. Although most things are available at all times, there are still some that remain seasonable. Garden peas in their pods can only be found for a very short time and it's the same with broad beans. Parsnips are non-existent and their local celery can be hard and stringy. Before coming to Greece I had never eaten a fresh apricot. When they came into season I found them one of the tastiest fruit I have ever tried. Sweet, firm and delicious, their skins are soft and smooth, not thick and furry, like they are in England. I could go on for ages discussing the wonders of the fruit and vegetables available because they are all so good.

A quick word of caution when purchasing loose vegetables: Whilst they are happy for you to pick out the fruit and vegetables of your choice, obviously avoiding any rotten looking ones, they will take offence if you stand and pick out the pea pods with the biggest peas inside. Please don't laugh, but we were witness to a man standing and feeling all the pods to see which ones had the bigger peas in as he only wanted to buy 20 pods enough for one meal. A kilo of peas would cost approximately one euro and, when shelled, would do two meals. This kind of behaviour is very insulting to the shopkeeper and bad luck for the poor person who has to buy all the empty pods left behind!

On the subject of fresh produce I feel I should quickly make mention of the dreaded cockroach and other pests you could take on board. Make sure you wash all produce well and store it safely. If you leave food lying around the decks you will be prey to the night time prowlers, the rats and cats. The rats may come and go with little trace but I can assure you if you entice a tomcat onto your boat you could regret it for some time if he chooses to mark the place where he found a cache of food. Of course, you also run the risk of rats deciding to stay too and this is a whole different ball game. You must catch the mouse before he eats through the wiring and foam around the boat. We have managed to escape all of this so far but we do not become complacent about it and remain forever watchful.

I am a strong believer in making sure the cupboard is full of packet sauce mixes or jars to make life very easy. We always have carbonara, cheese and napolitana in packets and sweet and sour in a jar. Soups and cuppa-soups are great to have at anytime especially when sailing in a cold spell. I would caution against getting too carried away with unnecessary herbs and cookery items that you would have in the cupboard at home. You just will not have the space to store it all on board a boat. Over the years I have become a little adventurous, as I like a good curry. When I find a source of a different powder I feel the need to have it on board, and with Rogan Josh, Masala, Tandoori and Tikka in addition to the normal hot curry and chilli, my spice cupboard is starting to burst.

Having laid the foundation of my newly acquired culinary prowess I would like to provide a few ORGANISED RECIPES for some of my favourite meals so you can hopefully try them, gain confidence from them and enjoy eating them. Most of all I want to do this simply to celebrate the fact that, after such a long time of battling and trying I finally managed to successfully do it. I DID IT!!

BERNIE'S ORGANISED RECIPES

Bernie's Bolo': On a chopping board chop 1 red pepper, 6-8 mushrooms and 1 medium onion. Peel and thinly slice 2 cloves of garlic and get out ready olive oil, a 450g tin of chopped tomatoes and 600g of mince beef. Boil some water ready to use and mix 1 heaped tablespoon of corn flour in a measuring jug with some cold water and a heaped dessertspoon of beef gravy mix. Make sure you have access to the salt, pepper, basil and oregano, and if not, get these out ready. (The oven ring will be lit on full and turned down slowly and gently until the flame size reduces for the first time – approximately half flame).

Using the oven setting detailed above take a saucepan and drizzle some of the olive oil in the bottom, add the onions and garlic and cook until they are both glazing and slightly turning brown. Add the mince and cook until no red meat can be seen then add the mushrooms and pepper and continue to cook until both slightly soften. Next add the tin of chopped tomatoes and a pinch of both basil and oregano. I tend not to add salt or pepper to my meals but now is the time to add whatever your tastes require. Stir for a few minutes before adding the corn flour mixture from the jug. As this mixture heats it will thicken the juices from the chopped tomatoes but if it becomes too thick add a little hot water previously boiled. You can keep adding water until you get a consistency you like; I prefer to eat mine quite stodgy and not too runny.

If you are going to eat the meal immediately after cooking, turn the heat down to its lowest setting and simmer the Bolo whilst cooking the spaghetti. I normally like to make this first thing in the morning or early afternoon so I can let it stand for a while as this allows the full flavour of the garlic and herbs to come through. The mixture is then re-heated for the 10-12 minutes it takes to boil the spaghetti pasta and it is ready to serve.

I have served this with hot garlic bread instead of pastas and it worked well. Also if, as I am prone to do, I have made too much for just Dudley and me, the leftovers are kept and re-cycled as per the following recipe.

Churned-In Chilli: Now don't mock this until you've tried it. As I said, if you've made too much bolo but you don't want to eat it for two days on the trot, this is what you do.

Boil the rice (I prefer Basmati) and whilst cooking this on the simmer for 15 minutes, take the left-over bolo and slowly heat it. Open and wash a 450g tin of red beans and add these to the bolo. Also add chilli powder or paste according to how hot you like your chilli. I like mine hot so I get carried away and also add a dash of Tabasco or some cayenne pepper and a little sprinkle of sugar. Stir this well and heat to boiling, then simmer until the rice is cooked.

It makes a tasty alternative to eating bolo two days running and, let's face it, we all get used to adulterating recipes when sailing, coping with what we have at the time.

Stifadho: This is one of my favourite Greek meals and is very easy to make. This one makes you get organised before your start the cooking as it all goes into the baking tin and straight into the oven.

To make a meal to serve 3 or 4 adults you will need 800g to 1kg of Stifadho beef. I am guessing that in England this is equivalent to chuck steak or stewing beef. This needs to be cut into sizeable chunks, as during the cooking it will shrink slightly.

Take a metal roasting tin and put the following ingredients into it, mixing them together well:-

3 Bay leaves, 3 level tablespoons parsley, 6 black pepper corns, 2 tablespoons of sugar, 3 oz. butter, 3 garlic cloves sliced or crushed, 7 tablespoons of olive oil, 4 tablespoons of tomato paste, 3 tablespoons of vinegar, 12 tablespoons of red wine and 200ml of water.

Now add the chunks of beef and mix them into the mixture and add salt to your personal taste. Cover the tin with foil and bake in a low oven for one and a half hours. I like to stir the ingredients every half hour to ensure not only an even cooking of the meat but to allow further water to be added if it looks to be too thick or too dry.

Peel approximately 15 baby onions (I tend to use more as I enjoy the onions more than the meat!). Add these to the mixture after 1 _ hours, stir them in and cook for a further 40 minutes. If the mixture looks too wet after this time, bake uncovered for a further ten minutes but be warned that this could dry out the beef.

Cooking this meal can be a bit of a juggling act, but after the first time you will get used to seeing the way the fluid levels change, and thereafter will appreciate that it is worth the effort as this rich, beefy meal is delicious served with boiled rice and salad or boiled potatoes. I have even tried it with garlic bread. No matter what it's served with it, it has always been very tasty and one of Dud's favourites.

Bernie's Belter Belt-line: The traditional English fry up made on two rings!!

This is only guidance as to how best to manage the cooking of a fry-up on board according to my experience. The quantities will be for you to gauge depending on how many you are cooking for.

Peel potatoes and slice them into half-inch thick rounds, place them into boiling water and parboil them for approximately 15 minutes. Once cooked, drain the water off and place aside in the drainer allowing them to dry off. Whilst this is happening get yourself organised, as once this process starts it is a relentlessly busy time that will leave you wishing you had more than one pair of hands.

Get the bacon out ready and the pack opened; have the eggs at hand; slice or halve the tomatoes however you like them and the same with the mushrooms. Open the tin of beans and place them in a small tin. Ensure you can get to the olive oil and butter when needed and pre-light the oven on its lowest setting and then line a roasting tin with a large piece of foil. Now the fun can begin.

Take two frying pans, one on each ring but if, like mine, one ring is bigger than the other, a little juggling will be required whilst cooking the potatoes. Put a good measure of olive oil in each pan and heat it well. When nicely hot place the potatoes in each pan and cook until brown and crispy. Swapping the pans onto the different sized rings at intervals will allow them to cook at the same rate. Once cooked, place the fritters in the foil, wrap them up and place them in the oven to keep warm.

Take the bacon and fry it on the bigger ring whilst heating the beans on the lower ring. Set aside the second pan to be used for the eggs. The beans will heat roughly in the time it takes the bacon to cook one side so turn the bacon, then remove the beans to stand aside and put the pan back on the heat with extra oil and cook the eggs. Remove the cooked bacon and pop it on top of the foil in the oven. In the same pan, add a little butter if needed and cook the mushrooms and tomatoes. This takes very little time at all so at this point I start to serve. The eggs will be cooked so these go onto the plate along with the beans, bacon and potatoes by which time the tomatoes and mushrooms are ready to serve.

Sometimes I find it a little less stressful leaving the eggs in the hot pan and simply serving them with the tomatoes and mushrooms and placing the backing tray of bacon and potatoes and the saucepan of bean on the table for people to help themselves. The trouble with this is that Dud likes a runny egg!!

I refuse to cook fried bread but if you like it I would suggest that you add a little butter to the bacon pan and soak up the bacon juices with the bread. This can then also be placed in the warm oven to crisp further whilst cooking the mushrooms and tomatoes – if you do this don't forget to delay the start of the egg cooking.

If you manage to follow that recipe and come out the other side in one piece I congratulate you. This is one meal I cook very rarely as, no matter how organised I get, it always seems to get very frantic and there is never quite enough room or enough hands. But I've found this is great to boost the energy levels after we've had a few days at sea.

Of course, being terribly English, it is obligatory to wash it down with a lovely cuppa tea!

Bernie's Buns: I've made these in exactly the same way but changed the flavours and they seem to work out whether you use currants, cherry pieces, coconut, vanilla, coffee or chocolate chip. Enjoy!

I have on board two hanging nets and inside each is a bowl that I use to store my fruit and vegetables. I also use these bowls for mixing when baking (with limited space everything on board should have a dual purpose!). I have a small compact set of scales, sieve, pastry cutters and a tiny roller. I've never needed anything extra when baking.

Take a mixing bowl and other implements such as scales, sieve etc. Place cases in a bun tin and pre-heat the oven on a half setting. I found that by turning my oven down very slowly I could find a medium size flame which is the setting you will require.

Measure 4 oz. butter and 4 oz. sugar and then place them in the bowl and mix together into a creamy texture. Break two eggs into a cup and beat them. These can be added, a little at a time, to the bowl and mixed in well. Measure 6 oz. of self-raising flour and sieve the flour into the mixing bowl. Fold the flour into the mixture and add a handful of currants.

Take a spoon and add a healthy blob of mixture into each bun case and place in the pre-heated oven to cook for approximately 16 minutes. I like to cook mine for 8 minutes then turn the tray around and cook for a further 8 minutes. I know they say you should not open the oven or else they go flat but I have never found this to be the case.

If you find that the eggs have not been big enough and the mixture is too doughy and thick I use a little milk to rinse round the cup the eggs were beaten in and add this to the mixture. One of my favourite versions of the buns is to add cocoa powder and choc chips but because of the extra powder I've always had to add a little milk to thin the mixture.

As you will be able to see, I really am no cook at all. For me it has all been trial and error and I've been very lucky that Dud has been very patient with me in my learning process. I can now confidently say that my fear of the boat oven has gone and over the years I have become quite fond of it, warts and all.

APPENDIX 2
EXPENDITURE

Having mentioned our financial predicament several times I feel it only right and fair for me to give you a detailed insight into what kind of budget we had to live on for the period this book covers, which is end of September to middle of May; approximately twenty months. We left England with no financial buffer believing the rental of our property would cover our outgoings and leave us approximately six hundred pounds a month to live on. We thought this would be more than enough for our needs. We never expected or wanted to be rich people but had estimated that this was a reasonable sum for our purposes.

I now realise that we were somewhat green in the ways of boating. As anyone who lives on board a boat or indeed owns a boat will tell you, repairs never end and neither does the financial commitment. We never imagined we would have the problems we had with letting the house and flats as this had been Dudley's profession. Even he did not foresee our agent letting a flat to people that after the first few months didn't pay the rent. It took us a full twelve months to finally, through the courts, get them evicted. Just before the court date they were arrested and imprisoned for burglary but we never saw a penny of compensation as our agent let us down very badly.

But enough of the stories of woe and on to the facts of life whilst living aboard. Because of the state of our finances we agreed, from the beginning, to record all expenditure under separate headings. These are detailed below to give you a clear idea of what the cost of living was like for us:-

BOAT EXPENDITURE

Fuse box	€49
Wood	€57
Boat lettering	€15
Second-hand dinghy	€140

Gas lamp	€13
Manual bilge pump	€13
Second-hand outboard	€150
Gas regulator	€18
Second-hand VHF radio	€40
Winch handle & waiter bailer	€26
Shore power lines	€24
Water hose & fog horn	€31
Stainless (screws, shackles, etc.)	€36
Varnish & cleaner	€66
Throttle cable	€70
Water filters	€56
Anchor light	€18
Sail needles and cord	€10
Solar vent (old stock sale)	€10
Alternator repair	€50
Winter jobs*	€800
Boom tent	€20
Engine spare	€32
Spinnaker pole fitting	€30
Battery master/booster	€850
Sundry D.I.Y (string, tilt, hooks, bungee)	€91
Deck netting	€150
Oven knobs	€5
Tools	€83
Mooring line & genoa sheets	€123
Non-slip strips	€17
Torch & leather apron (for helm)	€13
Oil & filters	€31
Ropes (fenders, etc.) & main haul	€40
Relay for windlass	€50
Silicone	€18
Oil pump	€20
Radiator & helm seat	€64
Floor mats	€18
Work on hull**	€567
Impellor pump & tiny fender	€31
Sail repairs	€130
Engine sound padding	€33
New Perspex & hatch repair	€373
TOTAL	€4,599

* Included life raft service, new shower head, cutlass bearing, gear cable, anodes, fire blanket, VHF aerial, Navtex and water pump.

** Included all fibreglass filler, rollers, sandpaper discs, protective mask and gloves, epoxy and anti-foul.

You may consider the expenditure under the heading of sundry D.I.Y. excessive but several small amounts of money for string, cord, bungee, plastic hooks, etc., soon mount up.

PORT FEES

Sailing permit & transit log	€95
Ragatta entrance fee	€16
Mooring fees	€130
Marina fee & haul out fee	€1,569
Port police	€17
TOTAL	€2,677

HIDDEN EXPENDITURE

Greek language classes	€50
Weight belt	€25
Christmas light	€6
Clothes	€72
Vet fees	€468
Cycle repairs	€30
Electric extension cables	€12
TV aerial	€19
TOTAL	€682

LIVING COSTS

Food & drink	€8,722
Water & gas	€135
Fuel	€591
Communications*	€655
TOTAL	€10,053

* Included postage, phone cards, mobile top ups and Internet usage.

All the above added together gives us a grand total of

€18,061 over a twenty month period. This calculates approximately to €903 a month or at the exchange rate at the time of writing £630. We had estimated an income of £12,000 that had not come to fruition for various reasons and we had been left with a serious shortfall. Somehow, by undertaking casual labour when the chance arose, we managed to make up the difference and remain solvent.

As can be seen, our actual living costs were fifty-six percent of our total expenditure, forty-four percent being used to maintain the boat. This only scratched the surface of what we needed to update our boat. We still had a very long list of things we needed such as radar reflectors, ball fenders, auto-helm, cockpit covers for winter etc. etc. When speaking to other people they assured us our list would never get any shorter and our pockets could never be deep enough to keep up with maintaining a boat and keeping it sailing safely on the water.

There have been many things I would have liked, especially new clothes, not that either of us needed them as we had so many clothes on board and we would not need to buy new ones for another twenty months. It's the not being able to afford things that makes them all the more attractive, and self-constraint and control can be very tiring when it is non-stop and unrelenting. I felt at the time that we would never be financially secure and that I would have to accept that I would never have money to spend. In amongst the depression of the realisation we did also accept that we had a wonderful life and were doing what we enjoyed most. We had both eaten well and enjoyed the company of many people, while managing to live on approximately £305 a month or £69 a week.

It had been a time of considering priorities and everything had been a compromise but we had managed to survive quite happily and were determined not to give in on this adventure. After all, twenty months was only the beginning of what we had planned.

Lightning Source UK Ltd.
Milton Keynes UK
25 January 2010
149077UK00001B/94/P